In *Even the Sparrow* ... well lived
and listened to, a li... ...ideserved,
extravagant grace. What is usually said ... ...iese is that
they helps us to better listen to our own lives. And I suppose that's
partly true. More importantly Jill's book awakens in selfish people
(like me) the desire to care enough to listen to the life of someone
else, to care as much about her story as my own.

MICHAEL CARD
BIBLE TEACHER, SONGWRITER

Jill Weber is part sage, part saint, but her life has been far from
easy. She laughs like a drain, prays like a saint and emanates
wisdom like Yoda. This remarkable, sassy memoir will inspire and
provoke you to live and love from the core. And because there is a
musicality to the way Jill writes, you may well be humming its tune
for many months to come.

PETE GREIG
24-7 PRAYER INTERNATIONAL AND EMMAUS RD, GUILDFORD

Even the Sparrow is the honest journey of the pilgrimage of prayer.
Each chapter is a window into the heart and soul of a life given
to devotion and the testimony of his great faithfulness. This book
is a must-read that will stir the heart with jealousy for the sweet
simplicity of devotion to Jesus.

AISHA REVENTAR
DIRECTOR OF THE TORONTO HOUSE OF PRAYER

This great book, written in such a compelling and wildly engaging
way, will capture your imagination and inspire you to explore both
ancient and fresh new ways to apprentice with and follow Christ. All
along the way, it offers spiritual fuel and practical input to catapult
your walk with God into something quite extraordinary, even in
the ordinary everyday life. I consider this a must-read for every
Christian who wants more out of their personal relationship with
Jesus and more from their missional walk in the world.

LISA KOONS
NATIONAL DIRECTOR OF 24-7 PRAYER USA

So many holy and incredible things have happened in and through the life of Jill Weber that it's tempting to file her away in the 'extraordinary saints' category, refusing to think her story has any relation to ours. And yet, Jill chronicles her journey with such disarming humour, earthy candour and lived wisdom that we can't help but be pulled along for the ride. In *Even the Sparrow*, Jill's friends become our friends, and we are reminded that her best friend—the God who has so claimed her heart—is the same God who invites us on the extraordinary adventure of 'doing whatever he says'.

CAROLYN ARENDS
RECORDING ARTIST, AUTHOR AND RENOVARÉ DIRECTOR OF EDUCATION

Those who have been involved in the prayer movement of Canada recognize Jill Weber as someone who has dedicated herself in helping people discover what is a truthful and dynamic prayer life. In *Even the Sparrow*, Jill opens her life and gives the reader a real and somewhat raw picture of the frustrations and challenges associated with personal prayer. But also, through the lens of Jill's real-life encounters, we meet a God who patiently draws us to his greater purposes. Therefore, he rebuilds us; heals our woundedness; and eventually redefines us into a people that could rightly be called a House of Prayer. This book is instructional and inspirational as it outlines Jill's personal prayer journey. We learn that God is seeking to develop us into a 'house of prayer', whether alone, or in company with others. In a building, or even a prayer truck, Jill removes the veil of religiosity and fear surrounding the subject of prayer and helps us to see that for Christians, prayer should be as natural as breathing.

ROB PARKER
NATIONAL HOUSE OF PRAYER OTTAWA, ONTARIO, CANADA

Even the Sparrow is the product of the thinking, searching, learning and praying of its wonderful author Jill Weber. Everything you read here will be the result of Jill's experience and she writes with that same practicality. I recommend it highly.

ANDY FREEMAN
CO-DIRECTOR, SPACE TO BREATHE

Jill Weber has given us a profound gift with her spiritual autobiography. Weaving her story and her community's story together within the pattern of Jesus' life and work calls to mind the celebrated stories of other saints throughout history. These devoted lives are studied not because they are heroic or worthy of worship, but because they make the connection between the Divine and the human more accessible to us all.

AARON WHITE
NATIONAL LEADER OF 24-7 PRAYER CANADA, AUTHOR OF REVOLUTION, THE HITCHHIKER'S GUIDE TO THE KINGDOM OF GOD AND RECOVERING

My friend Jill Weber manifests unbridled enthusiasm, childlike wonder and unpretentious courage. She is a pioneer who uniquely embodies ancient mystical wisdom, practical compassion and a heart for justice. Her story is a testament to how God can use the messy details of our lives to accomplish the extraordinary.

MARK SCANDRETTE
AUTHOR OF FREE, BELONGING AND BECOMING, PRACTICING THE WAY OF JESUS AND THE NINEFOLD PATH

Fascinating. It is impossible not to get caught up in Jill Weber's adventures with God. Down to earth and even funny, yet reflecting a deep and authentic spirituality as she grapples to understand and follow God's call while inviting the reader to do the same. An amazing spiritual journey.

EDWINA GATELEY
AUTHOR, POET, SOCIAL ACTIVIST AND PUBLIC SPEAKER

EVEN THE SPARROW

Muddy
Pearl

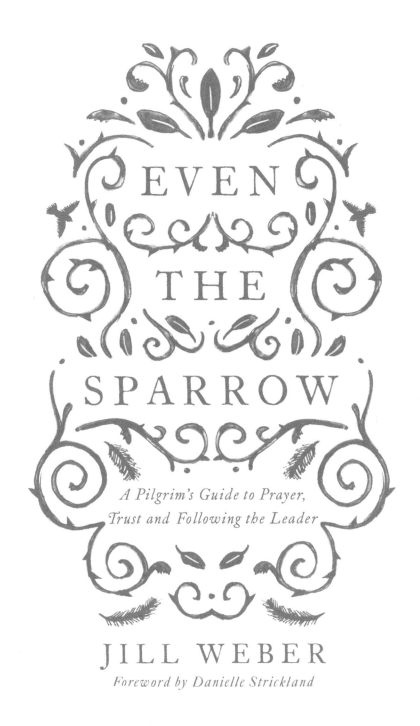

EVEN THE SPARROW

A Pilgrim's Guide to Prayer,
Trust and Following the Leader

JILL WEBER

Foreword by Danielle Strickland

Published in 2019 by
Muddy Pearl, Edinburgh, Scotland.
www.muddypearl.com
books@muddypearl.com

British Library Cataloguing in Publication Data
A catalogue record for this book is available from the British Library
ISBN 978-1-910012-71-0

Cover design by Lindy Martin
Typeset in Minion by Revo Creative Ltd, Lancaster
Printed in Great Britain by Bell and Bain Ltd, Glasgow

To Kirk and to Hannah, who have taught me that marriage and motherhood are sacred vocations.

CONTENTS

ACKNOWLEDGEMENTS

It is impossible to name everyone who contributed to this story and its writing, so please forgive the broad strokes.

Thanks to all of my fellow pilgrims – my travelling buddies on this epic journey – both those mentioned in the book and those not (sorry I couldn't fit you all in!). You have encouraged and sustained me, pointing the way, and sometimes dragging me out of the ditch, dusting me off and setting me back on the path.

To my family at the Greater Ontario House of Prayer, both past and present – you have shaped my heart and my life, our little prayer community, and our city and surrounding regions in incredible ways with your generosity to Jesus and to one another in our shared life of prayer, mission and justice. The people soup tastes so so good!

To my guides and mentors – Dale and Linda Bolton, Richard Long, Andy Freeman, Pete Greig, Kirk Bennett, Sandra Broadus, Dave Witt and the two Sues, amongst many others. You have seen me, made space for me, named me and marked my life. I thank God for you.

To Beth who didn't like my writing and told me to take more risks – I've tried to be courageous and, I think, managed it at points – you are a far better writing teacher than this manuscript demonstrates. To Stephanie and the Muddy Pearl team, thanks for giving me an opportunity to tell my story and helping bring it to birth.

To my mum and dad, who have been unwaveringly supportive through both the rough bits and the good bits. I feel like I've become an amalgam of the best of the two of you – the leader and the contemplative – and am so grateful for the legacy you've passed on to me.

And of course, to Jesus. I don't have a song unless you first sing it. I don't have a story unless you write it in me. Thanks for handing me the pen.

Jill Weber
www.JillWeber.com

FOREWORD

Urban missionary. Prayer champion. Contemplative. Activist. Theologian. Mother. Friend. I could go on. Jill Weber has packed a lot of depth and width into her one beautiful life. She has lived. Perhaps that's what I love most about reading this book.

I've heard a lot about Jill. From friends and people she has impacted over her years investing in the kingdom of God. A Canadian prophet, preacher, prayer-warrior and activist. People would ask me if I knew Jill and I would always respond that I wished I did. The way folks spoke of her made me long to know her. Years later, I would have an invitation to do exactly that – to get to know Jill. And now I am more intrigued than ever. Jill has a warm way of being herself. She's comfortable in her own skin. Something about her assurance of God's presence through every season of life makes it possible for me to be comfortable as well. Jill doesn't make me want to be more like her – she makes me want to be more like myself. And the secret to that is Jesus. Of this, Jill and I are both sure.

So many people can wax eloquent about God and their thoughts about how the spiritual life works, but they remain detached from the muck and mire of their real lives. Jill doesn't just contemplate God – she experiences God. She doesn't just believe in Jesus, she follows Jesus. For her that's meant a departure from business as usual. Far from the upwardly mobile masses, Jill has descended into the life of Christ. That's opened a place for her to embrace a risky, strange and beautiful life, enriched by its depth of relationships and encounters with God, and with others. Reading these reflections from a jam-packed life of sorrow, joy, pain, beauty, hope, truth, visions, feelings, friends, rejection and fear fills me with a sense of permission. Permission to be human. Permission to be a human who can encounter a living God. Permission to encounter this living God in the everyday – a God who is present in the here and the now. More present than we might ever dare to imagine.

I'm not sure what stage of life you are in right now. I'm imagining some young adults hoping to learn how to pray. This book will help you. This life will show you. I can picture someone seasoned in ministry, struggling with deep doubts and fears haunting you between your pastoral duties. This book will help you. This life will show you. I see folks who have been burnt out by religion, who have given up on church as usual, wondering if they can find God again. This book will help you. This life will show you. People in all kinds of life, misfits and business suits, leaders and teenagers, women and men, pagans and Christians, will find in these stories – in this life – an invitation to discover the God who is already with you. In finding this present God, you will lose your life. Jill helps you understand that you need not be afraid. This losing is the best way, the only way, to find your truest self. It's in this space that you too can be comfortable in your own skin, at any season of your life, knowing that the words Jesus spoke over 2000 years ago might apply to your frantic and anxiety-inducing pace of keeping up in this world. Even the sparrow is fed, cared for, held and provided for by a loving Father. Once you know that, you can let go and let God take over. Jill knows this, lives this, and is inviting you to join her.

Danielle Strickland
Speaker, Author and Social Justice Advocate

INTRODUCTION

We lost a friend of mine recently to illness – a young woman who was a worship leader in the early days of our House of Prayer. Rebekah was a songbird, a sweet sparrow nestled by the altar of God. Her sudden departure left us all reeling. Sorrow gripped me at unexpected times and places, leaving me a sodden mess in the middle of grocery stores and car parks. Now that I've moved and live an ocean away, I'm unable to attend her memorial service. So instead, I send a little consoling note to my former community. As I ponder what I want to say about Rebekah's life, I think about the times she sat down at the piano, smiled, stroked the keys and then began to play and sing, transporting us all into another realm. I find myself drawing from an image in the book of Revelation that feels appropriate.

> Rebekah was a doorway to heaven, and a voice
> saying, 'Come up here'.[1]

Our stories are like that. Doorways to heaven. Places of convergence where the eternal crashes into the now. Our stories call us upward, looking beyond the ground under our feet to a more expansive horizon. They can transport us and others to another realm.

---

1 Revelation 4:1.

Jesus understood the fine art of enfleshing spiritual truth in earthy matter, revealing heaven through ordinary stories of everyday lives. Writing to fledgling churches, the Apostle Paul challenged them to do the same. You are a living letter from Christ, he said: '… written not with ink but with the Spirit of the living God, not on tablets of stone but on tablets of human hearts.'[2] Stories matter. My story matters. So does Rebekah's. So does yours.

Here is my story – a portion of it, anyway. Let's consider for a moment how you might want to approach it: some people are cat people and others are dog people. If you're feeding a cat, you put the food in the bowl and, after a while, the feline saunters by and gives it the eye. When it's good and ready, it meanders over, grabs a dainty bite or two, purrs, licks its whiskers and then lies down in the sun to digest and snooze. If you're going to be away for a couple of days, you know you can leave food in the bowl and that, over time, the cat will nibble away as needed. Not so with dogs. They are entirely different. Put food in the bowl and they gallop over and gulp its contents in a few enthusiastic bites. Leave a dog with a bowl of food over the course of several days and it will be ravenous by lunchtime. I never really understood people who eat like cats and I am most definitely not one of them. When visiting a particular friend of mine, I see the same box of chocolates on her shelf week after week after week. How on earth is that even possible?

In the same way, some people are cat readers and others are dog readers. Some of you will nibble this book, then stop, put it down and ponder. Maybe even purr a bit. Others will consume it swiftly with enthusiasm. There is nothing wrong with either approach. I trust both will find it tasty! However, I'm hoping the speedy eaters will come back for a

2 2 Corinthians 3:3.

second look and spend some time on the reflection sections at the end of each chapter, entitled 'The Invitation'. They're designed to help you think about your own story – your life and journey with God. In them, I introduce some forms of prayer or other spiritual practices that may be unfamiliar to you but are time honoured in the Christian tradition. Some invitations are very practical, others are designed to help you explore your inner space, and others to deepen your connection with God.

As you read, imagine I'm sitting across the room from you in my office. The decor is simple, sparse, except for two paintings on the wall: replicas of Rembrandt's 'The Return of the Prodigal Son' and Klimt's 'The Kiss'. On the bookshelf, nestled within an array of volumes, is a little bird's nest rescued from the back garden – a weaving of twigs, moss and bits of bird fluff. You're in a comfy chair complete with plumped cushion and a little crochet blanket if you get chilly. We've both got a warm drink in hand. I'm a soy sugar-free hazelnut, extra hot latte, kinda person. Perhaps you prefer tea? I light the candle on the little round table between us – a reminder of the presence of Jesus in our midst. We sit and sip in silence for a minute or two, simply breathing and settling down into the quiet place in our souls to listen to whatever his invitation might be to us today.

The book has been designed with forty chapters (don't worry – they're short!) so you can use it during Lent or other seasons of retreat or devotion if you wish. My prayer is that as you read this story, and reflect on your own, you will see glimpses of God at work and you would hear his voice calling you to himself.

Chapter 1

FOLLOWING THE LEADER

My sheep listen to my voice; I know them, and they follow me. I give them eternal life, and they shall never perish; no one will snatch them out of my hand.

JOHN 10:27–28

It's a grey, drizzly day. I sit snuggled in the back of the moving van we've converted into a portable prayer room. Waiting. I love these moments the most. Making space for God. Asking him to fill it in whatever way he wishes.

Suddenly, four young men, half naked and fully intoxicated, leap into the truck. They look to be about 20 years old – big strapping boys. Tattooed, wild-eyed and fierce. 'I'm effing gonna do it – I'm gonna pray!' one declares. I find out later his street name is Ratchet. Pulse throbbing, I feel a shot of adrenaline course through me. My first impulse is to scooch over and sit on my rucksack, which holds my wallet and my mobile. Hopefully I won't get robbed. I scooch.

I am aware that I might be dealing with territory issues. The prayer truck is parked downtown in an alley. We are behind the Living Rock, a local youth centre. The teens tolerate the truck's presence out back but any signage that we set up in front of the centre gets torn down or destroyed.

That's their turf. The truck, however, is my domain. Really, it's God's – but at this moment, I'm the one he's put in charge.

'Well gentlemen, you're in the prayer truck. Are we gonna pray?' I sound much bolder than I feel. The ringleader swaggers over to the side of the truck, snatches one of the markers lying around and scrawls his gang tag on the wall with a flourish. He steps back to admire his handiwork and shoots a grin at his comrades. 'Fantastic!' I say. 'We've got little old ladies who come to the truck to pray. Now they're going to pray for your gang!'

Another boy grabs a marker and writes down the name of his son and his baby mama. In a moment they are all scribbling.

Except one.

He's young but his face is already weathered by street life. Pockmarked, grubby and stubbly.

'Can you help me read these?' he asks, pointing to the prayers written on the walls of the truck.

He sounds out the words he knows and together we decipher the heartfelt messages.

'Mom I can't stop hurting for you.'

'I love you. Simple. That is all.'

'Pray for everyone and everything.'

At the end of their visit the boys and I sit in a circle, heads bowed and eyes closed. We pray for two of them who are desperate to get into rehab but haven't yet been able to. 'I don't care about the weed. It's the hard stuff that's killin' me ...'

After a hearty 'Amen!' they leap to their feet, jump out of the van and careen across the car park like a playful pack of wolves, howling and yelping. I heave a sigh of relief, shaking the tension from my shoulders. That could have been bad. Really bad. But instead it was good. As my friend Sue would say in her British accent, 'Deeply good.'

The next morning, I'm at my post early and Ratchet lopes

up to where I'm sitting – in a lawn chair on the roadside in front of the truck. He parks himself in the chair beside me and as we watch the sunrise he begins to talk. 'I used to live in Toronto, but too many of my friends were getting killed in the gang fights. Hey, d'ya wanna see my scars?' I'm a bit taken aback, but before I can respond, he lifts his shirt. 'Here is where I got stabbed. And here, and here. Here is where my girlfriend skewered me with a screwdriver!'

After the scars have been duly viewed and admired, he settles back into the chair again. 'What I really want to do is be a doctor.' he says, 'But school is so friggin' hard! And teachers are stupid!' We sit in silence for a while. I ask questions. He talks. About everything and nothing. 'Hey, do you wanna hear a song? It's got a lot of F-bombs in it, but it's got an effin' awesome message.' Ratchet pulls out an iPod and flips me one of the earbuds. It's pink with a rhinestone in the centre, like those ones I see at the Dollar Store. He pops the other in his own ear and together we listen to the music, grooving a little to its beats, watching the city awaken.

After that I see Ratchet around the neighbourhood from time to time. Sometimes he ignores me. Other times, especially if he is a little tipsy, he runs up to me and gives me 'props' or a loose-limbed hug. 'Yo, it's the prayer lady!' Other times I go months without seeing him. I wonder if he's spending time in the local jail. Eventually, he disappears – skipping town perhaps. Hopefully nothing worse.

I never would have imagined that my career journey would have taken me to a U-Haul Truck in an alley in downtown Hamilton. Not every high schooler aspires to *kibitz* with drunken thugs in makeshift urban sanctuaries.

How on earth did I end up here?

It's dark and I'm fourteen, wandering the woods alone. All I can see around me are tree silhouettes, silent sentinels in the dusk. I pick one and nestle myself between rangy roots. 'Go out somewhere on your own and pray,' our camp director said. I'm not quite sure what he means. Rather, I'm not quite sure how to do what he's asked. Prayer seems like some foreign language that one only hears in bad *Kung Fu* or Godzilla movies. Other than reciting the 'Our Father' in school, I have neither experienced nor practised prayer. Unsure of what to do, what to say, I decide to begin with an introduction. I tip my face upward, because, well, that's where God is, right? 'Hi, I'm Jill,' I say.

What happens next takes years for me to wrap words around, even longer to understand. In fact, I'm not sure I understand it even now …

… all of a sudden, I'm not alone under that tree. The Presence is invisible but tangible. Palpable. I can feel the weight on my body. Shapeless, formless substance. It doesn't feel malevolent or friendly, necessarily. Just … there. Someone.

I do what any sensible teenager does when encountering invisible beings in the dark. I hightail it back to my cabin, shaken and wondering. What. Just. Happened?

The next day at camp they share the gospel with us – tell us who Jesus is – and invite us to become his disciples.

I had been trying to sort out this Jesus person for the previous year or so since my dad began going to church. He converted to Christianity after his quest for meaning in pop psychology and transcendental meditation. Transactional analysis[3] was popular at the time, and internal movements of the heart and internal dialogue were categorized as Warm 'Fuzzies' or Cold Prickles. As best as I could figure out, Jesus was a Warm Fuzzy sitting on my shoulder.

I found out that day that the Jesus revealed in the Bible is Someone else altogether. For me now, it's a no brainer. The only invisible person I know (and only very recently) is God. And if God wants me, who am I to say no? When the Creator of the universe issues you a personal invitation, it's pretty darn impolite to turn it down. So I say yes to that invisible Presence. I say yes to a lifetime of trying to love, listen to and follow Jesus.

Fast forward some thirty-odd years ...

'So what do you do?' It's a common question. I'm always hard pressed to answer. Usually I pause, assessing who my enquirer is and the best way to describe this unusual life I lead. Sometimes I say that I'm an urban missionary or pastor. Sometimes I say I'm a prayer missionary. Other times I say I'm an Abbess of a New Monastic community or I'm a musicianary. All of these are true.

The deepest truth?

I'm a lover. A listener and a follower. Or at least I try to be.

I'm nine and wandering through the woods, this time not by myself. I've always liked hiking. Forests are full of beauty and mystery and my heart feels at home in them. Skin dappled with tree shadows, I'm eyeing the stones that punctuate the stream. 'Step here and here and here.' My hike leader turns,

3 Transactional Analysis was a psychoanalytic theory and method of therapy developed in the late 1950s by Eric Berne and popularized by his book, *Games People Play*, published in 1964. www.ericberne.com/transactional-analysis.

pointing out the series of footholds. 'Careful, that one's a little slippery.' I've got one eye on my leader, one eye on the rocks. I'm tentative. Slow and steady makes for dry sneakers. 'There you go. That one, and that one, and grab my hand. You made it!' She gives me a congratulatory squeeze and we clamber up the riverbank together.

Following the leader. It's a child's game. Played out on wilderness hikes and in schoolyards.

'*Simon says, jump up and down!*'

'*Simon says, spin around!*'

'*Now stop! Ha! I didn't say Simon says!*'

But like the wrestling of wolf cubs, our childhood play is our training ground, preparing us for adulthood. I wonder sometimes if everything essential we need to know about following Jesus we learn in kindergarten.

John Dawson is a senior leader of Youth With A Mission, one of the largest mission agencies in the world. His work has global reach and he bears the weight of tremendous responsibility. Once at a conference I hear him say the most wonderful, liberating thing: 'Every morning I get out of bed like a little child.' His recipe for success, the key to a way of life that works in a world of complexity? Childlike simplicity.

'My sheep listen to my voice,' Jesus said. 'I know them, and they follow me.'[4] Listen and follow. It's all I know how to do. When everything is said and done, I'm surrounded by great 'unfixables'. My life is too big for me and I don't know how to navigate it. Listening and following are ultimately the stepping stones that have taken me from that first encounter under the tree to the back of an alley amongst the rubbish bins. It's been a fascinating (and sometimes perilous) journey.

4 John 10:27.

THE INVITATION

How do I pray? It's tempting to complicate prayer – we want to do it 'right'. We want our prayers to be effective. I'm often asked the question, 'Does prayer work?' I counter with another question, 'Does conversation with your husband, or your loved ones, work?'

Prayer is not a tool or a mechanistic process. We cannot measure its efficiency. It is not a technique we master in order to create our desired results. Prayer is simply this: communication and communion with the God who loves us more than we could ever hope for, and who is closer to us than we could ever imagine.

The only way to fail at prayer? By not praying.

Prayer is simple. Paradoxically it is also full of mystery. One of the wonderful mysteries of prayer is that God is the Great Initiator. In 1 John 4:19 it says: 'We love because he first loved us.' And in John 6:44 Jesus says: 'No one can come to me unless the Father who sent me draws them ...'

Our interest in God and our desire for him is an indicator that he is already at work in our lives, drawing us to himself. The fact that you've picked up this book and have begun to read it is because God himself has invited you on a journey. He has set your heart on pilgrimage.

Take some time to reflect about the following questions. It might be helpful to write in a journal.

1. Review the last few days and ask God to show you where he might be at work drawing you to himself. How might God be initiating contact and conversation with you? This can be as simple as those things we call 'common grace' – general indications of his goodness to all of us,

like the sun rising each day. Or are there instances in your day where God might be trying to get your attention? Situations? Conversations? Unusual occurrences?

2. What might happen if you took some time alone, in quiet, and initiated a conversation with him? If you've not spoken with him before, introduce yourself! If it's been a while, it's a great time to get caught up with him.

At the end of each invitation I will include a written prayer that you may join in with if you wish.

Jesus, thank you that you love us – that you have always loved us. Thank you that you are pursuing us even now – inviting us into communion and conversation. Thank you for the hunger and longing you have placed inside us and for the ways you are drawing us to yourself. Help us to be aware of your presence and activity in our lives today.

Chapter 2

VOCATION

*For we are God's handiwork, created in Christ Jesus to do
good works, which God prepared in advance for us to do.*

Ephesians 2:10

I love animals. As a child I want to be a vet. It is my soul
ambition. We have a happy, but not very bright, golden
Labrador named Brandy that we acquire the same year we
get my baby brother. I prefer Brandy. She is cuter and fuzzier
and much less 'screamy'.

We are supposed to leave Brandy in the basement to sleep
but I can't bear the thought of her down there by herself.
She's lonely! She needs me! The box itself is puppy-sized, not
toddler-sized, so I drape myself over its side, bum in the air,
blanket tented over us both. We're hidden and I'm sure my
trespassing will be undetected. My cheek is warm and tickly
as the puppy snuffs and nestles. We breathe and sigh together.

I'm in heaven and decide that animals are my thing. I
don't know how on earth my parents figure out where I am,
but it's not long before I'm ejected from heaven and sent to
my lonely bed.

Many years later, I'm in eighth grade in a special
accelerated programme for brainy kids. We do extra, extra-
curricular activities and I pursue anything they offer in the

area of animals and veterinary sciences. That is how I find myself stepping into a barn at the University of Manitoba. My assignment? To do an operation on a live pig. I'm told that I'm either going to do a C-section or an ovariectomy – birthing or sterilizing. Somehow holding a flaccid ovary in my palm doesn't hold the same allure as welcoming infants into the world, but unfortunately my timing is off and there are no piglets ripe for the plucking.

When I step over the threshold of the barn I'm hit by a wave of warm, fetid air. The smell of faeces, straw and warm pig washes over me, catching in my throat. I can taste it on my tongue. Being a city girl, the only pigs I have ever seen are in petting zoos and the illustrations of one of my favourite children's book, *Charlotte's Web*. As I look around for Wilbur's cousin, my eyes widen as I see what appears to be enormous pink horses. Horses? No, wait. On closer examination they are indeed pigs, but much, much larger than what I've imagined.

My patient, whom I call Wilma, is already strapped to the makeshift operating table. A hanging bag of anaesthetic drips slowly into the IV line attached to her thigh. Hairy chest rising and falling, Wilma dozes while I suit up in a full-body paper overall, mask and surgical gloves.

The attending veterinarian pulls the instrument tray close. 'Here's your scalpel.' He places it in my nervous fingers. 'I've drawn the incision line on the side of the pig, so just insert the knife and slice downwards.' I flatten my left hand on Wilma's belly to steady us both and make the first cut. Not so different to slicing ham, right?

Except hams don't shriek and kick.

Wilma hoofs me on the thigh and writhes on the table. Later I find that she has marked me with a dinner plate-sized bruise that lasts for weeks. The vet lunges for the IV line and I hobble out of harm's way. 'Shoot! Let's give the anaesthetic a little more time to work.'

Soon Wilma settles and I poke her side with the scalpel to ensure that she's completely under. No response. 'Alright then, let's give this a go.' The vet shifts into guide mode and begins to give me a tour of Wilma's innards. 'That's the intestines. Yeah, there's a lot of them. Make sure you don't nick them with the scalpel, or you'll kill her.' No pressure!

We root around for the womb and then follow the path of the fallopian tubes to the ovaries dangling at their ends. My arms are warm and wet. 'There you go. Just cut them ... there. You've got it.' The organs slop from my fingers into the metal bowl we have handy. 'Now, let me show you how to suture. Insert the needle here and cut and tie. And again ... Just a few more ... There. Finished! Now we close everything up again. Mind the bowel!' We back our way out of Wilma's cavernous belly, stitching as we go.

My first ever surgery successfully complete, I leave an eggless and snoozing Wilma on the table and go into the washroom to de-pig myself. I strip and scrub and scrub some more, thank the vet and proceed to the next part of my day.

Very conveniently, the annual Language Arts Festival is also at the University of Manitoba. I'm competing this year and I spend the afternoon going from one classroom to the next, presenting poetry and short stories. Winning a ribbon or two. Feeling satisfied and grateful. What other kid gets to perform an operation on a pig in the morning and compete in a poetry competition that same afternoon?

The classroom seats all around me are vacant but I don't notice. All the car windows are open on the ride home with all my schoolmates, even on the motorway, but again I'm oblivious, daydreaming about my future as a world-famous veterinarian and author. Just like James Herriot. It's only when I get home that I become aware that my life is over. 'Hey mum,' I slam the front door and doff my shoes. 'Amazing day!' My mother's voice floats from the kitchen, all the way on the other side of the house. 'Jill, what on earth have you done? You stink!'

I freeze. A sick lump thumps into the pit of my belly.

Stink?

Over the course of the morning in the barn, I must have become acclimatized to the reek. A cloud of Wilma and her companions had followed me all day like the cartoon character Pig-Pen in Charlie Brown. I was blissfully unaware of the low-lying weather system that surrounded me. Stinky piggy Jill standing at the front of the university classrooms, reading poetry. Stinky piggy Jill in a carful of my friends. Ex-friends, most likely, after today.

I'm in hell and not so sure now if animals are my thing. After the longest, scrubbiest shower in history, I decide that the most sensible course of action is to hide in my room forever and home school.

However, it isn't the stink incident that ends my short-lived veterinary career. It was that fateful night under the tree – the night of the invisible but unmistakable encounter – that changed the trajectory of my heart and my life. These decisions we make – the fateful 'yes'es. Not only moments in time and movements of the heart but actual transactions that reshape reality and unfurl new futures.

I slink back to school and join the Christian club. Post conversion, my reputation is ruined. It had already been ailing due to my being an overweight smarty pants. Now that I'm religious they call me the long-haired Jesus freak. Three strikes and I'm out – officially un-datable. So I decide that I might as well hang out with the handful of oddball disciples that meet and pray on Wednesday lunch hours.

There is Patrick, slender and androgynous. A shock of hair hangs to his chin, covering up one guy-linered eye. (These were the Boy George days.) It's whispered he is bisexual. During prayer meetings he scribbles and scrawls in his big black sketchbook. Black and purple are his colours of choice.

Then there is Andrew, who is working hard at growing a wispy moustache and goatee. His church is called 'The Church of God of Prophecy'. Serious and devout, he kneels in front of his chair and his prayers are loud, fervent and repetitive. 'Father God, we love you Father God, and Father God we ask, Father God, that you would bless the school Father God. Father God, would you help us all with exams, Father God, we bless everybody's families, Father God ...'

And there is Joel: affable, intelligent and open hearted. His Cerebral palsy crooks his grin and his left arm. You can recognize his shuffling, dragging gait all the way down the hall. One lunch hour, he falls down the stairs and lies unconscious in a pool of his own blood. Like rubberneckers passing a crash on the highway, we wall him in with our curiosity until the paramedics resurrect him and cart him away. He is back a couple of days later, lurching through the school and showing off his stitches.

The three musketeers need a wrangler and before I know it, I'm put in charge. What I lack in biblical knowledge I make up for in initiative, organization and my ability to bake cookies. Evidently, I'm a leader.

A Christian leader.

Am I supposed to be a pastor? Reverend Jill? Complete with dog collar and voluminous robes? It's a possibility.

I begin my investigation by examining the pastors in my life with the same curiosity and intensity with which we scrutinize amoeba under the microscope in science class.

There is Reverend Ian, pastor of our congregation and father of triplets. I have a vivid memory of him preaching one Sunday (it must have been near Halloween, is my best guess). The triplets are three at the time and are sporting matching lion costumes, complete with maned hoodies, painted noses and whiskers. Sunday school must have ended early because part way through the sermon the lions are let loose. They rush the altar growling and giggling and all three proceed to climb their father like he is a spreading Serengeti tree. Ian gamely tries to continue his sermon, but the impact of his teaching is dulled by the spectacle of three little lions swinging from his robes.

And then there is Reverend Frances, a minister from a church down the road who I know entirely too much about. On an unseasonably hot and drippy day, I visit her church and have the unfortunate opportunity to sit in the choir loft adjacent to the pulpit. As Frances raises her loosely robed arms in benediction at the end of the service, I happen to be at just the right angle to see that she has decided upon the, um, breezier option underneath her vestments.

Frances, despite her minimalistic clothing tendencies, does have very good advice about a career in ministry. 'Seminary won't actually teach you anything useful.' We are sharing fries at the local fast food joint. 'My first Sunday in my new parish I had to do a funeral for a baby. A baby! They didn't cover that in my theological education! Here's my best advice. If you feel called to the ministry, just run the other way. If you're supposed to be there, somehow you will end up there anyways.'

Ian is also helpful when I question him about pursuing a clerical career. 'The model we have is Jesus. And what Jesus modelled was servant leadership. When I'm standing in front of the congregation, I picture myself wrapped in a towel, just like Jesus when he washed his disciples' feet.' 'What about if you're a pastoral assistant?' I figure you start small and work your way up in the Reverend business. 'Ah, if you're a pastoral assistant, that just means you wear a smaller towel.' He grins.

My exploration is fuelled by the school aptitude tests we do in guidance class. Lots of multiple-choice questions that help us explore our interests and areas of giftedness. The answers are fed into the computer. Ingested and digested, then the Oracle of Wisdom spits out the results. The printout is on old style computer paper, one long foldable sheet with perforated edges. On it is a list of our best choice for careers. The sheet of paper that will define our professional lives.

Two vie for supremacy on the top of my sheet: pastor and horticulturalist. 'What a weird, unlikely combination,' I think. I have no idea how accurate the prediction will be.

THE INVITATION

Ephesians 2:10 says:

'For we are God's handiwork, created in Christ Jesus to do good works, which God prepared in advance for us to do.' The Greek word for workmanship is *poiema*. We are God's poem. His work of art. His masterpiece. We are fearfully and wonderfully made, the Psalmist declares.[5] The word vocation comes from the Latin word *vocare* which means to call. God calls us to live out of the uniqueness with which he has created and shaped us. He also calls us to live into his plans and purposes not only for our own lives but for his overarching plans and purposes for all of creation.

---

5 Psalm 139:14.

1. *Vocation ... comes from listening. I must listen to my life and try to understand what it is truly about.*[6]

   Take some time to listen to your own life. Explore your childhood passions and aspirations, your personal quirks and personality, your experiences both good and bad. You might want to do this through journaling. You might find it more helpful to draw your reflections using pictures or symbols. How might your passions, your personality, and your experiences inform your calling and vocation?

2. *By and large a good rule for finding out is this: the kind of work God usually calls you to is the kind of work (a) that you need most to do and (b) that the world most needs to have done. ... The place God calls you to is the place where your deep gladness and the world's deep hunger meet.*[7]

   In the previous question you identified your passions, your personality, your experiences. Where might those gifts intersect with the needs you see around you?

Jesus, I am so grateful for the shape of my being, for the way I have been uniquely crafted and created.
Your works are wonderful.
May I be attentive to your call in my life and may I respond with courage in those moments you invite me to follow.

6 Parker J. Palmer, *Let Your Life Speak: Listening for the Voice of Vocation* (Jossey-Bass, 2000), p.4.

7 Frederick Buechner, *Wishful Thinking* (Harper Collins, 1993), p.118–119.

Chapter 3

OK, NOW WHAT?

Let the morning bring me word of your unfailing love,
  for I have put my trust in you.
Show me the way I should go,
  for to you I entrust my life.

PSALM 143:8

I'm nineteen when my career as a religious professional begins. 'What kind of work do you want to do?' asks Reverend Ian. 'Just write it all out, send it in to the denomination, and see if any churches are interested in having you. The best way to learn is by doing!'

I'm sure my ad went something like this:

Position wanted:
Enthusiastic, naive and idealistic young adult seeking pastoral position far beyond her skill, education and ability. Will work for room and board.

A brave (or foolhardy) congregation in Ottawa recognize a good deal when they see it and snatch me up. My job title? Pastoral assistant.

'I'm calling you that so I can get you up front leading worship services without people getting cranky about it.' The

Reverend Gordon is a lanky Dutchman with a no-nonsense attitude coupled with a mischievous streak. My main task is to develop youth programmes. Reverend Gordon has lots on his own plate, so he gives me a long leash to explore, be creative and just get on with it.

A family from the church takes me in. Another family provides a vehicle. It's a proper youth leader car, suitably dilapidated. The windows get stuck in the rolled-down position, which is tricky in the bitter Canadian winter. The back doors are fused shut so youth have to climb over the front passenger seat to get in. It's a hit among the kids and I call it Bessie.

I learn lots in my six-month assignment:

1. When you finish a prayer in Jesus' name you don't pronounce it 'in Jesuses name'.
2. A peanut butter sandwich is a poor substitute for communion wafers. Who knew that just the smell of it could possibly send someone to the hospital?
3. Jolt Cola has twice the amount of caffeine as regular cola. A six-pack gets me through most weekends, but in the case of overnight youth retreats, a twelve-pack is required. I ignore my twitching eyelids and trembling hands as I chug one after the other so that I can be energetic, perky and chirpy.
4. Kids are actually interested in being and making disciples. I offer them a host of topics they can explore – dating, music, media? 'We want to learn about evangelism,' they respond. 'We want to be able to talk to our friends about Jesus.'

Several months in I'm sitting in a kitchen with a bunch of teenagers. We are decorating jeans, ripping out the knees and unravelling the denim. Then we decorate them with fabric paint. Remember it's the late 1980s: the era of Cyndi Lauper, Madonna, and MC Hammer who exhorts us to pray to make it today. Across my back jean pockets, I paint in gold glitter what is to become essential life-shaping words from 2 Corinthians 12:9, 'My grace is sufficient for you, for my power is made perfect in weakness.' I cling to that verse like those snug jeans cling to my backside.

I feel clueless – I have no idea what I'm doing. I am like a teenage mother – a baby raising babies. Some of the kids in the youth group are just a few months younger than I, and others definitely seem more mature. I'm in over my head and struggling. It feels like I'm back in my lifeguard training days. To develop strength and stamina we have to swim for ten minutes in the deep end of the pool, all the while holding a ten-pound brick out of the water. Our legs churn like mad and the water boils as we struggle to stay afloat and keep our burdens aloft.

I'm desperate. I don't want to drown and pull my growing gaggle of youth down with me. So I devour books on youth ministry and register for Bible School correspondence courses. I carry index cards of Scriptures in my rucksack that I memorize on my walks and in my spare minutes. The owner of the local Christian bookstore has a reputation for being 'youth flypaper' so I make regular pilgrimages to her shop, perch on a stool by her counter and pester her with questions.

Mostly I pray.

I learn the hard way that quiet times tucked under my quilt or on a comfy chair have the tendency to become entirely too quiet, until I startle awake with my head in my Bible and a dribble of drool on the page. So in the mornings I kneel by the side of the bed. Prayer is supposed to work better when you're kneeling, right?

Eyes squinched shut, I take some deep breaths and direct my heart towards heaven, or at the very least to the top right hand corner of my bedroom. My sense of responsibility and its twin brother, inadequacy, grapple inside me like Jacob and Esau wrestling in the womb. With all the internal turmoil my prayers are short and to the point.

'OK, now what?'

After I talk, I listen. I listen hard.

In retrospect, I wonder if the order of the words were important.

OK.

Now what?

Basically: yes. Yes to whatever God thinks I should do because he's obviously smarter, wiser, more creative than I am. Yes, because if he created the earth and the infrastructure of the universe then likely he can handle a handful of teenagers. Yes, because he knows the opportunity or peril lurking around the next corner. Yes, before he tells me what I'm saying yes to. I know – what was I thinking? Young and foolish.

Or was I?

I say yes then I listen with the intent to obey what I hear. Because it's all just a crazy big experiment anyway.

Much to my surprise, when my heart is pre-set to yes and I take time to listen, I hear stuff. I get creative ideas. Inspiration. My problem-solving abilities get amped up.

Things begin to happen.

By some miracle I don't blow up the church or kill peanut-allergic congregants. The youth group grows. And grows. And grows. Kids get excited about telling their friends about Jesus. The community I've been given to cultivate flourishes.

OK, now what?

Little do I know that this is going to my prayer and my modus operandi for the next thirty years of life and ministry.

THE INVITATION

In the book of Chronicles we see that King Jehoshaphat is in over his head. He is responsible for the welfare of his people in a complex and dangerous situation. His response? Prayer.

'We do not know what to do, but our eyes are on you,'[8] he says to God.

A couple thousand years later, Thomas Merton pens a similar prayer, albeit a little more poetically.

The Road Ahead

My Lord God,
I have no idea where I am going.
I do not see the road ahead of me.
I cannot know for certain where it will end.
Nor do I really know myself,
and the fact that I think that I am following your will
does not mean that I am actually doing so.
But I believe that the desire to please you
does in fact please you.
And I hope I have that desire in all that I am doing.
I hope that I will never do anything apart from that
desire.
And I know that if I do this
you will lead me by the right road, though I may know
nothing about it.
Therefore will I trust you always though I may seem to

8 2 Chronicles 20:12.

be lost and in the shadow of death.
I will not fear, for you are ever with me,
and you will never leave me to face my perils alone.
Amen.[9]

Read: Read Merton's poem out loud, slowly. Which words or phrases jump out at you?

Reflect: Reflect on those words or phrases. How do you relate to what Merton is expressing before God?

Respond: How might God be asking you to respond to what he is highlighting in the poem? What is his invitation to you?

Jesus, I'm so glad that you're stronger, smarter, wiser, more
loving and more capable than I am.
I ask your protection and care with complete abandon.
Show me the way I should go, for to you I entrust my life.
(Psalm 143:8)

---

9 'The Merton Prayer', https://reflections.yale.edu/article/seize-day-vocation-calling-work/merton-prayer.

Chapter 4

DETOUR

'Therefore I am now going to allure her;
I will lead her into the wilderness
and speak tenderly to her.
There I will give her back her vineyards,
and will make the Valley of Achor a door of hope.
There she will respond as in the days of her youth,
as in the days she came up out of Egypt.'

HOSEA 2:14–15

Flushed with the success of my first venture I create a life map and chart a path towards a career in the church. It is linear and straightforward. A to B to C. University for my Bachelor of Arts. Seminary for my Masters of Divinity. Ordination, dog collar and robes – et voila!

And then?

I meet a guy.

How many detours start with that sentence?

I'm standing in the doorway of the sanctuary, my dad on my arm. He's a bit furrowed but I chalk it up to his allergic reaction to the lapel rose. I look up at the stained glass above our heads. Sun shines through it, giving it a rosy glow. There is a bush and it's burning. A promise of God's presence, the supernatural breaking in upon the ordinary. God is with me. I smooth my pearled wedding dress, pat my dad's hand, smile at the young man standing down the other end of the aisle, and take my first fateful step.

Six months later I'm in a women's shelter.

We're sitting in a circle. Mothers and children. The room is quiet, weary, bruised. But also poised and intent. In the middle of the circle one of the women sits beside a pile of rubbish bags. They are full of donated clothes. She pulls out a dress. It's blue, calf length with flowers. Creased but promising. A hand shoots up. 'I like it.' First one to say it gets the prize. I learn to speak first and speculate on fit later.

I don't speak fast enough when it is time to choose our chores at the shelter but I'm relieved that the easy job has been left behind. How hard can it be to clean out and organize the kitchen cupboards? I learn that this depends upon how fussy you are about cockroaches. We compete for domination of the cupboards and ultimately, I am out-maneuvered and defeated. Disgusted, I slip out the back door of the shelter and hitchhike back to my husband.

Hidden between the mattresses of our bed at home are a couple of books on domestic violence. Occasionally I am able to snatch a few moments alone to read. I'm looking for understanding, support and solutions. How do I make it stop? I read that women usually get out early or they endure decades of abuse until, body and spirit broken, they seek escape. Often they leave and return, leave and return, over and over.

I go back five times.

Looking back, I know this is five times too many. But I'm drawn to him like the mayflies that career wildly and self-destructively around our porch light. Love hopes all things, believes all things, endures all things, right? And I want to have the confidence that I have given the mess of my marriage my best effort.

A year later I'm walking down the road, carrying all my belongings in two large shopping bags. My most precious possession is strapped tight to my bosom. She huffs, wheezes and makes 3-week-old snuffy baby noises, rubbing her nose and cheeks against my chest. She's peckish but patient. I rest my chin on her fuzzy head and sigh. He can have the flat, our camping gear, even my guitar. Everything actually. I've got all I need.

Out of the corner of my eye I see what looks like our car flash by. I tense and flinch, instinctively arching my body and its fragile burden away from the road. Was that him? Did he see us?

Evidently not. I trudge on.

It's a long walk but eventually we make it to the house of Faye and Ray, our church mom and dad. They are surprised to see us but, with experienced hospitality, quickly assess the situation and invite me in. I am unburdened, stripped first of the bags and then baby Hannah. Slumping into an overstuffed easy chair I begin to uncoil. Ray cradles Hannah like a football and coos her to sleep and Faye puts the kettle on.

My other burdens are also gently removed as, eyes lowered, I begin to tell my story. Parts of it at least – the bits that I can bear to tell. They are quiet and wet eyed. Every once in a while, they ask a question. We hold the tale together in stillness. And in that moment, we are aware that the silence has deepened and we are all being held.

'Can I read this to you?' Faye reaches for her Bible, thumbing through it. I tense again, wary. Recently some other well-meaning (maybe? Maybe not) Christians had bludgeoned me with verses about submission, silence and suffering. The bruises from that encounter ache almost as much as the ones on my throat. I feel like a feral cat trapped in a corner, unsure if the hands that are reaching for me are

friendly or not, but hungry and aching for touch.
    Her eyes are kind. I take a risk and nod.
    'Just close your eyes. Imagine God speaking this over you.'

'Do not be afraid; you will not be put to shame.
    Do not fear disgrace; you will not be humiliated.
You will forget the shame of your youth
    and remember no more the reproach of your
widowhood.
For your Maker is your husband –
    the LORD Almighty is his name –
the Holy One of Israel is your Redeemer;
    he is called the God of all the earth.
The LORD will call you back
    as if you were a wife deserted and distressed in spirit –
a wife who married young,
    only to be rejected,' says your God ...
'... yet my unfailing love for you will not be shaken
    nor my covenant of peace be removed,'
    says the LORD, who has compassion on you.

'Afflicted city, lashed by storms and not comforted,
    I will rebuild you ...
All your children will be taught by the LORD,
    and great will be their peace.
... tyranny will be far from you;
    you will have nothing to fear.
Terror will be far removed;
    it will not come near you.'

ISAIAH 54 (EXCERPTS)

The words alternatively sear and soothe me. See me. Name me. Mark me. Inscribe themselves beneath my skin. Half a century later I still trace their lines and feel their strength. My detour has taken me deep into the wilderness where I fell prey to the wild beasts in myself and in others.

As Faye reads and God speaks, hope cracks a doorway. I limp towards it, leaning.

THE INVITATION

It can be bewildering when plans go awry, when the pathway forward is obscured in the mists of challenge and confusion, when we find ourselves in the wilderness. Jesus was no stranger to the desert places. After he is called to ministry and affirmed by the Father, he is compelled into the wilderness where he is beset upon by his own frailty and the onslaught of the enemy. At one time or another all of our pathways detour through the desert.

1. Have you ever been in a wilderness season? What was its landscape? How would you describe the terrain? It can be helpful to draw a picture or a map of your wilderness and describe your experience either through words or symbols. Is it mountainous? Like a maze? A jungle?

'Therefore I am now going to allure her;
I will lead her into the wilderness
and speak tenderly to her.
There I will give her back her vineyards,
and will make the Valley of Achor a door of hope.

HOSEA 2:14−15A

2. The prophet Hosea promises that in the wilderness God will make the Valley of Achor (which means trouble) a door of hope.

Where might God be at work in your personal wilderness? How is he leading you and speaking to you? What is he restoring? What doorway of hope is opening for you?

> *Jesus I'm comforted by the fact that you are no stranger to the wilderness.*
> *You entered into our suffering – you entered into MY suffering – and in the desert you can, and will, bring your saving help. God of hope, please come and fill me with joy and peace in believing, that I might abound in hope by the power of your Holy Spirit.*
> *(Romans 15:13)*

Chapter 5

REBUILD

*For the L*ORD *will rebuild Zion*
and appear in his glory.
He will respond to the prayer of the destitute;
he will not despise their plea.

PSALM 102:16–17

'I will rebuild you.'

I stand at the ground zero of my life and survey the rubble. It takes about five years to sift through the tangle of debris and clear it out. If it weren't for Hannah, I'm pretty sure I would have just laid down in the dust. But she's depending on me. Somehow, I have to find a way to function.

We are inseparable. She doesn't want to be alone and neither do I, so we share a bed at night. I need my hands free for cooking, cleaning and all manner of other single-mother tasks, so during the day she is tied to my body in a sling. She peeks out the front like a baby kangaroo in its mother's pouch and flirts at passers-by when we are out and about.

My body is not my own. I am a mountain for her to climb, a tree for her to swing from and of course the source of breakfast, lunch and dinner. There is something visceral and life-giving about our physical connection. When I am empty and desolate, when the black hole yawns inside me and I feel like I'm spinning off into space, she tethers and grounds me. I'm shocked by the intensity of my adoration for her. I know that my parents loved me, but I had no idea that a mother's heart could be so wild and fierce.

'Are you going to put Hannah in day care and find work?' I'm asked.

'No.' I'm terse. Edgy. 'She's just lost one parent. She's not going to lose another.'

I hire myself out as a nanny and take Hannah along. Over the next few years, autumns are spent watching the trees change colour and hurl their leaves to the street as I push a baby pram and walk for miles and miles. I log countless wintry hours slumped on the couch watching Disney movies, kids tumbling like puppies around me. Springs and summers find me sitting on the edge of the sandbox in our local park – 'Hey, don't stick that up your nose!' – surrounded by Filipino nannies and the musical cadence of Tagalog.

I stumble through my days and months as best I can, but I'm still a mess. My head is full of a flock of crows. They rasp and cackle.

'I should have ...'

'If only I'd said ...'

'I can't believe he ...'

It's a dark swirl inside and I can see why they call it a murder.

One Sunday as the congregation filters out to find the coffee, I'm slumped alone in the pew. Head in my hands, I'm weeping again – bitter, angry tears. There is a gentle touch on my shoulder and I look up into the face of one of our pastors. 'Do you want to come to a back room and talk?' I let her take my hand. She leads me slowly like I'm fragile and breakable. Which I am.

We sit down together. Her husband joins us.

What happens next is perhaps the most healing, restorative event of my life. Years later as I look back, I mark it as a watershed, the tipping point where the boulder I had daily been rolling uphill finally crested the peak.

'You need to forgive,' they say. 'You need to let it go. But first you need to name it. Say it out loud. You need to be heard.'

'You don't have to feel forgiving – you don't have to feel anything at all. This isn't about letting him off the hook, it's about you – untangling you and setting you free so you can move on.'

Over the next hour and a half that's what I do. I recount every … single … detail. Every unkind word. Every impossible situation. Every act of neglect or cruelty and every hurt. Even the deepest and most shameful – things I never thought I would say out loud. The words jolt out of my mouth like shards of glass. I can't look at my silent witnesses, staring instead at a spot on the carpet.

At the end of each disclosure I pray a prayer of response they teach me: 'I forgive him, and I release him to you, Holy Spirit. And I take back the ground that has been stolen from me.'

Several times when I say it, I spit it through clenched teeth. My jaw twitches and aches. But I say it – over and over and over again, each time I recount another painful memory.

Finally, it's done. All the pieces have been sorted, named and reclaimed. As I look over them, I feel emotionally flat but clear somehow – detoxed. My pastors lay a sacramental hand on me and release me with blessing.

In the weeks that follow I begin to swing at the crows with my newfound weapon, 'I forgive him, and I release him to you, Holy Spirit.' Over and over and over I pray that prayer – sometimes a hundred times a day. It's time to fight for my brain space.

Months later, I'm in the shower washing my hair. As the water flows over me, I startle, suddenly alert. 'Waitaminit.' What was that? I tilt my soggy head to listen.

To silence. My internal space has – well, space.

I can breathe again – there is room to exhale. The crows have gone, flitting away when I wasn't looking. It's a miracle.

I'm reminded of Psalm 18, 'He brought me out into a spacious place; he rescued me because he delighted in me.'[10] Life continues as it did before but now my skin fits better. I'm able to be more present and give better attention to Hannah and the other kids in my care.

My husband takes one last swing and divorces me, proving that even from a distance he is able to inflict damage. 'No church will hire you now!' He's right it seems. My congregation does a great job caring for me. I'm the first single mother whose baby they dedicate. When I show up on Sundays, I'm handed rubbish bags full of baby clothes. One month I'm unable to pay my rent and someone writes a cheque, no questions asked. However, it seems I've also been neatly boxed and sorted. In their eyes, I'm Jill the single mum, Jill the victim of domestic violence, Jill the Wounded One. I bump my head against the glass ceiling several times before I figure it out. Jill the leader doesn't exist anymore.

I bury my ministry aspirations in an unmarked grave. After a year or two I can't even see where the ground had been disturbed. I've stopped asking God for direction. My confidence in my ability to hear his voice is shattered. Hadn't I felt completely peaceful about my decision to get married? Biggest decision of my life and I get it wrong. How on earth could I have messed up that badly? This is reinforced by the most frequent (and most obnoxious) question that comes my way: 'Weren't there any signs before you got married

10 Psalm 18:19.

that he was going to be violent? *Oh sure, I knowingly and willingly signed up for all this. 'Cause I'm that kind of girl and this is the kind life that I wanted for myself ... Yeesh.* Really?

Insensitive questions aside, I can't deny that whatever instrument panel I was referring to for life navigation was seriously flawed, if not completely broken. I had been flying blind and didn't even know it. I decided that I was grounded – no more crazy God-leadings for me. Common sense is going to have to be enough.

'The way to combat depression,' my therapist says, 'is just do the next right thing.' So I do the next right thing. And the next. And the next. Life is simple. Uncomplicated. Routine and uncluttered.

It was as if God was waiting for the ground to be cleared of debris. When the snarl of my internal weeds and brambles gives way to green space, he drops in a dream, pressing it deep into the loam to grow.

THE INVITATION

Clutter. Our lives are often cluttered. So, also, are our hearts and minds. Our internal world and our headspace can get filled up with all manner of mental and emotional debris – worry, fear and unforgiveness. Author Stephen Covey talks of how we can get stuck in the 'thick of thin things'.[11] We lose perspective. How can we de-clutter, clear the ground and create space for God's word to grow within us?

Read: this parable slowly, out loud if possible. As you read, pay attention to which words or phrases jump out at you.

---

11 Stephen R. Covey, *The 7 Habits of Highly Effective People: Powerful Lessons in Personal Change* (Simon and Schuster UK Ltd, 1989), p.9.

At about that same time Jesus left the house and sat on the beach. In no time at all a crowd gathered along the shoreline, forcing him to get into a boat. Using the boat as a pulpit, he addressed his congregation, telling stories. 'What do you make of this? A farmer planted seed. As he scattered the seed, some of it fell on the road, and birds ate it. Some fell in the gravel; it sprouted quickly but didn't put down roots, so when the sun came up it withered just as quickly. Some fell in the weeds; as it came up, it was strangled by the weeds. Some fell on good earth, and produced a harvest beyond his wildest dreams. ...'

MATTHEW 13:1–8 (MSG)

Reflect: Where do you find yourself in the story? Which kind of soil most describes your inner space right now?

Respond: How might God want to till the soil of your heart, to break up hard ground or to remove stones and stumps, to create space inside of you for his word to root and grow? How might you be a willing participant in that process?

> *Jesus, I need your presence.*
> *I need Your Spirit.*
> *I need the joy of my salvation once again.*
> *Grant me a willing spirit to sustain me.*
> *Help me to release all I need to let go of, and lay hold of all you have for me.*[12]

12 Psalm 51:11–12.

Chapter 6

STEP BY STEP

'All this,' David said, 'I have in writing as a result of the
Lord's hand on me, and he enabled me to understand all
the details of the plan.'

1 Chronicles 28:19

Once Hannah is old enough to start school, I begin to look around for other work. What can I do that will fit well with my life as a single mum?

'Jill, we're looking for people who will dress up as clowns for the community festival. What do you think? Want to help?' My pastor's grin and enthusiasm are infectious. 'Sure,' I say. Why not? I mean, who doesn't like dressing up and acting silly? I'm given a wig of white feathers and a bowler hat, a baggy white costume and gloves. 'Let's call you Angel.' The clown nose is glued on and I am transformed.

I start out shy, unsure. But children are open-hearted and responsive, especially the little ones. Over the course of the day as I work the crowd, handing out sweets and playing with kids, I discover my inner clown.

I wonder if there is something to this?

Craisy Daisy is birthed at home in the bath. I'm actually of the opinion that the bathroom is The Room of Revelation. God speaks to us there more than in other places, I have no idea why. Maybe it's the only place many of us get a little solitude? I'm soaking in the tub one day, minding my own business. Without warning, the entire business plan bursts into the room and lodges itself in my imagination.

Here is your clown character: her name is Craisy Daisy. Here is what her costume will look like. Here are your tricks and your shtick. Here's how you will market yourself. Here is how you are going to use her for God's purposes.

It takes about twenty minutes. When it's all over, I hop out of the bath, dry myself off and get to work.

In the beginning I market myself to my daughter's friends: 'I'm just learning, so how 'bout I come to your party for half price?' Then as I grow in confidence and ability, I hire myself out to agents and build my business. I'm not a gospel clown – I'm a corporate event and birthday party clown. Santa and I are buddies and Barney the Purple Dinosaur is a close personal friend.

I learn the importance of pre-emptive prayer before going into parties and I spend time in my car taking authority over spirits of lawlessness and chaos before I enter into the fray. A room full of clown haters hopped up on sugar can be a fearsome thing.

The money is good, but it's really about home invasions. I want to bring the presence of Jesus to my clients, even if I can't talk about him directly. One day my agent decides to spy on me in order to assess my skill level. She secretly sends a friend into one of my parties. 'She's got this wonderful aura about her,' the friend reports. 'A glow.' Ha.

Craisy Daisy is a hit. She develops a following of teeny fans and a reputation in the clown community.

Around this time, I also find myself drawn to the back garden where I had buried my dreams for a career in ministry, and begin to dig in the dust like an archaeologist.

Unearthing them with care, I hold them up to the light and am surprised to find them still intact. What might be possible for a divorced single mum? I don't know but I begin to explore. Another local church has a divorce recovery group, so I join it and begin to make friends. Warmly received by my new community, I decide I need to make a fresh start, and so I switch churches. My new pastors are unhampered by my sordid past, are quick to discern my knack for leadership and give me opportunities for growth and development. Before I know it, I'm on staff part time and begin training as a church planter. It's been a long way round to becoming a Reverend but I'm finally on the path again.

My friendship with Kirk, the handsome drummer on the church worship team, deepens. I knew him back when I was dating my first husband. Before my divorce is finalized, Kirk is quick to remind me that I'm only separated. 'No dating for you!' he exhorts.

A year or so after my marriage ends, Kirk and I feel the gravitational pull and we swing more and more into each other's orbit. It's complicated. We try dating, but I'm easily triggered, self-protective and jumpy. What if I make the same mistakes again? For about a year or so we are on again, off again as we try to sort out our mutual attraction in the midst of the complexities. Through it all we keep leaning into God, our close friends and our church leadership.

One day we're walking from the subway station to my house. Kirk is playing hide and seek with 4-year-old Hannah. She hasn't quite got the hang of it and is hiding *in front* of the trees with her forehead pressed against the bark. 'Where is she?' Kirk circles around the tree, ignoring her muffled giggles. I begin to wonder if he is father material.

Half a year later … It's Christmas Eve and I'm cranky.

Here's what you need to know about me. I get up early in the morning. Really, really early. Somehow, I've inherited my father's circadian rhythm and I've yet to decide if it's a blessing or a curse. Probably both. 'I'm a lark, not an owl,' I chirp to my friends. 'The early bird gets the anointing!' Early rising works great for my prayer life but it makes me a really boring companion in the evenings. My 'best before date' is 9pm; after that I go sour and rancid.

It's 9.30 when we pull up to Kirk's parents' house. Kirk promised it would be a short stop on the way home from a wedding we had just attended. 'Jill, you've just got to come in and see the Christmas tree,' he says. 'It's fantastic. You've never seen anything like it!' I'm comfy, nestled into the passenger seat of the car. The wedding was lovely and the bride was beautiful. It has been a great night, but I'm fuzzy headed with fatigue and out of sorts like a petulant toddler. 'I don't *want* to see the tree,' I pout. 'I just want to go home. 'Come. Inside. And. See. The. Tree.' He is thin lipped and his jaw juts.

I humph and flop out of the car, dragging my feet up the stairs to the house. The tree is, indeed, beautiful. Kirk's mum has elegant taste, and the tree looks like something out of a Martha Stewart magazine. I give it a quick glance.

'There. I've seen it. Can we go now?'

'Just sit down!'

I drop down onto the couch. Kirk pulls a small gift out from under the tree and hands it to me.

It's wrapped but I recognize the shape – it's a CD case. My anger flares. You cheap son of a gun! Dating for two and a half years and all you can buy me is a lousy CD? I mutter a cursory 'thanks' and begin to unwrap.

The CD has no sleeve in it and sitting on the centre

spindle is a ring. A diamond ring. My eyes widen. I'm not done being cranky though. 'Get on one knee and ask me!' It's a testament to Kirk's patience, kindness and long suffering that he doesn't chuck the ring at me or take it back. Instead he slips it on the finger of the most undeserving fiancée ever.

Hannah makes an adorable flower girl. Her hair is pixie-cut short – just a month before the wedding I come upstairs to find her, sewing scissors in hand, contemplating a rubbish bin full of blonde locks.

My hair is problematic as well. A week before the wedding I get lice, a surprise gift from a hat-borrowing friend. Kirk and I both have long locks, so on our wedding night he gets infested as well. We spend our honeymoon combing nits out of each other's hair for hours at a time. Romantic. Not the start I expected in this new season, but hey – all in all things are looking up, so who am I to complain?

THE INVITATION

A burst of creativity? Instructions from heaven? Or both? How do we know what plans are from God and what plans are from us? How do we tell the difference between the good idea and the God idea?

In the book of Nehemiah, the author claims that God has given him a plan to rebuild the city of Jerusalem. 'What my God had put in my heart to do,' he says of his plans in Nehemiah 2:12. King David was the same, he says this: 'All this ... I have in writing as a result of the LORD's hand on me, and he enabled me to understand all the details of the plan.' (1 Chronicles 28:19). I love that certainty! But how many of us feel that?

Here are some questions that might help us assess the plans we carry in our heart:

1. How does it fit with our overall direction and calling?
2. Does it bring a deep sense of life and freedom?
3. What are our deepest, most authentic desires?
4. What does the Scriptures say to this issue?
5. Does the life of Christ point towards a particular direction?
6. Will it develop our character growth and development?
7. What does love call for?[13]

My biggest challenge? My own grandiosity. How can I detect my own ego in the midst of making plans? What is the difference between confidence and striving, between boldness and arrogance? I've found the following steps helpful:

Ask: Search me O Lord and know my heart – see if there is any wicked way in me.
Notice (and repent if necessary):

- Am I comparing myself to others or am I subtly in competition with them?
- Am I striving – trying to 'figure things out', trying to 'make it happen'?
- Am I isolating myself in independence rather than leaning into others in interdependence?
- Who is being glorified? Do my plans make me look good, or do they make God look good?

Remember: God opposes the proud and gives grace to the humble.

13 Ruth Haley Barton, *Pursuing God's Will Together: A Discernment Practice for Leadership Groups* (InterVarsity Press, 2012), pp.68,69.

God, I offer myself to Thee – to build with me and to do with me as Thou wilt.
Relieve me of the bondage of self, that I may better do Thy will.
Take away my difficulties, that victory over them may bear witness to those I would help of Thy Power, Thy Love, and Thy Way of life.
May I do Thy will always![14]

---

14 3rd step prayer from Inc, A.A. World Services, *Alcoholics Anonymous, 4th Edition* (Alcoholics Anonymous World Services, Inc., 2001), p. 63.

Chapter 7

DANGEROUS PRAYERS

But even if I am being poured out like a drink offering on the sacrifice and service coming from your faith, I am glad and rejoice with all of you. So you too should be glad and rejoice with me.

PHILIPPIANS 2:17–18

It's midweek and the church is deserted. Alone in a pew, I'm enjoying a moment of solitude. I love the quiet that settles in holy spaces like mist – dampening sound, enfolding you. God walks on little cat feet.

I am feeling grateful. My anxieties about remarriage seemed unfounded and Kirk, Hannah and I have settled snugly into life together. My work at the church is challenging and interesting – I'm growing and being given more responsibilities. My clown business is flourishing. I'm in a season of what I can only describe as increased God consciousness. Some mornings I wake up and as soon as I open my eyes I feel like he's right there, saying 'good morning', not unlike the way my grandfather greeted his wife with a cup of tea at the start of each day. There is an intensity to his proximity and sometimes I am overwhelmed with a sense of his nearness. It feels like I'm a bathtub and someone has left the tap on and I'm full to the brim and beginning to overflow. I'm on track and the path before me looks fruitful and promising.

Back in the sanctuary I pray, 'You are so good, and have done so much. I'm grateful but I also know there's more. Lord, can you continue to pour yourself out in my life?' I'm not expecting a response. But there is a gentle nudge on the edge of my consciousness. Not an audible voice, *per se*. More like words taking shape like cloud formations in the sky.

'What if I want YOU to pour yourself out?'

At that moment I'm reminded of the passage in Philippians where Paul talks about being poured out like a drink offering, giving himself away in gratitude for all he has been given.[15]

You want *me* to pour myself out? Makes sense. I begin to hum. Then sing. *Pour it out, pour it out, pour it out O God.*

I've always had an affinity for music, tootling away on plastic flutes in my earlier school years, then a brief love affair with the piano. I pick up a guitar in my early teens and settle into learning how to use it. I also discover I've got a half-decent voice, and music becomes more and more a part of my life. I'm a voracious reader, and I gobble up the piles of books I bring home from the library each week. I begin writing stories, poems, and once I master the rudiments of guitar – songs.

I don't feel like a song writer, per se. More of a song 'birther'. Often songs feel like they get downloaded, sometimes in bits and bites, other times fully formed. Then they rattle and hum inside me and become my prayer assignment for a season.

Today in the sanctuary, this one rushes in all at once.

Make my life a prayer
Make my life a song
Make my life an offering to you

15 Philippians 2:17.

I wanna pour it out
Pour it out, pour it out, pour it out O God.
I wanna pour it out
I'm like the jar of alabaster
Broken to anoint my Master
Precious oil, my life's perfume
Is all I have to bring
I see it gently trickle down
Onto your head, your beard, your gown.
I'll spend it all, I'll give it all
I want to be an offering.

Little do I know what a dangerous prayer this is. You know, dangerous prayers? The ones you hold up to heaven, saying: 'Here you are Lord, take all of me.' And then want to immediately snatch back? 'You snooze you lose, Jesus – gotta be quicker to catch that one!'

Dangerous ones. Prayers of wholehearted abandon. Prayers that no one in their right mind would pray. At least no one with any sense of self-preservation and foresight.

Make my life a prayer
Make my life a song
Make my life an offering
I want to pour it out.

God snatches that prayer from my hands and lips before I can take it back, and adds to it his wholehearted yes.

THE INVITATION

The Methodist Covenant Prayer was written by Richard Alleine in the 1600s. On 11 August 1755, John Wesley used it in the first Methodist covenant service. To this day, Methodist ministers and congregations renew this dangerous prayer every year. Pray at your own risk!

> *I am no longer my own but yours.*
> *Put me to what you will,*
> *rank me with whom you will;*
> *put me to doing,*
> *put me to suffering;*
> *let me be employed for you,*
> *or laid aside for you,*
> *exalted for you,*
> *or brought low for you;*
> *let me be full,*
> *let me be empty,*
> *let me have all things,*
> *let me have nothing:*
> *I freely and wholeheartedly yield all things*
> *to your pleasure and disposal.*
> *And now, glorious and blessed God,*
> *Father, Son and Holy Spirit,*
> *you are mine and I am yours. So be it.*
> *And the covenant now made on earth, let it be ratified in*
> *heaven.*[16]

Read: Read the prayer out loud (if you dare!) Which words or phrases jump out at you?

Reflect: Reflect on those words or phrases. What do you resonate with? What do you feel resistant towards?

Respond: How might God be asking you to respond to what he is highlighting in the poem? What is his invitation to you?

16 *The Methodist Worship Book* (Methodist Publishing, 1999), p.290.

Chapter 8

INTER-WHATTER?

*And pray in the Spirit on all occasions with all kinds
of prayers and requests. With this in mind, be alert and
always keep on praying for all the Lord's people.*

EPHESIANS 6:18

We are warrior ninjas with prams. Our kids are tolerant and
long suffering, rolling their eyes and making faces at each
other as we trundle and jolt them over the rough terrain of
the housing estate. Townhouses peer with vacant eyes – half
lidded with sheets instead of curtains. Gardens are weedy
and dishevelled, strewn with rubbish. It's a tangle, an urban
jungle. At this early hour of the morning it's deserted.

My friend Shirley and I are prayer walking through one
of the poorest neighbourhoods of our city. If there had been
any onlookers, they may have thought we were somewhat
unhinged. We sing worship songs together as we walk.
Prayer is our powerful weapon.

Parking our buggies in front of a wall scrawled with
graffiti, we yell at the wall (well, really at the demons hiding
behind the wall), demanding the community's release. There
may even have been flags and shofars involved at some
point. We had teeny flags (pink, of course!) made for the
girls so they could join in.

I love that the Scriptures say that out of the mouth of babes you ordain praise to silence the foe and the avenger.[17] We are baby prayer warriors. We bluster and bumble our way forward, taking authority over this and that. What we lack in wisdom we make up for in zeal. We have no idea what we are doing, really. Two things we do know though. First, the earth is the Lord's – even the ghettos – and he wants it back. Second, we are Intercessors.

Two years before, it was my friend Sandy who first labelled me with the 'I-word'. I had just finished a two-month stint at a worship leading school in British Columbia, wee Hannah in tow. Before returning home we visit Sandy, her husband and their brood of kids. Hannah bounces for hours on their trampoline and I help Sandy's team of artists, musicians and evangelists as they prepare for a cross-Canada mission.

We had converted four tractor trailers into a portable theatre in the round, complete with stage and bleachers. Massive murals were painted on the sides of the trucks. A team of musicians and evangelists are assembled. The goal? Tour the mobile theatre through small communities all across Canada. Set it up in the centre of each town, throw a Wang Dang Doo (for the uninitiated, that means noisy musical party) and introduce people to Jesus.

One day we roll into a local community for a test run. Park the trucks. Get the word out to the neighbourhood. The techies scuttle about, assembling the theatre. Musicians tune up, actors and dancers rehearse. Hannah and the other kids bunny hop up and down the bleachers. New to the team, and a temporary member at that, I feel at a bit of a loose end.

17 Psalm 8:2.

'Sandy, how can I help?'

She looks around at the bustle of activity and thinks for a minute.

'Jill, you're an intercessor,' she declares.

An *inter-whatter*? I'd never heard the term before.

'What we really need you to do is stand in the corner – right over there.' She points to a nook where two trucks join. 'Before and during the meetings. Pay attention to what is going on in the space and with the people. Stand there, watch and pray.' I want Sandy to think I'm a team player so I do as I'm told. But I'm not happy. Intercessor. Great.

Intercessors, prayer warriors, whatever you call them – aren't they the weird uncles in God's family – the misfits? Nobody knows what to do with them. Mostly I had seen them relegated to some dingy little room in the back of the church, out from underfoot, out of sight and definitely out of mind. The job of praying belongs to those who don't have any real skills, right?

Not to mention that they look depressed all the time – carrying the weight of the burden of the Lord. Lamenting the woes of the nation and the sorry state of the church. Intercessor? Not me! I'm a worship leader! I get to be the happy one, not the gloomy one. I get to be the one up at the front on the platform, not cloistered away in a musty back closet.

Hmmph.

Standing in the corner I survey the crowd of the curious as they assemble to watch the show. Alrightee, Intercessor lady, how should we pray? *Bring the people, Lord. Help them to be open to you. Reveal Jesus.* I pray until I can pray no more. Spent, I stop and peek at my watch.

Five minutes had passed.

Great. Another two hours to go. I've used up all my words.

Then I remember. I don't need English words. I've got a

prayer language. I'm still in a non-charismatic church when I first start praying in tongues. In my late teens I investigate short-term mission projects and I find an interesting one that is going to Tijuana, Mexico. 'Candidates must be filled with the Holy Spirit and speak in tongues,' the application says. Tongues? Umm. Well darn. I had never heard of nor encountered the phenomenon before.

But the idea of loving underprivileged kids is alluring so I decide to do some investigating. I open up the book of Acts and find, much to my surprise, that many of the early Christians spoke in tongues! How come I never saw that before? Why haven't I ever heard of it? I write down all the Bible verses that have anything to do with the topic and ponder them. I've got questions. Lots of questions.

That week I'm in a chance meeting with a feisty Pentecostal pastor. During the worship his hands are in the air. A hand waver, eh? Maybe he's also a tongue speaker? Turns out he is. He tucks me under his wing as a potential Spirit-filled acolyte, fields all my questions and then guides me to The Moment. The Laying On of Hands. 'All you have to do is open up your mouth and start to speak. You might just get one word or two, so just repeat the ones you get and God will add more to them in time.'

I feel awkward. Just open my mouth? What if I'm just making it up? Spouting nonsense? Worse yet what if I say embarrassing things in some other language? I don't feel a thing when he prays for me but much to my surprise, when I open my mouth there is a torrent of words. Nothing English, or any other recognizable language I've ever heard. He is delighted and gives me a high five, but I'm still sceptical.

I take my prayer language home and tuck it in my back pocket, bringing it out only occasionally and in private. I find out that one of the sweet little old ladies at my Presbyterian church is a closet tongue speaker as well, but I'm too nervous to 'out' myself to her.

One night I'm standing at the bus stop. The street is empty and I'm still wrestling with the whole tongues thing. What if I'm being deceived? What if it's the devil making me speak instead of God? A lightbulb goes on. Ah, I know what to do! There's a way to test it! I had recently read in 1 John:

> *Dear friends, do not believe every spirit, but test the spirits to see whether they are from God, because many false prophets have gone out into the world. This is how you can recognise the Spirit of God: every spirit that acknowledges that Jesus Christ has come in the flesh is from God,*[18]

Stands to reason, then, if I speak in tongues, and then immediately after that blurt, 'Jesus is Lord' that should do the trick, right? If it's demons, I wouldn't be able to do that – would I?

I'm still alone at the bus stop so I try it out loud a number of times, just to be sure. My experiment is successful and I'm much relieved. Not demonized. Good. Still, there is not much room in our simple Presbyterian church service for tongues, so the gift lies dormant.

A couple of years later I wander into a Pentecostal church. Lots of hand wavers here. Some jumpers too, and lots of 'Amen'-ers. I'm shy and somewhat reserved but their enthusiasm is fascinating. I feel like an anthropologist observing some remote tribe.

Then, at the end of a particularly wavy and jumpy song, it happens.

They begin to sing in tongues.

All 500 of them.

18 1 John 4:1–2.

The nerve endings on my arms prickle and goose bump. It's the most beautiful thing I've ever heard. The melodies mingle, dance and twirl around each other. Dip and crescendo. It sounds like the heavens are open and angels are singing. It's otherworldly and overwhelming.

To be honest though, I'm pretty freaked out. I had the foresight to sit at the end of a pew so I decide to make my escape.

Back away ... Back away slowly ...

At the doorway to the sanctuary I pivot and bolt for the exit.

I'm stopped by a wizened Pentecostal granny. She's standing between me and the door. Her stockings are rumpled, her dress is flouncy and her veiled hat is at a cocky angle. She grabs my hand and holds it firmly between hers. Her skin is leathery, smooth and cool. 'God bless you, dear.' She holds my eyes with hers and I wonder how soon I can politely wiggle away. After an uncomfortable moment, her gaze and her grasp ground me and my insides settle. She gives me one last squeeze, lets me go, and I wander home wondering about tongues of men and angels.

When Hannah and I return back home from our west coast adventures with Sandy and her mission team, I begin to investigate and experiment with this whole intercession thing. Does prayer make a difference? Can we change things just by talking to God? I read about Abraham arguing God out of firebombing a city. About Moses' uplifted hands turning the tide of battle. About ten days of upper-room prayer catalysing the outpouring of the Holy Spirit and the birth of the church.

I find a co-conspirator – a prayer partner – in my friend Shirley. Together we begin to stir up holy dissatisfaction with the status quo. The kingdom of God suffers violence, and the violent take it by force. We wade into the fray.

THE INVITATION

1. We know ourselves only in part. One of the gifts of community is that, sometimes, those around us see aspects of us and gifts we carry that we are not yet aware of ourselves, like the way Sandy saw that I had a gift of intercession even before I did! Think about a time when someone has seen something latent, hidden in you, and told you what they saw. How did you feel? What was God's invitation to you in that moment? How has that informed your choices and influenced your journey?

2. Prayer has many expressions and the church has a rich and multifaceted, several thousand-year-old tradition of conversation and communion with God. Have you ever encountered a mode of prayer from another stream of the church that is entirely alien to you? What might happen if you dipped your toe in that stream and explored and experimented with an unfamiliar mode of prayer? How might you explore that?

Jesus, you see me and you know me.
As you put me in community you show me more of who I am
and how you want to grow me.
Give me an adventurous heart, ready to try new pathways and
to adopt new ways of seeing not only myself, but your work in
the world.

Chapter 9

GIRL, INTERRUPTED

*When the L*ORD *saw that he had gone over to look, God*
called to him from within the bush, 'Moses! Moses!'
And Moses said, 'Here I am.'

EXODUS 3:4

I've often said that God reserves the right to interrupt our lives and change their direction any time he likes. We are, after all, no longer our own but bought with a price. We belong to him. Don't you love it when the words you say turn around and bite you in the bum?

Life is humming along happily. My clown business is gaining momentum and my marriage is still in the rosy coloured honeymoon-ish stage. I'm working with a local congregation getting tooled up as a church planter. The path to my long-standing dream of becoming Reverend Jill is clear – I can see it ahead of me all shiny and gleaming, sparkling in the not-too-far distance.

And then, suddenly, my path zigs where it should have zagged.

It starts innocently enough.

My friend Shirley calls me up one day. 'Jill, there is a team from IHOP coming to town this week and next. Wanna go see them?' I've heard of the International House of Prayer

– a prayer missions base in Kansas City that had started a year or so ago. They had reputedly thrown away the keys to their building, claiming they were going to leave it open for prayer, twenty-four hours a day, seven days a week, until Jesus returns. 'Now there's a long-term plan,' I think.

I'm not sure what is involved in a prayer missions base – beyond prayer and, well, missions. But Shirley assures me that it will be well worth a night out. Maybe we will have another one of our excellent adventures. I leave Kirk to babysit. Curious and unsuspecting, I hop in the car and make the trip downtown.

The evening itself is a bit of a blur and I struggle to remember the details. I do, however, remember with great clarity how I felt. Stirred. Shaken. Vibrating. Every part of me.

When I was a child, my dad took my brother and I to the local science centre. There was an electric ball that caused your hair to stand on end when you touched it – super impressive for me because my hair reached almost to my waist at the time. There was also a display about sound waves and resonant frequency. In it was a picture of the corpse of Tacoma Narrows Bridge, shorn back and exposed, twisted and in pieces. A suspension bridge, opened in 1940, between Tacoma and the Kitsap Peninsula in Washington. At the time it was the third longest in the world. It lasted a few short months before it shimmied, gyrated, buckled and splintered to bits. 'The wind whipped through the canyon,' Dad said, 'and the engineers didn't anticipate the gusts would be the same resonant frequency as the steel cables. They began to vibrate like enormous guitar strings, and the whole thing fell apart.' My husband is a drummer, and drummers know a lot about resonant frequency. He works hard tuning his instrument to get the perfect tone. 'If you put your head right up to this drumhead, and hum at just the right pitch, it will start to vibrate!' He grins. 'Just like a tuning fork. Try it!'

That night in the church I'm like the bridge – quivering. I'm like the drumhead. God strikes a note and everything in me starts to hum.

The worship leader and singers have Bibles open and are singing Scriptures. Improvizing musically and lyrically. Weaving songs and prayers together with the worship team vamping around them like a seasoned jazz ensemble. The air is electric.

Prayer and worship together?

I've been diligently trying to grow in prayer and believe it's vital, but if I am honest, I find it hard work. What I am witnessing tonight is not that. Is it possible that there are ways to pray that are not boring, laborious and exhausting?

Could it be, *gasp*, fun?

My dear friend Shirley, who had been worshipping at the front, sprints to my chair.

'Jill!' She shouts, 'It all makes sense now! You – worship! Me – prayer! Together! This is what we've been looking for!' I realize is that I have just been interrupted. Captured. Apprehended. In that moment I slip off the career path I have been painstakingly carving out and slide onto a little side path leading ... who knows where?

At the end of the meeting I make my way to the front of the room and shake hands with the hostess. 'If you ever

decide to start something like this here, let me know.' I say.
'I'll be glad to help.'

I go back home and report to my husband Kirk what I
had seen, heard and experienced. The following Wednesday
the same team does another meeting, and this time he goes
while I watch Hannah.

Now, my husband is a thoughtful guy. He's a good balance
to me. Often, I'm the one with the foot to the floor and he's
the one with his on the brake. I'm the early adopter and he
takes a little more time to warm up to new ideas and settle
into decisions. But in this instance, he is clear.

'Yup, you're right,' he says upon his return. 'We need to
pursue this.'

THE INVITATION

1. The biblical story is full of instances where God interrupts
    the protagonist and invites them on both an internal
    and external journey with him. Abram is invited into a
    new identity when God says in Genesis 17:5 'No longer
    will you be called Abram; your name will be Abraham,
    for I have made you a father of many nations.' He is also
    invited on a journey to a new land that God promises
    to show him. Gideon is invited into a new identity: 'The
    LORD is with you, mighty warrior' (Judges 6:12b) and
    on a journey towards overcoming his oppressors. In the
    New Testament, Simon is invited into a new identity:
    'And I tell you that you are Peter, and on this rock I will
    build my church' (Matthew 16:18a) and on a journey
    with Jesus to see the kingdom of God established.
    Can you think of a time when God has interrupted you?
    What was your response to the interruption? What

might God's invitation to you be in the midst of that interruption? How might he be inviting you into a new identity and onto a journey with him?

2. Have you ever experienced a moment of 'resonant frequency?' Where you feel fully alive to yourself and to the presence of God and you know that you are in the right place at the right time, doing the right thing? Ignatius of Loyola, a sixteenth-century priest and theologian and the founder of the Jesuits, called such an experience *consolation*.[19] He asserts that it is an essential element to help us discern the presence and activity of God in our lives. Contemporary writer and spiritual director Margaret Silf gives these identifying signposts to consolation:

    - releases new energy in us
    - generates new inspiration and ideas
    - restores balance and refreshes our inner vision
    - shows us where God is active in our lives and where God is leading us
    - directs our focus outside and beyond ourselves
    - lifts our hearts so that we can see the joys and sorrows of other people
    - bonds us more closely to our human community.[20]

Think about a moment when you have experienced consolation. What were the circumstances surrounding that experience? What might God be inviting you to in and through that experience?

---

19 Ignatius of Loyola, *The Spiritual Exercises* (Beloved Publishing, 2016), p.73.

20 Margaret Silf, *Inner Compass: An Invitation to Ignatian Spirituality* (Loyola Press, 1999), pp. 84–85.

Jesus, you are the Way, the Truth, and the Life.
You see me.
You name me and call me your own.
You invite me on pathways of life.
I choose to receive my new name and follow you today.

Chapter 10

THE PASSING OF THE PEACE

*In their hearts humans plan their course,
but the LORD establishes their steps.*

PROVERBS 16:9

My career as a worship leader begins in the Presbyterian Church. I don't lead worship per se – that's the domain of the organist and choir director. They call my contribution 'pre-service songs'. The church is eager to find ways to involve youth, hoping to keep their interest within the community. I'm a kid with a guitar and a lot of enthusiasm and they create a new tradition so I have somewhere to plug in. In those days, if you knew three or four guitar chords you could play most contemporary choruses. I'm given ten minutes – the warm up act before the proper service begins.

Later on when I'm leading worship in my Baptist church, I graduate up to thirteen and a half minutes. Yep. Thirteen *and a half*. Verse, chorus, verse, verse chorus, bridge aaaand out! We time every song at rehearsal to make sure we don't create any afternoon luncheon disasters by dragging the service overtime. On the plus side, I'm leading worship in the actual service now.

When I join the Vineyard church, I'm delighted. They give me forty-five whole minutes! The service has its own shape and unspoken liturgy: fast song, fast song, slow song, slow song, fast song. I don't mind that. Because I've been given *forty-five whole minutes*! I feel like a dog on one of those zippy extendable leashes discovering I've got lots of room to roam. We can feast on the abundance of God's house, drink from the rivers of his delight and sing and sing and sing ...

We are down in Kansas City at the House of Prayer. We're at a conference to get some training and we're also being interviewed to join the staff team as prayer missionaries. As we step into the prayer room, the worship is under way. Ten minutes. Thirteen and a half minutes. Forty-five minutes. I'm in heaven.

At an hour and ten minutes I begin to get a bit twitchy and check my watch. Holy mackerel, they're still going!

That's the point, I guess. Continuous prayer. Continuous worship. The Catholics call it *Laus Perennis* – perpetual prayer. King David started it during his reign, assigning musicians to minister to God before the ark of the covenant, day and night. He says:

> *One thing I ask of the LORD,*
> *   this only do I seek:*
> *that I may dwell in the House of the LORD*
> *   all the days of my life,*
> *to gaze on the beauty of the LORD*
> *   and to seek him in his temple.*[21]

21 Psalm 27:4.

In the New Testament, the fire of Pentecost is sparked by ten days of continual prayer in the upper room.

In AD 400 there are Eastern Orthodox monks called *Acoemetae* (translated 'sleepless ones') – teams of monastics who take turns worshipping and praying day and night. In about AD 500 perpetual prayer exports to the West and in Saint-Maurice, Switzerland, *Laus Perennis* begins and continues to this day.

The first known Protestant continuous prayer began in 1727 by the Moravian Brethren in Herrnhut Germany, under Nikolaus von Zinzendorf's leadership. One hundred years of *Laus Perennis* sparks a missions-movement that sends Moravians all over the world.

Several hundred years later, the International House of Prayer in Kansas City, USA and 24-7 Prayer in Chichester, UK, find inspiration from Zinzendorf and the Moravians and relight the torch of night-and-day-prayer in the Protestant world. It's fascinating to note that both these 24-7 Prayer movements start in the same week of the same month, completely 'independent' of each other. Both go viral and both become global prayer movements.

Back in Kansas City, the music team winds down their two hours of worship and prayer, and is seamlessly replaced by another cohort of musicians. If our eyes were closed, we would not have noticed a break in the music at all. Continual worship. Continuous prayer.

Our trip down to the prayer-missions base confirms our suspicions. Yes. We're called to this. We feel peaceful and settled. Expectant. We apply to become staff, audition for the worship teams, and are accepted. We are officially 'musicianaries!'

We get ready to move. I train people to take over my various roles at my local church. We complete all the legal work required to move Hannah out of the country. Kirk gives notice at his job.

It's one month until moving day. Everything is in place. And then something unexpected happens. The peace we had been feeling about the decision slips away. Unease begins to buzz around the edges of Kirk's consciousness. He doesn't want to tell me about it – how would I feel? We've invested so much in this process and this transition.

In Colossians 3 Paul says 'Let the peace of Christ rule in your hearts.'[22] The word 'rule' in the original Greek is a judicial term: Paul is speaking of peace making a ruling, like a judge. And right now, the lack of peace is scowling down from the judicial bench like the ones on afternoon television. 'No peace for you!'

I'm lying in bed one night and Kirk is pacing back and forth at the foot of the bed. Agitated.

'I don't know what the peace of God that transcends understanding is, but this. is. not. it!' He blurts. 'You think maybe we're not supposed to go?' We are both surprised at how calm we feel when I say it out loud. *We're not supposed to go.*

Somehow, in the midst of our decision making, planning and execution, we have lost our way. But what to do? Not only had we not left a trail of breadcrumbs in the woods, we have actually burned the forest down behind us. We have already given notice at our jobs, already been replaced. There is no going back. So we do what all deeply intelligent, resourceful and spiritual people do. We retreat to the family cottage and pout.

22 Colossians 3:15.

This is one of a number of incidents in my life where it seems as if God points us in a certain direction, leading us on a certain path, only for us to find a dead end there. 'When God does that, I want to call him Jehovah Sneaky,' I say. 'I call it the bait and switch!' Kirk is less enthusiastic.

But it's only from the vantage point of this impasse that we are able to perceive a way forward. A way we would not have seen or noticed if we never went on the initial journey towards Kansas City.

While we are at the cottage, I get a phone call from a friend. 'My pastor has been meeting with a group of other pastors to pray together for the last six years. One of them recently went down to IHOP and they really want to see a House of Prayer established in Southern Ontario. Do you think you could help?'

THE INVITATION

Desolation is another spiritual dynamic that Ignatius of Loyola helped the church to understand. He primarily identifies desolation as the work of the enemy. The experience of desolation can also be a helpful indicator – like a warning light on the dashboard of your car. Something in your life needs attention and it's time to look under the hood.

Margaret Silf identifies these characteristics. Desolation:

- turns us in on ourselves.
- drives us down the spiral ever deeper into our own negative feelings.
- makes us want to give up on the things that used to be important to us.
- takes over our whole consciousness and crowds out our distant vision.

- covers up all our landmarks (the signs of our journey with God so far).
- drains us of energy.
- cuts us off from community.[23]

Where consolation can be symbolized as a person standing towards the sun, facing its warmth, desolation can be symbolized as a person with their back to the sun, looking at and feeling overwhelmed by their shadow.

1. Can you identify and describe an instance where you experienced desolation? What did it feel like? How did you move beyond it? Where did you see God at work through that experience, if at all? What might God be showing you through that experience?

Jesus, thank you that I was designed to face the sun.
When I feel caught and mired in shadow, help me to turn to face you again.
Help me to be attuned to the internal movements of my heart so that I can follow the pathways of peace.

23 Silf, *Inner Compass*, pp.84–85.

Chapter 11

THE DAY DAISY DIED

*When he reached a certain place, he stopped for the night
because the sun had set. Taking one of the stones there, he
put it under his head and lay down to sleep. He had a
dream in which he saw a stairway resting on the earth,
with its top reaching to heaven, and the angels of God were
ascending and descending on it. There above it stood the
LORD, and he said: 'I am the LORD, the God of your father
Abraham and the God of Isaac. I will give you and your
descendants the land on which you are lying.*

GENESIS 28:11-13

Craisy Daisy is 5 years old when God kills her.

'Upsy daisy, everyone!' The children all jump to their feet.
'Ooops, downsie daisy!' Giggles and thumps as they plop to
the floor again. 'O dear – so sorry – upsie daisy!' Now they're
all laughing – popping up and down in the merry chaos.

'Aaaand aroundsie daisy!' They spin and twirl, careening
into each other. When the show is over I'm swarmed. My
fans wiggle and yelp around me like a basketful of puppies.
Grubby fingers clutch the crinolines of my skirts. My pockets
are examined for treasures. Do my braids actually bounce?
Oh look they do!

Paul made tents; I make balloon shapes. I make daisies

(of course!), giraffes and dachshunds on a leash. I make a mean Viking helmet but flower crowns are my favourite. Clowning proves to be the perfect complement to pastoring. Wholehearted tomfoolery is cathartic. As I dance and sing with the kids I become loose limbed. The stress and responsibility of my congregational work slides off and disappears into the gleeful melee. The hours are flexible and the rates are fantastic. I'm being paid to play!

It's 2001. Kirk and I have responded to the call and agree to help start a House of Prayer in Southern Ontario. As prayer missionaries we have to raise our own support, trusting in God for financial provision. I look ahead to the transition and make plans. I will continue my clowning work and build the House of Prayer on the side. I'm confident I can make enough money in my business to support us.

Sensible. Logical and responsible.

One problem: I hadn't asked God his opinion.

One night I have a vivid dream.

Throughout the Scriptures, dreams are a vital way that God communicates to people. Jacob, sleeping with a rock for a pillow, dreams of angels ascending and descending in the place he later calls Bethel (house of God).[24] In the Old Testament, Joseph has dreams that foretell the unfolding of his life.[25] In the New Testament, Mary's husband Joseph is warned in a dream to leave Bethlehem when their family is in danger[26] and is then visited in a later dream when it is safe

---

24 Genesis 28:10–22.

25 Genesis 37:1–11.

26 Matthew 2:13.

to go back home.[27]

I'm not a prolific dreamer. Over my lifetime I can count on one hand the number of times that I have woken up in the morning knowing that it was definitively God who has spoken to me in my sleep (and that it wasn't just the pizza I ate before going to bed!). This dream is one of them. Eighteen years later I can still recall every detail with clarity – it's tattooed on my brain.

In my dream, I am Craisy Daisy and I'm at a summer camp. The sun is warm and a gentle breeze ruffles the nearby lake. I'm surrounded by a large crowd of children and am making them balloon animals. Without warning, the camp director walks up and says, 'You're done now.' En masse and without hesitation, the children all leave, jumping into canoes and paddling away. I'm left standing there, feeling somewhat confused.

'Follow me,' says the camp director. 'I'll take you to your vehicle.' She strides away with purpose, and not knowing what else to do, I follow. Our walk takes us to a narrow strip of grass flanked by two busy roads. Cars whizz back and forth. I find this disorienting and I wobble, trip and fall. As I lie on the ground I look up – to my dismay I see two planes falling out of the sky. They are hurtling towards me and I instinctively know that they are going to hit me. I brace for impact.

Everything goes dark, and the dream ends with a radio announcement: 'A satellite containing 24-7 prayer has fallen to the ground, and the only casualty is Craisy Daisy the Clown.'

Often dreams use symbolic language and can be mysterious and ambiguous. I'm not the sharpest tool in the shed and can be a little slow to clue in to things. But this message feels pretty darn clear. It's time to say goodbye to Daisy.

27 Matthew 2:19–20.

And just in case I didn't get it, or perhaps was not willing to obey, at the same time I 'happen' to seriously damage my vocal cords. For the next six months I am unable to speak without pain. I can't sing and I can't even talk much above a whisper. I don't fancy being a mime (they're a little creepy if you ask me – no disrespect to the profession). Without a voice it's impossible to wrangle thirty sugar-crazed toddlers and keep the room under control. My clowning career is over. Craisy Daisy has gone to the great clown 'beyond' where she can crack angel jokes and see if she can make solemn saints smile.

Why does God kill the clown? As I ponder the significance of the dream, my vocal injury and my inability to work in the field, I can only conclude one thing. He wants me to give myself one hundred per cent to the building of the House of Prayer. I'm comfortable paying my own way and supporting myself with my own business. Being a full-time missionary will massively stretch my faith and reliance on God to provide.

THE INVITATION

Our dreams can be doorways to revelation or doorways to the deep parts of our own hearts. Either way, it's good to pay attention to them. It can be helpful to have a dream journal that you keep by the side of your bed so you can write dreams down right away. Dennis Roy, senior leader with the Red Leaf House of Prayer in Canada, recommends these guiding principles to dream interpretation:

1. The Holy Spirit gives interpretation. It is primary that the Holy Spirit who gives the dream must be the one

to interpret the dream. Interpretation does not come from trying to figure the dream out. It comes from communing with God to reveal his message. When there is a true interpretation there is a sense of inspiration and life that comes from one's inner being (consolation) that accompanies the revelation.

2. Symbols. Dreams often use symbolic language and the symbols are often deeply personal. You can glean meanings from symbols either through how they are used in the Scriptures or through your own personal history with God – how he has spoken to you in the past through certain symbols. For example, a butterfly may represent a message of freedom to one person, while it may mean deep process to another. Both are correct!

In her course on dream interpretation, educator Autumn Mann recommends the following process:

1. Reduce the dream to its simplest form. Giving the dream a title can help. I called my dream 'The Clown Killing Dream'. (Kinda' morbid, eh?)
2. What is the main focus? Who/what is the centre of attention? Eliminate unnecessary details.
3. What is the overarching tone, feeling or attitude of the dream?[28]

Do you recall a dream that felt particularly potent or meaningful? Ask the Holy Spirit to help you interpret the dream. Apply these interpretation principles. Ask God what invitation your dream might contain.

---

28 Autumn Mann, *Unlocking Your Dreams*, p. 19, www.unlockingyourdreams.org (used with permission).

Jesus, thank you that you speak to us in so many ways.
I invite you to come and speak to me even when I'm sleeping.
Like the beloved in the Song of Solomon, may I say,
'I slept but my heart was awake.' (Song of Solomon 5:2)
Give me wisdom to understand.

Chapter 12

LAYING
FOUNDATIONS

*'Therefore everyone who hears these words of mine and puts
them into practice is like a wise man who built his house
on the rock. The rain came down, the streams rose, and the
winds blew and beat against that house; yet it did not fall,
because it had its foundation on the rock.'*

MATTHEW 7:24–25

Rivulets of rain dribble down my face. I button my coat, flip
up the collar and hunch against the cold drizzle. Why didn't
I bring an umbrella? Especially when just as I was leaving
the house I heard a clear nudge, *Bring an umbrella*. I was in
a rush and ignored the impulse, the Voice. Was it a Voice?

'You've got many voices in your head,' I recall a recent
workshop on listening to God. 'What you need to do is
discern between them. There is the voice of the enemy, the
accuser. There are your own thoughts. There are old tapes,
things from your past that you rehearse in your brain. And
then there is God's voice.'

God's voice. Is he interested in umbrellas, in keeping me
out of the rain? Seems kind of trivial if you ask me. Doesn't
God have more important things to talk to us about? I don't
want to be the kind of person who stands paralyzed in front

71

of my breakfast foods each morning. God, should I have a bagel? Or cereal? Or would eggs please you today?

One day I decide to experiment. I had read a passage in Isaiah and thought it would be interesting to try it out: 'Whether you turn to the right or to the left, your ears will hear a voice behind you, saying, "This is the way; walk in it."'[29]

I'll go wandering. Walk straight ahead until I hear a voice saying to turn one way or turn another.

So I walk. Listen. Respond to what I think I hear.

Get on the subway.

Get off at Bloor Station.

Turn left.

Turn right.

One more block.

Turn right.

As I round the final turn I stumble into a large flock of pigeons. Startled, they take flight and the air is full of a whirl of wings. They ascend, disburse and behind them I see a stately stone church. I glance at the church sign and I startle with recognition. Walmer Road Baptist.

I know this church and have been here before, although certainly not by this circuitous route. I didn't realize I was in the neighbourhood.

Go in.

I climb the steps and tug on the front door. To my surprise it's open and I step into the dimly-lit annex.

'Jill! What are you doing here?' My friend Renee is standing in the hallway, beaming a warm welcome.

'Um, I think God brought me here?'

'You're kidding me!'

---

29 Isaiah 30:21.

We have a great chat. I tell her about my experiment and its surprising results. We pray together. It feels like a divine appointment. I walk home bemused and wondering. Is it really that simple? All we have to do is listen, hear his voice and obey?

These questions are in the forefront of my mind as we begin to lay foundations for the House of Prayer. There are no local models to look at, nothing to imitate. Except IHOP. The Mother Ship down in Kansas City. Which I don't have the foggiest idea how to replicate.

To begin with, it's in the Bible Belt of the US Midwest, where Christianity is still very much in the centre of culture. Unlike here in Canada where we live much more on the fringes. IHOP is led by Mike Bickle – a twinkly-eyed, stocky former boxer who can fill a room with his charisma. His ministry has a global reach and he leads a mega church in his spare time. Right from the get-go they have gazillions of people and tons of resources. IHOP draws participants from all over the world, and at the time of our House of Prayer's beginning, the base down in Kansas City seems to have several thousand people participating already.

How on earth am I going to build something like that? I have no global platform. No megachurch. I am virtually unknown and untried. Mike Bickle I ain't. Not even close.

How to begin?

I begin by listening, straining all my attention towards heaven. 'Only build in response to revelation,' a mentor tells me. I stumble across a piece of Scripture that feels relevant:

Unless the LORD builds the house,
the builders labour in vain.
Unless the watches over the city,
the guards stand watch in vain.

PSALM 127:1

My question becomes, 'Lord what are you building?'

And much to my relief, as I listen, God responds – at least I'm pretty sure it's God. Two thoughts drop into my heart and land with a 'thunk'. They settle solidly inside me and become foundation stones that we build on.

First the voice says, *'In order to build a House of Prayer, you must become a House of Prayer.'* Makes sense in the light of what I understand the Scriptures to say about where God makes himself at home. In the Old Testament, the presence of God resides in a place. A tent of meeting. A tabernacle. A temple.

Then Jesus comes along. Almighty God wrapped in swaddling man. Jesus refers to himself as the temple in John 2:19, saying 'Destroy this temple, and I will raise it again in three days.' Earlier in his gospel, John says that the word became flesh and 'tabernacled' amongst us.[30] God resides in the person of Jesus.

But it doesn't end there.

On his departure and at Pentecost, Jesus gives us his Spirit to live within us. The church of the New Testament understands that, because of this, we become the temple of the Holy Spirit[31] – the tent of meeting. We become a house of prayer. God resides in a people.

Henri Nouwen wraps it in simple words: in the Old Testament God was for us. In Jesus, God was with us. And

30 John 1:14 (TLV).
31 I Corinthians 6:19–20.

now God is within us.[32] I am a House of Prayer. In some way I am also being made into a House of Prayer. Sounds exciting! I envisage Jesus coming into my soul house and freshening it up a bit. 'Hey, let's put up this kind of wallpaper! Had you ever considered moving this furniture around? Hmmm, maybe we should clean out those closets a bit – it's getting a bit cluttered in there ...'

What I don't realize at the time is that God isn't Martha Stewart. He's not interested in freshening things up and giving me a cool, hip new look. He's not even particularly interested in keeping things tidy. Over the next few years I come to understand (the hard way) that what God really intends is *Extreme Home Makeover*, bulldozer edition. Y'know – the one where they demolish the house right to the foundations and then rebuild? Story of the next eighteen years of my life. A good thing I didn't know it up front!

The second thing the voice says? *'You build a House of Prayer one person at a time.'* One person at a time? I can do THAT!

I like people. All kinds of people. Pretty much everybody I meet. I'm not sure why but I find humans fascinating and enjoyable. My introverted husband thinks it's weird, but he affectionately calls my gift 'the schmooze anointing'. There is something beautiful about gathering people around a common passion, a common cause, a Person. It's like stringing pearls on a necklace. Like neighbours cultivating a community garden, coming together to build something beautiful.

I've got my marching orders. My instructions. How to build the House of Prayer? Pray and make friends.

With this, we begin.

---

32 Henri Nouwen, *Bread for the Journey: A Daybook of Wisdom and Faith* (HarperCollins, 1996), p.76.

THE INVITATION

Jesus said, 'My sheep listen to my voice; I know them, and they follow me. I give them eternal life, and they shall never perish; no one will snatch them out of my hand' (John 10:27).

1. When was there a time when you thought you might have heard God's voice? What was the situation surrounding it? What did the voice sound like? What did you do in response to what you heard? What was the outcome?

   'Therefore everyone who hears these words of mine and puts them into practice is like a wise man who built his house on the rock. The rain came down, the streams rose, and the winds blew and beat against that house; yet it did not fall, because it had its foundation on the rock. But everyone who hears these words of mine and does not put them into practice is like a foolish man who built his house on sand. The rain came down, the streams rose, and the winds blew and beat against that house, and it fell with a great crash.'

   MATTHEW 7:24–27

2. What house are you building right now? Perhaps it's friendships or your family culture. Perhaps it's your career portfolio. Your philosophy of life and ministry. Your team at work.

   Foundations determine the shape and form of whatever you are building and give solidity and stability to the structure. How can you build what God is saying to you into your foundation?

*Jesus, I thank you that your words brings solidity and stability
to my life – that you still create and bring shape and form into
the world through your word.
In whatever I'm building, I want, like the Apostle Paul said, to
lay foundations as an expert builder.
So speak Lord, your servant is listening.
Come and build your house.*

Chapter 13

PROPHET SHARING

Follow the way of love and eagerly desire gifts of the Spirit,
especially prophecy ... the one who prophesies speaks to people
for their strengthening, encouraging, and comfort.

1 CORINTHIANS 14:1–3

We walk upstairs together and out into the cafe. The pastor at my side, wet eyed, turns to me. 'There is no way to describe what just happened down there, except that God was in the room,' he says. 'Their prophetic words for you, were they accurate?' I ask. He nods. 'That's fantastic. More importantly, did you feel safe and did you feel loved?'

We've been praying for and with pastors for seventeen years. Every week. We start with an hour of worship, then an hour of intercessory prayer for leaders in our city. Then in the third hour we invite a local pastor to join us. 'Would you find it helpful for a team who don't know you to pray for you?' I ask, 'People who are outside your immediate context?'

Our prayer team is skilled and seasoned. We've got systems – a secret code. If we are praying for a pastor who isn't particularly charismatic, when I introduce them to the team I say, 'We're going to spend a little time listening to God with pastor so and so ...' That way the team knows to soft sell what they are hearing, being gentle in their delivery. No 'Thus saith the Lord'. More like, 'Thus wonderith us'. And Bible verses – lots of Bible verses. However, if I know the pastor is more comfortable with charismatic expressions, I say, 'Now we're going to prophesy over pastor so and so'. That way the team knows they can just let it rip. And they do! (They still use lots of Scripture!)

We take praying for pastors seriously – it's a divine assignment we received at the very inception of the House of Prayer.

In almost every religious tradition, the birth of a new child is marked by a naming ceremony. At his son's dedication, the priest Zechariah declares, 'His name is John.'[33]

A prayer community in its infancy is like a child being named and dedicated. It's like a little chick emerging from the shell. That first season is critical for imprinting and impartation. God can shape and name who we are in a word, setting core DNA and putting us on a trajectory that can last years and in our case, decades.

A prophet from Kansas City is doing a series of strategic prayer events for the region. One of our friends engineers an audience and we are eager to hear what the Lord may want to say through him to our fledgling House of Prayer. He looks and sounds like a redneck, complete with bulbous nose, Arkansas accent and baggy plaid over-shirt with frayed cuffs. We cluster around him like a pack of dogs eagerly responding to the buzz whirr of the can opener. We are hanging on every word. Hungry.

'And the purpose for Jillian is so that pastors who are

---

33 Luke 1:63.

appointed to die can live. Oh boy. I mean it. There's men that's about to perish. Now, here, and what you do will make the difference between life and death. I mean you can stand between real death and life, and spiritual death and life.' He drawls. 'You seem awfully young for that kind of commission.' He looks my 30-year-old self up and down and we all laugh, albeit a little nervously.

'In ancient times, they put geese on the walls instead of men at night, you couldn't sneak up on them. The intercessors are the wild geese. And they fly in V formation. If the intercessors will line up behind you or whoever has the anointing, there's like a spearhead, there's a weight that drives the thing home. That's what this young woman is.' He points at me. 'You're the spearhead. You're the hardhead. Usually a wise mama goose in front – an old hand that knows the way.'

I don't feel like a wise mama goose. Or a spearhead. Or a hardhead for that matter. And I certainly don't feel like someone who can make the difference between life and death. But I do know that God can shape and name us through his words and, like it says in Romans 4:17, call 'into being things that were not.'

The assignment is given. The trajectory is set. We begin to pray for pastors.

Prophetic words we receive near the beginning of GOHOP not only set our course but also steady us when we feel wobbly. 'Jill, I had a strong dream about you and GOHOP,' my friend and co-conspirator Denni and I are sitting over a coffee. 'Can I tell it to you? I saw you placed on a wide but dry, parched land. It was so dry there were deep cracks and divisions across the whole land. You were carrying a spade. You tried to dig but the ground was too hard and resistant. I saw heaven open over you and audibly heard the Council of Heaven speaking. The voices said, "She has come to dig deeper to ready the soil for new seed. The frustration is because it is the wrong tool for the conditions. Give her a double pick-axe. There needs to be a ground-breaking work before it is ready for the deeper work." I then saw you standing with the double pick-axe. The Lord said, "It is a double anointing."

'I felt this double anointing reflected Elisha's request: it wasn't for personal glory or spiritual ambition. It was because he knew the spiritual condition, he knew what his nation and the land needed was more supernatural intervention.'

Certainly, at the front end, I have very little idea of what Denni's dream means. But as our House of Prayer start-up unfolds it becomes more and more clear. And when everything around us begins to shake and seemingly fall apart, I am held together by all these words and strengthened for the journey.

THE INVITATION

Follow the way of love and eagerly desire gifts of the Spirit, especially prophecy ... the one who prophesies speaks to people for their strengthening, encouraging and comfort.

1 CORINTHIANS 14:1–3

Someone prays or prophesies over you. Is God speaking?

How do you test, weigh or discern a prophetic word? I would suggest three tests:

1. Is it in agreement with God's word? A prophetic word would never contradict the word of God revealed in the Scriptures.
2. Does it reflect the nature and character of Jesus as revealed in the Bible?
3. Does it 'witness' with you inwardly? Often a prophetic word will confirm what God has already spoken in your heart. Sometimes it speaks of something new that God intends to do in your life. Do you have an inward peace about what has been spoken?

If it doesn't pass the tests don't be afraid to discard it. We all prophesy in part, the Scriptures say,[34] and those praying over you are human and fallible. At the very least you can give them credit for taking a risk and for trying to encourage you.

If the word 'passes the test' then it can be helpful to do the following things:

1. Write it down somewhere where you can find and access it down the road. Maybe your phone, journal or in a special file. Whenever I know that someone is going to prophesy over me, I record it on my voice app on my phone, then transcribe it later and put it in my journal. I then regularly review my journals to get an overarching view of how God might be speaking to me and how those words might be coming to fruition in my life.
2. Share the prophetic word received with spiritual friends, mentors, a spiritual director and/or pastors so that they can input their counsel, wisdom and discernment.

---

34 1 Corinthians 13:9.

3. Pray. The prophetic is 'the diving board into the pool of prayer,'[35] prophetic teacher Marc Dupont says. Pray over and through your prophetic words for yourself and others. Let them be fuel for your intercession.

4. Watch. Keep an eye open to see how God might be bringing that word to pass.

Jesus, I love that not only do you speak in the Scriptures, but that you continue to speak today through your people.
Thanks for all the edification, exhortation and comfort I have received through the prayers and words of others.
Continue to speak in the midst of our communities Lord.
We are listening.

---

35 Mark A. Dupont, *The Elijah Years* (Mantle of Praise Ministries, 1995), p.83.

Chapter 14

TREASURE IN THE FIELD

*'Suppose one of you wants to build a tower. Won't you first
sit down and estimate the cost to see if you have enough
money to complete it? For if you lay the foundation and
are not able to finish it, everyone who sees it will ridicule
you, saying, "This person began to build and wasn't able to
finish."'*

LUKE 14:28–30

For to me, to live is Christ and to die is gain.

PHILIPPIANS 1:21

Converted from a former theatre, the prayer room is black.
Black walls. Black ceiling. It would have felt oppressive but
for the front wall of windows and the fact that it is three
stories high. 'It's like a womb,' says one of our volunteers.
'Yeah, a womb with a view!' I quip in response.

Along the length of the room are cubicles, each set
out with prayer prompts and activities of various kinds –
prayer for children, for the city. The 'prayer for the harvest'
cubicle has a large sheaf of wheat and a bushel basket full of
vegetables. There is even a bridal chamber, a small enclosure
swathed in white, surrounded by lattice and vines. Inside

is a futon where people can settle and rest. At the front of the prayer room is a platform set up for times of corporate worship and prayer.

A black theatrical curtain separates us from the adjoining mailroom. Through it I hear the 'chunk, chunk, chunk' of the postal machines, and a dim refrain of Bob Marley on their radio telling me not to worry about a thing.

It's two years into the life of the House of Prayer and I'm alone in an empty prayer room.

Again.

My heart is a clenched fist, my prayers inarticulate groaning.

Our family is broke. The House of Prayer has no staff and has haemorrhaged volunteers. There are struggles with leadership and local churches. Personal health issues. Kirk and I are on edge with each other.

This is not what I signed up for.

The House of Prayer starts with such promise. We're offered free space at the Crossroads Centre, home to Canada's largest Christian television station. It is a hub of Christian life and ministry, a sprawling complex of studios and offices complete with 24-7 security. Perfect incubator for a House of Prayer. We have tremendous favour with its founder David Mainse, a nationally recognized and respected leader. Early on he hosts a breakfast for us so we can introduce the House of Prayer to local pastors with his warm endorsement. Much to our delight, about seventy leaders from across Southern Ontario show up.

'We're going to call it the Golden Horseshoe House of Prayer, GOHOP for short,' I announce. The Golden Horseshoe is the name of the region surrounding the western edge of Lake Ontario. A massive metropolitan complex comprised of multiple cities, it's home to about nine million people. We'll cover it in prayer. No problem.

In the back of the room, a pastor raises his hand. 'We're in Guelph, which is outside the Golden Horseshoe, and we want to be involved too. Could you call it something else? How about Greater Ontario instead?' And so, GOHOP is born.

We begin with lots of enthusiasm and buy-in. A team comes up from the House of Prayer in Kansas City and hundreds of people gather for a week of training. Of the hundreds, seventy willing souls sign up for regular slots in the prayer room.

There are three enemies of the prayer movement: the world, the flesh and the devil. One day when we are visiting another House of Prayer in Albany, New York, I notice a sign by its entrance: 'The battle is GETTING to pray'.

Early on in the life of GOHOP we bump into three problems. Problem number one: our love of novelty. We're always on the lookout for the new thing that is going to take us to the next level. It's biblical, right? 'See, I am doing a new thing,' says the Lord in Isaiah, 'do you not perceive it?'[36] The moment the novelty wears off is the moment when the real work begins. Mike Bickle is famous for saying, 'I don't need show horses for the House of Prayer. I need work horses.' It's no mistake that many of the Apostle Paul's prayers for the church are for patience and endurance. As an expert builder laying foundations for the work of God in a city, he understands what is necessary. Pioneering requires clearing the land, pulling out stumps and rocks, breaking up hard ground. It's difficult work, sometimes backbreaking and heart-breaking, often routine and mundane.

36 Isaiah 43:19.

What happens, then, when another novelty comes to town, another ministry or project that holds promise to take us to the next level? We're like small children playing football, the whole lot of us rushing willy nilly after the ball en masse. We all want to be part of the action but haven't yet learned how to hold our position.

Problem number two is related to problem number one. It's easy enough to add prayer to our to-do list but hard to keep it up. Our volunteers are well intentioned. But, well, life gets busy ...

Seventy becomes fifty.

Fifty becomes twenty.

Twenty becomes ten.

Finally, we whittle our team down to a steady two.

And then there is problem number three: regardless of your theology of spiritual warfare, most of us would agree that from time to time we experience what I call 'spiritual resistance'. In Ephesians it says,

> *For our struggle is not against flesh and blood, but against the rulers, against the authorities, against the powers of this dark world and against the spiritual forces of evil in the heavenly realms.*[37]

In these first few years it feels like there is a line-up of spiritual entities arrayed against us. No sooner do we successfully resist and wrestle one to the ground, than it 'taps out' and another one jumps into the ring.

Everything that could go wrong goes wrong. Very wrong. We are bruised, sore and bone weary.

Which brings me back to standing in an empty prayer room. With a heart that is a clenched fist. Praying without words because I don't even know what to pray anymore.

37 Ephesians 6:12.

Lord, if we're going to be always poor ...
If nobody joins us ...
If we are constantly embroiled in conflict ...
If we continue to be misunderstood and overlooked ...
If it doesn't appear fruitful and we don't see hoped-for answers to prayer ...
If this costs everything we have ...

In that moment I feel God stripping me naked. All my idealism, my great expectations and my external motivating forces fall to the floor and puddle at my feet. I take a deep breath.

I'm still in.

Because the bottom line is, he is worthy. He is worthy for incense, for night-and-day prayer to rise in this place.

According to Bob Marley, crooning behind the curtain, Everythings gonna be alright. I'm not sure that I believe him. But I am sure that I'm here to stay, nonetheless.

In 2 Samuel 24 we see King David the intercessor standing before God on behalf of the people of Israel. Here's the JPV (the Jill Paraphrase Version) of the event:

> *David: Hey Araunah, I want to buy your threshing floor. God told me I've got to offer a sacrifice there or our people are toast.*
> *Araunah: Buy it? You can have it! I'll even throw in the oxen and the wood!*
> *David: Not a chance, Araunah. I've got to pay for it. Why should I offer up to the Lord that which costs me nothing?*

Why should I offer to the Lord that which costs me nothing?

It is a costly 'yes'. The kind of yes that when I stumble over its threshold, I discover it is a doorway to inner freedom.

A number of years later I am in Uganda with a group of pastors. We have been invited to teach at a theological training school. It is a five-month course specifically designed for pastors in outlying villages who cannot afford conventional Bible College. 'They come mostly from the Congo,' says Anne, the school director. Some of them walk here. Edgar walked eleven days out of the bush to attend!'

The compound is in a dusty, labyrinthine neighbourhood in Kampala. The outdoor classroom is a large, striped tarpaulin hung over a metal frame. Students sit on plastic chairs and balance notepads on their knees. Behind the classroom there is an alley strung with hanging laundry and a cave-like dormitory where the students sleep on simple benches.

When we arrive, Pastor Kitumbe is teaching the gathered students in Lingala, the local language. He is tall and thin. Very, very thin. His trousers have a tenuous grip on his hips. I'm mildly concerned that if he moves too fast, he might lose them. His shirt is pressed, gleaming and immaculate, as I'd come to expect from the Ugandans I had met. I have no idea how they do it. Living in tin shacks with mud floors, red dust clinging to everything. And sparkling white, perfectly pressed shirts.

'Pastor Kitumbe, he is a true champion of the gospel,' Anne, our host, leads us from the classroom across the compound to her home. 'His congregation is too poor to pay him so he sleeps on a table at the church every night. They feed him when they can. ('Not enough,' I think.) But he counts it a privilege to be a minister of the gospel. It is a small price to pay.

'After his class, the students will give their field reports. They are just back from three weeks in remote villages. We drop them off, they begin to pray and to evangelize and after three weeks we expect a church to be planted.'

We sip sweet milky tea together in Anne's home and chat some more. After the break, we return to the classroom to hear the field reports. Pastors Kamuntu and Mwyseige swagger to the front. 'So they drop us off at the village, and our hosts show us the hut for us to sleep. We pray all the first night and then began to evangelize the next day. Later on that day they say to us, "You can't sleep in that hut anymore! You're disturbing the spirits!", but that night we sleep there anyway. In the middle of the night someone throws a large rock in the hut! Praise God!' Pastor Kamuntu's eyes twinkle and he flashes a grin. 'The rock misses us so we keep sleeping in the hut.'

His comrade pipes in. 'Then they said to us, "We won't feed you three times a day. Only two times." So we get to fast! Praise God!'

Praise God? For close encounters with large rocks and for being deprived of food? Far from being cowed, these pastors are delighted. The classmates cheer, clap and stomp as the pastors make their way back to their seats.

I leave Uganda with a whole new perspective on costly obedience. Humbled and sobered by the sacrifices they are willing to make to obey God and do his work, and their delight in the face of hardship. Which helps me when I finally go to the dentist after eight years of avoiding it. 'You've got eleven cavities,' he says. 'We're probably looking at a couple thousand dollars of dental work.' A couple thousand dollars? He might as well have said a million. If we manage to pay rent, buy food and our car insurance, we are doing well in a month.

The Sunday after receiving the bad news I stand at the front of the sanctuary at the end of the service. Overwhelmed. It's an unsolvable problem. Then it occurs to me. What if continuing as a prayer missionary means that I won't get the dental work done? I have lots of friends in my neighbourhood whose grins sport large gaps. Will standing in solidarity with them mean that I share their dental fate? The thought makes me shudder.

Then I'm reminded of the dedication of the pastors I met in Uganda, their readiness to sacrifice personal comfort, security and safety. In that moment willingness drops down into my spirit. If continuing my work with the House of Prayer means that I lose my teeth, then so be it. Praise God!

I pray my commitment, and joy bubbles up. The same kind of joy I observe in my Ugandan brothers and sisters as they sing and dance, loose-limbed.

Eh Yembela Yesu oyo! (Oh let us sing for Jesus!)

Eh azali malamu, atonda bolingo Nzambe oyo (For he is Good, this God is full of love)

Oh kumisa masaya eh! (O Let us praise the Lord!)

THE INVITATION

During the Nazi ascension to power in the early 1930s, German theologian Dietrich Bonhoeffer was a vocal opponent to Hitler and his regime. He left Germany in 1939, relocating to the United States, but soon regretted that decision. 'I must live through this difficult period in our national history with the people of Germany. I will have no right to participate in the reconstruction of Christian life in Germany after the war if I do not share the trials of this time with my people.'[38] He returns to Germany, and subsequently loses his life in a Nazi concentration camp in 1945.

---

38 Eberhard Bethge, *Dietrich Bonhoeffer: Eine Biographie* (Augsburg Fortress, 1999), p.736.

Such grace is costly because it calls us to follow, and it is grace because it calls us to follow Jesus Christ. It is costly because it costs a man his life, and it is grace because it gives a man the only true life ... Grace is costly because it compels a man to submit to the yoke of Christ and follow him; it is grace because Jesus says: 'My yoke is easy and my burden is light.'

DIETRICH BONHOEFFER[39]

Read: Read Bonhoeffer's quote out loud, slowly. Which words or phrases jump out at you?

Reflect: Reflect on those words or phrases. How do you relate to what Bonhoeffer is expressing before God?

Respond: How might God be asking you to respond to what he is highlighting in the passage? What is his invitation to you?

Jesus, I'm overwhelmed by the way you let go of position, prestige and power, emptied yourself, and joined me in my brokenness and suffering.
Lord, may I not shrink back from your mode of downward mobility.
Why should I offer to you that which costs me nothing?

---

39 Dietrich Bonhoeffer, *The Cost of Discipleship* (SCM Press Limited, 1959), p.45.

Chapter 15

RAVENS

*Then the word of the L*ORD *came to Elijah: 'Leave here, turn eastward and hide in the Kerith Ravine, east of the Jordan. You will drink from the brook, and I have instructed the ravens to supply you with food there.'*

*So he did what the L*ORD *had told him. He went to the Kerith Ravine, east of the Jordan, and stayed there. The ravens brought him bread and meat in the morning and bread and meat in the evening, and he drank from the brook.*

1 KINGS 17:2–6

I open the cupboard. There is a jar of Dijon mustard and a box of corn starch, some peanut butter scrapings and a couple of slices of bread. Right then, peanut butter sandwich it is – hold the mustard. I assemble Hannah's lunch, tuck it in her school bag and send her off to class with a hug. With the option of either Hannah or I getting to eat, the choice is obvious.

Kirk and I are both full-time prayer missionaries, and we have no financial plan B to fall back on. We live pretty simply. We might not always get what we want, but we tend to get what we need. Thus far God has been faithful – we've made rent every month and never fasted involuntarily. Until today.

'Ah well,' I think as I trudge to work, 'it *is* a ministry of fasting and prayer!'

When I arrive at the House of Prayer and open the door to my office I'm met with a delightful surprise. On my desk is a bag of home-baked muffins. 'The ravens! The ravens left me muffins!' I remember God's supernatural (and wing-borne) provision for Elijah[40] and dance a gleeful jig right then and there. Come lunchtime I munch muffins with gusto. Best muffins I've ever had. In all our years with GOHOP there has only been that one day when we've been completely out of food. And only one day when an anonymous food package is left on my desk.

I find the life of faith missions incongruous and amusing. In the famous 'Vision' poem by Pete Greig he writes, 'They could eat Caviar on Monday and crusts on Tuesday. They wouldn't even notice.'[41] I can't say I don't notice. The contrasts do make my head spin sometimes.

Monday – rice and beans, looking for coins under couch cushions. Ewww, when did we last clean under here?

Tuesday – oh look, I'm off to Dublin for a ministry trip!

I have story after story of God's gracious provision for our work, especially our national and international prayer assignments.

It begins like this. It is a national gathering of prayer leaders in Quebec City over an extended weekend. I am expected to be there, but the day before I'm due to leave I have no cash on me. Over the course of that afternoon two people pop by my office and I find myself with enough money for a train ticket.

'Kathy what should I do?' I ask one of our prayer missionaries, 'I've got enough to get there but no money

40 I Kings 17:2-6.
41 Pete Greig, *The Vision and the Vow* (Relevant Books, 2004), p.15.

for hotel or food, or even for the conference registration!' 'You've got money for a train ticket,' she says. 'Get on a train!'

'So, worst case scenario,' I'm thinking out loud, 'I take the train to Quebec City, sit in the conference hotel lobby, fast a little bit and sleep ... well I don't know where.' It's April, and in Canada that means it's a bit too chilly to sleep on a park bench. 'But if I do all of that, I've pleased him, haven't I?'

Hebrews 11:6 comes to mind: '... without faith it is impossible to please God'. Hmm, what if the inverse is true? That faith makes heaven smile? 'Makes sense to me,' she grins. I'm not sure if Kathy is pleased with my faith-filled logic or amused at the thought of my going off on a wild goose chase.

'Alrighty then. Train ticket it is!'

I'm tickled by the thought of it. Pleasing him by doing something that, in the natural, seems a bit crazy, nonsensical – even a bit irresponsible. Just because I believe he wants me to. I do the mental calculations and, no matter how I look at it, it turns out as a win. In the very worst case, even in epic failure, I will have a good story to tell!

The next day, crazy fool that I am, I hop on a passing train. I'm a bit giddy with the excitement of the adventure. Curious and expectant. What will God do? God doesn't waste any time, and my first surprise is that one of my colleagues gets on the train just a few stations down. He's on his way to Quebec City as well. 'Jill! Great to see you!'

We have nine hours to chat, and I wrestle with whether or not to share the details of my adventure. If I tell people will that be cheating? Will they feel compelled to help? Would I be skewing the outcome?

My dilemma is solved when my friend says, 'Hey, my buddy and I are driving back from these meetings – why don't you just cash in your return train ticket and come with us?' Wahoo! Provision! In part, at least.

When we arrive in Quebec City, I refund my return ticket and climb the hill to the venue. I have money to attend the meetings now and a little more faith that the other bits will sort themselves out.

'I would like to register please.' The welcome team is set up in the hotel lobby.

'Sure. What's your name?'

'Jill Weber.'

'Ah Jill, yes, we've got you registered already. Here is your room key. And your meal pass.'

Waitaminit. Room key? Meal pass?

'Um, I think you've got me mixed up with someone else? Jill Weber, with one 'B'. I'm from GOHOP?'

'Yes we've got you here. Looks like someone has paid your expenses, but the records don't tell me who. Enjoy the meetings!'

Chuckling to myself I make my way to my hotel room. I went with nothing but a little *chutzpah* and ended up fully funded with $200 extra in my pocket! I can feel God's smile beaming down, the pleasure of heaven.

'Give the extra money away,' the Voice says. *Of course* he would say that.

My daughter Hannah is an artist and in her early years went through what I lovingly call 'the zombie period', not unlike Picasso's cubism phase. The people in her drawings are scrawled circles with stick legs and massive dark eyes. Zombified or not, these pictures are precious, and with pride I stick them to the fridge.

This feels the same, somehow. My tentative, trembling, semi-faith filled response to God's invitation to take risks is just like that childlike scrawling. And I'm sure there is a picture of me stuck on a fridge in heaven somewhere.

THE INVITATION

And without faith it is impossible to please God, because anyone who comes to him must believe that he exists and that he rewards those who earnestly seek him.

HEBREWS 11:6

My former pastor, Bob Warriner, says, 'Faith is that thing that you do to demonstrate to God that you believe what he has said.'

1. When was the last time God asked you to step out in faith, to take a risk and, in response to his word, attempt something beyond your own personal resource and capacity?
2. If we are honest, it's likely that for most of us it's been a long time – if ever. What prevents us from taking risks? Reflect and journal on what your barriers to risk taking might be. After you journal them, hold them up to God and invite his help to 'be strong and of good courage'.
3. One of the challenges in risky responsiveness to God is our attachment to particular outcomes. I have a pretty good idea at what I think a positive outcome in the situation should look like, and I'm still deeply committed to my own comfort and security. What would it look like for me to let go of my preconceived opinion about and attachment to a particular outcome in a situation? What might happen if, instead, I re-orient my heart so that God's glory becomes my end goal and destination, regardless of outcome?

Jesus, I thank you for your promise that it's the Father's good pleasure to give us the kingdom.
I want to please you in every way, bear fruit in every good work, and grow in my knowledge of you.
Grant me the grace to step out of my comfort zone when you call me, to take risks, and to see you do immeasurably more than I can ever ask or imagine.

Chapter 16

STIR UP THE NEST

…like an eagle that stirs up its nest,
and hovers over its young,
that spreads its wings to catch them
and carries them on its pinions.
The LORD alone led him;
no foreign god was with him.

DEUTERONOMY 32:11–12

After having been pruned back to the nub, our House of Prayer team slowly begins to grow. We are anchored by the three musketeers, Denni, Kathy and Karen, who log countless hours in the prayer room. They are joined by volunteers from local churches. One of my favourite prayer meetings we call 'Mummyhop'. Mums bring their kids and have a great time interspersing prayer for families with 'The Wheels on the Bus go Round and Round'.

Richard, a pilgrim from the UK, finds us online and wings over to join us for nine months. He's an electronica composer so brings his gear with him, spinning soundscapes for us to pray along with. One of our early volunteers, Phyllis, returns back to Canada after a couple of years down at IHOP, and is eager to plug in. Then Tim swings into orbit. He's young, a fresh-faced and fiery-hearted revivalist who jumps into the deep end of HOP life, spending hour after hour in worship and meditating on Scriptures. 'It's better than Bible School!' he asserts.

The Crossroads Centre is the perfect incubator for our baby House of Prayer. Cloistered away in the recesses of what is essentially a Christian citadel, we feel like we are tucked into God's back pocket. We have support and security, comfort and easy access to the larger Christian community.

However, after about eight years or so we begin to wonder if comfort and security is what God wants for us long term. 'Eagles' nests are quite comfortable,' I am listening to a local Bible teacher. 'The branches and twigs are woven, entwined to create a cradle of sorts. It's lined with bird fluff, feathers and other soft materials. But if the nests stay that way then the eaglets don't grow into their next phase of maturity. If the nest is too comfy then why leave it? If you're getting fed all the time, what's the motivation to get out and provide for yourself?

'At some point the mother eagle begins to stir up the nest. Pulling out all the feathers and fluff. Tugging the sticks and twigs out of place. Bringing food with less frequency. The nest becomes inhospitable, motivating the eaglets to learn to fly.'

In the beginning it is our hearts that get stirred up. Our vision for the House of Prayer expands beyond what we are presently experiencing. How can we make GOHOP more accessible? Is this the best location for our next phase of life and ministry? We can sense that change is in the air but can't put our fingers on the exact nature of it.

Then the physical nest gets stirred up.

'We're so sorry,' the Crossroads folk say. 'We've got increasing demands on our space, so we need to reduce your footprint in the building a bit.' Initially they cut our room in half, using the other half for storage. Then they relocate us to a much smaller room in another corner of the building. There is a storage cupboard about the size of a walk-in wardrobe next to the prayer room, 'Could we empty this out and put our office in here?' we ask. 'We don't see why not.' They are eager to help us, wanting us to feel at home even in the reduced space.

We are grateful for their willingness to accommodate us and their desire to continue to have us in the building, but the walls are beginning to close in. We sense our days here are numbered.

I make a list.

'God, I want our next location to be at street level, accessible by bus and accessible to passers-by. And I want to be invited by a group of pastors who are working together. I want us to do something related to youth. And I want free rent again.'

Before the ink on my list dries, I find myself sitting across from my friend Pastor Bob, who facilitates the interdenominational pastors group in the nearby village of Waterdown. 'Would GOHOP be willing to relocate? We've got a house that we are redeveloping into a local youth outreach centre in the next couple years.' The pastors in the village would love to see the ground saturated in prayer before we build.

'It's on a corner right at a main town intersection. One of the upstairs rooms is allocated for offices for the youth ministry, but other than that you can use the whole house, rent free.'

Ha! Street level. The right invitation. Youth. And free rent! Four for four!

'Thanks for the offer. It's very ... interesting and timely. We will pray about it and get back to you.'

Right on cue, the Crossroads folks contact us again.

'We're so sorry,' they say. 'The demands on our space are

increasing. We love what you're doing, but we're afraid we just don't have room for you here anymore.'

I chuckle to myself. 'No problem whatsoever. We've already got somewhere to go.' Time for the eaglets to fly.

We settle into our new, albeit temporary, home in Waterdown. The house is cute and snug and it's all ours for a couple of years until planning permissions and sufficient funds are obtained to tear it down and build the youth centre. We settle in, paint and decorate, put up curtains and prayer stations and begin to mobilize locals to pray.

It's not unlike Elijah's situation in 1 Kings 17. He's hiding in a ravine and the Lord is supplying him daily. There is a brook to drink from and ravens bring bread and drink, morning and evening. But when it's time for Elijah's new assignment, time for him to move on, the brook dries up, compelling him to leave. He steps forward out of the security of daily provision into a much riskier venture.

Years later the 'live nest cam' comes into being. Webcams are set up next to eagles' nests so that curious folk can watch online and track the birth and development of eaglets. Now that we can see right into the nests, we discover that the phenomenon of the parent eagles 'stirring up the nest' is actually a myth.

Myth or no, our community has been stirred up and is ready to take flight. Transition is coming.

THE INVITATION

Some time later the brook dried up because there had been no rain in the land. Then the word of the LORD came to him: 'Go at once ...'

I KINGS I 7:7–9A

In this passage in 1 Kings, we find Elijah hiding in the wilderness. He is well provisioned – God supplies food through ravens and water through a stream. When it is time to transition, the stream dries up and God speaks – giving Elijah instructions for the next phase of his work.

Most of us like predictability, daily routine, support and structure. However, in the midst of 'business as usual' it can be very easy to default to automatic pilot.

Then a door of opportunity closes. Finances get tight. You feel a shift in some relationships. Is it spiritual warfare? The hardship of life on a fallen planet? Or is God trying to alert you to change?

1. Are you in a situation where your nest is stirred up or your stream has dried up? Take a few minutes to journal, reflect on and describe the situation.
2. Is it possible that God might be trying to get your attention, showing you that it's no longer business as usual?
3. How might God be wanting you to respond in the midst of the transition? What changes might be possible? New directions to explore? Take some time to listen, pray and journal.

Jesus, I thank you for all the ways you support, provision, lead and guide me.
You are the God who comforts the afflicted and afflicts the comfort.
I welcome both your comfort and your affliction.
Help me to be alert to shifts in seasons, for your unexpected invitations, and grant me the willingness and courage to say yes.

Chapter 17

IF THE SWEATER FITS

*And in him you too are being built together to become a
dwelling in which God lives by his Spirit.*

E P H E S I A N S 2 : 2 2

My best school friend and I have completely different
shopping modes. She's a butterfly browser. Drifting from
store to store, she flutters among the clothing racks. Alighting
briefly in one section, she slowly peruses its contents before
winging her way to another.

I, on the other hand, am a Trapdoor spider snatch-and-
grabber. I wait until just the right moment, quickly dart in,
seize my prey, and beat a rapid retreat. Consequently, I'm a
bit twitchy by the time we get to the fifth store on our quest
for The Perfect Sweater.

'What do you think?' Deanna pulls an item off the rack,
holds it up and smooths it against her torso, peeking in
the mirror. Definitely a contender. Fluffy without being
'velour-y'. Velour is still in fashion in the mid-eighties,
though many of us are beginning to sniff and turn up our
nose at it. Pale pink. Great colour for Deanna – she's the
pretty-in-pink, slightly-pouty-Barbie-doll type. Button nose
and hair that feathers like the girls on *Charlie's Angels* reruns.

I'm the rounded and flouncy, slightly-hippie-dippyearth-mother-y type. The long skirts, woolly socks and Birkenstocks type. She's an elf. I'm a hobbit. And there is nothing I want more than to be her. 'I'm going to try it on,' she skips into the changing room and emerges moments later, a vision of pink, fuzzy loveliness. Yes, it is indeed The Perfect Sweater.

'I think this is the winner!' She smiles sunnily. 'I'm just going to look there in the back corner, I think I see some socks that might match.' As she floats off on a quest for The Perfect Socks, I linger at the sweater rack and finger the fuzzy fabric. It really is beautiful. Y'know what? I'm going to try it on. Maybe we could have matching sweaters! Like two halves of a friendship locket, a declaration of our undying friendship. Sweater buddies!

I slip into the changing room and pull it over my head.

I look myself up and down in the mirror. Mirrors add ten pounds, right? Just like being on TV! I tug The Perfect Sweater down over my rounded middle. Hmmm, maybe the next size up? It's a low scoop neckline and my generous bosom feels dangerously untethered. Can I stretch it up a bit? And the pink, which made her cheeks flush prettily, just makes me look a little yellow-y. Urgh.

Yeah. Nope. Not gonna happen.

About eight years into the life of GOHOP, it feels almost like we're an awkward teenager standing in front of a mirror, tugging on the sweater edges. We love some of the spiritual DNA we've gleaned from the International House of Prayer: praying the Scriptures, the fusion of prayer and worship, the centrality of the person of Jesus, and a vocational call for some to a lifestyle of prayer. However, we are finding that the IHOP model isn't fitting us or our context the way we hoped. On us, the sweater doesn't fit our body well or look nearly as nice.

We begin to feel frustrated and discouraged. We can't seem to cobble together more than a handful of musicians, let alone the hundreds of staff required to fuel ongoing 24-7 worship and prayer. A yearning for something more, something other, stirs within us.

We love gathering charismatic Christians, but long to see a fuller representation of the Body engaging in prayer for the city. We want our Presbyterian friends to be just as comfortable in the prayer room as our Pentecostal ones. We want to see everyone praying more and we aren't sure how to help them.

We long to engage more in mission and justice, putting feet to our prayers. We wonder how we can create an expression that is meaningful and accessible to the urban poor. In our frustration and longing we begin to look for other models, for lifestyles and communities built around prayer, mission and justice.

Enter 24-7 Prayer, Andy Freeman and *Punk Monk*.

It's the first night of the Global 24-7 Prayer Gathering in Dublin. I hide behind the pillar in the restaurant and survey the chatting crowd. I don't know anyone. Not a single soul. But I'm on a mission. There is one single soul in the room I must meet.

Nervous, I approach a friendly looking stranger. 'Um, I'm looking for Andy Freeman. Can you point him out to me?'

'Sure, he's right there.' She points. 'Goatee and glasses – you can't miss him!'

For a few minutes I survey my quarry from afar, then summon my courage and calculate my trajectory of approach. Slowly sidle my way over to his table. *Try to look casual.* My palms are clammy.

The interchange is brief. 'Um, hi I'm Jill. I lead a House of Prayer in Canada. Your book, *Punk Monk*, has been really helpful for us – really influential. Just wanted to say thank you.' I also want to say about a million other things, but I'm shy and awkward and so is he. So I drop my little thank you and then beat a hasty exit.

It's my first 24-7 Prayer Gathering and also my first time staying in mixed gender bunkbed rooms in a youth hostel. Much to my relief our little gaggle of Canadian pilgrims fills up most of the dormitory. Sleeping with strangers, especially male strangers, is not high on my bucket list. I'm an early-to-bed, early-to-rise kind of girl, so as soon as I can slip away from the evening meeting, I tuck myself into a lower bunk in a corner.

As I'm drifting off the door opens, framing the silhouette of a stranger. Aghast, I realize it's *not* a stranger and, in a flash I pull my blanket over my head and scrunch myself as small as possible against the wall. I am *not* prepared to greet Andy Freeman in my jammies and tousled bed head.

I hide until morning and then, in the wee hours, gather my clothes and creep out to make myself more presentable.

'Heya, Jill, y'all right?' I'm sitting in the hostel cafeteria, nursing a cup of terrible coffee when Andy wanders in a couple hours later. Toast and more bad coffee help us overcome our shyness, and my story begins to tumble out. I tell him my frustrations. Our community longings. 'Your book, Andy, it's just what we're looking for. We got it a little while back and we're studying it now as a team.'

About the same time as we started GOHOP, across the pond in England, Andy, his buddy Wardie and a handful of other wannabe monastics embark on an experiment. 'Can we create a new monastic community built around the practices of prayer, mission and justice?' they wonder. *Punk Monk* is the story of the formation of the Reading Boiler Room, 24-7's first prayer community. Not only does it tell the 'what', but more helpfully for us, it tells the 'why' and the 'how'. In the book, we're introduced to a common Rule of Life – a way of living that shapes an entire community around the formational practices of prayer, creativity, learning, mission, mercy, justice and hospitality.

We've been famished, and it feels like Andy has handed us a recipe book and a load of groceries. Our GOHOP team can't wait to get cooking. Not gonna lie – we're gonna freestyle a bit as we cook – adjusting the taste for our context and our unique cast of characters.

THE INVITATION

We visit a church whose worship expression makes our heart sing. We have lunch at a friend's house and marvel at the beauty of her table and the scrumptiousness of its contents. Someone writes the most clever and comprehensive Bible study notes we've ever seen!

It's so tempting when we see something extraordinary modelled, to try and reproduce it. Imitation is the best form of flattery, right?

Here's the kicker, though.

The kingdom of God is not a franchise.

And when we try to live into someone else's gift, when we try to mirror our organizations on something we visited or read about in *Relevant* magazine, we set ourselves up for failure and disappointment.

God has not called us to live someone else's life. He's called us to live our own. He has not called us to recreate someone else's community, but to co-create our own with him: 'the kingdom of God is in your midst,' Jesus said in Luke 17:21.

1. In life and in ministry, are you metaphorically wearing someone else's sweater? How is it fitting?
2. How might you unravel it and knit something that fits better? What are the unique gifts and graces God has given you, given your community? What might those look like expressed in your context?
3. Who are you learning from these days? Books, teachers, podcasts? How can you incorporate your new learning by innovating, not imitating?

Jesus, I thank you that you created me for good works, which you prepared for me before I was born.
Please forgive me for the times I have tried to live someone else's life rather than my own.
I receive the gift of myself, the gift of my community.
Show us the story you are writing in our midst, so that we may inhabit it with authenticity, and be your unique word to the world.

Chapter 18

PRESBYANGLIBAPTI CATHOLICOSTAL

*Just as a body, though one, has many parts, but all its many
parts form one body, so it is with Christ. For we were all
baptised by one Spirit so as to form one body – whether Jews
or Gentiles, slave or free – and we were all given the one
Spirit to drink. And so the body is not made up of one part
but of many.*

1 CORINTHIANS 12:12–14

My longing for a prayer community with a broad
interdenominational reach is not surprising. I'm an
ecclesiastical mongrel – a mutt really. The ecumenical
impulse has been bred in the bone. In my early years of faith
I am discipled through interdenominational school and
university clubs. Right from the get-go I learn and grow with
Christians of all kinds. I wash feet on Anglican retreats and
date Mennonite boys. 'So, this pacifism thing, if someone
attacks me when we walk down the street, would you fight
to defend me?' I ask. 'Nope,' he responds with a grin.

I call myself a PresbyAngliBaptiCatholiCostal. To begin
with I've been baptized as an infant. And also as an adult. In
fact, I've been baptized three times. 'This is your christening
gown,' mum lifts up a tiny ivory dress. It's delicately

embroidered. Looks like it's for a baby doll. I reach out to touch the fabric. It crinkles under my fingers – smooth, slightly stiff with age, fragile. It seems disproportionately long for its size and parts of it are yellowing, water stained.

'All of your cousins were christened in this dress. Your brother too.' Tim? In a dress? I grin as I try to picture my baby brother dressed in drag. Too bad there are no pictures to blackmail him with.

My parents aren't properly Anglican – basically at the time they were Christmas and Easter people. But they were married in an Anglican Church and evidently Tim and I were baptized there too.

Later, aged 18, I visit my cousins in the States. They are Evangelicals, the kind of Christians who leave large Bibles lying around the house – Bibles marked up with notes and passages underlined in multicolour. They say *Amen* a lot and they are very smiley and go to lots of church meetings. They are excited about my new-found religion and ask me, 'Have you ever been baptized? You know, properly baptized after having made a confession of faith?' Properly baptized? I'm not sure. I decide to get baptized again, just in case the first one didn't count. Better safe than sorry.

The next Sunday I find myself in a church basement with several other baptism candidates. We receive a couple hours of instruction before the BIG event. I'm fascinated by the boy in the corner, trying not to stare at the angry red scar across his throat. 'He tried to commit suicide, but then God saved him,' my cousin whispers. The boy is withdrawn and quiet, his fingers tracing the other scars on his wrists. We listen together to the pastor talk about leaving our old lives behind, dying to the past and welcoming our new lives with Jesus after baptism.

The church mamas give me a choir robe to wear and hustle me up some stairs to a large tub built into the front of the church sanctuary. Pretty handy, I think, but what if it springs a leak?

As the congregation sings, I take the pastor's hand and join him in the water. Then I cross my arms over my chest and bow my head, nervous and shy. 'Do you believe Jesus Christ is your Lord? Do you receive him as your Saviour?' I nod and *fwoosh*, he tips me backwards into the water.

Dripping, I climb out of the tub and the church mamas immediately enfold me in towels and prayers. Like a little chick emerging from the shell, I'm ripe for impression.

This is the first time I ever receive what I would later come to understand as a personal prophecy. Seems normal to me now, but at the time I thought the mamas were a little bit unhinged.

'I see you wearing a Carmen Miranda hat,' coos one of the mamas. Carmen Miranda? I suppress the urge to reach up to see if a hat has indeed affixed itself to my head. 'It's a big hat piled high with fruit – all kinds of fruit. You're gonna have lotsa fruit – lotsa fruit for lotsa people. For one, a pineapple. For another, a banana. Lotsa gifts for lotsa people.' Weird. Haven't a clue what she's talking about, but it sounds somewhat encouraging.

The smiles and the towels are warm and so, wearing my invisible hat, I lean into their embrace.

I receive a lovely framed baptism certificate showing that I am now 'properly' baptized. With pride I present it to my parents. They are somewhat taken aback but humour me all the same. The invisible hat I don't mention, but rather tuck it into a dusty corner of my psyche. I chalk it up as an interesting but slightly bizarre cross-cultural religious experience.

Over twenty years later, when my daughter Hannah is herself eighteen, I am baptized for a third time.

We are on a whirlwind tour of religious sites in Israel. We skip rocks on the shores of Galilee, scale the heights of Masada and explore its ruins. We float in the Dead Sea, overseen by a wizened lifeguard sporting a little round *yarmulke* on his head, a belly-button length beard, a whistle and a speedo. 'Don't get your eyes wet,' he barks, 'it stings!'

We sneak into an off-limits mud pit and slather ourselves with Dead Sea mud. It prickles and tingles. 'Good for the skin!' Hannah exclaims. After a few minutes we notice a man slouched in the corner of the hole, almost submerged in the mud. Creepy. We crawl out of the pit, leaving its glowering guardian behind.

We climb David's En Gedi stronghold, its springs like a green slash across the arid landscape. We see desert rats the size of raccoons and goats that climb low-lying trees, calmly munching leaves, probably happy that they are out of reach of the rodents of unusual size. Finally, we arrive at the Jordan River.

'Would anyone like to be baptized here in the Jordan? Just like Jesus was?' My hand shoots up before my mind considers the maths. Baptism number three? Overkill? An act of faith or religious tourism? Hmmm maybe the latter, but I mean, who can resist the chance to be baptized in the Jordan River?

It's a bit touristy, but not obscene. You can hire a local photographer to capture your dunking. And rent a white robe. As I look around at other soggy devotees, I make a mental note – make sure you wear something underneath ...

Crowds swarm towards the banks as I expect they did in Jesus' day. The babble of multiple languages fills the air. Every skin colour on the planet seems to be represented, as is every variation of monastic habit. By the water, there is a changing room. The kaleidoscope of colourful pilgrims enters one door. They emerge from the other side all dressed in white, many silent and thoughtful as they approach the water. 'Nuns! I want to swim with the nuns!' Hannah points down the river towards a gaggle of Sisters dipping their toes.

Waiting for my turn I perch on a rock, arms wrapped around my knees. The Middle-Eastern sun warms my skin. I lift my face towards its rays and take a deep breath, inhaling the moment. The wind tousles my hair. My heart feels kissed awake.

It's time. I'm in the water surrounded by my travelling buddies. I startle as there is a small but sharp tug on my foot. And another. And another. Tiny Middle-Eastern piranhas? Probably the same kinds of fish that spas use to get rid of dead skin. I hop from one foot to another, trying to dissuade their exfoliation efforts and attempt to focus. *Fwoosh*, down I go, and bob up again, surrounded by the smiling faces of my companions.

All except Hannah. I look over my shoulder to see her floating on her back like a starfish, drifting nunward down the river.

My triple baptism and my interdenominational discipleship and dating set me on an ecumenical trajectory, and a dream I have in Hannah's early years certainly reinforces it. The dream is an actual at-night-time, while-I'm-sleeping dream. I wake in the morning and its outlines are still imprinted on the inside of my eyelids.

The landscape is in shadow. The glint and shimmer of the waning moon's rays bounce off little meandering tributaries. The streams begin to tangle and weave, tumbling together to congregate into a vast floodplain. On the edge of the watery expanse I see the darkened skyline of a city. There the dream pauses, holding its breath.

Shapes shift in the sky and it glimmers, glows and warms.

Light cracks on the horizon and spills over. The sun begins to rise, and everything is made new in its light.

The dream is a mystery. An invitation. At least I think it is. Over the next couple of years as I ponder its meaning, the vision slowly gives up its secrets. I pen them into a song.

Son of righteousness is rising
Darkness drifting away
Light of deliverance is dawning
Bursting forth, in glorious day.
All the streams combine, flowing as one river
All our hearts entwine, worshipping together
We watch the morning rise over our city
And we sing, we sing.
Arise, shine, for your light has come, your light has come
Arise, shine, for your King has come, your King has come.
And you will break forth, as the dawn,
As we unite in morning's song.

I can't shake it. Almost two decades later it still rumbles and rolls around inside me.

A chat with a Pentecostal friend reinforces my conviction. One day he tells me this story: 'I was worshipping one day, talking with the Lord, and I said to him, "I *love* your river, O God!"' Ron is passionate, eyes gleaming as he remembers the conversation. By the river, he means the presence and activity of God he was seeing around him.

'You haven't seen the river,' God replies. Ron is taken aback. 'Of course I have – I'm a river man! I love the river!'

'You've only seen a stream.' God says. *'There is a river whose streams make glad the city of God. Streams, not stream. You haven't yet seen the river.'*

THE INVITATION

Everything I have shared with you ... grows out of a deep conviction that a great, new gathering of the people of God is occurring in our day. The streams of faith that I have been describing – Contemplative, Holiness, Charismatic, Social Justice, Evangelical, Incarnational – are flowing together into a mighty movement of the Spirit ... a new thing is coming. God is gathering his people once again, creating of them an all-inclusive community of loving persons with Jesus Christ as the community's prime sustainer and most glorious inhabitant.[42]

Imagine your spiritual life as a pilgrimage and picture yourself wearing a rucksack that carries all your provisions for the journey. The contents of the rucksack include your favourite, most formative books or teachings. Spiritual practices that you have found particularly helpful or life giving. Stories or examples of inspiring leaders that spur you on.

1. Take some time, unpack the rucksack and examine its contents. Where have you picked them up along the way? How are they giving you strength, resolve and resource on your spiritual pathway?
2. In his book *Streams of Living Water*, Richard Foster identifies six streams of the church, each of which carries a particular emphasis and strength as it seeks to follow Jesus' life and teaching:
    *   The Contemplative Stream: the prayer-filled life
    *   The Holiness Stream: the virtuous life
    *   The Charismatic Stream: the Spirit-empowered life

42 Richard Foster, *Streams of Living Water: Celebrating the Great Traditions of Christian Faith*, (Hodder & Stoughton, 2017), p.273.

- The Social Justice Tradition: the compassionate life
- The Evangelical Tradition: the word-centred life
- The Incarnational Tradition: the sacramental life.

What streams of the church have shaped and influenced you as you have sought to practise the way of Jesus? How have they informed and formed you? Take some time to reflect with gratitude for all the gifts you have been given.

3. What might happen if you were to dip your toe in another stream of the church, to explore their teachings and particular practices? Try something new and reflect on your experience.

Jesus, your Church is so beautiful in all its diversity, reflecting many different aspects of your life and character.
Thank you for revealing yourself in your body.
Help me to embody you well.
Give me courage and curiosity to explore beyond my present experience and, as I do so, reveal yourself to me and through me,
Jesus.

Chapter 19

THE PERFECT STORM

Why, LORD do you stand far off?
Why do you hide yourself in times of trouble?

PSALM 10:1

I sit in my back garden, legs stretched out on the chair in front of me. I'm watching the squirrels. They chase one another, scolding and chittering on the branches of the sprawling maple that overshadows my garden. Daring leaps from one branch to another. Landing on 'branchlets', on tree fringes, then skittering higher to even more impossible exploits. I love their *chutzpah* and playfulness. The garden beside mine has a shed covered with plastic, and one day I watch a young squirrel jump up and down on top of the bubbling, air-filled tarpaulin like it was a trampoline, seemingly for the sheer joy of it.

I myself am more landlocked, fused to the lawn chair. I have spent the better part of my sabbatical in the garden. I'm cranky. I haven't opened my Bible for months. Even looking at Christian books makes my lip want to curl. I feel allergic to anything religious. From time to time I go to church, but sit in the back, arms folded. Prickly, resistant and defiant. 'I dare you to bless me!'

I'm a cabin shuttered behind storm windows. I've had enough tumult for the time being, thank you very much. And right now I don't trust God to blow a fairer breeze my way.

Several months before, the storm warning came in the form of the police knocking at my door. 'Are you Jill Weber? We're investigating some calls made about you.' Some calls. We eventually find it's 105 calls, to be exact. Death threats sent to my mother's workplace and also the prayer phone lines at the Crossroads Centre. The police ask me to listen to a recording so that I can identify my ex-husband's voice. His tone is calm, but his message and intent is chilling.

The local authorities have just established a local domestic violence unit, and excited to flex their new-found muscles, they spring into action on my behalf. They assess the risk. Evidently, I rate high on the 'you're probably going to get killed' scale, because the police issue me a special silent alarm to clip to my belt.

'That will bring the closest squad car to your home the moment you trigger it,' a blonde ponytailed officer says. We are sitting at our dinner table with a couple of officers who have been assigned to show us how to safeguard our home. 'Can I offer you a coffee? Some cookies?' I'm unsure what the etiquette is for police hospitality. 'No that's alright thanks. Let's talk about how you can fortify your front entrance.'

Beside the table, our little Christmas tree wobbles and tilts. I lunge to grab it before it completely falls over. Blonde ponytailed officer steps in, helping stabilize the tree while I re-attach it to its base. Christmas saved; we move on to discussions on how to create a safe room. How to back my car into parking spots to enable a quick getaway. Lockdown procedures for work.

Eventually my ex-husband is apprehended, but the ordeal takes its toll on us. I ask the GOHOP board for a sabbatical, a few months' rest to recover my equilibrium. I step back from the frontline.

It doesn't go as planned. Instead of feeling more centred, I spin out, twirl and fragment. I fortify my bruised heart and peer out at the world through the shutters, suspicious and angry. Angry at God, mostly. I would love to say that my resentment has purpose and reason but it's more like an amorphous cloud. A generalized simmering rage.

To make matters worse, in the midst of it all I can't hear his voice. Zip, nada, nothing. Maybe because he knows I'm pissed off. Maybe he's figured out that I need some space. But I don't need space really. Or maybe I do. I don't know. I'm conflicted.

'I can handle anything if I can hear God's voice,' I grouch to a long-suffering girlfriend. 'But when he's not talking, I don't know what to do with myself.'

I sometimes wonder if Moses stayed up on the mountain for forty days not because God wasn't speaking, but maybe because it just took Moses that long to dial down enough to listen! Not sure what a six-month time lag in his speaking says about me ...

On that squirrel-watching day in the garden near the very end of my sabbatical, God finally breaks the silence. The familiar voice, the one I had been alternatively mad at and longing for, finally sounds in my head.

I expected something nice, something comforting and sympathetic – 'There, there honey, I'm sorry that you have to look over your shoulder and that someone's out there wanting to kill you. Sorry for the toll that has taken on your family. Sorry that life is so hard.'

Nope, he doesn't do that at all.

Instead he issues a simple directive. A command really.

'I want you to raise up the next generation of champions.'
What???

I feel like Gideon hiding out in the winepress. Bruised

by the enemy, laying low and keeping his head down. Then God appears, calling him – of all things – 'mighty warrior', ignores Gideon's whining complaint, and, despite his protests, sends him on mission.[43]

'I want you to raise up the next generation of champions.' Like Gideon, I complain, whine and protest. Next generation of champions? Well, Lord, let me tell you: GOHOP isn't growing right now. We're like an aeroplane circling the airport waiting to land. Struggling along with just a handful of faithful intercessors holding the fort.

And when I try and plan prayer events, five middle-aged ladies with flags and shofars show up. I know it's the praying grandmas who make the world continue to spin on its axis, but I'm not sure that's what you are talking about in this instance.

And next generation? Young people? I know charismatic leaders who attract young people, and I know I'm not one of them. I'm not cool. I don't even have a nose ring!

Plus, I'm mad at you and done with ministry anyway. I think I'll go work for a library – they are nice and quiet. Or maybe a convenience store.

'I want you to raise up the next generation of champions.'

I wrestle. Grump and harrumph. I struggle but eventually succumb.

It's not my most gracious, faith-filled moment.

OK. Whatever. I have no idea how this might come about. But yes.

Ah, such a teeny word to have such massive catalytic effect! My little yes puts me in the path of oncoming grace. I can picture the great cloud of witnesses in heaven, watching with bated breath. 'Is she gonna do it? Say yes? Yeah! She did it! Wooohooo! Can't wait to see what happens next!'

43 Judges 6:11–14.

THE INVITATION

The genius of the Psalms is that David and the other psalmists not only gave us the language of worship, but also the language of lament. The Psalms give us permission to feel and to voice our sadness, fear and anger in God's presence.

> *Save me, O God,*
> *for the waters have come up to my neck.*
> *I sink in the miry depths,*
> *where there is no foothold.*
> *I have come into the deep waters;*
> *the floods engulf me.*
> *I am worn out calling for help;*
> *my throat is parched.*
> *My eyes fail,*
> *looking for my God.*
> *Those who hate me without reason*
> *outnumber the hairs of my head;*
> *many are my enemies without cause,*
> *those who seek to destroy me.*

PSALM 69:1–4A

Read: Read this portion of Psalm 69 out loud, slowly. Which words or phrases jump out at you?

Reflect: Reflect on those words or phrases. How do you relate to what David is expressing before God?

Respond: What might happen if you summon the courage to voice your lament and, as Ruth Haley Barton says, 'walk all the way into your sadness?' What might be possible if you invite God to meet you there?

Jesus, you are no stranger to suffering and to lament.
Thank you for entering into my adversity with me so that I am
not alone.
I hold my lament before you – how long, O Lord, how long?
Help me to discover your new mercies every morning, even in
the midst of my own misfortune.

Chapter 20

SPEAK FRIEND AND ENTER

I will place on his shoulder the key to the house of David;
what he opens no one can shut, and what he shuts no one
can open.

ISAIAH 22:22

I'm back from Sabbatical and starting to feel like my old self again. Interestingly enough, after I give God my begrudging yes, young leaders begin to contact me out of nowhere. They text. They 'friend' me on Facebook. I bump into them on the streets. I'm not any cooler. I still don't have a nose ring. But somehow, just my willingness puts something in motion. GOHOP begins to grow.

Its November-ish. It's 4.30am. In the predawn hours, I'm snuggled up in my prayer chair. Fluffy slippers on my feet. Warm and foamy latte in hand. Open on my lap is the book *Celtic Daily Prayer*. I like to use a prayer book instead of just selecting and parking on my favourite Bible passages. When I do, the Scriptures choose me rather than the other way around, they read me instead of me reading them. Often they illuminate something in my heart and life that God wants to address.

On this particular day, the Scripture is slightly less shiny: worn through regular use 'Ask and it will be given to you; seek and you will find; knock and the door will be opened to you.'[44] With my characteristic faith and spiritual acuity, I respond. 'Yeah, yeah, whatever. I'm a prayer person. I knock all the time!' However, I write the verse down in my prayer journal, because it does shimmer just a teeny bit.

Knock and the door will be opened.

It's January-ish. Our time is beginning to run out in Waterdown and our prayer community is watching and waiting for the go-ahead from God to relocate to the urban core of Hamilton.

It's 11am: I'm at a pastors' conference. In one of the sessions I feel a gentle hand on my shoulder. I look up. It's Faith, a friend of mine, and she is silently praying for me. When she is done I thank her. 'As I was listening to God, what came to mind was that he was going to open double doors ahead of you,' she says. Open doors? Hmm, hadn't I written something about that in my journal a couple of months before?

Over lunch I'm sitting with one of my girlfriends, reflecting on the coincidence. 'What do you think double doors mean?' I ask. 'Ha!' She chuckles, 'reminds me of the doors into the mountain in *The Lord of the Rings*!'

I scan my memory banks and the scene from the movie comes into focus. I remember the image of Frodo and the members of the Fellowship, huddled before the gates of the mines of Moria. It's their only way forward, but it's barred

44 Matthew 7:7.

and locked. Arched over the double doorways is Elfin script saying, 'Speak, friend, and enter.'[45]

'Oh yeah,' I respond, 'remember, they thought it would be all complicated and difficult to open the doors. They tried all kinds of things! Finally, they figure out that they only have to say the word 'friend' in Elvish and the doors just open!' As soon as the words are out of my mouth, something uncorks on the inside of my chest, bubbling over. I began to tremble at the table – literally. And I heard a quiet but clear internal voice say, *'Speak to your friends and enter the city.'*

I'm shaken. Bemused. I have a sense of receiving some kind of divine directive. Speak friend and enter. Can simply talking to people open up the way for us? Will it work? What could it hurt?

In subsequent weeks, I meet with friend after friend in Hamilton – sharing my heart to see GOHOP relocate to the downtown core. An urban monastery that would raise up a generation of young leaders generously giving themselves to Jesus in lifestyles marked by prayer, mission and justice. Prayer and evangelism coming together in synergistic ways.

April-ish. Lunchtime. Kirk and I are downtown renewing his passport. After standing in line for half an hour our mission is accomplished. Documents in hand, we head for the door. On our way out we are accosted by a uniformed security guard. He steps in front of us, chest puffed. He is scowling, his gaze intense. 'Isaiah 45:1!' He blurts. 'Excuse me?' Shocked, we stop in our tracks. 'What did you say?'

'Isaiah 45:1! God will open before you double doors; and

45 Peter Jackson, *The Lord of the Rings: The Fellowship of the Ring* (New Line Cinema and WingNut Films, 2001).

the gates shall not be shut!' Shock turns into incredulity. 'Who *are* you?' Passport tellers peer out of their cubicles, watching us as his story unfolds. Formerly a pastor in an underground church in the Middle East, he has returned to his native Canada and is now working as a security guard. He almost never shares prophetic words with people and certainly has never prophetically 'blurted' at someone on the job before. Today, however, when we pass by he can't contain himself – he's compelled to discharge his message.

When Kirk and I finally leave the passport office, we lean against the wall of the building, shocked and laughing. 'That was the craziest thing that's ever happened to me, like something out of a book!' Kirk says. When we get home, we run to our Bible to look up the passage.

> '*Thus says the* LORD *to His anointed,*
> *To Cyrus, whose right hand I have held –*
> *To subdue nations before him*
> *And loose the armor of kings,*
> *To open before him the double doors,*
> *So that the gates will not be shut* …'

ISAIAH 45:1 (NKJV)

Double doors. The gates to the city!

I love the symbolism of it all. There we are at a passport office, obtaining governmental permission to enter new territory, and God uses the security guard as a divine messenger. Even his name, Evangeliste, feels symbolic. From that moment on, door after door opens for us.

As part of our exploration of radical hospitality, Kirk and I decide to try a massive and potentially risky experiment. What would it look like for us to live in community? A community house with a bunch of others? I had pretty great experiences living with friends at camps in the summer, and Kirk has fond memories of dormitory life at university, so we decide to give it a go. We listen to an online 24-7 Prayer course on Christ-Centred Community. I read a number of books, including *The Intentional Christian Community Handbook.*[46]

I love the idea of life-on-life discipleship – living in close enough quarters with people so that I can find out if I am holy or merely undisturbed (just so ya know, I found out I am the latter). As a 'religious leader' I'm worried about having public persona that is different from how I am in private. Living with folks will help me build consistency and authenticity into my journey. Plus, sharing the day-to-day tasks of cooking and cleaning will make life a lot easier and sharing the cost of rent will make life a LOT cheaper.

We begin a quest for a house big enough for us to share with some friends. I refuse to look at adverts.

Speak to your friends and enter the city! I get the word out that we were looking for a place to live. Sure enough, within a week I receive an email from a friend who has just heard an announcement at their church: there is a Canadian missionary heading to Brazil who is looking for tenants for his house in Hamilton. Four bedrooms, two bathrooms. Downtown and walking distance from our prayer room. Perfect for what we have in mind for our first community house.

I set up an online video call. 'Hey Tom, we can give you first and last month's rent and a security deposit if you need it. I can get some references for you.'

'Not going to need any of that,' grins Tom. 'I know who you are. The house is yours!'

---

46 David Janzen, *The Intentional Christian Community Handbook: For Idealists, Hypocrites and Wannabe Disciples of Jesus* (Zondervan, 2013).

God opens other doors for us as well. A local church gives free prayer space in their community building. A citywide network, TrueCity, offers us free office space. Other friends give us access to their congregations and to their networks.

The city is wide open to us and GOHOP steps into the new space with confidence, knowing that God has gone before us to prepare the way.

THE INVITATION

In this chapter, we see a number of ways that God gives direction. Through reading and meditating on the Scriptures. Through prayerful discernment of friends. Through a still small voice. Through startling prophetic interruptions. Through unfolding circumstances. All of these things can work together to help us get a sense of where God is at work in our lives and how he might want to move us forward.

1. Where do I need direction in my life? Where do I need God to show me which way to go?
2. How is he leading me as I read the Bible? Are there any Scriptures that seem particularly relevant, or feel particularly potent?
3. Do I have prayerful friends who share with me what they discern on my behalf? What are they saying?
4. Do I have a sense of hearing God's voice pertaining to this issue? What might he be saying to me?
5. Are there any unexpected or specific situations or prophetic words spoken over me that speak into the situation?
6. How are life circumstances unfolding before me. Do they in some way confirm God's direction?

Jesus, you are our Way, our Truth and our Life.
Your word is a lamp unto our feet and a light unto our path.
Thank you for our communities that help us to hear you, that
bring encouragement and confirmation on the way forward.
We trust your good leadership and we commit ourselves to
following as you unfold your will and your desire for us.

Chapter 21

ZING!

'I have revealed you to those whom you gave me out of the world. They were yours; you gave them to me and they have obeyed your word ... I pray for them. I am not praying for the world, but for those you have given me, for they are yours.'

JOHN 17:6,9

I begin to invest more deeply in my Hamilton relationships but find it to be a little more complicated than I imagined.

Denni is a dear friend, a confidante. She's the Tweedledee to my Tweedledum. Over the last eight years as we've worked together in GOHOP, we've both frolicked in the sunshine of God's blessing and weathered the inevitable storms, hanging on to one another and to God when life gets rocky. She's seen me at my best and loved me at my worst. I can tell her anything.

Today I'm sheepish and shy. Embarrassed. I can't believe this is happening. Best to talk about it, nip it in the bud. 'Denni I think I may be attracted to someone! I just don't get it, though. He's totally not my type.' My type is a ponytailed drummer who is eighty-five per cent smartass and makes me laugh constantly. Who greets me at the door with enthusiasm and affection when I get home every day. Who is mostly allergic to cooking but can still make a mean omelette. Who still, after all these years, tucks me in every night.

'Every time I get together with this colleague to talk ministry stuff, there's some kind of electricity – some "zing" in the interaction. It feels like, right from our very first meeting, we are on the same wavelength and have been friends for decades! I totally get him, he totally gets me.

'I don't feel sexually attracted to him at all, and I'm super happy with Kirk, but there just seems to be something between us ...'

Within the safety of loving accountability and some other healthy boundaries (meeting only for work stuff and always in public places, and getting to know – and love! – his wife), I continue to explore what God might be doing through this relational chemistry.

Over the years I've come to understand a spiritual dynamic that I call 'zing'. Simply put, it's the life flow of the Holy Spirit in a relational connection. Without exception, every time I have 'zinged' with someone, that relationship ends up being essential to me and important in the purposes of God for GOHOP both locally and beyond.

There was Chris, who at the time led 24-7 Prayer in Canada. A broad-shouldered, rugby-loving Welshman with creased laughter lines and a perpetual five o'clock shadow, he repeatedly invites me to join the 24-7 Prayer national leadership team. Eventually, I say yes just to stop him pestering me. He opens up the door for GOHOP to dock in to 24-7 Prayer internationally, creating opportunities for international relationships and influence.

Then there is Dave. After my first meeting with him I go home to Kirk and say, 'Basically he is me, except a guy. And about twice as smart.' Understated but brilliant, Dave is particularly fond of wearing plaid. 'My wife does my shopping for me,' he says when I tease him about his limited fashion palate. Dave facilitates a movement of churches in Hamilton that work together for the good of the city. He teaches me how to translate 'Charismatic-ese' into Baptist and Presbyterian. 'Those words don't mean what you think they mean.' He is a patient teacher and guide.

'Jill, our churches are getting quite good at doing mission together, but we're not so good at praying together. Do you think that GOHOP can help us?' Dave asks. I pause for a moment, then respond. 'I expect you are far better at praying than you realize. You just need to understand what your prayer language is. But yes, we can help.' What follows is a friendship that enriches us both and a partnership that blesses and benefits both our organizations and networks. Respected in the city, Dave opens up door after door of opportunity and influence for our House of Prayer.

And there is Sue, a cheeky Brit with a silvery pixie cut. Thirty years in Canada and she's stubbornly held on to her posh London accent. She is equal parts fierce and tender. We first meet at a pastors' prayer retreat where we are assigned as roommates. We hit it off from the get-go, never realizing how tightly our lives would be wound together over the next decade and a half. It feels like we are a string of Christmas lights, and when we each get plugged in, we light up!

'Zing' still feels weird, random and potentially 'out there' to me, so I look for a biblical framework of understanding for the phenomenon. Is it the 'man of peace' that Jesus talks about in Luke 10? The God-ordained relational connection that opens up new opportunities for the Gospel? 'When you enter a house, first say, "Peace to this house." If someone who promotes peace is there, your peace will rest on them; if not, it will return to you.'[47] Maybe.

47 Luke 10:5–6.

Is it like the supernatural bond of affection between King David and Jonathan? 'After David had finished talking with Saul, Jonathan became one in spirit with David, and he loved him as himself ... And Jonathan made a covenant with David because he loved him as himself.'[48] Perhaps. It certainly feels like it.

One day when I'm studying John 17, the penny drops. In his prayer for the disciples, Jesus talks about relational assignments that have been given to him by the Father.

> 'I have revealed you to those whom you gave me out of the world. They were yours; you gave them to me and they have obeyed your word ... I pray for them. I am not praying for the world but for those you have given me, for they are yours.'[49]

Jesus knows that there are certain people that the Father has given him – people he will give his heart to and share his life with.

That is what I've been experiencing!

My recent foray into Ignatian spirituality also helps me understand the dynamic better. Ignatius founded the Jesuits in the 1500s and one of his contributions to faith tradition is to help us understand some of the visceral responses we have to people and to situations. Ignatius calls them 'desolation' and 'consolation'.

Desolation is a sense of darkness, confusion, being off centre and out of focus. Consolation is a sense of being awake, alive to the presence of God, centred and joyful. I realize that what I am experiencing in these relational connections is not a crush, not infatuation. It's consolation.

48 1 Samuel 18:1,3.
49 John 17:6,9.

An awareness of the presence of God infusing an anointed, ordained friendship with his grace and his goodness.

THE INVITATION

In the children's stories, *Anne of Green Gables*, the heroine Anne Shirley has a special name that she reserves for people with whom she feels a life-giving relational connection. She calls them 'kindred spirits'.

> *The old captain held out a sinewy hand to Anne; they smiled at each other and were friends from that moment. Kindred spirit flashed recognition to kindred spirit. 'I'm right down pleased to meet you, Mistress Blythe ... You're young and I'm old, but our souls are about the same age, I reckon. We both belong to the race that knows Joseph, as Cornelia Bryant would say.' 'The race that knows Joseph?' puzzled Anne. 'Yes. Cornelia divides all the folks in the world into two kinds – the race that knows Joseph and the race that don't. If a person sorter sees eye to eye with you, and has pretty much the same ideas about things, and the same taste in jokes – why, then he belongs to the race that knows Joseph.' 'Oh, I understand,' exclaimed Anne, light breaking in upon her. 'It's what I used to call – and still call in quotation marks "kindred spirits".*[50]

1. Reading this description of Anne's relationship with those she calls 'kindred spirits', do you recognize some similar spiritual relational and dynamics with people in your own life?

---

50 Lucy Maud Montgomery, *Anne's House of Dreams* (McClelland and Stewart, 1922), pp.26–38.

2. Have you experienced a 'kindred spirit connection'? How did that kind of connection change or impact your life?
3. What would it look like to explore that connection further to see what God has in store for you both?

Jesus, I thank you for the special and unique relational assignments you have given me, the constellation of friendships in my life that give me light and direction.
Help me to love well and to be open hearted to those you bring my way.
Show me where you are at work in the midst of these relationships and the unfolding of your will for us together.

Chapter 22

JEDI

Follow my example, as I follow the example of Christ.
1 CORINTHIANS 11:1

My 'zingy' relationship with Sue really kicks into gear one day over coffee. 'So GOHOP is trying to figure out how to grow in our spiritual practices of mission and justice, and it occurs to me that rather than reinventing the wheel and starting something up, maybe I should just chat with you. Can I follow you around a bit?' We're sitting in a local coffee shop. Sue is nursing her tea with milk. Her gaze is both sharp and warm. 'I'm not sure that I will be particularly helpful,' like a true Brit, she is self-deprecating. 'But if you would like to come and be with us that would be just fine.'

That Sunday I find myself outside the local homeless shelter and rehab centre where Sue serves as chaplain. A handful of smokers loiter outside – they stare at me as I approach. I take a deep breath and run the gauntlet to the front door. (Note to self: next time wear baggier clothes.)

The staircase leads downstairs to the hall where the chapel service is held. It smells vaguely of sweat and something else, slightly sour and undefinable. 'Glad you could come!' Sue beams and shows me around. 'Here is the kitchenette, there is the ratty little storage closet. And here is my office.

Probably a good idea to leave your valuables in here.'

On her door is a painting of Lucy from the *Peanuts* comic strip, sitting at her booth with a sign that says, 'The doctor is in.' There is a line through the word 'doctor' and the word 'chaplain' has been written in instead. 'My daughter painted that for me,' Sue laughs.

'About seven years ago the mission asked me to start a Sunday Bible study, and my first thought was, 'Darn, there go my weekends.' Since then we've outgrown the little room we were in, and now they have us here. I never wanted to be a pastor and I never meant for this to become a church. I told my people "we will just practise church together until you want to go to a proper church". Then one day, someone asked me what we were, and I asked the group. "We're a church, of course." So here we are.'

Some of the residents arrive and briskly set up chairs and put Bibles and songbooks onto them. 'We use songbooks and they choose the songs. It's important that they choose – there is so much going on in their lives that they can't fix, where there aren't choices and options. Mostly they like songs that they heard at their parents' funerals. Those are the ones that they remember.'

The songs are led by Jared, a seminary student on placement. He is over six feet tall and about ninety-seven pounds soaking wet, topped with a shock of red hair. When not serenading our crew, he dresses up in a hot dog suit and sells organic 'street meat' downtown. Today, however, he is playing an old steel guitar, lustily pounding out 'The Old Rugged Cross' and 'There is Power in the Blood'.

'Number one! I want number one!' Jackie's hand shoots in the air. She's quick on the draw, so we sing number one, which is 'Amazing Grace', Sunday after Sunday after Sunday. After the worship, Sue leads a discussion through the

Scriptures. My job is to pray in the back, sometimes quite fervently, depending on how many of our congregants are drunk and disorderly. I also help with refreshments.

I spend the first year hiding behind the coffee table. It provides a safe distance from this group of unkempt strangers but also gives me an opportunity to meet each one of them as they line up for cup after cup of coffee, which they take with spoonful after spoonful of sugar.

They arrive hungry and, before long, I am spending the week baking in preparation. The treats are well received, especially the cupcakes decorated as spiders and hedgehogs. I become an expert forager, gathering leftovers and snacks for our little flock.

'Is there a full moon tonight? Everybody's restless.' It's just one of those days when everything feels out of joint. One of the congregants is particularly agitated and while Sue attempts to preach, he lurches out of his seat. Swaying on his feet, he mumbles an invocation, sweeping his arms towards the four directions of the room. The crowd loses patience and begin to heckle.

'Shut the &%#$ up!'

'Get out the &$* way! We want to hear Pastor Sue!'

Sue breaks into the rumble.

'No one gets kicked out of my chapel!'

Cowed, the crowd quietens.

Sue then waits until he finishes, gently encourages him back to his seat, and proceeds with the sermon. I'm in awe. She may look like a tiny Englishwoman, but I see through her disguise. She's really a Jedi.

I become Sue's Padawan, her apprentice and shadow. Making coffee. Setting out and stacking chairs. Following her around. Watching everything she does and chatting with her about why she does it that way. Over the course of the next few years I get an indispensable education. How to cultivate safe, welcoming and inclusive space. How to honour the dignity of each individual and how to coax them to share their gifts with each other. I am wrecked for 'regular' churchy church.

The next time I visit the International House of Prayer in Kansas City I really struggle. The prayer room is squeaky clean and orderly. The music is high calibre and expertly mixed. Everything is beautiful, professional, well ordered. And I feel distinctly ill at ease and out of place.

That night I have dinner with one of my friends there and tell him my experience. 'Ah what you need to do is visit Hope City, our inner-city House of Prayer!' He says. 'I'll arrange a ride for you.'

The next day I am dropped off in a neighbourhood that seems to be very much on the wrong side of the tracks. The front door opens to a hall where a bunch of scruffy men are sitting at tables, clutching coffee cups. 'Here is where we have the soup kitchen and food bank,' my host is showing me around. 'Over there we have laundry machines so people can do their wash for free. And we've got a clothing bank as well, mainly for the men. Socks are always in demand.'

At the entrance of the prayer room itself there is an ancient and wispy woman swaying back and forth to the music. She has the gentle and vacant look of someone with dementia. Inside, a few African American children are playing tag amongst the seats and someone is passed out on a pew in the back. On the platform one of the singers is nursing her baby as she sings into the microphone. The worship is interspersed with rap and spoken word.

Ah, much better. With a sigh of relief, I settle into a chair. Best pick a wooden chair, don't know what crawly creatures might be living in the padded ones. My heart feels at home.

She's brown haired and grey-blue eyed. Wearing a warm woolly sweater and big bulky scarf wrapped around her neck, she's sitting on the other end of the couch and interviewing me for a class project on leadership. People study me for school. Weird. One day I'm invited to a seminary class by a local professor. 'Am I coming as a teacher or a specimen to be examined?' I ask.

New Monasticism is growing in its profile and popularity, and students are curious. Shira is a seminary student at the university down the road. We first meet in Winnipeg at their local House of Prayer. I'm there speaking and when I'm done she approaches me. 'I'm coming to Hamilton this fall to go to school,' she says. 'I would love to connect with you!' 'Sure, c'mon over and visit,' I respond. I make a mental note. Young person: check. Loves the Bible: check. Worship leader: check. Into the prayer movement: check ... iiiinteresting ...

Several months later she's over at our place. After the interview, she poses a question. 'Any chance I can do my school placement at GOHOP? Basically, follow you around for a year or so?' I chuckle to myself. I'm not sure that I'm a Jedi yet, but happy to have a Padawan for a season.

THE INVITATION

The shape of first-century Rabbinical education was much more about imitation and apprenticeship than it was classroom type learning. Discipleship was life-on-life spiritual formation – Jesus' disciples immersed themselves in his lifestyle and teachings, towards the goal of becoming more like him. Jesus himself said: *'Follow me, and I will make you fishers of men'*(MATTHEW 4:19 ESV)

His disciples 'came and followed him' literally being with him and hanging out with him – making adjustments in their lifestyles so that they could learn from him. Then he began to shape and form them: 'I will make you.' Then ministry began to flow out of lives that had been shaped and formed by Jesus and his teachings. They became 'fishers of men'.

1. Who have been the most formative role models and mentors in your life? Take some time to meditate on their contribution towards your discipleship. (Note that in this chapter, I did not ask Sue to come to me to teach me. I relocated myself so as to immerse myself in her lifestyle and teachings. I wanted to become more like her and ultimately more like Jesus.)

2. Who has God presently put in your life for you to learn from? Do you need to make some changes in order to immerse yourself in their lifestyle and teachings so that you can grow spiritually? How might you do this?

Jesus, I thank you for all those faithful disciples who have gone before me.
Thank you for those in my life who demonstrate to me your lifestyle and teachings.
Show me how I might make space in my life to follow them and to follow you.
Jesus, I come to you.
Make me, shape me, form me and set me on mission.

Chapter 23

PRAY AT YOUR OWN RISK

*For the word of God is alive and active. Sharper than any
double-edged sword ...*

HEBREWS 4:12A

I look up at the stage. Slack jawed. Two of my favourite and
most respected worship leaders have just done the unthinkable.
'Whaddaya think? Key of D?' One turns to the other. 'Sure!'
He begins to sound out a simple chord progression, noodling
his way around the piano keys. 'I think I feel like Psalm 84
today. Let's do that one!' They then proceed to sing the Psalm,
making up their own melody and vamping their way through
the chords and through the words.

Making up their own song? To the Bible? Is that even
allowed? Not only is it allowed, it is actually a time-
honoured tradition. In Judaism the Torah is chanted both
by rabbis and nervous teens being *Bar Mitzvah-ed*. In the
Christian tradition, monastics have chanted and sung their
way through the Psalms for millennia.

GOHOP is fortunate enough to have its very own
Benedictine in our community. A lanky and loose-limbed
troubadour, Brother David Peter waltzes and sashays with
his stick dulcimer as he sings. Today we are circled for

morning prayer, which we call 'Heartwatch', chanting the Psalms to a distinctly reggae-ish cadence.

When the Lord delivered Zion from bondage
It seemed like a dream.
Then was our mouth filled with laughter
On our lips there were songs.[51]

Peter is a Benedictine Oblate, a lay monastic who is living out the Benedictine Rule in the context of his ordinary life. His day job for many years was to provide and to care for indoor plants in buildings across Hamilton, including our Central Library and the Central Police Station. 'I do prayer invasions', he says.

Like me he is a pray-er and cultivator. Unlike me he has played a key role in the prayer movement in Hamilton for over three decades. Part of Peter's spiritual practice is incorporating psalm chanting into his daily routines. At regular intervals he presses pause on his workday and takes some time to sing the Scriptures. 'Peter, what benefits are you finding from it?' I ask one day. He is quick to respond.

'The main benefit is the regular imprinting of the living and active word on one's spirit ... these words themselves prove to be a whole lot more beneficial than all the Dylan lyrics I've committed to memory. And the benefits of being David to one's own, not always so mentally-balanced, Saul have been undeniable in my experience, by keeping up the regular practice of singing over my own soul.'

Imprinting the word on our spirit. Singing over our own souls. I've been friends with Brother David Peter for a long time and have seen first hand the benefit he's received from habitually singing the Scriptures. Beneficial, yes. Potentially dangerous as well? Also yes.

---

51 Psalm 126:1–2 (The Grail Translation). The Grail Psalms were first published in 1963. Originally, they were translated from the Hebrew for use by the Grail community in their daily prayer. Since then, the original version Grail Psalms has been published in several editions, world wide. They are also used in Roman Catholic liturgy throughout the English-speaking world. *The Grail Psalms, a New Translation* (Collins, 1985).

Our first location in Hamilton is a former library in the North End of the city, right across the street from a social housing complex. A local Baptist church graciously offers us some space to pray. By then our team has grown, and Phyllis, Andy, Josiah, Abraham and a few others gather together regularly to worship and to sing and pray our way through the Scriptures. Today we are singing our way through the parable of the great banquet in Luke 14.

> … *'A certain man was preparing a great banquet and invited many guests. At the time of the banquet he sent his servant to tell those who had been invited, "Come, for everything is now ready."*
> *'But they all alike began to make excuses. The first said, "I have just bought a field, and I must go and see it. Please excuse me."*
> *'Another said, "I have just bought five yoke of oxen, and I'm on my way to try them out. Please excuse me."*
> *'Still another said, "I have just got married, so I can't come."*
> *'The servant came back and reported this to his master. Then the owner of the house became angry and ordered his servant, "Go out quickly into the streets and alleys of the town and bring in the poor, the crippled, the blind and the lame."'*

LUKE 14:16–21

For someone who mobilizes prayer and plans prayer meetings, the story feels vaguely familiar. We set a table of the Lord's presence. Choice food and wine. It's a party and it's going to be great! We let folks know that it's time to begin – people who have already said they are coming.

And then?

We get all the excuses.

Too busy.

Other stuff going on.

And we're left with empty chairs around the banquet table.

God's solution to the dilemma? Go out to the highways and to the byways! Find the poor, the marginalized, the sick, and compel them to come in! That day as we pray our way through this passage, the Lord gives our community a gentle chiropractic adjustment and issues us a special invitation. What if he wants us to stop worrying about whether 'nice' or 'regular' churchy people come, but instead wants us to invite folks from the margins, make friends with all the 'wrong' people? Addicts. Ex-offenders. The handicapped. Those on disability allowance.

A couple of years later I look around our prayer circle, both bemused and deeply glad. To my right is Chuck, a Nigerian student who had suffered a brain injury and who is living in our community house while he recovers. He loves to worship, and at points abruptly jolts to his feet and bellows out the song in his rich, deep, mellifluous voice. The problem is his short-term memory is shot so he inevitably shouts out the wrong words to the songs that both drown out and draw in the rest of us. His worship is wonderful.

Next to him is Mildred, a hairy-chinned senior who comes mainly for the lunch and snores through most of the prayer meetings. From time to time she wakes with a start, offers stuttered prayers for the Royal Family, and then dozes off again.

Then there is bushy-bearded Joe in his Led Zeppelin T-shirt, worshipping with his eyes closed and playing air guitar with great dexterity. Beside him? Janey with her long skirts, shawls and seventies protest songs. Her face is radiant as she sings. It looks like she's not only been transported from another time, but also to another place.

And then there is my dear friend Sally. Also brain

147

injured. 'I want to sit beside you!' She pouts. 'Can I play guitar too?' Whatever I do Sally wants to do. 'OK Sally, here's your guitar. Do you have the guitar pick I gave you?' 'No, I left it at home.' Over that season I go through a few dozen guitar picks. I suspect she's secretly building a collection. As we begin to sing Sally 'plays' her guitar, either pounding on the instrument or clutching the neck like a hockey stick and strumming with vigour.

One week I'm away, so I invite my buddy Aaron Weafer to be a substitute worship leader. I want to see how he does with our motley crew, whether he is able to enter into worship in the midst of all their colourful expression. 'How did it go?' I ask him the next day. 'It was a trip!' He grins. 'Sally asked for a guitar so I got her one. I was tuning mine, so asked her if hers needed tuning as well.' 'Does that mean you need to use these little knobby things?' she pointed to the tuning pegs. 'I said to her, "Um, do you actually know how to play the guitar? Play me a G." "Geeeeeee!" She sang, strumming the strings with a flourish.' Aaron passes the test.

Not only does our prayer room get a little more unique and interesting, but so does our dinner table. Our neighbourhood is, shall we say, lively. You don't actually have to watch TV; you can just sit on the front porch and watch the police chasing bad guys up and down our street! One day our front porch is crowded with friends hanging out after dinner, and our attention is riveted on another police takedown in the car park opposite our house. A ragged man is facing off with several police officers, his arms slightly extended. Rocking from one foot to another, he has a cheeky grin on his face. We can't hear what he is saying but it seems to be riling the police up a bit. Suddenly, he spins around and makes a break for it. The officers pile on him, taking him to the ground and cuffing him.

Our porch erupts in cheers and catcalls.

'Yeah, go officer!'

'Get him!'

'Filthy pigs! Leave him alone!'

'Police brutality! I'm gonna film this on my phone!'

I realize that the line of demarcation between the front porch cheerleaders and the cat callers is between those of us who have gone to jail, and those of us who have not. In fact, for a season, you almost have to be an ex-offender to be one of our worship leaders. Only misfits need apply.

Praying the Bible? Yep, it's dangerous. It will take you to all your 'never never lands', accompanied by extraordinary travelling buddies, and will open your life to unexpected horizons.

THE INVITATION

That triggered a response from one of the guests: 'How fortunate the one who gets to eat dinner in God's kingdom!'

Jesus followed up. 'Yes. For there was once a man who threw a great dinner party and invited many. When it was time for dinner, he sent out his servant to the invited guests, saying, 'Come on in; the food's on the table.'

'Then they all began to beg off, one after another making excuses. The first said, "I bought a piece of property and need to look it over. Send my regrets."

'Another said, "I just bought five teams of oxen, and I really need to check them out. Send my regrets."

'And yet another said, "I just got married and need to get home to my wife."

'The servant went back and told the master what had

*happened. He was outraged and told the servant,
"Quickly, get out into the city streets and alleys. Collect
all who look like they need a square meal, all the misfits
and homeless and wretched you can lay your hands on,
and bring them here."
'The servant reported back, "Master, I did what you
commanded – and there's still room."
'The master said, 'Then go to the country roads. Whoever
you find, drag them in. I want my house full! Let me tell
you, not one of those originally invited is going to get so
much as a bite at my dinner party.'"*

LUKE 14:15–24 (MSG)

Read: Read this portion of Luke out loud, slowly. Which
words or phrases jump out at you?

Reflect: Reflect on those words or phrases. How do you relate
to what Jesus is teaching?

Respond: How might God be asking you to respond to what
he is highlighting in the story? What is his invitation to you?

*Jesus, I'm so grateful that your word is living, active and sharp.
Thank you that as I read it, it reads me.
As I master it, I am mastered by it.
Let your word come and do its good work in me and shape me
in a way that pleases you.*

Chapter 24

PILGRIMAGE

Blessed are those whose strength is in you,
whose hearts are set on pilgrimage.

PSALM 84:5

Our journey to explore how a House of Prayer can grow in mission, justice and hospitality takes me on pilgrimage to the west coast city of Vancouver. The Downtown East Side of Vancouver, to be precise. It's about six blocks by six blocks, home to about ten thousand drug addicts, Aaron and Cherie White, and 614, a 24-7 Community.

Here was my chance to see everything I had read in *Punk Monk* enfleshed in real time and place. I've been sent by my team at GOHOP, and they are eager for me to report back. My goal? To step out of my regular context and routines and go on a quest for Jesus. To sleep on Aaron and Cherie's couch for five days and immerse myself in the context and rhythms of their community.

My first day.

My parents are nervous when they drop me off across the street from the bright orange Hells Angels strip club. 'Be careful – watch out for bedbugs,' they warn. As casually as I can, I mention their concern to Aaron. 'Oh don't worry' he says. 'We threw that couch out last week.' He's joking. I think.

The sky is grey. So are the rundown buildings. So is the crush of humanity on the sidewalks. I trail behind Aaron as we weave our way through the crowd. We're passing the bottle return depot, local entrepreneurs lined up toting large bags of recyclables. Cans are big business it seems. 'Watch your stuff,' he warns. I tighten my grip on my satchel bag as we break through the crowd to the other side.

Aaron is taking me on a 'Tour of Beauty' through the neighbourhood. 'If you don't love it, you won't fight for it.' He points to a room high up in one of the many slum hotels in the area. 'That's where we had our five years of 24-7 prayer for the neighbourhood. You can see Carnegie Centre, the main drug dealing corner, from the window. We stand there and pray for our friends when we see them.'

We pass by a community garden, tucked in between two high rises. It's locked behind a high fence topped with razor wire. 'We had to restrict access to the garden – people kept planting weed. Over there is where we set up a tent city during the Olympics. They wanted to clean out the streets, hide everyone away from the tourists. That was the centre of resistance.

'Here is Oppenheimer Park. They used to call it "Needle Park", but over the years we started cleaning it out and got a children's playground built. We're slowly reclaiming it.

'When Noah was born, we took him out to the park for his baby dedication. Gathered all our neighbourhood friends and passed the baby around the circle, asking them to bless him. Some folks were nervous – didn't want to do it. I challenged them, "So you're not going to bless my baby?" After that he became everybody's baby.'

'Do you feel safe, raising your children here?'

'Absolutely,' he responds. 'If anybody hurt my kids, it's quite possible some of my neighbours would actually kill them. And my kids are never going to touch drugs – they've seen where that road takes you. Actually, they are far safer here than if they were living beside a shopping centre – now there's a dangerous location!'

Aaron, his family and a bunch of friends have all moved into the Downtown East Side. 'We don't see "being missional" as sustainable. We're incarnational. We've moved into the neighbourhood. We're here to stay. We're here to love our neighbours and pray for them.' They live in local co-ops, shared apartments and houses. Many of the community work part-time jobs in the neighbourhood, often with the multitude of agencies that serve the desperate needs in this, the poorest of postal codes in Canada. They make friends with the prostitutes, the drug addicted, the down and out. By the end of the first day, they are my heroes.

My third day.

There is an African proverb that says, 'The first day you are a guest. The second day you are a guest. The third day we hand you a hoe.' Time for me to pitch in. I've been assigned to cook the community meal. The two centres of gravity for this community are the prayer room and the family table. 'I started our community dinners because I hate cooking so much,' Cherie laughs. 'Because we are Salvation Army, we understand that every time we eat together we are celebrating the Lord's supper. We break bread together and remember him.'

Six nights a week, different members of the community come to their house and cook up enough grub for anywhere between ten to twenty people. As they make friends in the neighbourhood, they invite them over for dinner. In an area saturated with soup kitchens, the family table brings a whole other level of belonging.

Dinner is in the oven and things are starting to smell yummy when my first guest arrives. Sam swaggers into the space with the confidence born of long familiarity. It's his home away from home. With faded jeans, leather jacket, missing teeth and mullet, Sam is a little rough looking. I'm nervous, but wanting to be hospitable, I try to make polite conversation, 'Sooo, what do you like about Vancouver?' 'The crack is really cheap here,' he grins. I guess he's figured out I'm a newbie, and decides to give me a rough time. However, it doesn't take us long to settle into friendly banter.

'Woman, get me my coffee!'

'Get your own damn coffee!' The beginnings of friendship is born.

My last day.

I head over to the coffee shop I've been frequenting each morning. Part of the way to make friends in a neighbourhood like this is to have a routine so people know where and when to find you. Just before I enter the cafe I bump into Anne, as I've done almost every day this week. 'Someone stole my coffee! I put it down for just a minute and someone grabbed it and walked off with it! I can't believe it!' She's flustered. 'No problem, let's go get you another one.' We head into the shop and smile at the baristas. I comment on the beautiful blue dress Anne is wearing and find out that this morning her boyfriend is graduating from his recovery programme. We chat over coffee and then she heads off to celebrate with him.

When she's gone, I get to work. My table is strewn with my laptop, journal and a bunch of papers. After a few minutes, nature calls and I am beginning to tidy up my portable study when Sam reappears. 'How's it going?' He asks. 'Yeah, good thanks. Sorry, just got to make a little trip to the ladies' room.' 'I can watch your stuff for you if you like.' I freeze for just a moment, my mind swirling. I've been spending the week building rapport with Sam. Do I trust him with my laptop? As far as I know, he's still active in his addiction. Here is where the rubber hits the road, doesn't it?

I take a deep breath.

'Sure,' I say, sounding more casual than I feel. 'Thanks.' Much to my relief, both Sam and my stuff are waiting for me at the table when I return.

I come back to Hamilton bubbling with enthusiasm and grand plans. 'Kirk we should do community dinners! Six nights a week!'

'I'll give you one night,' he counters. In that moment, Spaghetti Tuesday is born.

THE INVITATION

Pilgrimage in its truest sense is religiously motivated travel for the purpose of meeting and experiencing God with hopes of being shaped and changed by that encounter. Pilgrimages are often concretely physical – journeying to a particular place, perhaps with some extraordinary expense and exertion – and spiritual – one hopes to meet God in this travel ... Pilgrimage sites are not merely an end to

> *themselves. They are not strictly speaking even necessary. They richly symbolize the fact that our lives are to be a journey with and to God.*

ARTHUR BOERS[52]

Pilgrimage can be as long as the 500 mile walk on the Camino de Santiago in Spain, or as short as a stroll to the park bench on the corner. When we step out of our regular routine and explore new territory we can experience massive shifts in perspective.

Pilgrimage Planning

Plan a pilgrimage and go somewhere unfamiliar. It can be for a few hours' walk in a local park or a few weeks overseas!

Go with a spirit of openness, hoping to encounter God and anticipating the growth that this encounter invites.

Disconnect from your regular responsibilities and routines – from the familiar demands of work, television, internet, media and smartphones.

Connect with God through trying some new formational practices/spiritual disciplines. Maybe begin journaling? How about a photo essay of the place you are visiting? Perhaps bring a devotional book written by an unfamiliar author and utilize it to shape your quiet times on the journey.

---

52 Arthur Boers, *The Way is Made by Walking: A Pilgrimage Along the Camino de Santiago* (IVP, 2007), pp.41–42.

Reflect on your pilgrimage once it is completed. What did you learn? How did God reveal himself to you? Did you leave anything behind on the journey? Did you bring anything home with you?

Jesus, thank you that you are always inviting me further in and farther up.
Help me to let go of all that is familiar and join you on the journey.
I set my heart on pilgrimage today.

Chapter 25

SPAGHETTI

Do not forget to show hospitality to strangers, for by so doing some people have shown hospitality to angels without knowing it.

Hebrews 13:2

It takes six months to train our friends. In North America we're not enculturated to just show up for dinner.

'Just come over. Tuesday. Any Tuesday.'

'Really? Any Tuesday?'

'Yep, every Tuesday except for Christmas Eve and Christmas Day. Six o'clock!'

We make spaghetti. Lots of spaghetti. Kirk does the maths, and over the six years of our community dinners we serve over a half ton of pasta. It's cheap and easy. We fine tune a special sauce recipe.

'The secret spice – that's what makes it!' Kirk is proud of his culinary creation.

'What's the spice?' Friends are curious.

'If I told ya I'd have to kill ya,' he grins.

Eventually people get the hang of popping in unannounced and soon our Tuesday community expands beyond our dining room table, into the living room, the kitchen, and in the summer, the front and back porches.

Jason comes early, keen to help. He's almost blind but quickly finds his way around our space, blustering about the kitchen like a whirlwind. 'I'll put the glasses out!' Miraculously, the glasses survive. 'You need more napkins! Is there garlic bread today?' Hopeful, he opens the oven door to squint inside and sniff.

There is a knock on the door and I answer. Margaret is there with her uncle Mike and a gaggle of friends. She's wearing a pink toque with kitty cat ears. 'Put the walkers in the garage!' she barks. Below on the parking pad is a small flotilla of walking aids. I'm not entirely sure they are all necessary medically, but they do have multiple uses. It's free to get on a bus if you have one. Plus, you can carry lots of stuff on them. Mike's walker is a deluxe model – it has been kitted out with all manner of nautical paraphernalia. He's captain of the ship, and his cap is perched on his head at a cocky angle.

'I made you a Trouble board!' He hands it to me, proud. It's made of scrap wood and is hand painted with love. 'And I made you dice too! Lookit!' I feel the heft of the golf ball-sized dice in my palm – each hole has been hand drilled. 'You gonna play with us?' he asks.

We set the Trouble board up at one end of the table and the crew gets to it. Board games are serious business. 'Awwww, you got me!' Mike cries. Margaret grins wickedly as she moves her pawn around the board. 'I always get you!' She crows. 'Roll the dice!'

'I know this house,' our other guest Terry looks around, bemused. 'Used to live here back in my recovery days. Looks different now though! Ahh, if these walls could talk ...'

Our second community house has a chequered history. Initially it was a crack house – with as many as five guys living in the damp low-ceilinged basement alone. When they left, they stripped the home of all its phone wires for the copper. The house was bought by a bunch of Baptists who lovingly renovated it back to life and then used it for a number of social projects, including a guys' recovery centre and also a transitional home for women.

It falls into our hands just when we need to relocate. Our landlord gives us notice at our first community house when a family crisis brings him unexpectedly back to Canada. 'Sorry guys, I need my house back.' A chance encounter with some friends in a local grocery store opens the way for the new location. Kirk and I live there with three friends, leaving one bedroom free for pilgrims, guests and those in housing transitions.

I wander from the dining room into the kitchen. Matt is up to his elbows in suds, washing up the mountain of spaghetti dishes. Aaron is camped out at the small kitchen table, arguing politics with Shira. We've declared the dining room a 'Trump Free Zone', so he's taken the debate to the kitchen. 'Whaddaya think Jill?' He flashes me a cheeky grin. 'No comment!' I breeze into the living room.

Chris, one of my housemates, has a guitar in hand, and is leaning back on the couch, lazily strumming some chords. 'Check out my new haircut,' he says, lifting his bright blue cap. 'She put zigzag lines in it this time.' His hair is cropped close, and, as mentioned, zig zaggy. 'Nice!'

'Hey, there's someone walking around outside!' Chris peers out the window and then heads for the door. He returns with a slight, moustached stranger. He's shy, but after a few minutes I'm able to eke out his story. 'My mum is friends with a friend of yours and when I moved to town she told me to look for you guys. I bought a house just a couple of blocks away and am renovating it. I'm a Luthier – I build guitars.' Turns out he had been walking up and down in front of our house for a few minutes, summoning enough courage to knock on a stranger's door to invite himself over for dinner. 'Amazing! That is so cool! Let me introduce you to some folks.' I grab a plate of spaghetti and strategically set him at the table with some other musicians.

Our favourite Spaghetti Tuesday is the last Tuesday before Christmas. We call it 'Spaghetti Tuesday – Elf Edition'. In Kirk's favourite Christmas movie, Buddy the elf says, 'We elves try to stick to the four main food groups: candy, candy canes, candy corns and syrup.'[53] We supply the maple syrup and the guests bring their own candy for spaghetti toppings. We pour syrup over the spaghetti and top it with sweets. The kids love it.

'I want smarties, and gummy bears and skittles!' 'On spaghetti? Gross!' One adult friend wrinkles her nose. 'Actually, with the maple syrup on it the spaghetti tastes a bit like French toast,' I comment. 'Not bad!'

After eating our candy-laden spaghetti, we turn all the couches around to create a mini theatre area and watch the movie together. Kirk insists on this tradition every year, and truth be told, no matter how many times I watch it, I still laugh out loud every time.

At a critical juncture in the story, we stop the show and pull out a twelve-pack of Coke cans. It's time for the belching contest. Our friend Naomi is the presiding champion and, true to form, she blows the competition out of the water again this year.

I survey the room and I feel full – deeply satisfied. We are a colourful conglomeration of housemates, friends, the strange and the stranger. Living together, hanging out and eating spaghetti together. It truly is a feast, in every sense of the word.

53 Jon Favreau, *Elf* (New Line Cinema, 2003).

THE INVITATION

In her book, *Making Room*, Christine Pohl urges a return to the forms of hospitality that characterized the early church. Hospitality is not optional for Christians, nor is it limited to those who are specially gifted for it. It is, instead, a necessary practice in the community of faith. One of the key Greek words for hospitality, *philoxenia*, combines the general word for love or affection for people who are connected by kinship or faith (*phileo*) and the word for stranger (*xenos*).[54] Because *philoxenia* includes the word for stranger, hospitality's orientation toward strangers is also more apparent in Greek than in English.[55]

Biblical hospitality is not the same as setting a fine table and entertaining your friends. Jesus says in Luke 14:12–14:

> '*When you give a luncheon or dinner, do not invite your friends, your brothers or sisters, your relatives, or your rich neighbours; if you do, they may invite you back and so you will be repaid. But when you give a banquet, invite the poor, the crippled, the lame, the blind, and you will be blessed. Although they cannot repay you, you will be repaid at the resurrection of the righteous.*'

The problem with inviting Jesus into your life and your personal space is that he wants to bring his friends with him! Biblical hospitality is opening your hearts and homes to the other – the stranger – the one who is unlike you. And in doing so being blessed. As we practise hospitality we can also experience the mystery that Christ is in the midst of these human encounters.

54 Christine D. Pohl, *Making Room: Recovering Hospitality as a Christian Tradition* (William B. Eerdmans, 1999), p.31.

55 Ibid.

1. Reflect with gratitude on how God has created a space for you at his table – how has God demonstrated hospitality towards you? How has he made a space for you by his altar, the way he does the sparrow in Psalm 84:3?
2. How have you been blessed by strangers? How have you encountered the presence of Jesus amongst those who are unlike you?
3. How might you expand your circle of welcome to those who might not normally grace your table? How might God be inviting you to make space for the stranger in your life? It can be as simple as inviting a newcomer to your home for lunch after church. Perhaps you can frequent a new coffee shop and, loitering with intent, become a regular and making friends there.

Jesus, thank you that you made room for me at your table and invited me join you.
Help me to see and take the opportunity to make space for others at the table as well, particularly the one who is not like me.
As I encounter the other, may I also encounter you, Jesus.

Chapter 26

WHAT DO YOU HAVE IN YOUR HAND?

'And afterwards,
I will pour out my Spirit on all people.
Your sons and daughters will prophesy,
your old men will dream dreams,
your young men will see visions.'

JOEL 2:28

My friend Sue invites me to a Baptist Pastors Convention. I innocently tag along, not knowing that at this conference I would have one of my strangest encounters with God ever.

'We're going to take five minutes of silence,' the teacher says. 'Settle into a posture of receptivity, quieten your heart and invite God to meet you.' I plant my feet flat on the floor, straighten my back and lay open hands on my knees. Eyes closed. I inhale deeply. The muscles across the back of my shoulders relax. My arms feel heavier as my body settles.

Just breathe.

What the …?

I startle as, suddenly, I felt the weight and heft of something long, narrow and cylindrical on my palms. I crack an eyelid. Is someone playing a trick on me?

My eyes widen. There is nothing there. And yet … I can feel it.

Weird.

I close my eyes again, take another deep breath and focus on the sensation. What do I have in my hands? It feels solid, substantial. Like wood. Some irregularities, knobbly bits.

Not a broomstick.

Maybe, a ... a staff?

Cool, I've got some weird invisible ghost staff in my hands. Call me crazy.

'Well, Lord I asked you to meet me in the silence, so whatever this is, OK – I receive it.'

The next day I'm back at the conference, listening to the lecturer again. After what happened yesterday, she's got my full attention. 'Moses encounters the Lord at the burning bush,' she says, 'and the Lord says to Moses, "What have you got in your hands?"'[56]

Whaaaat? A jolt in my chest as a rush of adrenaline hits. I nearly bounce off my seat. What have you got in your hands? A staff! A staff! Moses had a staff! I had a staff yesterday! I did!

For the next few months I ponder what I can only describe as a mystical experience. What's the significance of the staff? Is it a sign of Moses' authority? God taking something ordinary and transforming it into something extraordinary?

I realize that my little brain isn't going to be able to make sense of it all, so I stop trying to figure it out. More will be revealed, I feel certain. I shelve it in the 'weird but wonderful' department and just get on with things.

About six months later, in a random flash of insight I understand the *double entendre*.

What is it I have in my hands?

A staff?

My staff!

56 Exodus 4:2.

Ooooooh, I get it. My staff team at the House of Prayer! That is what God has given me! That's what I've got in my hands! I'm a little slow, but I get there eventually. I take that as God's encouragement to receive my staff team as a gift from him and to continue to prioritize cultivating them – to try and bring out the best in each one.

As a young teenager, I enjoy reading the fantasy genre. Hey, who doesn't want a pet dragon, I mean really? There is one author I enjoy in particular. His books are set in an enchanted land where every citizen has a magical talent of some sort or another. Some can levitate. Others can understand the language of animals. Everybody's talent is unique. Whoever has the Most Powerful Magic is appointed king of the country and the rulership changes when new talents emerge.

One year a little girl, 6 years old, becomes king. All the people are amazed. How could one so little exercise so much power? What is her magic ability anyway?

The secret to her strength is this: whenever anyone steps within a ten-foot radius of the child, their own magical abilities are magnified and enhanced. Her magic is that she makes everyone whose life she touches more magical. At 13 years old I find that utterly compelling and decide that I want the Most Powerful Magic.

'Thank you, Jesus, for our luuuuunch, Aaaaaaamen Amen!' Andy's children chirp and warble the sung grace. We all sing along. I sit back in my chair and look around the table, tummy and heart full. (Why does everything in GOHOP seem to happen around tables?) It's our weekly team gathering where we pray together, eat together, and learn and scheme together. There are a dozen or so having lunch, ranging from 2 to 72 years of age. We call our community 'people soup'. Lotsa flavours – some of them quite spicy – but all together we make a nice blend. When someone new jumps in the pot things take on a whole new taste. It means our community is constantly evolving, changing shape and flavour. I love the complexity and fluidity of it.

Youngest and (almost) oldest are at the end of the table. Elijah is in his high chair, laughing hysterically as he tries to shove a bagel into Abraham's mouth. Elijah gets his middle name when his father Andy reads Athanasius's treatise *On the Incarnation* (leave it to our monkish scholar to name his child after a third century theologian).

'Eat the bagel!' Elijah Athanasius demands. Abraham grins and pretends to eat it, grabbing at it with big beefy fingers. He flashes a smile and throws his head back to laugh. 'Ah, ah, ah! I et it!' He teases. A Congolese missionary to Canada, Abraham is full of faith, love of prayer, and has the most hospitable heart I've ever encountered. 'Aaay! My sister! Welcome! Your house is my house!' he exclaims, arms stretched wide, whenever pilgrims come to visit.

Down the table, Andy smiles at their banter as his daughter snuggles in his arms. His wife, Gwen, pregnant with their fourth child, potters in the kitchen before lowering herself onto a bench at the end of the table. I always think women are at their most beautiful when they are pregnant and Gwen is radiant, despite looking a bit weary.

Doug is our oldest member. He was with YWAM (Youth With A Mission) for twenty-seven years before he and his wife relocate to Hamilton to be close to his grandchildren.

He 'accidentally' stumbles across our community and is quickly drawn into the adventure. Like 80-year-old Caleb in the book of Joshua, he's ready to take new territory.

'Peter, can you pass the spaghetti?' He asks. 'I'll give you a penne for your thoughts,' Peter responds, reaching the bowl across the table. We all groan. Peter grins, satisfied. You can count on Peter to insert a terrible joke into every conversation. He leads our internship training and last year was delighted to find out that two of the interns were also punsters. Evenings often deteriorated into silly wordplay as they sparred verbally with one another.

'OK everybody, let's check in. Where did you all see God this week?' Andy asks. It's our regular practice as a community – an *Examen* of sorts. We're trying to be attentive to the presence and activity of God in and around us in the midst of monastic life.

'I really saw God at work at the cafe this week,' Shira starts us off. 'Jenn decided to ask our community to help create a daily prayer, so we collected prayer requests from our regulars. She compiled them and now they pray it every morning together when the cafe opens!'

'Amazing! Love it. Anybody else?'

'Our friend Joe is back in town,' Doug chimes in. 'We've been emailing and calling him but he seemed to have dropped off the planet. We were really concerned and praying. But yesterday he just showed up at the front door!'

'My back patio is finally done,' chimes in Gloria. 'The barbecue is ready. The gazebo is up with the outdoor seating. The gas fire pit has been installed. Ready now for some guests. It's the party yard!' Gloria has one of the strongest gifts of hospitality I know. I'm surprised and delighted when she purchases a house three doors down and sets it up as a guest home. 'For pilgrims who visit and for caring for women leaders.' Gloria beams.

'I really saw God at work in the prayer room,' Phyllis has an extraordinary grace for pursuing God's presence. In another time and in another denomination, she could very well have been a nun. In GOHOP she's found a place to explore her vocation of intercession. 'This week some of our interns came down to visit and it was wonderful to pray for them!'

We continue around the table, everybody sharing their stories, and I'm reminded of Psalm 128. The psalmist declares when we walk in obedience to the Lord the result is that those closest to us become fruitful vines and olive shoots around our table.[57] It seems to me the House of Prayer is like a greenhouse. My job is to cultivate, hopefully creating conditions for extraordinary growth.

The staff team are fruitful. And flourishing.

It's magical.

THE INVITATION

Mystical experiences are not uncommon in the biblical story. Throughout the Old Testament, God spoke to his people in visions and dreams. Mary and Joseph, even the shepherds in the fields around Bethlehem experienced angelic visitations. In Acts 10, Peter falls into a trance and experiences a vision.[58] Paul talks about being caught up to the third heaven, where he had visions and revelations from the Lord.[59]

The history of the church abounds with tales of unusual, mystical supernatural encounters. Joan of Arc hears voices that lead her to victory in battle. John Wesley's heart is

57 Psalm 128:1–3.
58 Acts 10:9–16.
59 2 Corinthians 12:1.

'strangely warmed'.[60] Blaise Pascal experienced a dramatic conversion through a profound mystical experience. He wrote about his experience, took the piece of paper and carefully sewed it inside his jacket – he kept it with him the rest of his life. It wasn't discovered until after his death. Here is a portion of his account.

> *The year of grace 1654,*
> *Monday, 23 November, feast of St. Clement, pope and martyr, and others in the martyrology. Vigil of St. Chrysogonus, martyr, and others. From about half past ten at night until about half past midnight,*
> *FIRE.*
> *GOD of Abraham, GOD of Isaac, GOD of Jacob*
> *not of the philosophers and of the learned.*
> *Certitude. Certitude. Feeling. Joy. Peace.*
> *GOD of Jesus Christ.*
> *My God and your God.*
> *Your GOD will be my God …*
> *Joy, joy, joy, tears of joy.*[61]

1. Have you ever had unusual experiences in prayer? What were they? What was the long-term result or fruit of those experiences?

2. Take some time in quiet and open your hands before God. Listen to his question to you: 'What do you have in your hand?' Be still and receptive for a few minutes. After you are done, write down anything that came to your mind and heart during that time.

---

60 John Wesley, *The Journal of John Wesley* (Independently Published, 2016), p.38.
61 http://www.users.csbsju.edu/~eknuth/pascal.html.

Jesus, I thank you that you are the giver of all good gifts, and I receive with gratitude all that you have for me.
Thank you for all that you have put into my hands.
May I be a good steward of what is entrusted to me, for the sake of others but ultimately for your glory.

Chapter 27

WHERE IS MY PRAYER TRUCK?

Every good and perfect gift is from above, coming down from the Father of the heavenly lights, who does not change like shifting shadows.

JAMES 1:17

I continue to consider God's question to me, 'What do you have in your hand?' and resolve to pay attention to whatever resource he may send our way.

The next gift is completely unexpected. 'I've got a U-Haul truck, a seventeen-footer,' I'm on the phone with my friend Nick, a local mechanic. 'We just drove it across the country to move my buddy, but now it's just sitting in my yard. Do you need it for anything?' A moving van? What on earth would I do with that? Does God want us to start up a social enterprise? A moving company with some of our neighbourhood friends? I shudder at the thought of all the bedbugs we might come into contact with if we start moving furniture in our area. Here I am Lord, send someone else. Not knowing the exact nature of God's invitation, I shelve the truck offer for a couple of weeks.

One day I'm looking at the 24-7 website and a story catches my eye. In Toronto a group of folks hire a moving van, kit it out as a mobile prayer room and set it up in a car park outside a church missions conference. Over the course of the weekend, conference participants sign up for an hour in the prayer truck and pray for the nations.

A truck! A prayer truck? A pop up prayer room! Seems doable ... I call Nick back and tell him we will take the truck for a couple of weeks in July. We park it behind the Living Rock. The Rock runs breakfast, housing and employment programmes for youth in the area. Several years before, when we wanted to find ways as a community to practise more justice and mercy as a House of Prayer, we contacted them to see how we might help. 'Al, can we come over and help every week?' I ask their Director. 'We can clean bathrooms, help in the kitchen. Whatever you need.' 'Actually, we really could use prayer,' he responds.

From that point on, every Wednesday, our team went to the Rock, participating in their weekly Gathering and praying for and with the youth and staff at the centre. By the time the Prayer Truck appears on the scene, we've been there for a few years. The Rock seems to me to be the ideal location for us to park. 'You can use the bin alley,' says Al. 'We'll just push the wheelie bins right to the edge and then you can park it so the back of the truck lines up with the pavement.'

The bins are full and the day is warm. I sniff. There is a pong in the air. Thinking better of sniffing again, I kick the mummified remains of a rat under the bush at the edge of the alley. 'It's perfect.' I love the idea of getting our team out of what had become a pretty comfy prayer room and into the thick of things in downtown Hamilton. God comforts the afflicted and he also afflicts the comfortable, and I am interested to see how a little discomfort will grow us as a prayer community. GOHOP is going on mission.

The day we are due to begin, the phone rings. It's 9am. 'Hi Jill, Sara's here at Living Rock, wanting to know where her prayer truck is.' I laugh. 'Tell her she's early! We're opening at 8 o'clock tonight.' Sara has been joining our weekly prayer meetings at the Rock. She loves the free lunch, the community and the worship. When it's her turn to pray she pretends to be shy, 'What she said!' She ducks her chin and flaps her hand at me.

It's 7.30pm on the first night and Sara shows up. She parks her Walking Frame beside the truck and slowly eases into one of the folding chairs. 'I wanna get in the truck!' She says, eyeing the prayer room inside. The storage area of the truck is carpeted, and large throw pillows are propped against walls that have been papered with newsprint. A large cross leans in one corner, a guitar and hand drum beside it. Art supplies and Bibles litter the space.

'I don't think you can climb in Sara,' I respond. 'Remember you can't do stairs? Plus, we need you here at the front, handing out water.' Sara folds her arms, hummmphs and pouts, but soon cheerfully settles into greeting passers-by and handing out bottles. She sits by the truck all day, every day. At 10pm each night, I send her back to her group home. 'It's the rules, Sara. No women alone out here at night!'

Once I realize she is going to be a permanent fixture, I put her to work. 'You see those people walking by?' I point. 'Let's pray for them. And those people on mobility scooters?' (I'm pretty sure that Hamilton is the scooter capital of Canada.) 'Let's pray that God heals them so they don't need them anymore. And see the car park across the street? Let's pray that no cars get broken into.'

She catches on right away. When I arrive midday the next day, she's sitting happily with Phyllis and exclaims, 'I'm a prayer warrior! I prayed over all those cars in the car park!

I love the prayer truck! It's MY prayer truck!'

Sara isn't the only one who claims the truck as her own. Halfway through the second week, two teenage girls warily circle the truck before entering it. They are heavily tattooed and pierced, one tucked deep in her hooded sweatshirt. The other is clutching a creased and dog-eared picture of a dark-eyed young woman smoking a cigarette. 'Candy died this week,' she says, showing us the photo. 'We just knew we had to come to the truck and pray – we've gotta get some good energy released.' We glue Candy's picture to the inside wall of the truck, and they write memories and prayers around it. Over the rest of the week, a small but steady stream of youth come by to grieve and to pray. The truck is their sanctuary.

Later on in the week my daughter Hannah swings by with two buddies. Her friends are hesitant. 'Come and check it out!' she says, climbing inside. Natalie leans her bike against the truck entrance. It's a recent gift from her mum, expensive and precious. Today she's taken it out for her first test ride. They follow Hannah into the truck and began to examine the prayers and art scrawled on the walls. Suddenly there is a scuffle outside and, looking up, Natalie sees that her bike has disappeared. An opportunistic and very bold thief brazenly grabs it right in front of us and is tearing away down the street.

Chaos ensues. Hannah's boyfriend jumps on his own bike and shoots down the street in pursuit. Natalie is distraught. 'We came here looking for God and then he lets my bike get taken!'

Hannah is on the phone with the police. 'They've taken off down Wilson Street, oh now they've turned left on Rebecca!' Natalie's friend Breyanne takes a deep breath. 'We're in a prayer truck. What we need to do is pray.' They collect themselves, hold hands, then she prays her first ever out-loud prayer. 'God, can you please return Natalie's bike?' While they are praying the phone rings and Hannah picks it up. 'It's the police!' she crows, 'They've got your bike! Tears turn to joy. 'God did it! He got our bike back!' The girls hug each other and wait in their prayer truck for the return of the bike.

On my last day at the truck, a young man slouches up. Sullen, he slumps into the lawn chair. I've seen him on and off all week, mostly when he is fuming and pacing the sidewalk, blowing off steam after some debacle or other at the youth centre. I give him his space. He glances up and scowls at me. 'You know you can pray for me, right?'

'Um, sure!' I scooch over to where he is sitting and bow my head to pray.

'You're not doing it right!' He snaps. 'You've got to put your hand on my shoulder!' I smile to myself, lay hands on him and began to pray. It's his prayer truck.

That year the Prayer Truck makes it into the local paper. The headline reads, 'Hamilton has a cupcake truck, a grilled cheese truck and now a prayer truck.'

THE INVITATION

In a recent Christmas advert, we see an ageing Elton John, world famous musician and composer, sitting at a piano playing some simple notes. As he plays, the commercial flashes back through his life and musical career. The timeline goes all the way back to when he is a young child, coming down the stairs on Christmas Day to find that his parents have given him a piano. The tagline of the commercial is 'Some gifts are more than just a gift.' Elton's gift from his parents sets him on a trajectory that shapes his future and enriches many.[62]

62 The John Lewis & Partners Christmas Advert 2018.

Sometimes God invites you in a new direction by giving you an unexpected gift. In opening it we begin to unpack unexpected blessings that he might have for us and for others.

1. What unexpected gifts have come your way recently?
2. How might these gifts contain/point toward an invitation from God to you?
3. How might these gifts be a blessing to those around you? If you've come into some unexpected money, how might you share it? If your time has freed up a little, how might you use it to serve others?

Jesus, you are full of surprises and I thank you for the way you unexpectedly show up in my life with gifts and invitations. Help me to perceive and receive these invitations and gifts when they come.
As you open up new space before me, new opportunities and new spiritual territory, may I step forward into it with confidence and trust.

Chapter 28

WARLOCK

When he was at the table with them, he took bread, gave thanks, broke it and began to give it to them. Then their eyes were opened and they recognized him.

LUKE 24: 30–31A

'Can I siddown?' He jerks his head towards the empty lawn chair. I am perched on the truck bumper. 'Sure!' His shoes are duck taped around the toes, his pant cuffs frayed. Fingertips are stained from tobacco, as are his teeth. 'Ahh!' He leans back in the chair, stretching his lets out. Passers-by skivvy around his feet as they made their way down the sidewalk. 'Woke up on the floor of the peep show this morning,' he said. 'Don't rememba getting' there, but it must have been one helluva night! Got a cigarette? Name's Joey,' he says. 'Ima warlock. Bet ya never met one. Learned it from my granmother.'

At the Prayer Truck we chat with passers-by and ask them if they would like prayer. It's amazing how many do. Muslims, agnostics, and now, evidently, even warlocks! Not only do they want prayer, they want to talk. Mother Theresa said that the greatest poverty is loneliness, and my experience in the truck tells me that is true.

Joey talks. And talks and talks. And talks some more. It is amazing, and a little bewildering how many words he can get out without seeming to take a breath. Normally in conversation I need to egg folks on a little. 'Um-hum,' 'Really?' 'Wow what do you think about that?' Joey doesn't need any help at all. He just motors up the conversational onramp to Route 66 and settles in for a day-long journey. I am eager to steer things towards prayer. Where can I jump in? How can I shape the conversation? It's like trying to grab a vehicle bumper on a busy motorway. Joey is on a roll and isn't pausing anytime soon.

I end up listening to his monologue for six hours. SIX HOURS. After a while I despair of getting a word in edgewise and just sit there nodding, wrestling inwardly. Is this helpful? Effective at all? I'm pinned to the truck as a captive audience as Joey's musings meander through the corruption in city hall, his childhood back at home, the hazards of shelter life ('No way! I'm gunna sleep by the train tracks!') the meanings of cloud formations and his favorite kinds of beer, wine, liquor, etc. etc. etc. Anytime I ask him if he needs prayer for whatever it is he is talking about, his eyes and conversation skitter sideways.

My attention drifts. After the first hour or two his voice begins to sound like the teacher from the Charlie Brown cartoons, 'Wa wa wa wa wa waaaaa.' Lord, how do you want me to deal with this? Not knowing what else to do, I end up just speaking in tongues under my breath while Joey continues to chatter. How can I attentive not only to Joey but also to the presence of Jesus in the conversation?

Little do I know this is the beginning of my career in spiritual direction. Joey proves to be the doorman, rolling out the red carpet and inviting me to explore the art of being attentive to the presence and activity of God while being present to another.

My friend Andy defines spiritual direction this way. 'Spiritual direction is two people having a conversation together about one person's relationship with Jesus.' For centuries, it was the primary domain of the Catholics, but in the last fifty years Protestants have discovered the treasure of spiritual direction and how helpful it can be to one's spiritual journey. The job of a director is to help the directee be attentive to the presence and the activity of God in their life.

'The most helpful way to think about it,' says Andy, 'is to picture three chairs in a room. You are in one chair. The directee is in another. And God is in the third. What is God up to in the third chair?' Ultimately the Holy Spirit is the Director, and if the spiritual director and the directee are both paying attention to the presence of God in the midst of the conversation, it can be transformative.

Julian of Norwich was an anchoress in Norwich England in the 1400s. She lived in a little bricked alcove on the side of her church and spent her life in prayer. She also listened to pilgrims as they stopped by her window to seek God and explore their spiritual journey with her. She is famous for saying. 'I look at you. I look at God. I look at you.' She understood the art of soul accompaniment.

At one point in Joey's monologue, ominous clouds begin to cluster overhead.

'No problem! I got it!' Joey gestures dramatically to the sky and mutters a brief incantation. 'Those clouds gunna pass right over.'

Instead it rains. Just a little bit though.

'It would've been much worse if I didn't do my thing!' He flashes a cheeky grin.

Finally, my Prayer Truck shift is over and a bit wild eyed, I hand Joey off to the next truck volunteer. 'Have fun!' I make my escape.

Am I able to be really present and attentive to both Joey and to God in that instance? Yeah, nope. Probably not.

THE INVITATION

Spiritual direction is an ancient form of Christian soul care that goes back to the earliest days of the church. It has never really gone away. It is just that large sectors of the Christian church have forgotten their own heritage. In its classical form, spiritual direction is a one-on-one relationship organized around prayer and conversation directed toward deepening intimacy with God. As we shall see, spiritual directors are not experts, nor do they direct. They do not follow a standardized curriculum or implement a pre-packaged programme. Rather, they journey with others who, like themselves, are committed to the process of spiritual transformation in Christ. And most importantly, they seek to help those with whom they journey discern the presence and leading of the Spirit of God, the One Jesus sent as our true Spiritual Director.[63]

It can be very helpful to have someone outside of your immediate context and familiar denominational tradition to help you examine and explore your relationship with Jesus with fresh eyes.

1. Have you ever experienced an awareness of the presence and activity of God in the midst of a conversation with another person? What was it like? What happened?
2. Do you have someone in your life at present who accompanies you on your spiritual journey, helping you to be attentive to the presence and activity of the

63 David G. Benner, *Sacred Companions: The Gift of Spiritual Friendship & Direction* (InterVarsity Press, 2002), p.17.

Holy Spirit in your life? What do you think might be the benefits of having someone like that?

You can find a spiritual director through Spiritual Directors International, https://www.sdiworld.org. However, do note that spiritual direction is a spiritual practice that is utilized by many faith traditions, so if you decide to contact SDI, make sure to clarify that you are looking for a Christian spiritual director. Many local Anglican Dioceses have Spiritual Direction departments and have lists of spiritual directors. Many seminaries now train spiritual directors and have lists of trained spiritual directors available on their websites. And many retreat centres also offer spiritual direction and have lists of spiritual directors available.

Jesus, thank you that you are present in every human interaction and in every conversation.
Give me eyes to see you even in the midst of 'the least of these'.
Help me to be attentive to your presence and to be able to hear your voice.
Awaken me to your presence and activity in my life and in the lives of those around me.

Chapter 29

NOONDAY DEMONS

My heart is in anguish within me;
the terrors of death have fallen on me.
Fear and trembling have beset me;
horror has overwhelmed me.
I said, 'Oh, that I had the wings of a dove!
I would fly away and be at rest.
I would flee far away
and stay in the desert;
I would hurry to my place of shelter,
far from the tempest and storm.

PSALM 55:4–8

I'm no stranger to receiving spiritual direction myself, and enjoy its benefits. I've been seeing Sue (a different Sue!) every month for years. Versed in Ignatian spirituality, she is a loving companion and guide on my journey. She helps me pay attention to the presence and the activity of God deep in my soul and in my life. Over the years, Sue has become very familiar with the contours of my soul, even its shadows.

'I think I'm depressed – I'm feeling really low.' I'm sitting across from Sue. I'm in a springy canvas chair with a pillow tucked behind my lower back. To my left is Sue's bookcase, crammed full of books on prayer, spiritual formation and church leadership. And tea. Dozens and dozens of boxes of tea. Sue's head is framed from behind by the stained-glass panel hanging from her wall – grapes and a chalice. I'm enjoying the warmth both of her presence, and of the mug of mystery tea (you pick a flavour, Sue – surprise me!) I have cupped in my hand.

I'm no stranger to depression. The black dog sits outside my door and sometimes scratches and whines, wanting to be let in.

I'm nineteen when I experience my first episode. In my second year of university, I move away from home, trying life on my own for the first time. On the back end of a messy breakup with my boyfriend, I start to fray around the edges, I begin to self-medicate with binge drinking, and then I fully unravel. It isn't long before I find myself in the local psychiatry ward staring at the wall across from me.

My family visits. My brother smuggles in a small feral kitten we had recently rescued from a friend's garage. It was undersized and vicious, a bundle of needle-sharp teeth and claws. In a moment of heightened creativity, he named it Kat. It rode into the hospital peeking out of the top of his coat pocket, before exploring my bed and trying to gnaw on my fingertips.

Some genius had created a large open-concept hospital ward with little curtained cubicles around the edges. Several times I wake in the morning with a gaunt elderly lady standing over my bed, staring at me with wide eyes.

My companion in the hospital is Steve Bell, a local folk artist. Someone gives me a cassette of his latest album and we spend many hours together with him crooning to me through my headset. 'Comfort, my people, comfort, my people, says the Lord.'[64] Yeah, a little comfort would be good right now.

64 Steve Bell, 'Comfort My People' (Signpost Music, 1989).

My very first introduction to contemplative prayer comes from the head of psychiatry at the hospital, of all places. Turns out he used to be a Jesuit. White haired with long, elegant fingers and eyes creased with compassion, he leans across his desk. 'You might find it helpful to try meditation. Just sit comfortably in a chair, feet on the floor, hands open on your lap. Take a posture of receptivity. And then just say the name 'Jesus' over and over.'

After three weeks I regain some vestiges of my sanity and about twenty pounds from eating the Peak Freans cookies the hospital leaves in baskets everywhere, hoping to tempt the anorexics to snack.

Some vestiges, but not all. I drop out of university but spend a lot of time that year hanging out on campus, sitting by myself in the hallways or slinking in late to university Bible studies. I don't want to be alone but I don't want to have to interact with anybody. At the end of one of the Bible studies, I am cornered by a small woman, fierce in bangles and bright colours. 'I been praying for you, and wat I think you need is deliverance. The Lord wants to deliver you from the demon of depression! I can pray for you and cast it out?' I flinch and involuntarily step backwards. 'Um, no, that's OK, thanks,' I flee the room.

On my return home, I wonder if I do, indeed, need deliverance from something besides overzealous exorcists. The Frank Peretti book, *This Present Darkness*, is sitting on my bedside table. I've just spent a few weeks immersed in its graphic dramatizations of epic battles between good and evil in the invisible realm. I'm Presbyterian and we all know that Presbyterians, with their Scottish sensibilities, don't have demons. But after reading this book I begin to wonder.

That night I have a vivid dream. I am standing alone in a dark house. It is pitch black and the air is heavy, weighing on my shoulders and in my throat. I hear the whir of wings and, suddenly, I am being dive-bombed, attacked from all sides by invisible, malevolent creatures.

I awake in a sweat and tangled in my bedsheets. Perhaps there is something to this demon business? I decide to attempt deliverance on myself. What can it hurt? Worst case scenario I'll just feel foolish. So with the most authoritative tone I can muster, I command depression to go, in the name of Jesus.

Astonishingly, it does.

The effect is immediate and dramatic. Like when a birth caul is torn from over an infant's face. Suddenly, everything that was smothered and obscure comes into clarity. I am reborn into the light.

The depression doesn't re-occur until several years later. One day I find myself plastered against the wall of the Toronto subway. Breathe, just breathe. I'm fighting the almost overwhelming impulse to jump in front of the train. Stay away from the edge. O Lord, make haste to help me ...

Self-service deliverance doesn't work this time, so I opt for antidepressants and group therapy. In time the flood waters recede. Over the ensuing twenty-five years, the tide does roll in from time to time, but attention to diet, exercise and rest seem to give me what I need and keep me from getting caught in the current.

Sue gets out of her chair and pulls an orange book off her shelf. 'Have you ever read *Acedia & Me* by Kathleen Norris?'[65] she asks. I tuck the book into my rucksack and take home what ends up being a vital companion to my mental health journey. As I delve into Kathleen's book, I am interested to discover that the monastics were no strangers to dark moods. A millennium before Freud and Jung, they had a name for it – the Noonday Demon, or acedia.

---

65 Kathleen Norris, *Acedia & Me: A Marriage, Monks, and a Writer's life* (Riverhead Books, 2008).

The life of prayer necessitates an inward journey, and we all have nameless creatures flying about the dark houses of our souls. That's why we avoid silence, solitude and stillness. We don't want to go into the deep waters because we know, or suspect at least, what lies beneath.

The Desert Fathers used the language of spiritual warfare to describe their interior battles, but the jury is still out if these are real entities or psychological forces that they grappled with. I think it's both. One way or another, the battle is real. At least it has been for me, and continues to be so, although thankfully with ever decreasing frequency.

There are times (not recently, thank God) when I have woken up and my day faces me like the slathering maw of some beast out of a Star Wars movie. I suspect I'll be devoured the minute I step out of bed. I feel blank, like someone has erased my internal hard drive. It's hard to focus. My thoughts skitter like roaches when you turn the kitchen light on. I feel like a wind-up toy slumped where I'm standing, having run out of juice.

An essential element in the Desert Father's prescription for depression? Manual labour. I call it the spiritual practice of puttering. There is something about working quietly with my hands that I find so helpful. Can I say, centring? It roots me in the moment and in my body. When I'm puttering around the house, cleaning or cooking, I can drop down inside myself and rest there. I can hold my soul in the presence of God and receive whatever grace is available in that moment.

I have stilled and quietened my soul ...

When I feel frozen like the Tin Man in *The Wizard of Oz* after a rain shower, a little mindful motion eases oil into my joints and I begin to live again.

THE INVITATION

Spiritual or mental oppression. Depression. Acedia. The inner workings of our hearts are complex and it can be difficult to diagnose the roots of our malaise. Sometimes, we might need therapy and medication. Other times, some warfare prayer brings us out of the nosedive. Other times rest, solitude, silence and simple work with our hands can restore our equilibrium.

In her book, *Strengthening the Soul of Your Leadership*, Ruth Haley Barton outlines some warning lights on the dashboard of our souls that can be indicators that we need to give our inner world some attention:

- Irritability or hypersensitivity: things that normally wouldn't bother us put us over the edge.
- Restlessness: a vague sense that something is not quite right. Broken sleep or an inability to settle into rest.
- Compulsive overworking: inability to regulate work habits or unplug completely when appropriate.
- Emotional numbness: we can't feel anything, good or bad.
- Escapist behaviours: we succumb to compulsive eating, television, internet surfing, etc. and don't have energy to choose activities that are life giving.
- Disconnection from identity and calling: we find ourselves just going through the motions.
- Unable to attend to human needs: exercise, eating right, sleep, going to the doctor, etc.
- Hoarding energy: we feel the need to become overly self-protective and even repulsive in our attempts to hoard the few resources we do have.

- Slippage in our spiritual practices: practices that are normally life giving, like solitude and silence and prayer, become burdensome and we don't have energy for them even though we know they are good for us.[66]

1. Do you recognize yourself in any of the above mentioned symptoms?
2. It can be tempting to jump into 'fix it' mode, which can, in itself, be another level of striving. Take some time in God's presence and name your struggle. Ask him, 'What shall we do about this?' Listen for his response.
3. Talking with a pastor, spiritual director or counsellor can help you look at what your soul and your life are trying to tell you and what a life-giving pathway forward might be.

In the Morning

This is another day, O Lord.
I know not what it will bring forth, but make me ready, Lord, for whatever it may be.
If I am to stand up, help me to stand bravely.
If I am to sit still, help me to sit quietly.
If I am to lie low, help me to do it patiently.
And if I am to do nothing, let me do it gallantly.
Make these words more than words and give me the Spirit of Jesus.
Amen.[67]

---

66 Ruth Haley Barton, *Strengthening the Soul of Your Leadership*: Seeking God in the Crucible of Ministry (IVP, 2008), pp.103–105.

67 'In the Morning', *The Book of Common Prayer and Administration of the Sacraments and Other Rites and Ceremonies of the Church* (Church Publishing Incorporated, 2007), p.461.

Chapter 30

LUMINOUS

Those who look to him are radiant;
their faces are never covered with shame.

PSALM 34:5

My journey has, at times, led me to wrestle with my shadow in dark corners. Other times, however an unexpected turn leaves me blinking in the light.

What. Just. Happened?

I'm on my way home from an international 24-7 Prayer gathering. Six of us had gone from GOHOP, combining it with a pilgrimage to a bunch of monastic sites in the UK. The conference is good but it's the leaders' training day that leaves me shaking. I don't remember the bulk of the material we cover but I can't get over the effect it has on me.

I feel alive. Like really, really alive. Activated and catalyzed.

It's like in those car race films when two cars are neck and neck and then, all of a sudden, one of the drivers hits a secret button and his vehicle leaps forward, functioning at a whole new level and leaving the other in the dust.

Feeling 'zoomy', I look at myself and ask, 'Who *are* you, and what have you done to Jill?' It's an invitation. Something has been activated within and demands response.

I begin to look around at leadership development programmes. 'Hey Kirk, what do you think? Tyndale has a good Masters of Divinity programme. Or what about this one? It's a training course for Christian Executive Directors?' There are tons of great options, a bewildering array of choices. How to decide?

Then it hits me.

I need to begin with the end in mind. What kind of leader do I want to become?

Who are the leaders who inspire me? Who do I want to be when I grow up?

Do I want to be a C.S. Lewis, with logic, intellect and killer storytelling skills? Steve Jobs – creative and organizational mastermind? Rosa Parks with courage and dogged determination?

After some deliberation and soul searching I make my decision. I want to be Henri Nouwen, founder of L'Arche, when I grow up. Or someone very much like him. I want to be a luminous soul. Like Jean, or like Catherine, a woman I meet at a prayer gathering. She carries a curious mixture of vulnerability and strength. Her skin looks almost translucent. Eyes no stranger to sorrow, but also creased with joy. She is slight, even a little fragile. But somehow also solid. Grounded. She is quiet, observant. Attentive and present. You can tell that she is just as aware of the Other in attendance at the table as she is the rest of us. She doesn't speak much – she chooses her moments carefully. But when she does weigh into the conversation, her words carry heft and substance. I can't take my eyes off her, and I hang onto every word. This woman has been with Jesus. She has gravitas.

Craig Barnes, in his book, *The Pastor as Minor Poet,* describes it this way:

The old seminary professors used to speak about a necessary trait for pastoral ministry called gravitas. It refers to a soul that has developed enough spiritual mass to be attractive, like gravity. It makes the soul appear old, but gravitas has nothing to do with age. It has everything to do with wounds that have healed well, failures that have been redeemed, sins that have been forgiven, and thorns that have settled into the flesh. These severe experiences with life expand the soul until it appears larger than the body that contains it. Then it is large enough to contain a holy joy, which is what makes the pastor's soul so attractive. The early church found gravitas through persecution. The desert fathers and monks found it by abandoning comfort and dedicating themselves to a vocation of prayer for the world.[68]

I long for gravitas, to become someone who carries spiritual weight and substance. Who changes the spiritual atmosphere in a room when they walk into it. My friend Shira says, 'You don't always remember what a leader says, but you remember how they make you feel.' I want people to feel loved – fully and unconditionally loved, by both God and by me. I want to learn how to be fully present and fully loving. To quiet my internal noise so that I can be a hospitable space – a place of belonging and rest for people. I want to be people's Sabbath place, their Sabbath person.

But luminosity is elusive – a tricky thing. The journey to the depth of the soul is fraught with peril. These things come with a price. And I'm wondering whether I may not need a

68 Craig Barnes, *The Pastor as Minor Poet: Texts and Subtexts in the Ministerial Life* (William. B. Eerdmans, 2009), p.49.

school so much as a guide. Someone who knows the territory, the contours of the soul and of the deep places of the heart.

That quest takes me to a monastery just outside Chicago.

It is like something out of a *Lord of the Rings* film. The lake is still, completely calm. Across the arching surface I can see the stretch of the monastery boathouse, rising out of the water like an Elfin palace. The pathway takes me through the woods, past the lake and over arched stone bridges with carved pillars.

I walk through sun-dappled woods, stopping each time I happen across a herd of deer. Used to priests and pilgrims, they stand unafraid and curious. They watch me with calm eyes as they chew and flip their tails.

As I sit on by the stone cupola overlooking the lake and watch the sunrise, a school of carp boil in the water at my feet. They splash and thrash at the edge of the pier. Above me, sparrows chatter and scold as they negotiate access to the twiggy bird houses tucked under the cupola eaves. It is calm and quiet. No one is awake yet besides me and nature in her various forms, and the guard who patrols the grounds, waving at me and chatting each time our paths cross.

'Are you with the Transforming Centre?' he asks.

'Yeah, I'm staying at the monastery till Tuesday.'

'Alrightee, just checking,' he waves and drives off.

I am on a quest for depth, eager to move out of the realm of information into the realms of formation and transformation. My syllabus over the next two years of quarterly retreats? To explore various spiritual practices from the breadth of the Christian tradition. Through reading, spiritual direction and lectures, I hope to find wise guides who understand the topography of the soul and who will point me in the direction where treasure lies. X marks the spot. Here's a shovel. Now dig.

'God wants to be with you in a particular way,' one teacher says. 'What is his invitation to you today?' Paul says:

> *And we all, who with unveiled faces contemplate the Lord's glory, are being transformed into his image with ever-increasing glory, which comes from the Lord, who is the Spirit.*

2 CORINTHIANS 3:18

The pathway to luminosity? Paul would say the contemplation of God's glory. British poet William Blake says, 'We become what we behold.'[69] What might happen if I search for God's glory in all its multiple manifestations around me? In the Scriptures and in a walk around the lake? In the faces and lives of those I love? What if I set my heart on a quest for his beauty and when I find it, stop? Look. Listen. Take it all in. Let it invade the inner chambers of my heart and fill them with light.

Might I become luminous?

THE INVITATION

1. Think about the leaders you have encountered that have most influenced you. What was it about them that made them so impactful?
2. What kind of leader do you want to become? What might be the journey towards that becoming?

69 William Blake, *Jerusalem, the Emanation of the Giant Albion* (Kessinger Publishing, 2010) p.57.

3. Read this poem out loud, slowly once or twice. Which words or phrases jump out at you? How does your heart respond to what you read? What might God be saying to you?

Communion

I drop into silence
like the bottom of a well.
Sit in the darkness
and let my eyes adjust.
I see the etchings
the scratches
of my ancestors.
Hieroglyphics shimmer
Stories of long ago.
My fingers trace the ridges of their narrative.
My palms feel the heat
that radiates and pulses.
Their stories enter my skin.
Our hearts thrum together
The ancient rhythm
In the shadows of the earth.
JILL WEBER

Jesus, I'm grateful that I am not shaping myself but rather being formed by you.
Not only are you my guide but also my pathway.
You are the treasure and you are also the tool that helps me uncover it.
Take me deeper.

Chapter 31

I SEE YOU

She gave this name to the Lord who spoke to her: 'You are the God who sees me,' for she said, 'I have now seen the One who sees me.'

Genesis 16:13

It's the first session of my spiritual formation training. I'm in a room with pastors and leaders from all over North America. 'I want you to leave behind your titles, the ways you define yourself by what you do,' our hostess says. 'In this space can we just be souls in the presence of God?'

I'm standing at the edge of the crowd, coffee in hand. Holding it high in front of me like a shield. Without the body armour of my title and CV, I feel quite vulnerable. If the mug is big enough, maybe I can hide behind it. Do I make eye contact? Smile? I feel like an awkward teenager standing against the wall at the school prom. Hmmm, maybe the hospitality team needs help with cleaning up the coffee and snacks. Or maybe I should just go to my seat and organize my papers and notebooks ...

I'm shy. Sometimes painfully so. But I also want to be seen. I want everybody to know what a wonderful, unique person I am. I'm special! Delightful, even! You should get to know me! Like Donkey in the movie *Shrek*, my insides hop up and down, bleating, 'Pick me! Pick me!'

Over the years I've become aware of the contours of that particular neurosis, so I'm quick to notice and resist it. But it's persistent and keeps popping up, like rodents in a Whack-a-Mole game at the carnival. As I survey the room, the Whack-a-Moles are stirring, restless. 'Leaders. Lots of leaders. Maybe new friends? Maybe important contacts?' they chitter.

I whack the mole. Why does this still bother me? I'm a grownup, for goodness sake! But the moment feels physically painful – I feel scooped out inside. Raw and vulnerable in my loneliness and my need for human connection and affirmation. My need to be seen.

All of a sudden, a clear and loving voice bursts into my consciousness. The Voice.

'I see you. My eye is on you.'

It is a quiet, calming word. Peace unfurls within.

'I see you. My eye is on you.'

It's a holy moment. Years later I feel it in my body with the same strength and intensity. 'You are the God who sees me,' says Hagar in the desert.[70] And Jill in the monastery.

A word from the Lord changes everything, and this briefest of encounters reconfigures my insides. And it radically and permanently changes how I react in these types of social situations. Now when I'm in a crowd of strangers my prayer is, 'Lord, hide me from those I'm meant to be hidden from. Reveal me to those you want me to connect with.'

Gone is the striving and the need to be seen. I trust that whatever relational connections happen are the ones ordained to be. And I don't fuss when I'm overlooked and ignored (as slightly plump middle-aged women can be).

Years earlier, I'm sitting across from one of my mentors in a restaurant in Kansas City, wrestling with the shape of

70 Genesis 16:13.

my vocation. Building a local prayer community is part of it, but my spheres of influence and concern are both expanding and I'm not sure how to engage with God's invitation to inhabit the larger space. 'Just think of it this way,' he says, 'What you do is fly from one House of Prayer to the next. You dip in and gather sweetness from one and you take it to the other – cross pollinating! You're a honeybee!'

Honeybee.

The word is weighty with affection. It's one of those moments when someone's lips are moving, but in actuality it is God speaking. I can see the crinkle in God's eye. Hear the tenderness in his voice. I feel like I'm about 5 years old and have just been scooped up onto his lap.

These are profoundly orienting moments where I am seen. Named. Blessed. Shaped and formed by his word.

In the beginning God said, 'Let there be Jill', and then there was Jill. He speaks me into existence.

The present is wrapped in a small, stiff brown envelope, tied tight with yellow, shimmery ribbon. 'I want you to open it in front of me,' Hannah says. 'But read the note first.'

The card is home-made, just like they are every year. I've kept them all, tucked away where I bury my treasures. On the front is a detailed illustration of a honeybee. 'I find you to be sweetly delicious,' the card reads. 'Remember always who you are made to bee.' Untying the ribbon, I pull out a necklace. It's a honeycomb-shaped pendant hanging from a black cord. Inside is a small, fuzzy insect encased in glass.

'A honeybee!' I wrap my hand around the pendant and hold it close. It feels warm to the touch. I buzz and hum in response. My eyes glisten and I shut them for a moment. She sees me.

I'm reminded of the story in the first chapter of the book Luke – the story of Mary and Elizabeth. Having said a dangerous 'yes' to God, Mary finds herself pregnant and goes to look for shelter and support from one of her relatives.[71]

I imagine the scene. Mary is cautious, tentative. Will she be welcome? Hand resting protectively on her still-flat midriff, she stands at the entrance of her cousin's home. She needs to be hidden and she needs to be seen. Will she be safe here?

The moment they meet is a holy moment. Heavy with child herself, Elizabeth sucks in a breath as she is filled with the Holy Spirit. The baby leaps an acrobatic amen within her. Somehow Elizabeth perceives she is witnessing a miracle. Mary is carrying hidden treasure.

'Blessed are you!' Elizabeth exclaims, 'And blessed is the child you will bear!'[72]

I see you, Mary. My eye is on you.

Her hidden yes and her secret treasure is seen, blessed and affirmed.

Mary is safe. Seen and known. Named and blessed.

It doesn't end there. For not only is Mary carrying a baby, but she is also carrying a melody. When Mary is safe, when the hidden work of God in her is seen, when she is blessed and affirmed, then and only then does the melody of her heart, the song of her life come forth.[73] Like a sparrow in God's hand she sings, and for two thousand years we've been enjoying her song.

71 Luke 1:39–45.
72 Luke 1:42.
73 Luke 1: 46–55.

THE INVITATION

1. Reflect on a time when you have felt safe. When God's hidden work in you has been seen. When you have been blessed and affirmed. Offer that instance and situation back to God in gratitude.

2. Numerous times in the Scriptures, God has given people new names that held keys to the essence of who they were and who they were becoming. Abram becomes Abraham – father of many nations. (Genesis 17:5). Jacob becomes Israel, one who has struggled with God and with humans and has overcome (Genesis 32:28). Gideon is called 'Mighty Warrior'(Judges 6:12). Simon is renamed Peter (Matthew 16:18), the rock. In Revelation 2:17 it is declared that some will be given a new name, known only to the one who receives it. Have you ever been named by God in a personal way? It might be a nickname, a demonstration of his affection towards you and his concern for you ('Do not be afraid, *little flock*, for your Father has been pleased to give you the kingdom.'[74]) It might be a name that holds keys to who you are and who you are becoming. (Like Gideon being called 'Mighty Warrior'.)

3. Try this creative exercise: gather a bunch of magazines. Ask God, 'Who do you say I am?' Then go through the magazines and cut out pictures that speak the answer to that question. Don't think too hard, just see which pictures you are attracted to. Then compile them together in a collage.

---

74 Luke 12:32.

Jesus, I thank you that you are the author and perfecter of my faith.
Ultimately I begin and end with you.
You know me.
You see me.
You name me.
I receive your word to me.
Let it be done to me as you have said.

Chapter 32

THE BELLY OF THE WHALE

'Very truly I tell you, unless a grain of wheat falls to the
ground and dies, it remains only a single seed. But if it dies,
it produces many seeds.'

JOHN 12:24

Kenosis

I didn't think it would feel like dying.
The leaf falling to the ground
Crumpled and spent
Brittle
Veins popping.
The seed falling in the ground
Cold and dark
Split.
The new life emerging
Tears me apart.
Resurrection plunges upward,
Leaving me in its wake.
A torn husk,
Forgotten and still.
I didn't think it would feel like dying.

JILL WEBER

Autumn 2014. I undergo a major surgery. 'You will have three days in the hospital,' the doctor says, 'three weeks in bed and two months off work.'

My journal entries before the surgery are full of naive excitement. I'm going to have time! Lots of time! I want to read books! Lots of books! Have an extended spiritual retreat. Get back to my regular writing and blogging. It will be a creative time! A productive time! A deeply spiritual time! Tucked in alongside my optimistic forecasts is a nudge, a teeny sense that my surgery recovery might just bring me a different gift. One day I feel inspired to write down in my journal, 'Very truly I tell you, unless a kernel of wheat falls to the ground ...' With naivety, I assume I understand what that means.

It's probably a good thing that I don't.

Upon my return from the hospital, I'm a wreck. The pain is easily managed but I have no energy, no mental focus or concentration. I sleep and sleep and sleep. My brief waking hours are preoccupied with learning new regimes of drinking, eating and managing secondary infections. With glazed eyes I mindlessly scroll for hours through social media feeds. Prayer takes more mental and emotional energy that I am able to muster. I want God, but in the darkness of this season he is completely imperceptible. In silence I stare blankly at walls or out of window for hours on end. I feel vacant. Hollowed out. The lights are on, but nobody is home ...

My daughter Hannah says, 'Everything else in nature goes through times of dormancy. Why should humans think they are somehow exempt?'

After a couple of months, the fog clears, and bit by bit, life begins to flow back. My faculties return with excruciating slowness. Simple day-to-day self-care doesn't take up the same amount of brain space and eventually I am able to resume my regular routines of spiritual reading, prayer and meditation. The season of dormancy ended up being just that – a season. I'm relieved it's over, but troubled and perplexed. I had completely shut down. What was that all about?

Seeking to understand what felt like a dark night, I dive into my spiritual formation textbooks, combing them for clues. I find some interesting perspectives. Catherine Doherty is a writer who explores the Russian Orthodox tradition. In her in her book, *Poustinia*, she says:

> *One cannot enter into the mystery of the Incarnation without first doing a hidden stripping of self. Then follows a lifetime of continued stripping, of emptying oneself ...*[75]

Emptying oneself – what the Russian Orthodox call 'Kenosis'. I know that in Philippians 2 we are invited to follow the descending, self-emptying path of Jesus. However, I wonder, is this Orthodox perspective on *Kenosis* a bit extreme? Hasn't God given me my intellect, my personality, my gifts? Doesn't he want me to use them in obedience to his leadership? But, on the other hand, what if his leadership requires I lay them down from time to time? When we ask God to fill us, are we first willing and able to empty out, to make room? What if he then fills me with something far greater than my own inherit capacities? I wrestle and question.

In his book, *Everything Belongs*, the Franciscan friar Richard Rohr also wraps words around my experience. He talks about going inside the belly of the beast.

---

75 Catherine Dougherty, *Poustinia: Encountering God in Silence, Solitude and Prayer* (Madonna House, 1993), p.121.

Christians call it the paschal mystery, but we are all
pointing to the same necessity of both descent and ascent.
The paschal mystery is the pattern of transformation.
We are transformed through death and rising, probably
many times. There seems to be no other cauldron of
growth and transformation. We seldom go freely into the
belly of the beast.[76]

He goes on to say,

We must learn to stay with the pain of life, without
answers, without conclusions, and some days without
meaning. That is the path, the periods dark path of true
prayer ... we avoid God, who works in the darkness –
where we are not in control.[77]

The dark path of true prayer. The path beyond words, even
beyond emotions. The place where God works imperceptibly
in darkness.

Looking back, I wonder, was God at work in me during
this season? Hard to say. I find it interesting though, that
since that time, I'm less wordy in my prayers. I settle more
easily into silence. On the far-flung edge of conversation,
I've discovered communion.

THE INVITATION

The dark night of the soul is not restricted to holy people.
It can happen to anyone. I believe that in some ways it
happens to everyone. Yet it is much more significant than
simple misfortune. It is a deep transformation,

76 Richard Rohr, *Everything Belongs: The Gift of Contemplative Prayer* (The Crossroad Publishing Company, 2003), p.45.

77 Ibid, p. 46.

*a movement towards indescribable freedom and joy.
And in truth, it doesn't always have to be unpleasant!
... The dark night is a profoundly good thing. It is an
ongoing spiritual process in which we are liberated from
attachments and compulsions and empowered to live and
love more freely. Sometimes this letting go of old ways is
painful, occasionally even devastating. But this is not why
the night is called 'dark'. The darkness of the night implies
nothing sinister, only that the liberation takes place in
hidden ways, beneath our knowledge and understanding.
It happens mysteriously, in secret, and beyond our conscious
control. For that reason it can be disturbing or even scary,
but in the end it always works to our benefit.*[78]

1. When have you experienced a 'dark night'? What were
   the circumstances? What did it feel like? How long did
   it last?
   John Mark Comer, pastor of Bridgetown Church in
   Portland, gives this advice for weathering dark nights in
   our soul:

1. Don't try harder.
2. Rest.
3. Wait patiently.
4. Trust.
5. Slow down.
6. Pay attention to beauty.
7. Resist doubt.
8. Release the illusion of control.

---

78 Gerald G. May, *The Dark Night of the Soul: A Psychiatrist Explores the Connection Between Darkness and Spiritual Growth* (HarperCollins, 2009), pp.4–5.

*Jesus, help me to follow you on the hidden path towards death
and resurrection.
Release me from all those things I cling to.
May I stand in the darkness unafraid, knowing you are with me.
Amen.*

Chapter 33

ABBESS

I will fulfil my vows to the LORD
in the presence of all his people ...

PSALM 116:18

El Escorial, Spain

It's warm for October, but it is Spain, after all. We are sitting in a circle in the gardens of a monastery outside Madrid. The Brits, in particular, are enjoying being outside, lifting their faces to the sun, soaking up the Spanish warmth before heading back to their drizzly isle. I look around the circle. People I've admired from afar for many years. Do I belong here?

That's what we're trying to figure out. I've been invited to join a group of leaders from across the 24-7 Prayer movement who help bring support and structure to our growing number of communities that are swinging into their orbit. Pete Greig, co-founder and team leader of 24-7 Prayer, has asked me to help cultivate the Houses of Prayer that are beginning to emerge. I say yes to this meeting, but it's a bit like a first date where we're all uncomfortable and shy, sussing each other out to see if we're a good fit.

'When we look at the history of the church over the millennia,' I am sharing about Houses of Prayer, 'it's these little groups of monastics – the ones who have given themselves in extravagant ways in prayer and loving the poor, these are the ones that have preserved thought and culture, these are the ones who evangelized Europe and changed history!'

As I talk, the team's cautious observation relaxes and warms into welcome. At the end of the meeting, they gather around, lay hands on me and pray for me. Pete Greig speaks authoritatively over me in his Benedict Cumberbatch voice (basically you can say pretty much anything to me in a Benedict Cumberbatch voice and I'll do as I'm told).

'You will be an Abbess to many.' He declares.

Herrnhut, Germany

My daughter and I, Shira, Sue and some other friends are wandering through 'God's Acre', the famous Moravian cemetery in Herrnhut, Germany. I stand over Zinzendorf's grave, a stone cairn engraved with his name.

He's shorter than I thought. I mentally take the measure of the man. I've heard tales of people lying on top of the cairn, asking God for an impartation of his anointing. Hmm, maybe not. I give the stone top a little rub instead. *Hi Nikolaus! Pleased to meet you!*

We climb the staircase inside the prayer tower on the edge of the graveyard and congregate at the top. Hannah pulls out her camera and takes pictures of the sleepy village that sprawls before us. Flaming red and orange leaves crown the village like a monastic tonsure.

It looks ... normal. Like all the other sleepy little German villages we can see from our vantage point. 'It could be anywhere, couldn't it?' Sue is thoughtful. 'Just an ordinary place, full of ordinary people.' *Ordinary people with an extraordinary commitment to prayer,* I think.

Nikolaus Ludwig Von Zinzendorf is serious about following Jesus. And aware that he needs help to do so. In 1716 he is 16 years old and just about to enter La Halle university. He gathers some friends and they decide on some shared commitments and spiritual practices. Sometime later they have rings made to remind them of their vows. The rings are imprinted with the verse 'no one lives unto themselves'.[79] The Order of the Mustard Seed is born.

Over his lifetime, the Order provides Zinzendorf the support he needs to maintain an extraordinary commitment to the gospel. Their vows? To be true to Christ, kind to people and to take the gospel to the nations.

After Zinzendorf's death, the Order of the Mustard Seed fades into history. It is planted into the ground. Almost four centuries later, some leaders in 24-7 Prayer and YWAM dig it up and dust it off. Is there any life in the seed?

Turns out there is. On a cold February evening in 2005, around one hundred people gather at Holy Trinity Clapham in London. Many take vows, and don their rings. The Order of the Mustard Seed is reborn.

Back at home in my house in Hamilton, I have the most beautiful rose bush. The soil is shallow and sandy, but right in front of my porch it gets lots of sun. In June the bush

79 Romans 14:7.

explodes into a riot of colour – a wall of crimson blooms. I cut it back every spring, but come summer it grows and grows to monstrous proportions. Eventually it gets overwhelmed by its own weight and flops forward onto our driveway. I lovingly call it Audrey[80] and I problem solve about how to keep her from attacking my neighbours and housemates as they enter the house.

'You've got to tie it up!' Kirk says. 'Get it under control.'

With a little twine and a lot of prickled fingers, I'm able to tie Audrey to the porch railing. She strains against the twine, but remains contained.

My spiritual life, too, often feels floppy, sprawling, slightly carnivorous and in need of support. When I hear about Zinzendorf, his vows and the formational practices that shape the members of the OMS, I wonder whether I should join the fellowship of the ring.

Colorado, USA

The 24-7 Leadership Team is sitting in the basement of a log chalet tucked deep in the Colorado Rockies. Some folk are sprawled on the beanbag chairs. Others are snugged onto the couches. I'm perched on a wooden stool in the back of the room. Pete is filling us in on the latest initiatives unfolding on the 24-7 landscape.

'As you know, many of us took vows in the Order of the Mustard Seed about ten years ago,' Pete says. 'We've just been contacted by the office of the Archbishop of Canterbury. When Justin Welby came into his role, he set the revival of prayer and the religious life as one of his top priorities. We've been asked to consider formalizing and expanding the Order. We're going to need to develop a novitiate year of

---

80 The carnivorous plant from *Little Shop of Horrors*.

sorts – a year of preparation for people before they take their vows, and also start to build some systems and structures around it all.'

'Hmm,' I think. 'We could probably help with that.' I've been leading our House of Prayer for fourteen years now, so have a little bit of experience. I'm sure our team of monkish theologians can help shape a preparation process.

Geneva, Switzerland

Fool that I am, I vow all that I have and all that I am to be true to Christ in the grace of our Holy Spirit for every day the Father grants me.

So help me God.

Weak as I am, I vow to be kind to people: to see Christ in others, to serve Christ in others and to show Christ to others in the joy of the Holy Spirit for the glory of our Father.

So help me God.

Small as I am and wherever I am, I vow to serve the Gospel of Christ.

Today, together, we offer to spend ourselves on behalf of the broken and poor in the power of the Spirit, giving our whole life that Christ might be loved in every language, tribe and nation in our generation for the glory of our Father.

We will not live for ourselves.

So help us God.

I look at the ring on the table in front of me and sink to my knees. It's a sacred moment. I'm not sure why it feels so potent – all I'm doing is promising to be a Christian, really. But somehow, it's another level of 'yes'. Of giving permission. Putting myself in the path of oncoming grace. It feels like I'm stepping over a threshold into somewhere completely new.

I put on my ring, take a deep breath, clear my throat and make my way back to my seat, joining the other members of the Order. Shira and Abraham, Peter, Doug and most of our gang are here. We're on the journey together. *Cymbrogi* – companions of the heart.

Surrey, UK

The team that had been responsible to get the Order of the Mustard Seed up and running is at a retreat centre that overlooks the ruins of an ancient monastery. Pete is across from me, leaning forward in his seat, elbows on his knees. One eyebrow cocked the way it does when he's feeling mischievous.

'Jill, we would like to invite you to be the first Global Convenor of the Order of the Mustard Seed.' My eyes widen and I shoot a questioning glance around the room at my colleagues. They are smiling, nodding, intent on my response.

Earlier in the day we wondered what to call the leader of the Order. Abbot? Guardian? Mucky muck? Zinzendorf himself believed in non-hierarchical servant leadership so we want to follow his example. 'I like the word "convenor,"' Pete interjects. 'Someone to convene – to gather the community. A Global Convenor!'

The OMS is a disbursed Order which means our members are scattered all over the world, from Adelaide,

Australia to Cape Town, South Africa. From Southeast Asia to Afghanistan and across Europe and North America.

I thought we were just going to spend the day sorting out leadership and governance, put the systems and structures in place so we could pick a leader a couple of years down the road. I had somebody in mind already that I thought would be a good candidate, so I was unprepared for the ambush.

In a flash of hindsight, I see the stepping stones that led to this moment. First, the invitation from the Lord to strengthen my leadership – to dig into God. 'You've got to go deep before you go wide,' he said to me years back. Followed by several years of study, pilgrimage, spiritual excavation and exploration. Next the invitation from Pete to serve the international leadership team. And then the invitation to join and help establish the Order. And now, well, here we are.

I have no aspiration for a larger circle of influence – I'm happy with the little plot of soil that God had given me to cultivate in Hamilton. Life in our community is rich and satisfying.

I wonder though, is being Convenor really all that different from what I've been doing back home? Slightly bigger garden to putter about in. But still praying. Still making friends.

While they are waiting for my response, Pete points to the window behind us. 'Look at that!' We all swivel. Just at that moment three Canada geese fly past in perfect formation before landing on the lawn outside.

An 18-year-old prophetic word floats through my head. 'Usually a wise mama goose in front – an old hand that knows the way.' I smile at my friends around the circle and say yes.

THE INVITATION

A rule of life is a spiritual practice that has been used over the centuries to help people bring shape and support to their spiritual lives. In the Order of the Mustard Seed, members of the Order build a rule of life around six spiritual disciplines (prayer, creativity, learning and hospitality, mercy and justice, and mission) that help us to live into our vows.

Ruth Haley Barton, in her book *Invitation to Retreat*, outlines a helpful process for establishing a rule of life.

A rule of life (is) a practice that responds to two questions: Who do I want to be? and How do I want to live?

Hopefully you have worked through a process for establishing your own sacred rhythms and are seeking to live faithfully within them. Such a process involves getting in touch with your deepest spiritual desires, exposing spiritual practices ... that correspond to those desires, and then asking God to guide you in putting them together in a rhythm that works for you ... [81]

1. Take a retreat or an extended time of solitude. It can be an hour locked in your bathroom, a half day (or multi-day) visit to a local monastery or a hike in a local park. Ask yourself the questions, 'Who do I want to be?' and 'How do I want to live?' A helpful exercise can be to look forward and to think about what kind of legacy you want to leave behind you. What kind of eulogies would you like to be shared at your funeral?

---

81 Ruth Haley Barton, *Invitation to Retreat: The Gift and Necessity of Time Away with God* (InterVarsity Press, 2018), p.98.

2. Barton defines sacred rhythms as 'patterns of attitudes, practices, and behaviours set apart for the sacred purpose of keeping us open and available to the transforming presence of Christ'.[82] I like the term 'formational practices', which I learned from Marc Gauvreau, one of my spiritual formation instructors. The word 'formational' means that these are things that I'm doing that actually shape and form me personally, and shape and form my internal and external world. The word 'practices' means that these are things that I'm practising, that I'm exploring, experimenting with and learning. Take a personal inventory. What sacred rhythms or formational practices do you already have in place in your life?

3. Take some time to ask God how he might be inviting you to adjust or expand your sacred rhythms or formational practices.

Jesus, thank you that you invite us to live freely and lightly in the unforced rhythms of grace.
Thank you for the varied sacred rhythms and formational practices that we can explore as a means to grace, a way to create space to encounter you in transformational ways.
How shall I live?
I invite you to show me the pathways of life.

---

82 Ibid.

Chapter 34

BARTON STREET

For the LORD is good and his love endures for ever;
his faithfulness continues through all generations.

PSALM 100:5

The beauty of prayer is that it is portable. Prayer can happen anywhere, any way, any time.

Several times over the years, faith-filled friends say, 'I'm praying for a building for GOHOP!' 'You can pray for that if you like,' I respond, 'but it's not likely to happen while I'm in charge.'

I'm not keen on buildings. A lot of time, money and energy goes towards brick and mortar that I would much rather direct towards the development of people and the cultivation of prayer. Plus, we are professional prayer squatters. Since our inception we've never paid rent for our prayer room.

After a few months praying in the former library in the North End of Hamilton, we move right to the centre of the city. For a couple of years we set up shop at the Vine, a building adjacent to the main inner-city shopping centre and farmers market, surrounded by homeless shelters. Our team prays there 9–5 most days, and sometimes invites the city to join us for weeks of 24-7 prayer. From there we migrate eastwards to the basement of a social enterprise cafe on Barton Street.

Barton Street is infamous. Once, it was a thriving hub of economy close to booming and productive steel plants. But when the bottom drops out of the manufacturing industry and the plants close, the neighbourhood slips into disrepair and then despair. The street is lined with many dilapidated shopfronts and heaps of illegal flats. At certain times of the day, women work the street corners.

Barton Street has been the focus of prayer for many years. About ten years ago, a local intercessor and her team commit to pray for every business on the street. Every business, including the strip club and the massage parlours. Diane goes from shopfront to shopfront, collecting prayer requests. 'I've got a prayer team back at the church who will pray for you,' she says.

One day she drops in to a local massage parlour. 'Can we pray for you guys for anything?' Diane asks. The young woman at the front counter pauses a moment. 'Well, Joe here is having some trouble with his eye.' Diane turns to Joe, a big, beefy, broad-shouldered guy. Joe's lid droops over a reddened eye. 'Can I pray for you?' Diane is feisty and bold, quite comfortable praying for bouncers in sex trade establishments. He shrugs grudging permission. She prays a simple prayer and continues her rounds.

The next time she checks in at the massage parlour, the front counter girl just about jumps up and down in excitement on her arrival. 'His eye got better! Right away! You healed him!' She chirps. 'Jesus healed him, actually.' Diane responds.

Diane and her team blanket Barton in prayer for a couple of years, and then the baton is passed to a young man named Thomas. For the next two years, Thomas takes a prayer-walking team up and down Barton from 11pm–3am every Thursday to Sunday. During that time, Christian outreach to sex trade workers begins to emerge on the street. Several organizations begin handing out toiletries, sweets (to help with the jitters between hits) and clothes. People begin moving into the neighbourhood with missional intention.

And then, after years of different teams saturating Barton Street in prayer, asking for God to bring transformation to the neighbourhood, God plants a beachhead in the community.

'Hey Jill! Howzit going?

'Pretty good, Ellis! You busking at all these days?'

'Naw, it's too cold. Maybe when spring rolls around.'

'Jill! How'arya doin!' Fred always speaks with exclamation points. 'Didja get your walk in today? I got my run in! Nine miles!'

We're standing outside the cafe with the morning crowd. At about quarter to seven, they all line up outside the door. We're stamping our feet, arms wrapped around ourselves, and we're surrounded by the mist of our own breath. It's a chilly one today.

Seven in the morning is my favourite time in the cafe. It's when our regulars congregate, our neighbourhood friends. Many of them don't have stoves in their rooming house accommodation so they make a beeline to 541 for an early cup of 'joe' and a free breakfast.

Seven on the dot, Jenn opens the door. She's tiny, pixie-like. Topped with short curls and rosy cheeks. Her love for good food, great coffee and her passion for this neighbourhood converge in her co-conspiring in the establishment of the 541 Eatery and Exchange – a social enterprise cafe right in the middle of what I call a 'vulnerable but resilient' community.

The crew crowds in and lines up. As they reach the front, they grab a handful of buttons from the jar on the counter. The cafe uses buttons as currency. You can buy a button for a dollar and then it goes in the jar for someone else to use if they need it. Last time I checked, neighbours were feeding one another to the tune of ten thousand buttons a month.

It's my turn at the counter.

'How are you doing Jenn? Any disasters yesterday?'

'Apart from the state of the toilets and the dishwasher breaking down for the umpteenth time, no I think we did OK.' She grins. 'Do you want a soy latte?'

'Yeah, thanks.'

As Jenn makes my coffee I look around the cafe. Some of its residents are quiet, bleary eyed from last night's shenanigans. They quietly cup their coffee close to their chests. Charlotte is sitting at a table, poring over her schoolwork. She looks to be about 50 or so – it's hard to say really. 'Gonna get that high school diploma, maybe this year,' she says. Wild-bearded Arthur looks up at me and smiles a shy welcome. I smile back. Ellis has tied an apron around his waist and is already bustling mugs to the back. The cafe keeps food prices low by employing hundreds of volunteers.

'Hey Jill! C'mere!' I pay for my coffee and head over to Fred's table. 'Jill, you gotta pray for me! That place where I'm staying is just killing me! I had to call the cops last night – my housemates were all shouting and screaming at each other! I'm just not feeling safe there! Pray that I get a new place, OK?' 'Yeah, Fred, I can do that.' I'm mentally calculating how many new homes I've prayed in for Fred.

I chat with a few more of the regulars and then head to

what looks like the door of a storage cupboard. In actuality it's the doorway to our basement prayer room. Making my way downstairs, I turn on the lights. The room is small and cosy. Near the entrance are a number of creative prayer stations and activities. A bulletin board covered with pictures of all of our interns. We have a shelf full of books on prayer and tons of art supplies. There is a whiteboard on one wall with prayer requests for the cafe scrawled on it. I write down 'a home for Fred'. In the back end of the room is a little worship circle with a keyboard, a couple of guitars and some hand drums. I switch on the fake fireplace (the basement is chilly in the winter) and settle into the space. I'm not alone long. Soon, members of our prayer community arrive.

It's crowded today – we have to grab a couple of folding chairs from the back and shoehorn them into the circle. Sandy settles at the keyboard. 'Do you all have songbooks?' she asks. Her husband Peter hands them out. 'Let's turn to number 47, "*Da Pacem Domine*".'

It's Wednesday morning so time for our Taizé prayer set. Many years ago we felt God challenging us through Paul's exhortation in Ephesians 6 to lift up all kinds of prayer.[83] So we begin to explore and experiment. Sometimes we do 'Harp & Bowl' a worship and prayer fusion we learned from our friends at IHOP. Other times we do prayer art – quietly illustrating Scriptures with all kinds of art supplies. Shira often pulls out the prayer books to do morning and afternoon liturgical prayers. One of our worship leaders is a real Holy Spirit guy. He comes in with his guitar, sniffs to see which way the Spirit is blowing and then jumps in for a couple hours of free-flow spontaneous worship.

We cover all kinds of topics. Prayer for pastors and leaders, creation care and environmental issues, prayer for

83 Ephesians 6:18.

the persecuted church and for our community. On Fridays, Shira leads prayer for the establishment of a YWAM base in town. Little mini-prayer communities build up around different modalities of prayer and prayer focuses. An underground prayer furnace – a boiler room.

'It changes the spiritual atmosphere,' says Sue, who also helps run the cafe. 'People walk into the space and say it feels different. Prayer in the basement makes all the difference.'

In the Message paraphrase of John 1, it says that the Word was made flesh and moved into the neighbourhood.[84] I love that our little House of Prayer is not cloistered away in its own building, apart from everything else. I love that we're embedded in this cafe hub, planted right in the heart of our community.

541 PRAYERS OF THE PEOPLE

(Gathered from volunteers and members of the 541 community and prayed each day as a morning liturgy at the cafe)

Lord Jesus,
You invite all people to eat at your table.
Thank you for bringing 541 to Barton Street so it can open its arms of light and love to all who enter.
Lynda

Thank you that those who come here find it 'a fine service that is generous and personal'.
And that it is a privilege to 'be a part of each day'.
Laurie

Bless this family at 541 and bless those outside of 541.
John

84 John 1:14 (MSG).

Bless the food that is eaten here.
Bless those who grow and prepare the food.
Grant

May it keep everyone happy and healthy.
Maurice

We pray for each person who walks through our doors, that they would find your love in this place.
We pray for those dealing with mental illness that they would find peace and support here.
Sarah

Help us not to become weary in well-doing.
Todd

Thank you for having the Virgin Mary bear Jesus Christ your son.
Kim

Help us to remember it is in your strength and not our own that we serve this day.
Work through us and in us this day and restore us to our original divine.
Karen

May your kingdom come at 541 today and keep us open for many more days.
Frank

Amen.

THE INVITATION

Community transformation is not measured in months or even in years, but in decades. We're all part of a relay race.

Sometimes we're looking back with gratitude at those who got us this far. Other times we're cheering on the next ones who are running a lap. Always we are fixing our eyes on Jesus.

It helps, now and then, to step back and take a long view.
The kingdom is not only beyond our efforts,
it is even beyond our vision.
We accomplish in our lifetime
only a tiny fraction
of the magnificent enterprise
that is God's work.
Nothing we do is complete,
which is another way of saying
that the Kingdom always lies beyond us.
No statement says all that could be said.
No prayer fully expresses our faith.
No confession brings perfection.
No pastoral visit brings wholeness.
No programme
accomplishes the Church's mission.
No set of goals and objectives
includes everything.
That is what we are about.
We plant a seed that will one day grow.
We water seeds already planted,
knowing that they hold future promise.
We lay foundations
that will need further development.
We provide yeast that produces effects
far beyond our capabilities.
We cannot do everything,
and there is a sense of liberation
in realising that.

This enables us to do something,
and to do it very well.
It may be incomplete,
but it is a beginning,
a step along the way,
an opportunity for the Lord's grace
to enter and do the rest.
We may never see the end results,
but that is the difference
between the master builder and the worker.
We are workers, not master builders,
ministers, not messiahs.
We are prophets of a future not our own.[85]

Read: Read this prayer, out loud slowly. Which words or phrases jump out at you?

Reflect: Reflect on those words or phrases. Why did they jump out at you? How do you relate to them? What do they mean to you specifically?

Respond: How might God be asking you to respond to what he is highlighting? What is his invitation to you? Pray some prayers of response.

Jesus, I thank you that I am a part of the larger story of your
faithfulness towards many, many generations.
I celebrate those who have gone before me.
I look with anticipation for those who I might encourage on the
next leg of the journey.
We look together for a city whose builder and architect is God.

---

85 This prayer was composed by Bishop Ken Untener of Saginaw, drafted for an homily by Cardinal John Dearden in November 1979 for a celebration of departed priests.

Chapter 35

DESOLATION

*For our struggle is not against flesh and blood, but against
the rulers, against the authorities, against the powers of this
dark world and against the spiritual forces of evil in the
heavenly realms ... and after you have done everything, to
stand.*

EPHESIANS 6:12–13

I love it except when I hate it.

Most days I'm OK, but every once in a while, the bottom
drops out and I lose heart. Today I have to get the hell out
of dodge. I just start driving. Anywhere but here. I point the
car towards the beautiful town just down the road, looking
for cathedral-arched trees on spotless side streets.

I woke up this morning feeling punched in the gut. Like
a deflated balloon lying flaccid on the floor.

Last night I discovered that one of my dear friends was
sliding further into addiction and making some dangerous
choices. I've watched her journey and rejoiced in every
step towards greater health and stability. To witness the
devolution, the disintegration is so discouraging. I know
that I'm not a mental-health professional. I'm not a service
provider. I'm not her pastor, her therapist. Her mother.
I'm her friend who prays. Who offers accompaniment and

hospitality, and maybe a different narrative of what life can look like.

Sometimes I wish I was the kind of prayer missionary who lives tucked away in a monastery somewhere. Safe behind walls. But we are right in the thick of it, embedded like journalists on the front lines of combat zones. Walking through my neighbourhood I see dead eyes, hollow cheeks, bedbug-pocked ankles and cowering Rottweilers on choke chains.

And if I'm honest, I sometimes feel like I'm looking into an old, tarnished mirror at distorted reflections of my own inner abyss. My own compulsions, my own insatiable hungers. My own small cruelties and half healed scars.

I run out of words. I run out of prayers.

Lord have mercy.

Christ have mercy.

Lord have mercy.

I feel helpless, hollowed out like somebody scooped out my insides. My usual drive, verve and determination dissipate.

You pray differently when you're embedded on the front lines. When human trafficking has a face, has a name. When you see her come into the cafe every day, this morning with bruises around her throat.

You pray differently for homelessness when dear friends of yours come to church wild eyed, unshaven and dishevelled, roaches skittering across the back of their jacket.

You pray differently when your friend shows you the bruises from her most recent rape and tells how the judge dismissed the case because she wasn't a reliable witness.

You don't pray from your head or your theology or even from the Scriptures. You pray from your gut with groaning. You sit across the room from a tormented soul. You look at them and they look at you and behind their eyes you can see an unnamed malevolent force staring at you, mocking.

You glare it down.

The Lord rebuke you.

You pray differently when you are praying in the midst.

Sometimes it feels like a python has wrapped itself around you and is squeezing your life away and all you can do is breathe out pleas for deliverance.

And I often think of Kevin Prosch's song:

I feel like I am failing
There is a hole in my trampoline
And I'm falling down.[86]

And I know that unless the Lord builds the house I'm building in vain and unless he's guarding the city, watching over it, we are praying in vain.

I know that it's too big for me.

Too dark for me.

Too complex for me.

Too heartbreaking for me.

All I can do is stand my ground and groan, having done all, then stand. And sometimes I can't even stand my ground. I have to get out of town and go breathe different air.

I pull up to the water's edge. Get out of my car and sit on the bench. I turn my face to the autumn sun that still carries some warmth and let the breeze embrace me, twirling through my hair and brushing my cheek.

I want to say to myself like the Psalmist, 'Why, my soul, are you downcast? ... Put your hope in God.'[87] But hope feels like a balloon that I accidentally let go of and is rapidly

86 The Black Peppercorns, 'Tumbling Ground' (7th Time Music, 1995).
87 Psalm 42:11.

ascending beyond my reach. All I can do is watch it float away.

And so, instead, I hold the burden inside that kicks and twists in my abdomen like a late-term child. I hold it and I name it. Try to summon the courage to walk all the way into my sadness, into the chaos twisting violently within.

To invoke the Presence of the One into my tiny soul-boat pitching in the storm.

THE INVITATION

Jesus didn't watch and pray for the world from the side lines. He entered into our mess. He joined us in our suffering.

> *During the days of Jesus' life on earth, he offered up prayers and petitions with fervent cries and tears to the one who could save him from death, and he was heard because of his reverent submission. Son though he was, he learned obedience from what he suffered and, once made perfect, he became the source of eternal salvation for all who obey him.*
>
> HEBREWS 5:7–9

His prayer warfare on our behalf was marked by submission and resistance. Submission and obedience to the Father and resistance to the forces of evil. James echoes these movements in his letter: 'Submit yourselves, then, to God. Resist the devil, and he will flee from you' (James 4:7).

1. Have I been playing it safe in prayer? What might it look like for me to, as the writer of Galatians in chapter 6 verse 2 says, 'Carry each other's burdens, and in this way

you will fulfil the law of Christ.'? To wade into the fray. To enter into someone's suffering with them? To pray embedded on the front lines rather than dispassionately from a distance?

2. How is God inviting me to submit to him today? Is there something specific he is asking me to do, or even to stop doing?

3. How is God inviting me to resist the forces of evil in and around me? Might I be able to 'act in the opposite spirit' and return good for evil, a kind word for a curse? Are there systemic forms of evil in our culture and economy that I can abstain from and resist?

Jesus, I'm so deeply grateful that you saw that I was a sheep without a shepherd and had compassion on me.
You drew near and entered into the mess, bore the weight of my suffering.
You carried me, held me close to your heart, and you still do.
Grant me the courage, resilience and endurance needed to enter into the suffering of others.
God of all hope, fill me with joy and peace in believing, that I might abound in hope by the power of your Holy Spirit.

Chapter 36

LIFE IS NOT AN EMERGENCY

Then a great and powerful wind tore the mountains apart
and shattered the rocks before the LORD, but the LORD was
not in the wind. After the wind there was an earthquake,
but the LORD was not in the earthquake.

1 KINGS 19:11B

'You've got to be kidding me!' My head is jangling – the cacophony of fire alarms rattling my brains. Layers of foils float around my face, and the sharp tang of hair colorant catches my nostrils. I'm in the salon at the local shopping centre, covering up my ageing hair with blond-ish highlights. Kirk and I have ongoing hair colour debates. He would like me to go grey gracefully and walk around with hair *au natural*. 'It looks good on *me!*' he says proudly. And it does. He's got a white superman swoosh and salt and peppery stubble beard. I'm holding my ground for now. I don't mind wrinkles. 'You have smiley eyes, mama!' says my daughter. However, I'm still in a pitched battle with age spots and grey hair. Thus, the salon trip.

I look up at the hairstylist, who sets her jaw and increases her pace. Her fingers are flying. 'Do you think we should stop?' I ask. 'I'm comfortable going on if you are.' I have visions of half-highlighted, or worse, over-processed hair burning to a frizzle as I shiver outside, waiting for the all clear. 'I'm good,' she says, glancing up at the salon owner. 'I'll keep going till she tells me to stop.'

'It's the restaurant at the other end of the centre!' one of the hairstylists has gone scouting. 'There's a little smoke down that way, and all kinds of fire engines outside!' Shops begin to close, and flocks of disappointed Saturday shoppers make a beeline for the exits. My stylist's fingers became a blur as she races against time and possible evacuation. She confers with her manager and they make a plan. They close our salon, and all of the hairdressers, myself, and one lady in the middle of a manicure slouch low behind a counter so as to be out of sight from the hallway. Perhaps the firemen won't notice us. All the while the alarms bleat and blare. 'We'll stop if we smell smoke.' says the manager.

In the book, *Don't Sweat the Small Stuff*, by Richard Carlson, one of the chapters is entitled 'Life Isn't an Emergency'.[88] That phrase has become one of my favourite mantras, and for me has become a key to developing resilience. In our intense urban-missions context, situations arise weekly, sometimes even daily, that trigger my adrenaline, my flight or fight response. Whether it's a national issue requiring fervent prayer, bills that are coming due or another neighbouring friend having a health or bedbug infestation crisis, my internal alarms can crowd out other sounds.

'There is no panic in heaven, only plans,' says my friend Denni. I'm learning to dial down my response, hunker down and find the secret place. Learning to just keep 'steady as she goes', one eye on the Boss and awaiting further instruction. At the salon, the alarms are loud but the danger isn't imminent.

---

88 Richard Carlson, *Don't Sweat the Small Stuff: Simple Ways to Keep the Little Things from Taking Over Your Life* (Hodder & Stoughton, 2008).

We were alert but we stayed on course. The enemy's plans to wreck my day and hair were 'foiled'. (Ha! couldn't resist!)

Life is not an emergency.

'We're not the largest House of Prayer in Canada,' I'm leading a workshop for House of Prayer leaders, talking about our work in Hamilton. 'Nor are we the most successful. However, I would argue that we are the most stubborn!' The crowd chuckles. It's a joke, and I usually get a good laugh when I tell it. But I'm also deadly serious. We are battling for the lives and souls of our friends and our communities. And to be honest, often I feel like I've got my hands full just wrestling with my own attitudes and habits! The stakes are high, as is the cost. In this line of work many of us, if we've been at it any time at all, carry battle scars that still ache. But we're resilient, reaching beyond panic and reactivity to receive the plans of heaven.

In preparation for writing this book, I'm at a spiritual memoir writing workshop. 'I want you to write a poem about your spiritual journey,' the teacher says. 'Use some kind of nature metaphor. The wind. A mountain. Whatever comes to mind.'

I open my journal, tap my pen a couple of times on the desk and scrabble the opening refrain that I learned from another writing teacher and which I often write at the top of new writing projects.

Write what you know.
Write what you don't know.
Find your voice.

Hmm, my life as a river? Naw, that's been done to death. An ocean? Hmm. Nope.

A little yellow weed springs up out of my unconscious.

A dandelion?

Hey, why not?

My Life as a Dandelion

Weedy and seedy, that's me.
Not wedding bouquet material
But I adorn the heads of children
As milky fingered
They weave me into a crown
And regally wave to passers-by.
My husband's name is William,
Pronounced 'Vill-helm' if we were properly German – which we're not!
Vill-helm means helm of resolution.
'You're stubborn!' I chastise.
'Not stubborn! Resolute!' He grins.
Resolute. Stubborn.
Like the dandelions proliferating in our backyard.
Mow em down, they spring up again.
Mow em down, they spring up again.
Like the old man in the Monty Python movie,
'I'm not dead yet! Really, I'm feeling quite fine!'
Or the soldier whose opponent systematically hacks off all his limbs.
'It's only a flesh wound!' I cry.
It's only a flesh wound.
Weedy and seedy.
How many of my companions clutch me in their grasp.
Faint of breath but blowing their wishes.

Their dreams and disappointments
Trace curlicues in flight.
They flutter and twirl, land and curl
Their way into the receptive earth.
Don't cry.
It's not dead.
It's a seed.
Watch and wait for the unveiling.
It will spring up again.

THE INVITATION

The ability to subordinate an impulse to a value is the
essence of the proactive person. Reactive people are
driven by feelings, by circumstances, by conditions,
by their environment. Proactive people are driven
by values – carefully thought about, selected and
internalized values. Proactive people are still influenced
by external stimuli, whether physical, social, or
psychological. But their response to the stimuli, conscious
or unconscious, is a value-based choice or response.

STEPHEN R. COVEY[89]

Are we reactive or proactive? Have we cultivated space between stimulus and response? How do we even do that? I would suggest that the spiritual practices of solitude, silence, retreat and journaling can be helpful. Meeting regularly with our spiritual director. Taking time to think about our values and to do the work of orienting our lives around them.

1. Is there a situation in my life right now that feels like an

---

89 Stephen R. Covey, *The 7 Habits of Highly Effective People: Powerful Lessons in Personal Change* (Rosetta Books, 1989), p.79.

emergency? How might I cultivate some space between stimulus and response?

2. Have I taken time to think about and articulate the values and principles that shape and direct my life? It can be helpful to take a half or full day retreat and reflect on what matters most, and how those values can inform my response to urgent and difficult situations.

Jesus, help me to step back, make space and take stock when life feels like a flurry.
Give me your perspective.
I thank you for all the resources of heaven that are available to me and that you strengthen me on the inside by the power of your Spirit.

Chapter 37

ENGLISH GARDEN

*The word of the L*ORD* came to me again: 'What do you see?'*
JEREMIAH 1:13A

'Can you tell us what you see God doing in the prayer movement?' I'm often asked that question. I guess because of all my years with the House of Prayer and also because I visit so many prayer communities in far-flung places. People assume that I must have some sense of what is going on from a God's-eye view. When asked, I nod my head and try to look wise. But inside I have a little panic and pray a frantic prayer, 'OK, God, tell me what to say!'

It has come up so many times that I've decided I should take time to reflect on what I think the prayer movement looks like right now.

It looks like an English Garden – to my eyes, at least.

Not a French one like the ones I've seen outside the Palace of Versailles or the Louvre in Paris. There everything is orderly. Symmetrical. Landscape architected and meticulously groomed.

But an English Garden ... You've seen them, I'm sure. Wild and chaotic – flowers and grasses exploding every which way – multiple layers of colour and texture. There seems to be no rhyme or reason – a garden having a riotous (and righteous!) bad hair day. But what seems to be cacophonic is actually a symphony to the appreciative observer.

I think the prayer movement is like that.

In the early days of the House of Prayer, one of my mentors cautioned me against trying to 'broker' the prayer movement, against being the 'go-to girl', for prayer in our city. I learned right from the get-go that you don't build the prayer movement in a locale. Instead, you discern it. It's a bit like moving into a new home with a big garden in the middle of winter. When things appear to be fallow, it's tempting to dig is all up, start from scratch and try and build and shape it to your preferences and expectations. But how much more miraculous to wait for a season or two to see what springs up out of the ground! In Hamilton we saw all kinds of creative, interesting and beautiful expressions we would never have been able to think up ourselves: prayer walking up and down Barton Street, prayer cycling around the Hamilton harbour, prayer drives around the circumference of the city. Extended times (sometimes up to forty-five consecutive hours!) of worship. Home-grown liturgies from our cafe regulars at 541. Ecumenical prayer for the marginalized in our city, on a park bench shared with a bronze statue of Jesus disguised as a homeless person.

We make a decision in the earliest stages of GOHOP: will we expend all our energy building our own little organization, or instead would we try to shape the larger culture? Would we landscape architect and try and plant all the little flowers into rows, or would we take handfuls of seed and scatter them wherever we go – knowing that some would blow away but that others will take root and grow – sometimes higgledy-piggledy? Will we build an institution, or will we aspire, instead, to be infectious? We choose the latter.

Over the years, we wander from patch to patch, sowing seed, watering and speaking encouragement (plants like it when you talk to them!). My mentor even cautions me against weeding, because some of those weeds are just as pretty as the plants, and who gets to decide what is a weed and what is a plant anyways? I think the designation is somewhat arbitrary, myself. Children know that dandelions are flowers, and clutch them in bouquets and make crowns with them.

Right now, I'm seeing prayer bloom all over the Western world and it's exciting! Multiple and diverse 24-7 prayer movements creating resources for local churches, denominations and national prayer initiatives. Houses of Prayer and experimental new monastic communities popping up across North America, Europe, the UK and beyond. On Pentecost Sunday in Salzburg, Austria, thousands of charismatic Catholic young adults gather to encounter God through his Holy Spirit. The same day, thousands of Anglican Cathedrals across several continents overflow with worshippers asking for God's kingdom to come. Evangelicals and Charismatics are exploring ancient Christian traditions and re-discovering treasures lost during the Reformation. Prayer trucks, pop-up prayer rooms, prayer busses and prayer caravans rolling up to and parking in campuses, festivals and urban alleys. Prayer Spaces in schools across the UK and now growing across Europe, where over a million children have encountered God through creative prayer activities in their classroom environments.

It's a wildly blooming proliferation, with more springing up all the time. The Church and the earth are being beautified right now as we cultivate the presence of God and the flourishing of our cities through prayer.

THE INVITATION

What do we see? What is the view from where we stand? It's so easy when God puts a dream in our hearts, to just put our hand to it right away and begin to work. What might happen if we take the time to pause, to watch and to listen, to see where God is already at work around us and to discern how we might supplement and support with our unique contribution?

1. Is there something in particular that you sense God is asking you to do? Perhaps it's something in your church, like providing more support for single mums in the congregation. Perhaps it is some contribution to your community, like supporting refugees or new arrivals. Maybe it's helping out at your children's school.

    Before you begin anything, take some time to research what is already happening. Do some internet searching. Find out who the key people in your locale are, what is already in place and what the needs are. Build relationships with others with the same passion and vision. Then ask God how you might supplement and support what is already happening.

Jesus, you say that your Father is always working.
Help me to discern the house that you are building, so that I
don't labour in vain.
Grant me humility and surround me with favour.
Help me to find travelling buddies and co-conspirators as we
follow you.
Amen.

Chapter 38

CORACLE

It seemed good to the Holy Spirit and to us …
ACTS 15:28A

I'm surrounded by the illuminated pillars of the upper rooms at St Blasius Church in Salzburg, Austria. I'm visiting my friends in the Loretto movement, 24-7's charismatic Catholic cousin. This is the 'honeybee' part of my work with 24-7. Visiting other Houses of Prayer. Dipping into them to gather sweetness so that I can cross pollinate.

Music swirls and wraps around us, but suddenly the room falls into a hush. It's one of those moments when the air feels weighty, pregnant and expectant.

One by one, and then *en masse*, everyone kneels. Waiting in quiet adoration.

God is here.

I too am kneeling, forehead touching the floor.

I like to get low. I think body matters. Posture matters. Something happens inside us when we kneel, when we lie prostrate before God.

With my body I Thee worship …

I startle as, suddenly, something begins to happen in and to my worshipping body.

Here's where it gets difficult to describe.

It is tempting to avoid recounting mystical experiences. I'm afraid I'll be written off as a weirdo fanatic and thrown in the 'fruits, nuts and flakes' category. But the reality is that, sometimes, unusual things happen in prayer. If nobody talks about them, then no one else knows how to process their own out-of-the-box God moments. We need to de-mystify the mystical and realize that extraordinary things can be an ordinary part of our life in God.

Kneeling there, I have the sense of the molecules of my body shifting and re-arranging. I feel concave – scooped out. I have a sense of movement, like rocking on invisible waters. I'm a … boat? A little boat! The word 'coracle' floats out of my mental mist and bobs up and down on the waters of my consciousness.

I imagine my colleague Peter punning 'I'm a-boat my Father's business.' And I can hear the theme song of one of my favourite childhood Saturday cartoons running through my head, 'Transformers, more than meets the eye …' I've learned from experience that it's good in these instances just to say yes to God and figure it all out later.

The moment passes and I get to my feet – perplexed but with a sense of deep peace.

On the flight home I pull out my new prayer book – a gift from a friend. Cracking it open to a random section, I begin to read. The writer is speaking of Celtic monasticism. Right away the word 'coracle' catches my eye.

'The emphasis upon the cell (the contemplative place of seeking, of withdrawal and being alone before God) and the image of the coracle (with its emphasis upon the apostolic, the missional, the going out and engaging and serving the world) are key elements ...'[90]

90 The Northumbria Community, *Celtic Daily Prayer: Book Two: Further Up and Further In* (William Collins, 2015), p.853.

Coracles. Missional. Going out and engaging the world. Historically, when it was time to start a new prayer community, the Celtic monastics would hop in small boats and push off from shore without sails or oars. Wherever the wind took them became the home of their new House of Prayer.

When I get home I share the story with a couple of friends. The kind of friends who won't write me off as a kook, or at the very least would love me in spite of my kookiness. I also tell Sue, my spiritual director. Sue has a high 'weird-spiritual-thing-that-happened-to-me' threshold and is the queen of killer questions. She knows how to get to the heart of the matter.

'So what is God's invitation in that encounter, d'you think?'

'Well ...' I pause. Two things come to mind.

I'm reminded again that I've often said that God reserves the right to interrupt our lives and change their direction any time he likes. And my mind also flicks back to a conversation I had recently with Pete Grieg. I was visiting him in the UK and we were walking together through a grassy field by the woods – a site we were considering for a new monastic community. A Mother House for the Order of the Mustard Seed and also the 24-7 movement.

'The housing will be up there in the woods. Over here could be your refectory, where we could take meals together,' he sweeps his arm to the right. And over there is where we could build your chapel!' There is a spring in his step. He is full of zip, zing and vision and, with warm hospitality, invites me to live into the dream.

My refectory, My chapel. I smile to myself. *Ha. Good sales pitch, Pete.* 'Sue, you know that Pete has been asking me to move to the UK and work for 24-7 Prayer. Help start new prayer communities. Right off I told him "no". ... I mean,

I've been labouring in prayer for Hamilton the last sixteen years – the ground has my blood, sweat and tears in it. And now, finally, things are starting to shift.'

Things had, indeed, changed dramatically. The Hamilton I began working in sixteen years ago was not the same city we are living in now. We've seen significant developments. Churches working together for a decade and a half, collaborating in all kinds of missional outreach and discipleship. Wrestling through the complexities of finding ways to work together in the midst of divergent theological perspectives. Solid friendships amongst pastors holding the tensions and providing the impetus for collaboration and growth.

The cultural and musical scene in town is flourishing, with Christian artists embedded at the very core, creating all sorts of fantastic art and music. Entrepreneurialism running rampant, again with Christian businesspeople taking the lead in food co-ops, architecture and creative enterprise. Millennials and post millennials swapping the American (Canadian) dream for lifestyles that create all kinds of space for creative kingdom exploration. Christians living together in intentional and unintentional communities. Just within three blocks of our house alone I could name six houses where friends live, pray and play together.

A church plant gets established in our end of town and its congregants buy houses in the area with the purpose of living in missional intention. Missional communities pop up out of the ground like weeds and congregants wade into the messy and complex realities of loving their neighbours in our tumbledown neighbourhood. Getting involved in community development hubs, politics, city development and, of course, the cafe, which is proving to be a hub of kingdom activity.

Folks are deliberately choosing to move into the core of

the city with the view of seeing it transformed spiritually, culturally and economically. A decade and a half of prayers were being answered.

There's a change in spiritual atmosphere. Even my non-charismatic friends can feel it. It's like Hamilton is a pot of water on the stove, with bubbles forming on the bottom. Any time now, it could burst into a rolling boil! All around life and hope are springing up from the ground.

It's just getting good! And there is still so much more work to be done. We can't leave now – can we?

Can we?

'When it's time to start a new prayer community, the monks get into coracles and push off from the shore.' I can't get it out of my head. Kirk and I begin to discuss the prospect of moving. I spend hours exploring the idea in meetings with my mentors and GOHOP Board members. We send emails out to all of my prophetic friends.

'Can you pray for Kirk and I and listen to what God might be saying to us?'

'About what?'

'Not telling. Just listen and let us know what he has to say.'

Prophetic words start to trickle in. Startling in their clarity. Confirmation.

My friend Sara emails me from British Columbia. 'I laugh because after emailing you, I was washing the dishes Sunday night after our community dinner and the Lord spoke to my heart, "*Jill has been asked to move to Europe and offered a position with 24-7.*" That was all he said, but with it came a strong sense that it was good and fitting with the timing of the massive shift in season we are observing globally. I hope this helps. I submit this to you, as my hearing and discerning.'

One day, Kirk and I are looking at Google maps on a big screen. We zoom in on the 'Surrey Hills – Area of Outstanding Natural Beauty' and peruse our possible new British home from above. Out of nowhere, Kirk begins to laugh.

'What are you laughing at?' I look at him.

'Oh nothing.' He's cagey and continues to chuckle.

A week later he comes clean.

'When we were looking at the map, all of a sudden I heard God say "*You know you're going, right?*" I didn't want to tell you right away, but I realize that it's important you know.'

After about a year of discernment with our mentors, family and community, I find myself sitting across from Pete, this time to say yes. 'With all due respect Pete, we're not coming because you asked us, we're coming because Jesus is asking us.' Good enough for him.

Later, I am on a day retreat with Pete and some other friends when I decide to share the whole Jill-morphing-into-a-coracle story. These are risky, vulnerable moments – moments when you put yourself out there then sit back in your chair, exhale the breath you've been holding and await their response. Are they going to think I'm a nutter and regret hiring me?

Pete pulls out his iPad and begins to scroll.

Not the response I was expecting. 'Look here,' he says, 'I'm on Wikipedia. Coracle – in Ireland they call it a *curragh*. It's a Gaelic word. D'you know what it means?'

He looks up at me.

'Little female saint. Little holy one.'

It's one of those moments when God speaks through another. I'm safe and seen. Known, named and blessed. The soul-boat is christened and pushes off from shore.

THE INVITATION

Over the years, my husband and I have learned together to be a community of discernment. We are learning together how to discern the presence and activity of God not only in our ordinary day to day lives, but also to discern God's invitations in our larger decisions.

Ruth Haley Barton, in her Book, *Invitation to Retreat*, outlines some helpful criteria for discernment, both for individuals and couples:

- Direction and Calling: how does this choice fit with the overall direction and calling of God upon our lives?
- Consolation and Desolation: which choice brings the deepest sense of life, inner peace and freedom for love? Does this choice (or some aspect of it) confuse us, drain life from us or leave us feeling disconnected from God, from love, from our most authentic selves?
- Desire: if Jesus were standing before us asking, 'What do you want me to do for you?' how would we respond?
- Scripture: is there a particular Scripture God is bringing to us relative to this choice – especially one that is surprising or unplanned?
- Life of Christ: is this choice consistent with what we know about the mind and heart of Christ and his redemptive purposes in the world?
- Character Growth and Spiritual Formation: where is God most clearly at work in our character and spiritual transformation? Which choice would give God the most opportunity to nurture this growth?
- Love: what does love call for? What would be the most loving choice for ourselves and those around us?[91]

91 Barton, *Invitation to Retreat*, pp.90, 91.

1. Are there any decisions that seem pressing in your life in this season? Identify a particular question for discernment. Then take some time to filter it through the above mentioned criteria. Does the way forward become clearer?

2. In Western individualistic culture, we cling to our autonomy, our 'right' to make decisions for ourselves. What might it look like, in the face of a larger life decision, to create a community of discernment around you – and discern together what God might be up to concerning that decision?

Jesus, I'm thankful that I don't have to face life and all its decisions on my own.
I have your Spirit, your word, your example to guide me, and the community you have given me to accompany me.
Show me your ways.
Teach me your paths.
Give me the courage to say yes.

Chapter 39

EVEN THE SPARROW

Are not two sparrows sold for a penny? Yet not one of them will fall to the ground outside your Father's care.

MATTHEW 10:29

Of all the things I'll miss in Hamilton, Prayer Truck is one of the things I will miss the most. It's in the truck that I most feel like a monastic. Quiet. Receptive. Holding space for God and for others. Expecting the unexpected and delighted (mostly) when it happens. In the truck my life and work distils to its basic essence. I pray and I make friends.

I love the little birds that hop and peck on the pavement outside. We have a bag of birdseed on board and I often throw a handful onto the street, just to see the flurry of feathered activity that ensues. I especially love the babies. They are 'flighted' already but still smallish, dun coloured and fluffy, with little feathers askance on top of their heads. They cheep at their mother, scolding and cajoling with open mouths and fluttering wings until she scoops up some seeds and feeds them.

I contemplate the birds and contemplate the other 'sparrows' that flit about the prayer truck and nest a while inside. There is Aaron, who uses the space as his living room. Often he stretches out for an afternoon on the pillows and reads. Leonard Ravenhill is his favourite. 'The pastor who is not praying is playing,' the words have their own cadence, and Aaron chants them from memory. 'The people who are not praying are straying. We have many organizers, but few agonizers; many players and payers, few pray-ers ...'[92]

And there is Mike. He peers out from under his hoodie with a cheeky smile. Early in the day he drops his gym bag at the truck before he makes his forays into the neighbourhood. Coming back to chill out, he flirts with pretty girls, shadowboxes and freestyles to beats hidden within his earbuds.

Frank is my personal bodyguard. Big, bearded and blustery, he perches on the back bumper of the truck, gleefully passing out ice lollies in the heat. He's got a black eye. 'I'm in all kinds of trouble!' He says with a grin. 'I can't stay out of it – everyone wants to rumble with me!' 'Frank, you know you love it,' I chide. 'Why don't you just take up boxing?'

Many who struggle with their mental health gravitate around us. Some just need company. Others need to talk. Many ask for prayer. Often, agitated ones calm right down, and even quietly weep, as we gather around them to pray. Some sit silently in the truck, eyes closed, breathing deeply like they are oxygen starved. One summer, a young man sleeps on cardboard under the truck at night – I hear his quiet chuckles in the morning when I come to set up. The wanderers come. The persecuted and the lonely. The truck is a sanctuary in the fullest sense of the word.

92 Leonard Ravenhill, *Why Revival Tarries* (Bethany House Publishers, 1959), p.25.

I feel at home amongst the sparrows because I am one myself. There is something in me – something visceral deep inside – that needs to be small, even in the face of expanding influence and responsibility. 'Do not be afraid, little flock, for your Father has been pleased to give you the kingdom.'[93]

A bird in the hand, that's what I am. Often hidden and nested in his palm. I relish the darkness. The containment. 'You hem me in behind and before, … you lay your hand upon me.'[94]

When Hannah is a baby, we swaddle her – wind her own little arms around herself when she's flailing and wailing. Wrap her tight. We call her the baby burrito. It stills and quiets her soul.

Sometimes I'm still and quiet, hidden in his hand. Other times he holds me aloft and I cheep and flap a bit. I know he likes my little song. He said so in Song of Solomon: 'show me your face, let me hear your voice,' he says, 'for your voice is sweet, and your face is lovely.'[95]

It's a sleepy day in the truck. I am tucked away in the back, praying. The heat is having its soporific effect and realize that my praying is turning into nodding (and possibly drooling). To help me stay awake, I grab my guitar and perch on the lip of the truck. I noodle on the strings. Hum a bit. Then begin to write.

Often inarticulate prayers roll around my insides, and slowly – sometimes very slowly – they clothe themselves with words. I feel the weight of them, and ponderous and

93 Luke 12:32.
94 Psalm 139:5.
95 Song of Songs 2:14.

wobbly, I carry them around inside me for days, sometimes weeks before bringing them to birth. This one has been on its way for a while and I am overdue.

Even the sparrows find a place near your altar,
Even the wanderers who roam.
Even the fatherless are embraced by the Father
We're coming home, coming home.
The table is set
We will sit down
Surrounded by friends
And feast ...

The next day, one of our neighbourhood friends stops by for a chat. We've come to know him because he sleeps on a flattened cardboard box on the pavement across the street.

'Look!' he says, lifting his baseball cap. Under the cap, on top of his head, perches a tuft of feathers topped with calm blinking eyes. 'I've impressed a baby bird! Isn't he cute?' He reaches up and the bird calmly steps onto his fingers.

In Alcoholics Anonymous they say that co-incidence is God's way of being anonymous. I think he blew his cover on that one.

Even the sparrows find a home, a place near your altar.

It's autumn. We're wandering through the German forest, just outside the village. The glory is passing, and the ground is a splendid carpet of dying leaves. 'It's here, or maybe, I think it's over here.'

Some friends and I are on another reconnaissance mission to Herrnhut – checking out possible facilities in preparation to bring members of the Order of the Mustard

Seed on pilgrimage. God orchestrates a meeting with a zealous young church history buff with an encyclopaedic knowledge of all things Zinzendorf and Moravian. We've been hiking all afternoon as he takes us to various hidden dells and nooks in the woods where, hundreds of years ago, the Moravians met for prayer and study. We're moving towards our final destination, a monument erected deep in the forest.

'The Moravians had been persecuted literally for generations,' our guide says. 'Hundreds of years. They were wandering, looking for a home. In Herrnhut, Zinzendorf permitted religious liberty. The Moravians knew that for the first time in centuries, they could finally settle and worship in freedom. So they put up a monument to celebrate. Ah, here it is!'

We veer to the left and, sure enough, a large stone structure looms through the trees. The words inscribed on it say:

On 17 June, 1722
At this location
For the building
Of Herrnhut
The first tree
Was felled by Christian David
Psalm 84:4

'The German Bible numbers the Psalms differently than the English one,' our guide comments. 'The verse is actually Psalm 84:3 in the English Bible.'

Even the sparrow has found a home,
*   and the swallow a nest for herself,*
*   where she may have her young –*
a place near your altar,
*   LORD Almighty, my King and my God.*

Even the sparrow ... You coulda knocked me over with a feather! My companions look at me and grin and I try not to laugh out loud as deep joy overtakes me like a sudden cloudburst.

The Prayer Truck, indeed the whole myriad of expressions of our House of Prayer, from community dinners and houses, to interdenominational internships, from social enterprise cafes to basement prayer rooms, they are the nest. A place by his altar. A sanctuary. It is our privilege to weave it.

THE INVITATION

The righteous will flourish like a palm tree,
they will grow like a cedar of Lebanon;
planted in the house of the LORD,
they will flourish in the courts of our God.

PSALM 92:12–13

A House of Prayer is a people. A community gathered around the person of Jesus, who give themselves generously to him through prayer, mission and justice.

A House of Prayer is a laboratory. A place of exploration and experimentation. Mike Bickle says 'the Prayer Room is a classroom.'

A House of Prayer is a greenhouse. It's a sheltered place that offers conditions conducive for optimal spiritual growth and formation.

A House of Prayer is a womb. Where God's dreams are incubated and cultivated. Where we are enlarged in the waiting. Where we labour and travail and birth God's purposes.

A House of prayer is a nest. Where sparrows can come, be sheltered, fed and nurtured. Learn to sing and to fly.

1. Which of these metaphors most describes where and how God is at work in your life? How has God been building your own life, your own soul into a House of Prayer?
2. How do these metaphors apply to and describe your spiritual community? How is God building you together into a House of Prayer?

Jesus, I come to you, the living Stone.
I delight in the fact that we, like living stones, are being built
into a spiritual house to be a holy priesthood, offering spiritual
sacrifices acceptable to God through Jesus Christ.
Come and build your house.

Chapter 40

FIND YOURSELF IN THE STORY

> *Yes Lord*
> *I believe.*
> *Yes Lord*
> *I receive*
> *All that You have promised.*
> *Your Spirit hovers*
> *Over my chaos*
> *Uncertainty and questions.*
> *Light beams into the deep.*
> *A gift is given.*
> *Pregnant with Divine intention*
> *I bear it.*
> *I bear You.*
> *Senses attuned*
> *To hear it.*
> *I hear you.*
> *Body breathless, poised and waiting*
> *To feel Your movement within.*
> *Internal*
> *Eternal Dance.*

You spin like the galaxy.
I grow heavy with expectation.
The weight of Glory
Slows me.
Show me
All that You have promised.

JILL WEBER

I think about Mary. A lot. Of all the characters in the biblical drama, she's the one I relate to the most. I find myself in her story and I try to crawl inside her skin.

I can picture the scene. It's dark and she's in her mid-teens. Awake in the stable – listening in the musky silence to the snort and breath of her furry roommates. All she can see around her are their silhouettes – silent sentinels in the dusk. She's exhausted. Achy and tender from the exertion of childbirth. Nestled in a corner, she's tucked beside the trough with its precious contents. She's sequestered away in the secret place. Hidden from the public eye.

Except, somehow, the shepherds found them. Her unkempt guests have just left. An unlikely flock of ragged and wild-eyed worshippers, they had fluttered about the manger, eager to see, longing to touch. Raving about angels, carrying prophetic proclamations that strangely resonate with the message she's pondering in her own heart.

Her eyes scan her unlikely accommodations and she smiles wryly. Not what she expected. But the whole journey's been unexpected, hasn't it?

It began with divine interruption. Risky invitation.

Will you say yes? Not gonna lie – it's gonna to be costly. Both to you and to your family. Will you carry the dream of God?

She is the sparrow and her body is host and nest and altar.

Nine months later she looks in wonder at God's word to her enfleshed – watching his little chest rise and fall underneath swaddled cloth.

Wouldya look at that. A baby. A real live flesh-and-blood baby.

She reaches down to smooth the tousled hair on his forehead.

Perfect in every way.

I share Mary's consternation when, twelve years later, on her journey home from Jerusalem, she realizes she left Jesus behind three days ago and didn't even notice! Yup. Been there. Done that. Off on my merry old way, oblivious to the fact that I've left God behind. Then comes the moment of realization, the quick 'about face' and frantic scramble to find him again.

I share Mary's hope and trepidation as she approaches Elizabeth and Zechariah's home, leaning into community in a time of vulnerability. And I share her surprise and delight when, in the midst of that community, she is received. Seen. Named and blessed. I join in with the worship that bursts forth from her like a champagne fizzing. *Our souls doth glorify the Lord ...*[96]

And I feel like Mary at the wedding of Cana. If you ask me, she comes across as a bit bossy in this particular story.

96 Luke 1:46.

'They have no wine,' she tells her son. It's her first recorded act of intercession, asking Jesus to exert his power on behalf of others. At first he seems disinclined to respond, but she persists, telling the servants, 'Whatever he tells you to do, do it.'[97]

Whatever he tells you ...

Mary hears and recognizes God's voice. In the Scriptures. Through angelic visitation. In the sanctuary of her own soul. In day-to-day life with him. In the midst of community.

My life message, if I had one, would be Mary's exhortation. 'Whatever he tells you, do it ...'

These words aren't spoken lightly, but with the authority that comes from hard-won experience. She knows obedience is costly. She's got stretch marks etched on her body and the scars of Egyptian exile in her heart. And she carries within her the prophecy of more wounds to come: 'And a sword will pierce your soul too ...'[98]

I knock at the back door of the Mother House. Sister Ann is waiting, beaming a welcome, and shuffles over to the door to let me in.

I've been hanging out with the Sisters for a few years now. Sue, my spiritual director, affectionately calls them 'the Pistols', and was eager for us to meet. There are two kinds of nuns. Cloistered nuns, those who are tucked away behind closed walls and who give themselves primarily to a lifestyle of prayer. And then there are what they call Apostolic nuns. I call them the 'getting things done nuns'. They too are anchored in rhythms of prayer, but they also serve in

97 John 2:5.
98 Luke 2:35.

other capacities: as nurses, teachers, missionaries and the like. Sister Ann is a 'getting things done nun', and at 85 she's still active in her community, teaching contemplative prayer in thirty-five Catholic schools across Hamilton and working with refugees.

Ann threads her arm through mine and gives my hand a pat. 'I love it when the young people come and visit,' she says with a smile. I chuckle to myself. Forty-seven years old and I'm a 'young person'. Guess it's all about perspective, eh?

Ann and the members of her community have given me a lot of perspective. Some of them have been in full time ministry since they entered their Order in their late teens – so that is seventy years – a lifetime of faithful obedience to Jesus. They have risen to the height of their powers – some of them serving as hospital administrators, school principals and Mother Superiors to their community – and then as they aged, gear back to 'lesser' roles. Their vocation is not their career. Their vocation is Jesus. And the different jobs and roles along the way are simply assignments, one not necessarily more important than the other. Each assignment is merely an opportunity for them to say yes to him.

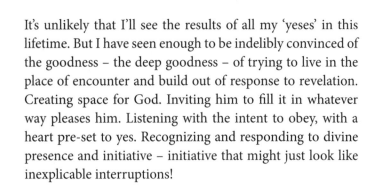

It's unlikely that I'll see the results of all my 'yeses' in this lifetime. But I have seen enough to be indelibly convinced of the goodness – the deep goodness – of trying to live in the place of encounter and build out of response to revelation. Creating space for God. Inviting him to fill it in whatever way pleases him. Listening with the intent to obey, with a heart pre-set to yes. Recognizing and responding to divine presence and initiative – initiative that might just look like inexplicable interruptions!

'Whatever he tells you to do, do it.'

Just say yes. Put yourself in that path of oncoming grace. When you do it, expect the unexpected!

THE INVITATION

My modus operandi for the last thirty or so years has been, as much as possible, to:

- create space for God,
- ask him to fill it in a way that pleases him,
- listen with the intent to obey, confident in his good leadership,
- respond to divine invitations and interruptions.

1. How can you create space in your life? Perhaps that is practising a weekly Sabbath, or regular retreats. Perhaps that is leaving margin in your daytimes. Maybe taking data apps off your phone to give you space from electronic white noise.

2. What are your barriers to asking God to come and fill that space in a way that pleases him? Sometimes we don't trust his goodness or his leadership. Other times we have unhealthy attachments to our own plans, goals and ideals for our lives. Often we don't know how to listen and we aren't sure it's his voice we are hearing. Be honest with God about what hinders your ability to listen with the intent to obey and to respond in confidence to his good leadership.

3. A large percentage of Jesus' ministry was comprised of his response to interruptions in his schedule. How open are you to interruption? What might happen if we responded with curiosity to interruption, looking to see what divine invitation might be embedded in it?

4. Where do you find yourself in the biblical story? Whose life in the Scriptures has a life whose overarching themes, overarching narrative or journey parallels yours? Don't try to figure it out, necessarily. Just take some time to ponder the question and ask God to reveal it to you. It might be that a specific story or instance speaks to a particular experience or season in your life. Or there might be a biblical character whose story speaks to your own.

I want to finish not with my own prayer, but a beautiful spoken-word piece of surrender and commitment written by my friend Chris.

Now how about the beauty in the suffering,
We all know that it's rough and sometimes we have too
much of it
And when the goings gets tough we start to crumble
But the secret to our strength is knowing that we won't
put up with it
Constant thoughts keep haunting me
Lock me up and off the key
Often we unlock decent then we be like we forgot that
God could free
See God sees things in us we do not see – what we call
weakness he calls strong
And that's beyond me
Why is everything obsolete?
When we share our thoughts we make sure they're
always coffin deep

Beauty to me is an excuse to be free
It's how we move to a groove as if it's all that we breathe
It's like the dirt surrounding flowers how it nurtures the
seeds
It's how we sit and talk for hours with the person that
we believe will sleep by our dreams Redeemed by vows
that keep us worthy of the love that they bring
Even things that come to hurt me
Suffering can be a good thing
Memories act as a lesson for the blessings of mercy
A message for pedestrians that are thirsty
I'm guessing our reflection looks the same if we look in
the right direction
It hurts me to say that we're always second guessing
But I guess that's the beauty in the question
Knowing we're all the same but making no connections
We're growing apart today yet hoping to see a
resurrection
And as we conquer the pain we can develop awesome
friendship
'Cause the impossible has ended.

2015 CHRIS MCGILLIVARY

BIBLIOGRAPHY AND RESOURCES

I am keenly aware that we've covered a lot of ground together in this book. I've only given a taster, an appetizer, really. For those of you who are hungry for more, here is some additional reading that I recommend:

IGNATIAN SPIRITUALITY

Thomas H. Green, S.J., *A Vacation with the Lord* (Ave Maria Press, 1986)

Margaret Silf, *Inner Compass: An Invitation to Ignatian Spirituality* (Loyola Press, 1999)

INTENTIONAL COMMUNITY

Dietrich Bonhoeffer, *Life Together* (Harper, 2008)

David Janzen, *The Intentional Christian Community Handbook: For Idealists, Hypocrites, and Wannabe Disciples of Jesus* (Paraclete Press, 2012)

Jean Vanier, *Community and Growth* (Paulist Press, 1989)

LEADERSHIP

Robert Clinton, *The Making of a Leader: Recognizing the Lessons and Stages of Leadership Development* (NavPress, 2012)

Ruth Haley Barton, *Pursuing God's Will Together: A Discernment Practice for Leadership Groups* (InterVarsity

Press, 2012)

Ruth Haley Barton, *Strengthening the Soul of Your Leadership: Strengthening the Souls of Your Leadership* (InterVarsity Press, 2008)

NEW MONASTICISM

Andy Freeman and Pete Greig, *Punk Monk: New Monasticism and the Ancient Art of Breathing* (Regal Books, 2007)

Ian Mobsby and Mark Berry, *A New Monastic Handbook: From Vision to Practice* (Canterbury Press, 2014)

Jonathan Wilson-Hartgrove, *New Monasticism: What it Has to Say to Today's Church* (Brazos Press, 2008)

ORDER OF THE MUSTARD SEED AND 24-7 PRAYER

Phil Anderson, *The Lord of the Ring: A journey in search of Count Zinzendorf (Muddy Pearl 2020)*

Pete Greig, *Dirty Glory: Go Where Your Best Prayers Take You* (Hodder and Stoughton, 2018)

Pete Greig, *Red Moon Rising: How 24-7 Prayer is Awakening a Generation* (David C. Cook, 2015)

Pete Greig, *The Vision and the Vow*, (Survivor/Kingsway Communications Ltd, 2004)

PRAYER

Catherine Doherty, *Poustinia: Encountering God in Silence, Solitude and Prayer* (Madonna House Publications, 2000)

Richard Foster, *Prayer: Finding the Heart's True Home* (Hodder and Stoughton, 2008)

Pete Greig, *How to Pray: A Simple Guide for Normal People* (Hodder and Stoughton, 2019)

Thomas Merton, *New Seeds of Contemplation* (Abbey of Gethsemani, Inc., 1961)

RETREAT AND SABBATH

Ruth Haley Barton, *Invitation to Retreat* (InterVarsity Press, 2018)

Ruth Haley Barton, *Invitation to Solitude and Silence* (InterVarsity Press, 2011)

John Mark Comer, *The Ruthless Elimination of Hurry: How to Stay Emotionally Healthy and Spiritually Alive in the Chaos of the Modern Word* (Waterbrook Press, 2019)

Wayne Muller, *Sabbath: Finding Rest, Renewal, and Delight in Our Busy Lives* (Bantam, 2000)

SPIRITUAL DISCIPLINES

Richard Foster, *Celebration of Discipline* (Harper Collins, 1978)

Eugene Peterson, *Eat This Book: A Conversation in the Art of Spiritual Reading* (Hodder and Stoughton, 2008)

Christine Pohl, *Making Room: Recovering Hospitality as a Christian Tradition* (Willian B. Eerdmans Publishing, 1999)

Michael Yankoski, *The Sacred Year; Mapping the Soulscape of Spiritual Practice – How Contemplating Apples, Living in a Cave and Befriending a Dying Woman Revived My Life* (Thomas Nelson, 2014)

SPIRITUAL DIRECTION

David G. Benner, *Sacred Companions: The Gift of Spiritual Friendship and Direction* (InterVarsity Press, 2002)

Rose Mary Dougherty, S.S.N.D, *Group Spiritual Direction: Community for Discernment* (Paulist Press, 1995)

Margaret Guenther, *Holy Listening: The Art of Spiritual Direction* (Darton, Longman & Todd Ltd, 1992)

SPIRITUAL FORMATION

Ruth Haley Barton, *Sacred Rhythms: Arranging Our Lives for Spiritual Transformation* (InterVarsity Press, 2006)

David G. Benner, *Surrender to Love: Discovering the Heart of Christian Spirituality* (InterVarsity Press, 2015)

Robert M. Mulholland, *Invitation to a Journey: A Road Map for Spiritual Formation* (InterVarsity Press, 1993)

Dallas Willard, *Spirit of the Disciplines: Understanding How God Changes Lives* (Harper, 1991)

DARK NIGHT OF THE SOUL

Thomas H. Green, S.J., *When the Well Runs Dry: Prayer Beyond the Beginnings* (Ave Maria Press, 2007)

Kathleen Norris, *Acedia & Me: A Marriage, Monks, and a Writer's Life* (Riverhead Books, 2010)

Gerald May, *The Dark Night of the Soul* (Bravo Ltd, 2013)

Mark Scandrette, *Practicing the Way of Jesus: Life Together in the Kingdom of Love* (InterVarsity Press, 2011)

Alain Emerson, *Luminous Dark* (Muddy Pearl, 2017)

MORE FROM THE
24-7 PRAYER COMMUNITY

www.orderofthemustardseed.com

The Order of the Mustard Seed is a lay, ecumenical religious order that seeks
to inspire and equip disciples of Jesus to be true to Christ, kind to people, and
take the gospel to the nations.

www.24-7prayer.com

24-7 Prayer is a movement dedicated to reviving the church and rewiring
the culture through non-stop night and day prayer. It started in 1999 when
a simple, student-led prayer vigil suddenly went viral. Today, 24-7 Prayer
is an international, interdenominational movement of prayer, mission and
justice; a non-stop prayer meeting that has continued for every minute of this
century so far, in over half the countries on Earth.

Prayer Spaces
in **Schools**

www.prayerspacesinschools.com

Prayer Spaces in Schools is a resource hub for the growing network of
practitioners running prayer or reflective spaces in schools. These prayer
spaces are rooted in broadly Christian traditions of prayer – in the teachings
and the ministry, the life and example of Jesus – while allowing children and
young people to respond individually and draw their own conclusions.

Dragon and Ceremony
God's Many Forms

3

Ichimei Tsukushi

ILLUSTRATION BY

Enji

©Enji

CONTENTS

DRAGON AND CEREMONY
Presented by Ichimei Tsukushi

©Enji

Ix

Apprentice wandmaker.

Yuui

Girl with the dragon

vand.

©Enji

Dragon and Ceremony

God's
Many Forms

3

Ichimei Tsukushi

ILLUSTRATION BY **Enji**

YEN
ON

New York

DRAGON AND CEREMONY
ICHIMEI TSUKUSHI

Translation by Jordan Taylor
Cover art by Enji

RYU TO SAIREI Vol. 3 -KAMI NO SHOKEITAI-
Copyright © 2020 Ichimei Tsukushi
Illustrations copyright © 2020 Enji
All rights reserved.
Original Japanese edition published in 2020 by SB Creative Corp.

This English edition is published by arrangement with SB Creative Corp., Tokyo in care of Tuttle-Mori Agency, Inc., Tokyo.

English translation © 2022 by Yen Press, LLC

Yen On
150 West 30th Street, 19th Floor
New York, NY 10001

Visit us at yenpress.com
facebook.com/yenpress
twitter.com/yenpress
yenpress.tumblr.com
instagram.com/yenpress

First Yen On Edition: September 2022
Edited by Yen On Editorial: Maya Deutsch
Designed by Yen Press Design: Andy Swist

Yen On is an imprint of Yen Press, LLC.
The Yen On name and logo are trademarks of Yen Press, LLC.

Library of Congress Cataloging-in-Publication Data
Names: Tsukushi, Ichimei, author. | Enji, illustrator. | Taylor, Jordan (Translator), translator.
Title: Dragon and ceremony / Ichimei Tsukushi ; illustration by Enji ; translation by Jordan Taylor.
Other titles: Ryū to sairei. English
Description: First Yen On edition. | New York, NY : Yen On, 2022-
Identifiers: LCCN 2021046140 | ISBN 9781975336936 (v. 1 ; trade paperback.) | ISBN 9781975336950 (v. 2 ; trade paperback) | ISBN 9781975336974 (v. 3 ; trade paperback)
Subjects: CYAC: Fantasy. | Dragons—Fiction. | Quests (Expeditions)—Fiction. | LCGFT: Fantasy fiction. | Light novels.
Classification: LCC PZ7.1.T7826 Dr 2022 | DDC [Fic]—dc23
LC record available at https://lccn.loc.gov/2021046140

ISBNs: 978-1-9753-3697-4 (paperback)
        978-1-9753-3698-1 (ebook)

10 9 8 7 6 5 4 3 2 1

LSC-C

Printed in the United States of America

In a town near the eastern border of the kingdom, a girl waited. The town was called Estosha, and the girl was called Riess. Ix was familiar with the village, but this was his first time meeting her. But somehow, she'd known his name.

Cloaked in the cold air, everything in the area lost its color, as though it were the backdrop to a dream. Winter was always like this. People would hole themselves up in their homes, and sleep would descend upon the town. Just about everything would come to a stop as the snowflakes flitted through the air. It would stay that way until the snow melted.

There weren't any passengers in the carriage besides Ix. The depressed-looking coachman told him it would be the last journey of the year as he handed him his luggage.

As Ix disembarked into the station, which was already shutting down for the end of the year, he saw someone sitting in a chair by the wall. Her back was perfectly straight, and her eyes were glassy and vacant. Her soft, light-colored hair stood out against her navy-blue clothing. As he moved closer, she turned to face him. This was Riess.

"Welcome to the City of God," she said in a tone that hardly suited a child not even ten years old.

"The City of God?" he asked back, his head tilted.

"Yes. Our community is closest to God."

"Sorry, I don't know much about Marayism."

"This is your first time visiting, right?" She trained her unfocused eyes on him. "Coming here is every wand craftsman's dream."

"I'm no craftsman, just an apprentice."

"But you came here to make wands."

"That's true, but..."

"Then you must know about the legend of Rednoff. Did you bring your Declaration of Equivalency?" Riess tilted her head slightly before clasping her hands in front of her chest. "Never mind. I'm sorry. I just wanted to talk to you a bit. I'll show you the way. Would you mind chatting while we walk?"

"There was a map included with the letter. I can go alone."

"But you'll get lost on your own. This town is very complicated. The other person got here a long time ago, so I'd feel bad making them wait in the cold."

"Aren't you chilly, Riess?"

Though the girl was wearing a few layers, she didn't have a coat on. Ix wondered if the frigid winds blowing through here every now and then were too much for her.

"Yeah. I'm not feeling so good, either," she said, narrowing her eyes as if from a bright light, despite the fact that the sky was still covered behind a layer of gray clouds. "Can I get in your coat?"

The girl didn't wait for a response before she moved toward him, wrapped the bottom flaps of his coat around herself, and disappeared beneath them.

Thinking it would be a pain to resist now, Ix didn't protest when she told him to move, though it was tricky adjusting his stride to hers.

Estosha's streets were just as complex as Riess had claimed. The roads twisted and curved, so you couldn't tell where they led. Ix would have ended up walking in circles had he gone off alone.

"It's like this because we're close to the border," Riess told him. "They built the city this way on purpose, to confuse invaders if they get inside."

"What's the point of making it so bewildering? They should strengthen the outer defenses instead," replied Ix.

"They couldn't improve the ramparts or the wand wall any more than they already had, so they turned to the interior. Besides, people get used to things being a little messy. No one who lives here gets lost."

"Have you ever been invaded?"

"Thankfully, no one's made it inside." Ix could feel her shaking her head under his jacket. "But what's aboveground doesn't matter. The heart of defense is below."

"Below?" She must have meant underground.

"I doubt anyone remembers, but that's how it was originally."

Ix couldn't help glancing at the pavement, but it was solidly built and didn't look like it was in danger of collapsing anytime soon.

Riess had told him she wanted to talk, but it seemed like she was more interested in telling him idle gossip than asking him anything. The few people who passed them on the street gave Ix suspicious looks as he addressed his coat.

"Thinking about it," started Ix, suddenly realizing something and taking his turn to speak, "you mentioned another person earlier. Does that mean they only called two people?"

"No, there are three in total, including you. I said 'the other person' because they're the other apprentice," she replied evenly. "They should have a Declaration of Equivalency, too."

In accordance with kingdom law, only those who achieved the title of craftsman were permitted to make wands. However, it wasn't realistic for this limited number of people to churn out every single wand, which was why shops off-loaded some of the work onto apprentices. This was allowed because a wand created under the supervision of a craftsman was considered the same as having been crafted by the craftsman themselves.

There were a few rare instances, however, when apprentices would carry something called a Declaration of Equivalency to make wands outside of their instructor's shop. It was a letter stating that the craftsman and apprentice were one and the same. That being said, these declarations were few and far between because they made the craftsman liable for whomever they gave them to. In practice, they were used in only the rarest of circumstances, such as grave emergencies or as a means of testing apprentices looking to become independent.

"There'll be one craftsman and two apprentices? Hope it goes well...," murmured Ix.

"Your master must have been busy," said Riess.

"No, she's just the worst shut-in you've ever seen. And she's not my master; she just studied under the same teacher I did. I also don't have any plans to go independent."

"So she really trusts you?"

"No...," Ix responded. He thought back to Morna as she'd scribbled out the declaration. "I imagine she just didn't put much thought into it. Or she didn't want to go outside. Could be both."

The person who'd gotten here before him was probably close to going independent. Ix, on the other hand, would have nowhere to go if he set off by himself, and he didn't have the funds to start a shop. He was lacking on all fronts. And without a store of his own, he wouldn't be allowed to work independently.

There came the sudden ringing of bells.

The high-pitched sound rang out multiple times, echoing throughout the town. It was so loud that, for a moment, it was all Ix could hear. Oddly, though, it didn't grate on his ears. Looking in the direction of the noise, he saw a bell tower peeking out from among the houses.

"That's Estosha Chapel," stated Riess. "And that was the noon bell. You're just passing through now, but you should take a look inside when you have time. It vies for the position of first- or second-most historical building in the kingdom."

"First or second?"

"Something about that interest you?"

"I heard the same thing said about the capital's cathedral."

"Exactly. It's vying with the capital's cathedral."

Maybe it was just because the town was so old, but it seemed like Riess had a new tale or historical fact to rattle off every time they turned a corner. Her stories ranged from what sounded like real history to entirely unfounded rumor.

"But…," said Ix, tilting his head. They were passing through a square where a knight had supposedly ended his hundred-person killing spree by slaying his lover. "You're telling me way too many things for this trip to be accidental."

"Maybe."

"Did you intentionally take me this way?"

"It was just a little detour," she said, unconcerned. "I'm sorry. I just wanted to walk with you a bit, even though I knew it would cause you trouble."

"And what about the other person who arrived earlier?"

"I'll apologize. But I suspect they'll be forgiving. I am a child, after all."

"Not if you put it like that, they won't."

"You think? If that happens, you can cover for me," Riess said lightly. Ix couldn't tell if she was joking or not. "All right, now I'll tell you what I've been saving for last."

"You still have more?" asked Ix, slightly exasperated.

"I'm at the age when I want to talk about the things I remember. I won't take you on any more detours once it's over."

"I guess it's fine, then," said Ix with a shrug.

"Why do you think people worship the sky?"

"Sky? …Oh, you're talking about Heaven's Worship?" Ix remembered the Marayist festival. "That's the one where they all gather at the end of the year and gaze at the sky, right…? It's held around this time of year, too, now that you mention it."

"It's curious," Riess remarked as if she was talking to herself. "The only thing in the sky, besides the moon, are the stars above it. It's not like God lives up there."

"Is that all you wanted to tell me? That you think the event is weird?"

"No, I think it's a very beautiful ritual."

"...So what's this thing you saved for last, then?"

"You are impatient, huh?"

"I'm at the age when I can't put up with anything."

Riess nodded in resignation.

"During Heaven's Worship, everyone in Estosha wishes on the stars. Since this town is the closest to God...," She pointed a slender finger toward the sky. "...our voices carry from the Estosha Chapel up to the sky. That's why there are so many stories in this city. Everyone talks because they want God to hear them. They tell all sorts of silly, pointless tales. But they shine like stars, so God draws near to listen. People say we're close to God, but it's actually the opposite—it's God who gets close to us."

"Is that what you were waiting to tell me?"

"...Will you come to Heaven's Worship with me?" inquired Riess, looking up at Ix from inside his coat. She sounded a little unsure of herself for a change. But a moment later, she returned to her normal tone and said, "Ah, I got nervous. I was saving the invitation for last. So how about it?"

He wasn't so sure what to think about that last part.

"You're jumping the gun asking me to come with you, Riess," he replied. "How do you even know who I am? Why are you inviting me to the festival? I don't know how to reply to an invitation like that."

"Don't worry, I'm done talking now." She closed her eyes for a moment. "What do you want to wish for on the stars? Think it over."

At that, she fell silent.

Just as Riess said, the path forward was completely straight. In fact, they were outside the city limits. Apparently, the city only had walls on the side that faced the border to the neighboring nation. The other sides had fences only to prevent animals coming near. The area probably had hardly any magic beasts living in it, either, which was why Estosha had been able to expand over the years.

At the base of a far-off hill was a small forest, which surrounded a stone building. Though the white walls of the structure were conspicuous, it still looked oddly harmonious against the natural backdrop. Ix could easily guess it was the Lus Monastery. That was where his most recent request had come from and where he would be working over the winter.

He noticed a fine sweat on his palms. He was nervous.

Riess's words ran through his mind over and over: *the City of God*.

She was right; this city wasn't just significant to the Marayists. The names Estosha and Rednoff had special meaning to wandmakers as well.

Rednoff was the legendary craftsman who'd developed the fundamentals for crafting man-made wands. When the world finally acknowledged the value of his creations, Rednoff's skills had reached their peak. It was then that he came to this town, Estosha, and was never heard from again. Though there were a number of stories about his fate, ranging from him committing suicide to secretly slipping away and leading a life of solitude, there was not a single clue as to his whereabouts. There was a grave for him in the capital, but the casket was empty.

There was, however, a legend passed down among wandmakers, told as though it was true:

Rednoff had crafted the ultimate wand in this town.

That's what they said.

No one knew who'd first told the story or if they had any proof. It was obviously just a tall tale. But the reason this story was told over and over was because it held some sort of irresistible magic of its own.

The ultimate wand. There wasn't a single craftsman who didn't dream of it, who didn't aspire to forge it.

That's why they worked day in and day out to improve their craft, why they constantly thought: *Would the ultimate magic catalyst be a wand? Or a staff? What wood would it take? What material would comprise its core? What adoption method would you use to create it? What kind of person could make a wand like that? Could that person be...me?*

People had high hopes that Munzil, Ix's master, would forge that fabled catalyst. But in the end, he'd only ever made "excellent wands," never "the ultimate wand."

There was an alluring quality to a story that said that, while all these wandmakers may come and go, Rednoff, their inspiration and genesis, had actually already achieved the impossible. It also provided a potential explanation as to his disappearance. Needless to say, a craftsman who made the ultimate wand would no longer have a reason to go on living.

In other words, Rednoff was to wandmakers as God was to ordinary people, which was why they, too, considered Estosha significant. There were even a few ludicrous stories about the ultimate wand being hidden somewhere in the city or a neighboring country stealing it during a war.

Ix obviously didn't put stock in those tales. Rednoff had accomplished great things, but his time had long passed. These days, his crafting techniques were quite inefficient. It had taken years of improvements upon his methods to birth modern wands; there was no way Rednoff could have been just a single step away from producing the ultimate catalyst. Assuming such an item even existed.

Still, Ix was a member of the wandmaker community, if only barely, so he was aware of Estosha and even felt drawn to the place. Hearing the history surrounding the town had only amplified those feelings.

Just as he decided to thank Riess for showing him around, Ix realized she had disappeared at some point. It seemed he'd been too lost in thought to notice when she'd slipped out from under his jacket.

The monastery had looked far away when he exited the city, but the walk actually wasn't that bad. The sheer size of the building, along with the abnormal quiet of the place, took Ix aback as he approached. He'd heard a lot of people lived here, but the only thing he could make out now was the rustle of the wind in the trees. There were no sounds of life.

Save for an abrupt shout.

"Ah, you're here! Finally!"

Someone stood by the monastery's entrance, one hand on their hip and the other pointing at Ix, who walked up to respond.

"Seriously! Give some consideration to the person you made wait this whole time!" The person's almond-shaped red eyes angled even more as they continued to rattle on. They had sky-blue hair. "I was so excited about another apprentice coming, but you just never showed. Were you not looking forward to meeting another apprentice at all?!"

"Sorry, were you cold?" Ix managed to say, despite being overwhelmed by the person's force.

"Cold? What the hell are you on about? You made me wait! Who cares about the weather?! I was thinking we could have lunch together, but you never came, so I had to eat alone, which makes my stomach hurt. And when you *still* didn't turn up after that, I got worried that you'd been in an accident. The waiting was the worst part!"

"...Oh."

"Maybe you should actually think about what you've done. Eh, whatever. I'm Shuno. Nice to meet you." They held out their right hand, still in its thick glove.

"Yeah. I'm—"

"Ix."

"Huh?"

In the brief moment Ix was thrown off, Shuno reached up and brushed both of his shoulders.

"You okay? You're not cold?" they asked, their expression serious as they brought their face closer. "This is what happens when you stop to smell the roses every five steps."

Ix shook his head, not understanding what they were saying at all. That's when he saw the snow—his namesake—piled on his shoulders. He glanced around, wondering when it had started to fall. The fluttering white flakes that filled his vision looked like shuno flowers—their namesake—dancing on the wind.

1

Bells rang in two locations: from inside the monastery and from the bell tower in the town of Estosha. They were announcing the time.

Once the ringing stopped, the sound of work could be heard throughout the monastery. Wood being cut, liquid being stirred, heavy objects being dragged. But what you couldn't hear was conversation. The monk showing them the way didn't say a single word, nor did his steps make any noise as he continued down the corridor.

Just like the town of Estosha, Lus Monastery had a long history. It had been built hundreds of years ago and served as the home for devout Marayist believers who longed for a quiet life. The sprawling complex contained its own farmland, which allowed it to be self-sufficient. The monks oversaw a variety of tasks, including carpentry, smithing, and medicine making. They sold what they made in town to raise the funds to keep the place running. Every person within the monastery worked hard to serve the Lord, so the goods they created were both higher quality and lower priced than average. There were even some merchants who purchased their products cheap to sell at a profit in other cities.

The building showed obvious signs of disrepair; it was actually a miracle how long it had lasted, considering when it had been built. For a place that housed tens of people, it was also surprisingly clean. That was undoubtedly a by-product of their ascetic lifestyle.

While Ix and Shuno followed along, they passed a number of monks, each giving a polite bow. None of them said a single word.

"H-hey," whispered Shuno, walking beside Ix. "This is my first time in a monastery. Will they get angry if we talk?"

"Dunno…," said Ix vaguely with a tilt of his head.

"Have you been here before?"

"Nope."

"R-really? You seem pretty calm… Ah, you just look that way, don't you? Bet you're all anxious inside."

"Maybe."

"I—I thought so! Don't think you have to bottle it all up. You can talk to me if you're nervous. 'Cause I'm not at all."

"I appreciate it."

"All right, then. But, you know, it's super quiet even though there are fifty people living here…"

By this point, Shuno had forgotten to whisper and was speaking at their normal volume. The monk guiding them turned back and cleared his throat loudly.

"Ah, s-sorry…" They immediately scrunched up their shoulders. "Guess they really will get mad at us. Make sure you're careful, too, Ix."

Shuno shot a serious look at the other apprentice, who nodded reluctantly.

This was what it had been like since they'd met at the monastery's entrance and briefly introduced themselves to each other. Shuno had been given a Declaration of Equivalency as a test, which they would need to pass before going independent. Once they learned that Ix was still just an apprentice, and younger on top of that, they'd been acting like they were his mentor or something.

"Oh yeah. I know I'm the more experienced of us, but you don't have to treat me like your superior or anything, Ix. I'm still an apprentice, just like you." Despite having just angered the monks, Shuno kept on babbling. "But if you ever run into trouble, feel free to come to me for help. I should be able to figure something out as the senior wandmaker."

Far from making fun of Ix, Shuno seemed genuinely concerned for him. At one point, with complete sincerity, they even said, "If your master gets in trouble, it'll partly be because I didn't keep a close enough eye on you. In that case, I'll come with you to apologize."

Ix didn't know how to respond to most of this, so he stuck with giving noncommittal replies. However, his tone turned oddly weak in response to that last comment from Shuno.

"B-but don't get me wrong. I'm not worried about your skill. Master said you could be trusted, after all."

"Your master?"

"Y-yeah. Wait, you didn't hear? He's the one who recommended you for this job..."

"All that was delivered to me was a letter from the monastery. What's your master's name?"

"Marlan. You really don't know him? That's weird. Why'd he recommend you for this, then? He told me he met you somewhere in Leirest, and you evaluated a lot of wands with just a glance. Only a seasoned craftsman could've done something like that..."

Ix turned the name Marlan over and over in his mind and came back with nothing. He did remember evaluating a bunch of wands once, during the incident he'd been dragged into at the party last fall. Marlan must have been one of the attendees. But what Ix didn't understand was why anyone would think highly of what he'd done. Abnormal situation aside, even an apprentice who'd just started their training could have accomplished that.

"That's why I've been looking forward to meeting you so much," continued Shuno. "I'm itching to see you make a wand. Mind if I watch?"

"I don't really mind, but..."

"...But what?" Shuno asked, eyes darting side to side and a stiff smile coming to their lips. Ix wasn't sure how they'd taken his momentary hesitation. "Seems like you've been annoyed with me for a while. I-I'm getting on your nerves with all this talking, aren't I...? I am; I know I am. I get it; it's distracting to have someone jabbering away nonstop. I'll shut my mouth..."

"It's not a big deal."

"R-really?"

Ix nodded. It was true that the conversation was a little tedious, but he suspected things would get even more tedious if he told Shuno that. There was no real harm in them chatting with him.

"O-oh!" Shuno's expression immediately brightened. "You should have said something if it made you that happy."

"Huh?"

"Since you don't show anything on your face, Ix."

Just as he was about to protest that he hadn't said anything about being happy, the monk in front of them came to a halt and turned around.

"Ah, s-sorry...," said Shuno, squeezing their eyes shut.

"Wait here, please," said the monk, pointing at a door next to him while ignoring Shuno. "It seems the craftsman will be late. The abbot will come to greet you shortly. We've also arranged for someone to assist you while you're here. Please ask him any questions you have regarding your work or daily lives."

"O-oh. Thanks... Ha-ha-ha," said Shuno.

The monk bowed and left.

They had been brought to a simple room. Ix couldn't tell what it was used for normally. Several long tables lined the chamber, and there were many chairs against the wall. A fireplace near the front of the room had been lit, so it was already warm. So warm, in fact, that Ix was starting to sweat in his coat. The place was also thoroughly cleaned, without a single speck of dust on the floor.

They each grabbed a chair, set them next to each other, and sat down. Shuno had been roving their eyes around nervously from the moment they entered the room.

"H-huh...so the craftsman's going to be late? At least we weren't the last ones here."

"Do you know who's coming?" asked Ix.

"No, I just heard they're a wandmaker based in Estosha. The pay's not great when you do jobs for a place like this, and the assignments usually end up being pretty tough, too, so only locals or apprentices like us are willing to take them. Anyway, I hope this person is nice."

"A craftsman based in Estosha..."

"Hmm, you think you know who it might be?"

"There's someone I sort of know." This was rare for Ix, since he had so few connections to other people in the industry. "A letter came to my master's shop a few years ago. It was from a wandmaker named Coaku."

The man had left an impression on Ix because Munzil had exchanged several letters with him, a rarity for his master. Though technically it had been Ix who had read and replied to the correspondences after Munzil put him up to it. He recalled being nervous at the prospect of responding to an older craftsman. Incidentally, Ix had first learned of Heaven's Worship through those exchanges.

As he thought back to that time, Shuno stared at him with shock, then asked, "Coaku? Do you mean Coaku Shtah?!"

"...Is he famous?"

"Uh, yeah, well." Shuno looked away in embarrassment. "I heard the name from Master Marlan. Coaku's the most experienced craftsman in Estosha right now. S-someone as important as him wouldn't come for this job. Well, I don't actually know if he's all that, but you'd think the most senior wandmaker in the city would be pretty important. Probably."

"You don't seem so sure…"

"But your master lives in Leirest, right? Their connections must run pretty deep if they know a craftsman all the way out here. Would you mind introducing me later? I might even know their name already."

"You ask for an introduction, but I'm not sure you could really say my master lives in Leirest…"

It would be too annoying to explain that Munzil had passed and that he was only working as an apprentice under another wandmaker who'd learned from his old master. Besides, Ix had a hunch that telling Shuno this would lead to some overblown comments on their part. The truth of the matter was that he was just taking advantage of Morna's generosity and living in her shop. That wasn't something to be proud of.

As Ix considered what to say, there was a knock on the door.

"Is everyone all right? I heard a shout," came the voice of a young man from the other side of the entrance.

"Ah, everything's fine!" Shuno made a big show of clearing their throat. "I, um, just sneezed really loudly. With all this cold, the snow falling, and everything."

"I am so sorry. Is the room not warm enough?"

"O-oh, no, it's not your fault. The chill from outside just got in my bones is all." Shuno's convoluted response was both an expression of concern for the other person and an attempt to hide their own embarrassment. "Anyway, why don't you just come in?"

2

The young monk entered the room. He looked to still be in his teens; though he was tall, his freckled face still showed signs of youth. The boy's head was shaved close, and his habit seemed to be a hand-me-down, since it fit too snugly on his body.

"My name is Beter," he said with a polite bow. "I've been tasked with caring for you while you work. If you have need of anything during your stay, please just ask."

"Thanks," said Shuno, standing up and offering a hand.

"Ummm..." Beter stared at their outstretched palm with uncertainty.

"Ah, I forgot to introduce myself. I'm Shuno."

"Ah, Shuno. Very nice to meet you. And you are...?" asked Beter, looking at Ix.

"Ix," he replied from his seat.

"N-nice to meet you, Ix—"

"Oh, he's not angry or anything, so don't worry," interjected Shuno somewhat boastfully. "He's just the kind of person who doesn't show much emotion on his face. But inside, he's overjoyed to meet you."

"Is that so?"

"Yep. Hey, why don't you have a seat, too?"

"No thank you, I'm fine as I am. Now then...," said Beter before launching into a quick overview of the monastery's structure and rules.

The two apprentices would mostly work in this room, and they were to avoid wandering around the monastery. They would also need to refrain from speaking with the monks and shouting. Essentially, they would have to steer clear of the residents as much as possible so as to not interrupt them.

"Ummm...," said Shuno quietly. "Does that mean we shouldn't really talk to each other, either?"

"No, not at all. You are welcome to converse with each other. These rules apply to us, not you. Also, since this is currently part of my job, there's no issue with speaking to me, either," explained Beter.

"R-really?" Shuno smiled and looked at Ix. "So we can still chat. Wait, but then why did they get angry with me earlier?"

"Because you shouted," said Ix.

"…Hmm." Shuno closed their eyes and gave a small cough.

Since the craftsman was going to be late, Beter decided to show the two around the monastery. Cold air swept their fire-warmed cheeks the moment they stepped out of the room. The hallway ran along the outer edge of the building and gave them an excellent view of the surrounding scenery. Snow was pouring down outside, and the field that led to town was being swallowed by white.

"It's really piling up…," murmured Shuno.

"This way," said Beter as he walked down the hall. "At this time of day, everyone will be reading in their rooms. We probably won't bump into anyone else."

Staring at the blanket of white, the pair followed along. There was nothing around them, and it was unnaturally quiet outside, as if the snow swallowed all sound.

Actually, that silence was to be expected. The monastery was a world of purity, separated from the rest of society. A world dedicated to God. It was like a bubble rising up through the water. That was why no sound carried here.

On the first floor, they peered into several workrooms. Some were lined with large barrels while others were filled with tools. Despite the fact that these chambers were used for labor, the tools were perfectly arranged in neat rows. Things were so orderly that even Shuno shut their mouth and stopped fidgeting on the tour. This level also contained a kitchen and a library, but there was no one to be found in them at the moment.

The back exit of the kitchen led to a garden. It had been cleared of trees to form a large vegetable plot. Though white snow was piling on the black soil, there were still some plants that hadn't been harvested. They had to be winter vegetables.

At the entrance to the monastery was a silver bell. Beter explained it was to chime the hour.

Farther in was a staircase that led up to the second floor, crisscrossing twice as it climbed.

The upper level seemed to primarily consist of dormitories, their narrow entrances packed tightly along the hallway. The door to each cell contained a small window you could peer into, revealing only a bed, a small table, and an elderly monk flipping the pages of a book. None of the residents turned to glance at them as they passed through the hallway.

At some point, they passed another person in the hall. He must have been old, as his back was hunched over. The man's face and form were hidden beneath rags, and he was pushing a cart laden with books. Instead of saying anything to him, Beter simply made eye contact in greeting. Just as the man passed Ix, the wheel of his cart caught on a small lip in the floor, causing one of the books to fall.

Ix picked it up and gave it back but predictably received silence in response. The man accepted the tome and continued along at a steady clip.

The majority of the rooms were occupied, but the last two were empty, and their doors were open. Some daily necessities were still there, though.

"People were in those cells until just recently," said Beter as they went back to the first floor. "They were two lay brothers who had just entered the monastery in the fall. They ran away a few days ago."

"Well, I'm sure there're some people who just aren't suited to this kind of life," remarked Shuno. "Might be rude of me to assume so, but I imagine that kind of thing happens a lot."

"Ah, well…" Beter nodded with a pained smile. "These two were passionate, though, so I was sure they would be fine. They said they wanted to live a quiet life of faith to atone for the harm they'd brought to others… Apparently, they were originally adventurers. We came to rely on them for jobs that required strength. Their departure was so sudden, too…"

"You seem really bothered by it. Were you close with them?" asked Shuno, who seemed like they were having a hard time understanding.

"As close as I was with any of the others, I thought..." Beter furrowed his brow in worry. "But the thing is, they said they saw a ghost."

"Ghost?" murmured Ix.

"Yes, that's what they claimed before fleeing the monastery," said Beter, nodding. "I would get it if they'd admitted the life was too difficult for them. But a specter..."

"They were adventurers, yeah?" said Shuno with a frown. "I mean, I'm not trying to disparage them, but I bet they were so used to living a life of freedom that having all these restrictions just became too much. The ghost stuff was probably just an excuse."

"We don't chase people who leave the monastery. You don't need a reason to abandon this life. Which is why I find it strange they would go to the effort of concocting such an unbelievable excuse," replied Beter.

Shuno nodded in agreement, since it made sense, and the conversation ended there.

After taking a trip around the building, they went back to the chamber they'd started in to find seven monks waiting. One was an elderly man with white hair and a beard. The other six monks looked to be in their twenties or thirties. They stood side by side in a line, gazing at Ix and Shuno as they entered the room.

"Ah, wh-what?" gasped Shuno, recoiling from the stares.

"I am the abbot," the elderly man announced in a mild tone. "Beter, we've received notice that he won't be coming today and that we should ask these two to begin work without him."

"Understood," said Beter with a nod.

"I apologize for the short greeting, but I must be on my way." The abbot gave a short thank-you and quickly left the room.

Ix waited for the door to close, then asked, "What he just said, did he mean the craftsman isn't coming? I thought this assignment was for the three of us, though…"

"Yes, that is the case. It seems he's tied up with another assignment at the moment," responded Beter, nodding.

"But he also said to go ahead with the job, right? Which means these people lined up here"—Shuno snapped their fingers—"are the people we're going to be making staffs for?"

The monks nodded in silence.

"…Uh, I was hoping for a more energetic response," Shuno said.

"You're going to make them angry again," said Ix with a snort.

3

All six of the men had only just recently been promoted to monk from lay brother. To accomplish this, they'd needed to get a recommendation from the abbot and pass a standardized test. Magic-wielding was on the exam, and if they were promoted, they would receive permission to carry a staff of their own in public. Ix had accepted a commission to make those staffs.

This kind of work came often during winter, and it was actually nice to have, since there was little else to do during the season. Even so, most craftsmen refused to take this sort of job. Not only were monasteries unlikely to have a large pool of funds available to compensate who they hired, but they were also aware that commissions dried up for wandmakers in winter. These factors put monasteries in a better position to negotiate good rates. All in all, the payment just wasn't worth the effort. Besides, monks had little opportunity to fight, so their staffs would go almost entirely unused after their creation. They were more of a commemorative item. Obviously, no wandmaker wanted their work to go unused, so anyone skilled refused the work.

Despite all that, most craftsmen hated jobs from monasteries for a separate reason.

"Thank you for your help," said the monks as they showed Ix and Shuno what they held.

Each monk was carrying a branch of artey, its twigs and bark removed, of different thicknesses and lengths. Some of them even had holes from bugs chewing on the wood.

Ix held back a sigh.

Monks had to "choose their staff" by preparing their own wood and core material as part of their training. They cut the wood from the nearby forests before doing a small amount of work to it. Getting core material wasn't as easy, so each person brought theirs when they joined the monastery. The wandmaker would have to produce a staff from these components.

No one but a craftsman would understand how much of a pain this was. There were even people who thought the way the monks did it was easier, figuring that the wandmaker just needed to put the materials together, since they were already prepped. Obviously, it wasn't that simple. In fact, making a wand or staff from preselected ingredients was far more difficult than adjusting a stock wand or crafting a staff to individual specifications. Wood and core materials had certain compatibilities, as did the user. If they weren't in alignment, the wielder's mana could be greatly decreased, or they might even end up with a product that couldn't cast a spell.

The monks studied a little wandmaking before preparing the materials for their staffs, but they were still amateurs. Despite having learned only the most basic of the basics, they often convinced themselves they understood everything, leading them to select unacceptable wood. Then there was the work they did to it, which you could call nothing better than haphazard.

Ix shook his head, thinking about how annoying the job would be. Shuno must have felt the same, because they took one glance at the wood and gave an unambiguous groan.

"R-right, Ix, there are six of them. So, you take three, and I take three," they said, trying to pull themselves together. "You can decide who you want to work with. Since I'm the more—"

"I'm not the one who should determine that," interrupted Ix. "Beter, have them choose who they want to work with."

"Oh, okay," he acquiesced.

The six monks hesitated for a moment, but Beter gave them a look, and they gathered together to discuss things quietly.

"You sure about this?" Shuno whispered as they came over to Ix, who was staring at the monks in the corner. "And after I tried to give you the choice, too."

"The working on their wood is equally terrible. It wouldn't have made a difference who I picked," said Ix.

"Huh? No, that's not what I mean." Shuno shrugged. "If you let them decide who they want, they'll, you know, all choose me."

"…If that happens, you can make them all. I'll just provide support."

"Seriously? But I'll feel bad for you."

"Craftsmen shouldn't force their problems on the clients."

"So that's what it's about…" Shuno smiled. "All right, what you said just now is enough to tell me everything. If no one chooses you, I'll just have to explain to them how reliable you are."

"A wandmaker's personality has nothing to do with their reliability."

"Well, obviously. If they were connected, you would have failed long ago."

"…You're probably right."

"Uh, wait, I'm sorry—that was a seriously mean joke. Really, I'm sorry." Shuno spread their hands. "But, you know, it might be good for you to show your emotions a little more, Ix."

As the two of them chatted, the monks finished their discussion.

"Um…," Beter spoke up hesitantly.

"Oh, they've decided?" Shuno turned toward him.

"Well, they've each said which person they would prefer, but…" Beter cast his eyes down, having difficulty getting the words out. "Their decisions are a bit lopsided."

"Wait, you can't mean they all chose one of us?"

"I'm afraid so."

"What, really?" Shuno's eyes opened wide. "Oooh, no, that's not good…"

"Everyone wants Ix to make their staff," revealed Beter.

"…What?"

It was Ix who'd said that.

He simply couldn't understand why the monks had picked him. This was his first time meeting them, and they didn't know anything about his level of skill or experience, so they shouldn't have leaned toward him so heavily. Shuno was obviously surprised as well and stood there with a look of disbelief on their face for a few moments.

"W-w…" They moved their mouth wordlessly as they tried to respond. "Wait a minute, why are all of you choosing Ix? I mean, he is reliable, and if you really want it, I'll just support your selection…but this… It's a bit hurtful, you know?" Tears started to form in their eyes.

"No, they probably just don't know our station," said Ix. "Let me explain, everyone. Shuno's older and more experienced than I am. I'm just an apprentice, but they're about to go independent, so they're closer to being an actual craftsman. I think you should reconsider."

After saying that, the six monks looked at one another. They'd probably figured the opposite was true. People often assumed Ix was older than he was due to the color of his hair.

"N-no, Ix, you don't have to worry about me," said Shuno. "Now you'll be the one who's left out. But it does make me happy that you care."

"I'm not worried about you; I'm just stating the truth."

"That's because you care. You would lie if you didn't," said Shuno with a smile.

"...No, it's just that's the way it has to be to satisfy the client. I'll support you with everything I've got."

"U-um...," interjected one of the monks as he raised his hand. "Excuse me, may we have another moment to discuss this?"

"Huh? I don't mind...," said Ix.

It seemed the revelation that Shuno was about to go independent had changed things. Even if the monks wouldn't have much opportunity to use their catalysts, it was only natural for them to want a good craftsman to make them. Ultimately, the conversation ended with Ix and Shuno each being assigned to three of the six men.

The apprentices got straight to work, dividing the space between themselves. Shuno and Ix sat with their backs to each other in the room they'd split in half.

"From now on, this is my crafting space. You can come over to watch me every once in a while," said Shuno while laying out tools. "Since I'll swing by to see what you're up to sometimes, too."

Ix gathered the three monks he was now in charge of and asked them to show him the wood and core materials they'd prepared. He wouldn't get anywhere without checking those first.

But...

He furrowed his brow as he examined the wood.

Monks traditionally wielded staffs, though there weren't actually any rules that demanded they do so. The three men who'd chosen Ix all wanted staffs and had prepared long cuts of wood accordingly.

"Um... What do you think?" asked the monk who was sitting across from Ix.

"What do I think?" asked Ix back, his eyes never leaving the stick in the man's hands.

"Well, I just wondered if there's a problem with the work I did on it."

Ix removed the magnifying lens from his left eye and stared at the monk. Behind him, he could hear Shuno saying, "Huh?! Ah, i-it's so well-made, ha-ha-ha..." They must have been checking the wood as well. And from the sound of Shuno complimenting the monks, it seemed those three were also interested in how they'd done.

"It's all right. You didn't completely botch it," said Ix, trying to reassure his client. "The mistakes on the other two aren't too bad, either. I should be able to make staffs out of these."

"M-mistakes?" The monk looked slightly insulted. "I worked so carefully, though."

"You made some unnecessary adjustments to it. This sort of prep is for wands, not staffs. But fortunately, it's not so bad that I can't do anything with it."

"...Oh."

"Show me your core materials."

Despite what Ix had just said, if there was a problem, it was going to be with the core material. Since the monks of this monastery traditionally selected wood from the same species of tree, it was guaranteed to be suitable for staffs. But that wasn't the case with the core material. Ix was on edge because there were so many options the monks could have chosen from, and he didn't know what they might pull out.

He took the materials one after the other and inspected them. They were all stone-type cores, which set Ix at ease, since they had few quirks and wide compatibility.

Today they would be doing only a simple check of the components. As Ix returned them to the monks, Beter came over and said, "You've worked hard today. Will you start crafting tomorrow?"

"No, it'll take a while to design the staffs. I'll start making them after that. Shuno will probably do the same."

"Ah, Shuno...," said Beter with a quick glance in their direction.

Ix turned back to find Shuno groaning, core material in hand. The monk standing across from them looked concerned.

"Um, is there a prob—?" he started.

"Wait," Shuno interjected, holding a hand up to the monk. "I'm thinking right now."

"O-oh..."

Curious, Ix went over to check out what was going on and saw that Shuno was holding a clump of some milky-white substance. They were so focused, they didn't notice Ix watching from behind. Looking closely at their hand, Ix saw a strangely twisted lump, which might have been stone.

Ix couldn't help bringing a hand to his mouth.

It was moma.

This was actually his first time seeing it in person. It was an incredibly uncommon resource, so rare he hadn't even seen it in his master's shop. That didn't mean it was particularly powerful or valuable, but the material did explain Shuno's worries.

Based on what wandmaking literature had to say about moma's disposition, it had poor compatibility with artey, the wood all the monks were using. Ix quickly ran through a few possible methods for getting the two substances to work together, but he didn't think any of them would bear fruit. But Shuno couldn't very well tell the monk to switch to a different core material at this point in the process.

Noticing Ix's consternation as he stood there silently, the monk grew even more uneasy.

Just then, however, Shuno gave a shout.

"All right!" With an exaggerated nod, they returned the moma back to the monk. "Yep, it's not a problem. Here, you hold on to this for now."

"Huh? A-all right," he said, his eyes wide as he accepted the material.

"Okay, now I've checked everyone's materials, right? Oh, Ix. You didn't have any problems, did you?" said Shuno once they noticed Ix standing right behind them.

"No, nothing on my side, but—"

"Great, looks like we're both getting off to a good start."

Shuno smiled in satisfaction, cutting off Ix as he tried to ask if they really didn't have any issues.

Though it didn't feel like much time had passed since the noon bell, night fell early in winter, and it was already getting darker outside. Each of the monks expressed their gratitude and left the room.

That left the three of them in the workroom. Beter bowed his head as he said, "I apologize for any burden we place on you."

"Nah, it's no problem, but...," Shuno replied, glancing around the room. "Uh, where are we going to be staying for the night? I heard you'd be preparing us lodgings. Are you going to let us use this room?"

"Um, about that...," said Beter, who sounded like he was having trouble getting his words out. "We've made arrangements for you to stay in Estosha..."

"You're saying we have to walk all the way back there now? Urgh, that's kind of a pain."

"Well, I suppose we do have those empty rooms you saw on the tour."

"Oh, the ones that used to belong to the guys who ran away?" Shuno clapped a fist into their palm. "They're a bit small, but it's better than walking back and forth."

"Yes, if you would like to use those rooms, you may, but..." Beter looked away from the two of them.

"Is there some sort of a problem?" asked Ix.

"An issue? Well, no, not with you, Ix," replied Beter.

"Um, is it a problem with me, then?" asked Shuno, blinking in surprise.

"Well, there's just one thing I need to confirm first." Beter cleared his throat, steeled himself, and asked, "Shuno, are you a man?"

"I don't see how that's relevant," they replied with a smile.

"It is very important," said Beter carefully. "Just as men are not allowed in a nunnery, women are not allowed in a monastery. The same holds true anywhere. We need this arrangement for our life of abstinence. Of course, there are exceptions, like now. While we don't have any issue with inviting special craftspeople into the building, staying overnight is a completely different story. I also believe that this has something to do with why all the monks picked Ix at first..."

"Ah, I see," said Shuno, staring up at the ceiling with their arms crossed. "Hmm... Yeah, uh, I don't feel like telling you that information just for this. I'll stay in Estosha."

"Understood," said Beter with a nod. "And you, Ix?"

"I'll go back there, too."

As Ix said that, he noticed Shuno nodding slightly out of the corner of his eye.

4

They borrowed two lamps and returned to Estosha. The snow was falling only lightly, but the field was already coated with white, and the road back to town was completely concealed. They would certainly have lost their way had it not been for the lights of the city.

Compared to Ix, who was wearing the bare minimum, Shuno looked massive in their big coat and oversized rain hat. Every part of their body was covered in protective clothing.

"Ix, are you curious about me?" asked Shuno as they walked beside Ix.

"No, not really." He shook his head. "Honestly, I don't care."

"Ha-ha, that's very like you... Why didn't you stay in the monastery? Wait, did you want to be with me?"

Glancing sideways, Ix saw Shuno in profile, white breath coming out with their every exhalation. They were lit up from below, from the lamp in their hand.

Ix hadn't noticed until Beter pointed it out, but he really couldn't tell Shuno's gender. Their voice and face were both androgynous, and their winter clothing obscured their body. Shuno could claim they were a man or a woman, and Ix would take them at their word either way.

But that had zero influence on their job right now. What mattered here was their wandmaking skills. Ix had no interest in anything but that.

"Yeah," he said with a nod.

"Huh? What are you agreeing with?"

"I want to talk to you."

"H-huh?" stuttered Shuno, looking around for some reason. But they had nothing to lay eyes on except a snow-covered field. "H-how am I supposed to respond to something so direct...?"

"The moma. How can you combine that with the artey?" asked Ix.

"Huh?"

"I can't come up with any way to use moma in a staff made of artey. But you decided it wasn't going to be a problem earlier. How are you going to make it into a staff? Have you worked with it before?"

Shuno stared at Ix, at a loss for a while, then let out a sigh, as if all strength had left them. "W-wand talk...? No, today was my first time seeing moma."

"I've been thinking about how to get it to work this whole time but can't come up with anything. No matter what you do, you'll get a defect at the conduit junction..."

"Oh yeah, you'll definitely get a leak." Shuno immediately echoed Ix's concerns. "But if you put in, like, a balancing mechanism sort of thing, or something, in the inlet for the leakage, then... Ummm, I mean, it's sort of like a reverse Rednoff-Seiquan-style thing. I've got it all worked out in my head, but it's hard to explain... Anyway, I think it won't be a problem if I do it that way."

It took a few seconds for Shuno's explanation to unfurl in Ix's mind.

But as he thought it over, goose bumps slowly formed on his skin. This wasn't because of the cold; if anything, Ix felt hot. It was intuitive. The solution Shuno had devised would work perfectly for making a staff. But...

"...Did you invent this procedure, Shuno?" asked Ix.

"*'Invent'* makes it sound like a big deal. That guy went to all the trouble of getting his core material, and I would feel bad telling him I didn't need it. That's why I came up with the technique."

That's impossible, Ix nearly blurted out.

In simple terms, the process Shuno explained essentially involved swapping the mana input and output on the staff. It wasn't a particularly complex idea. Just saying that much was enough for someone to understand. Yet, as far as Ix was aware, that sort of technique didn't exist anywhere in the world currently. It was actually an incredibly abnormal thought for a wandmaker to have. It was a total departure from commonsense wandmaking.

This discovery would only be applicable in very rare cases, but if Shuno really had developed it in such a short time...

They would be nothing short of a genius.

Ix's legs trembled.

Up until this point, he had met several people who could rightfully be called geniuses, but he never expected one to waltz into his life as casually as you might say *good morning*. To think he would find someone so gifted on this job of all things...

"Anyway, were you really honest with that one guy?" asked Shuno in a light tone, holding up a finger. They didn't seem aware of how incredible they really were.

"…What are you talking about?" Ix managed to say, still reeling from shock.

"You know, the monk who did some seriously crazy work on his wood. There's no way you'll finish before winter ends if you have to redo everything. I was about to jump in and help if you started complaining."

"No, it was fine…" Ix cocked his head in confusion. "Oh, you probably didn't see it up close like I did. It wasn't in that bad of shape. I'm planning on using it as is."

"Huh…? But he'd worked it like it was going to be a wand, didn't he? Or did he only half finish?"

"He finished. Seems he's hardworking, for better or worse."

"Wait… Wait, wait, wait." Shuno brought a hand to their temple. "Uh, how the heck are you going to turn a stick in that condition into a staff? I don't remember learning anything like that."

"I doubt it's the kind of technique you'd be taught."

"Wh-what do you mean by that?"

"I don't mean anything…" Ix frowned. He didn't understand why Shuno was so invested in this line of conversation. "It's just combining a few basic principles. Anyway, that doesn't matter; I want to hear more about your tech—"

"Nope, wait. Just hold up." Shuno grabbed Ix's wrist. "Hang on. We obviously need to talk about this before we talk about that. So tell me."

"All it is is…"

It wasn't a difficult concept at all, so it didn't take long for Ix to explain it. Yet after hearing it, Shuno just walked on in silence for a while, lost in thought. Ix was losing his patience; he wanted to hear more about Shuno's technique as soon as possible.

"So that's it… I'd thought you might be able to join two, but three…?" muttered Shuno before they raised their head and stared straight at Ix. "…You're incredible."

"Huh?" said Ix loudly in response to the abrupt, ludicrous praise.

He looked the other apprentice in the eye, trying to decide if they were being sarcastic, but they seemed serious as they stared back. Maybe Shuno just thought it was amazing because they didn't happen to come up with it themself. No matter how you sliced it, their idea was far superior.

"What are you talking about? You're the genius here," replied Ix, his voice somewhat hoarse.

"Wh-what?" Shuno asked back. "How can you say that? I mean, it makes me happy you think I'm so talented, but I don't remember doing anything worthy of being called that. You're not talking about the moma thing, are you? Anybody could've come up with that. But what you proposed isn't so simple. You couldn't develop a solution like yours without an incredibly thorough understanding of wandmaking theories. You just went and formulated a way of joining three base theories like it was nothing—that's super complicated! *That's* something a genius would do. You could give a lecture on it at the Academy."

"Are you serious? What I did was as simple as addition or subtraction. A child could do the same thing as long as they thought it through. And it's not like I came up with it in an instant like you. All I did was tweak the application of something I've been researching lately."

Recently, Ix had been looking into making wands that could withstand actual use despite being crudely worked. That research had led him to his idea. It was just dumb luck; it had nothing to do with ability or talent.

"Most importantly," continued Ix, "this is just a way to get something out of a worthless wand, not a path to forging an excellent one. Which means it's practically worthless for wandmaking as a whole. But your idea's the opposite. Not just anyone could have come up with it. No matter how much knowledge someone

builds up, they're never going to have a breakthrough like that without a little bit of genius. Plus, your method could lead to all sorts of advancements. You've opened up a new path toward the future of wandmaking, Shuno."

"H-h-hey now, you're clearly exaggerating," they countered, looking away and placing a hand on their cheek. "That's over-board, even for flattery… Okay, so listen, this is what I'm saying…"

Their discussion continued unabated, even when they arrived in Estosha and made it to their lodging. Since they were staying in separate rooms, they would have to drop the conversation.

They'd arrived at the doors to their rooms just as Ix was launching into a fervent explanation as to why Shuno's idea was so valuable.

"All right, Ix, we'll have to pick this up again tomorrow," said Shuno, pointing a finger at him. "I'm not going to let this end while you're ahead."

"Just give up already." He shook his head. "Assuming you're understanding what I'm saying, you should realize by now that you're the genius here."

"Hmph. Well, whatever. You can think that for now. Tomor-row, I'm going to give such a good argument that you won't be able to refute the fact that it's *you* who's the brilliant one."

"I have no idea what makes you think you'll be able to do that."

"What did you just say?"

The pair stood there, hands on the doorknobs of their respec-tive rooms, glaring at each other. Behind them, another guest passed by with a look of bewilderment.

5

In the end, their discussion stopped there because they shifted to a different topic the next day.

The monastery had arranged for Ix and Shuno to stay in a cheap inn, but it was run by a friendly elderly couple who kept the rooms spotless. Ix went to bed early after doing some routine maintenance on his tools. But in the time between him closing his eyes and actually falling asleep, he came up with a perfect counterargument.

At first, he thought he would just bring it up with Shuno the next day, but he couldn't hold back the urge to say something now. They were probably still up now anyway. With that in mind, he moved to the door of his room. Just when he was about to leave, a knock came from the other side. There stood Shuno, having had the exact same thought.

Both of them pointed out flaws in the other's argument, so they were unable to reach a conclusion. But that discussion lit a fire beneath a different debate, which continued until dawn broke. By the time they realized it, the two of them were collapsed on the floor, rays from the sunrise filtering through the window.

A thin morning mist shrouded the world.

The brisk outside air roused them as they walked to the monastery. A thin layer of snow coated the ground, and their feet left clear tracks as they traveled.

The sounds of labor greeted the pair at their destination; the day had already begun at the monastery.

"You don't have to bring the monks here today," Shuno told Beter, who was waiting for them at the entrance. "We did our measurements yesterday. We'll check them again once we finish our designs, but we'll work on our own until then."

"Understood." Beter nodded. "By the way, it seems he's arrived today."

"Huh? Who?" asked Shuno.

"The, um, craftsman."

"...Oh, right. We were supposed to have a real wandmaker here. Urgh... H-hey, Ix, you seem a bit nervous. I'm not, though. Not at all."

"No, I'm not really anxious," replied Ix.

"Oh man, you really do put on a brave face. It's actually pretty reassuring."

After being led to the same room as the day before, they started working on designs.

The two apprentices brought several tables together to form a simple work surface, since the designs for a staff were normally made on large sheets of paper that were formed by attaching several smaller sheets together. Here they would jot down details and determine the final structure of the staffs.

The general design for each was already set, but they needed to iron out the details. You didn't need any of the ideas or inventions like the ones they'd developed the day before for this process—it was just moving your hand and filling the page. Long ago, craftsmen wouldn't do this sort of preparation. Most of them would just take the materials and jump right into forging the final product. In those days, lack of planning was proof of your skill as a craftsman.

But in modern wandmaking theory, it wasn't possible to make a wand without a design first. The principles of crafting wands had advanced to the point where you needed to do tricky calculations and construct elaborate conduits. It was impossible to handle all that in your head.

Ix worked in silence. He realized he was becoming absorbed in his task, and when his hand stopped moving, he felt like he'd forgotten to breathe the entire time. After listening for a few seconds to the crackle of the fire and the sound of a pencil on paper, he would turn back to his work.

Beter made an appearance before the lunch bell rang. Even though Ix had been at it all morning, he didn't have much of a design yet. It was taking longer than usual. He realized that for all his ability to focus, he'd been doing a lot of roundabout calculations.

"You must be tired," said Beter. "We have prepared lunch for you in the cafeteria, though it's just a simple dish."

"Huh, so you do a full three meals a day here?" said Shuno.

"It's important to eat enough to complete your work. But before that, I wanted to let you know that he's finally arrived."

"Huh? Who?"

"The craftsman."

"...Oh, right! You did mention that."

"I'll go get him now. Please wait here a moment," Beter said before leaving the chamber.

Shuno slowly turned to Ix. "Wh-what do we do?"

"You forgot again?" asked Ix.

"N-no way, I've been waiting on pins and needles for him to get here. You're the one who's worried, Ix—that's you. Are you okay?"

"Why wouldn't I be?"

Not long after that, Beter returned. Behind him was a small elderly man.

"Let me introduce you to Mr. Coaku Shtah. He runs a wand shop in Estosha," announced Beter. Then he pointed to the two apprentices and said, "This is Shuno and Ix. They aren't full-fledged craftspeople yet, but they're skilled enough to have received Declarations of Equivalency. They've already begun working."

The old man's face was serene. He peered out of nearly closed eyes from behind his round spectacles. He was short enough that Ix had to look down at him, and his legs must have been weak because he walked with a cane. His outfit and hat were spotless. He looked less like a wandmaker and more like an elderly gentleman.

"I-I'm pleased to meet you," said Shuno, while Ix bowed.

"Yes, yes, very pleased indeed to meet you two," said Coaku as he took off his hat and held it in front of his chest. His tone was just as warm as his appearance suggested. Coaku held out a small hand, and the two of them each shook it. "They call me a crafts-man, but I'm half-retired anyway, so no need to feel nervous."

"Ah, no, it's fine..." Shuno gave a big wave. "Uh...are there more than six monks? We've already sort of started the designs for the staffs, Master Coaku..."

"Oh, no worries. I don't plan on doing much," the craftsman responded. "I've asked to just oversee your work. I don't think an old fart like me can do much anyway. Just think of me as a flower in a vase or a good luck charm."

"I—I appreciate it... Ha-ha-ha!" Shuno smiled before their face instantly turned grim as they came close to Ix and whispered, "So we're going to have an experienced craftsman staring at us the whole time?"

"That's reassuring," said Ix.

"R-right, totally..."

Coaku apologized for arriving late. Apparently, he'd been asked to help with something in Estosha and found someone to substitute for him only yesterday.

"Well, just think of me as someone you can come to for advice on wands. At my age, you can't just give up on things because you've got a prior arrangement." He rubbed his head with his hand. The little hair he had left was white, and the top of his head was completely bald.

"You found a replacement without any issue?" asked Shuno.

"I did. They were nearby and studied under someone I knew a long time ago. Should be good for the job."

Ix listened silently to Shuno and Coaku chatting. He was wondering if he should tell the craftsman that he'd apprenticed under Munzil, but he couldn't think of how to say it, and he wasn't sure it would make a difference if he brought it up. He'd probably just wonder why Ix bothered telling him.

In the end, Ix held his tongue, and the conversation drew to a close.

"Now then, I'm going to say hello to the abbot," said Coaku with a bow. "Will we be in this room again in the afternoon?"

"Y-yes," said Shuno with a nod.

"I shall see you both again, then."

"I will show you the way," offered Beter as he opened the door.

As the two left, Shuno sighed and muttered, "I can't believe Coaku really came."

But Ix didn't hear.

On the other side of the doorway that Beter and Coaku were exiting through stood a small figure. Ix hadn't been able to see her from behind the two men beforehand.

She pointed to herself.

"I'm his assistant."

That's what Riess said before chasing after Beter and Coaku with light footsteps. The sound of her running was blotted out by the chime of the noon bell.

6

Shuno had some cleaning up to do, so Ix headed off to get lunch first on his own.

The dining hall was already filled with monks. They were lined up neatly on the benches that ran on either side of the rows of long tables. Ix even saw the man who'd been pushing the book cart the day before. Even now, he was still wearing his rags, so Ix couldn't make out his face. There wasn't one word of conversation in the cafeteria, just the clinking of utensils against dishes.

Everyone received the exact same amount of food, and dishes had already been set out, each with a single serving. There were exactly as many plates as there were monks.

Ix didn't feel like sitting with the brothers, so he took his meal to the courtyard instead. Not only did he feel out of place in the dining hall, but it seemed like even choking would be frowned upon there. He didn't think he could get used to the silence. Besides, the monastery rules didn't apply to him anyway.

A cutting wind assailed his cheeks once Ix exited the back door of the cafeteria. He headed down the path under the eaves and sat in a place that looked as good enough as any. The sun lit up the silver fields in the distance.

As he tore off a piece of bread and brought it to his mouth, a shadow suddenly fell into his view.

"Hello."

His gaze met a pair of blank eyes. It was Riess. She was bent over, looking at him, a plate just like Ix's in her hands.

"Can I sit with you?" she asked.

"Don't mind," he replied, expressionless.

Riess passed in front of him and sat to his left.

"It's really bright here," she remarked, squinting against the glare from the snow and raising a hand above her eyes. "Doesn't it bother you?"

"Not particularly."

"Really…? Maybe it's because you're taller," murmured Riess, standing up to test her hypothesis. "No, that's not any better. It's still bright. Maybe I'm just sensitive to light? Or you're insensitive? What do you think?"

"Both options mean the same thing," replied Ix immediately.

"What a great answer." Riess sat back down again, then looked up at Ix and said, "Nope, I don't think that's the kind of thing a monk would say."

"What do you mean?"

"In other words, they're thinking about God."

Ix didn't know what the "*in other words*" was referring to, but he kept listening without saying anything. Words spilled from the girl's mouth. He knew another child who conversed in a similar fashion, though their words leaped in a slightly different way.

"Because God decides if something is considered bright or not," continued Riess in almost a whisper. "Everyone living in the monastery uses God as their point of reference. Or at least they're trying to find God in everything. But you're not. You don't think in those terms, do you?"

"Is that a question?"

"No, sorry. It doesn't matter what you think, that's just what I've decided in my head."

"...Are you Coaku's apprentice?" asked Ix, changing the subject.

"I told you, didn't I? I'm his assistant."

"Did he tell you my name?"

"Yep."

"And did he tell you to meet me at the station?"

"I just did that because I was curious."

"So he's heard of me?"

"Yeah. But he doesn't have to bring it up. Or do you want him to? If you do, I can ask him to."

"...No, it's fine."

The conversation stopped there, and they ate in silence.

Riess sat with her knees bent, chewing away at some bread with her small mouth. Even though Ix had learned who she was and how she knew his name, she still had a mysterious aura about her. Why was she talking to him so much?

Around the time they were clearing their dishes, there was a commotion from inside the monastery. Ix hadn't heard a bell ring, but he supposed the noise meant it was the end of lunch.

When he stood up, though, he heard a shout.

"Ah, so that's where you ran off to! Why are you eating outside? You should have said something to me." Shuno emerged from the back of the dining hall and headed over. "I was looking for you, you know. Thought you might be lonely."

"You ate inside?" asked Ix.

"Yeah. All by myself in silence." Shuno put their hands on

their hips. "But anyway, could you hear the noise from out here, too? What do you think's going on?"

"...I just thought it was the afternoon bell."

"It wasn't." Shuno grinned. "Do you remember what Beter said? About the ghost?"

"What about it?" Ix tilted his head.

"The ghost showed up, is what I'm saying."

"Huh?"

"Wow, it's not often I see emotions on your face. I knew you'd be surprised."

"No, I honestly just don't get what you're saying. Who saw this spirit?"

"Well, it's not that anyone saw it... Right, I should start from the beginning," said Shuno, playing with their bangs. "It just happened a second ago. I gave up looking for you and started eating lunch. The abbot, Coaku, and Beter were there, too. Since it was so late, they were the last three people to get their food. The thing is, there were only two servings left."

"...And?" Ix furrowed his brow. "You can't be trying to say that a specter took the food?"

"That's exactly what they're saying happened." Shuno nodded gravely. "They prepare the exact number of servings they need for the number of people who are in the monastery. It's impossible for them to be short. Which is why this quiet bunch is making a huge racket. They say there's a ghost mixed in with the people and causing trouble."

"They probably just got the number of people eating wrong. Maybe they forgot to include the guests."

"That's what I thought, too. But they insist they took all the visitors into account and made enough for everyone. Apparently, they've never once miscounted and made the incorrect amount of food." Shuno held up a finger and continued. "Besides, there's one other problem."

"What's that?"

"The lay brothers who ran off, the ones Beter told us about. They said they saw the ghost in the same place, in the kitchen. That's the other reason everyone's freaking out. The abbot's trying to get the place back under control."

Ix nodded now that he had the full picture, but he still didn't think it was a real issue. It was just a couple of coincidences coming together, and no real harm had been done. Was a missing serving of food really something to make a big fuss over?

Unless...

Perhaps there's some legend about ghosts in the building or in town? That thought struck Ix. A city this old was bound to have a few tales.

But this was a monastery. They wouldn't allow such rumors, not openly at least, which could explain their reaction. When he thought about it like that, it made how Beter talked yesterday seem strange. Ix didn't have a single shred of evidence to back this up, though. It was just speculation.

If there was a local legend, Riess would probably know a lot about it. Just as he thought to ask her about it, he found that she'd disappeared from his side. She must have left after she finished eating.

"Hmm? You got something over there?" asked Shuno, looking confused as they peered beside Ix.

7

They were supposed to start working with Coaku that afternoon, but the man made no move to do any work. He just said, "Don't overdo it, you two," before sitting down in a cloth-covered chair near the fireplace. He didn't move a muscle after that. Since he was facing away from their worktable, there was no way he would be able to check their progress. Ix and Shuno kept shooting him glances, but his white-haired head remained bowed. What was the old man doing? The occasional snores they heard made it obvious that he was sleeping at least some of the time.

That was how their day passed. Coaku had given them neither words of advice nor warning. Rising to his feet in time with the evening bell, he said, "I shall see you tomorrow, then," and left, without ever even glancing at their designs.

The two apprentices had been wondering how harsh the craftsman's evaluation would be, but now they felt somewhat underwhelmed, or maybe a bit discouraged. "The heck was that about?" Shuno muttered spontaneously, standing there bewildered with Ix.

Coaku was exactly the same the next day. He didn't lift a finger. Ix and Shuno discussed among themselves what they should do and agreed that the only real conclusion was to accept how things were and push on with the job. Pretending as if the silent elderly man wasn't there, they continued with their original plans.

Thus began their days of going back and forth between Estosha and the monastery.

Ix found the quiet of the monastery suited him more than he'd imagined. From the moment he rose in the morning to the moment his head hit the pillow at night, he thought of nothing but wands. Leirest was a pretty similar environment, but he had to do chores around the shop, since he was just a lodger there.

But here, there was nothing to get in the way of wandmaking. There was literally no background noise. He just needed to focus on the materials in front of him. Every wandmaker must have dreamed of crafting in a place like this.

Their work continued unabated for ten days, at which point the staff designs were complete. They hadn't aimed to finish at the same time, but as it happened, both Shuno and Ix finalized them in tandem.

Small problems cropped up during the design phase, as was to be expected, but Ix managed to draw on a combination of his experience and knowledge to work out all the kinks. Next, he would at last begin to actually craft the staffs. Not only did he feel confident from how well everything had gone until now, but he was also enjoying the assignment. That struck him as strange.

When he brought that up to Shuno, they looked at him inquisitively.

"What about that is weird?" they asked.

"Well, it's just..." Ix brought a hand to his mouth. "Wandmaking is a means to make a living for me. That's the only thing I can do. Obviously, I get excited when I see rare materials and I even sometimes get a sense of satisfaction from my work, but that's not why I do the job. So—"

"You're always so complicated," said Shuno with a sigh, turning back to their worktable.

Today as usual, they left the monastery and returned to the inn, where they picked up their conversation in Shuno's room.

The floor was littered with detailed notes and writing utensils, so there was barely a place for the two of them to step.

"Forget about that—look here," said Shuno, holding out a scrap of paper they'd scribbled something on. "I finished fixing it. It's just like I said before. If you go along with this calculation, you can push down the transmission efficiency attenuation to two percent. It can have a more widespread application."

"You missed something important." Ix glanced at the note and pointed to one spot. "You can cut down on this waste so you don't have to worry about leakage. That should bring the attenuation down to one percent."

"Oh, you're right... No, wait. Can you really use it if you do that? Remember, we talked about this the day before yesterday..." Shuno got on the ground and shuffled through the scattered papers. "Huh? It's not here. Is it in the other room?"

"Who knows..."

While the argument they'd had on the day they met was trivial, their subsequent discussions had led to a variety of debates on all sorts of topics. The primary theme, however, revolved entirely around wandmaking techniques.

They chatted while walking to and from the monastery, while they were eating, and basically every other spare moment when they weren't working. Once they returned to their lodgings, Ix would find topic after topic he wanted to discuss, and he'd knock on Shuno's door. They would often come over to Ix's room as well. Neither of them could remember whose room was whose at this point. Both were equally messy, and since their debates continued until they passed out from exhaustion, they would sleep in the same room together every night.

Now that he thought about it, Ix realized he'd never spoken to someone in the same position as Shuno. Everyone in his life was either a craftsman one or two steps ahead of him or a customer. When it came to talking about wandmaking, he was either being taught or doing the teaching. This was his first time having a peer he could debate with on even footing.

Though it might be going too far to say they were on equal ground. Ix was keenly aware that he was the one learning more often than not. After being with Shuno for days on end, his belief in their genius had only solidified. Their imaginative capacity was leaps and bounds ahead of Ix's, and though the things they said sounded strange at first, they eventually made a lot of sense. How had they developed that mindset?

On the other hand, Shuno wasn't very knowledgeable about wandmaking theory for some reason. Or rather, you could say that they knew about as much as your average craftsman; it was just that Ix's volume of knowledge overwhelmed Shuno's.

"So, back to our previous conversation," said Shuno, looking at Ix.

"The one about bypassing the conduit? Or the one about variable techniques?"

"No, not those. The one where you said it was weird that you enjoyed crafting." Shuno rested their chin on their hands and glanced outside, where it was growing dark. The window was open. Their rooms were on the second floor, and they could clearly see the roof of the building on the opposite side of the street. "I guess that does happen—people become craftsmen even if it's not something they want for themselves. So you started working without any sort of reason or goal in mind, and you've just kept going. I guess you could call that strange, right?"

"Were you different? You weren't put into an apprenticeship when you were a child or anything, were you?"

"Me? I... Yeah, I decided to become an apprentice myself."

"Did you have a reason for doing that? Or a goal...? Like wanting to craft the ultimate wand or something?"

"The ultimate wand? You're bringing up Rednoff again?" Shuno frowned every time someone brought up that name.

But they were staying in Estosha, so Rednoff was bound to come up every once in a while.

"That was just an example. It's not like I think the ultimate wand actually exists," replied Ix.

"You don't? Well, that's interesting, too. I thought it was normal for all craftsmen, apprentices or not, to study as hard as they can because they've got the ultimate wand in their sights. Is that not the case for you, Ix?"

He couldn't find an answer. He'd never considered it before.

Shuno was right—all craftsmen aimed for the ultimate wand. That's why they polished their skills and increased their knowledge. But had he ever really thought of doing that himself...?

"But really, what *is* the ultimate wand?" asked Ix with a tilt of his head. "What would be the criteria by which you determine that? Function? Or the materials you use to make it? Say...if you forge a wand with a dragon heart, would that make it the ultimate wand?"

"A dragon heart? I didn't realize you had some childish wonder in you, Ix," teased Shuno with amusement before continuing.

"You know, though, one thing that's certain is that Rednoff was a genius. In those days, the era of natural wands, there was no such thing as a wandmaker, just woodcutters picking up branches. And magic was so weak that you'd barely even need someone to craft wands. Yet despite the conditions at the time, a single man found a way of recreating artificial 'life' in the sticks that had been cut. With the birth of man-made wands, craftsmen appeared, with the woodcutters becoming the first ones. I've said it before, but someone that good might truly have made the ultimate wand."

"You really admire him," said Ix.

"It's not that I admire him. I'm just calling him what he is. Incredible."

"But wandmaking's already started to make distinctions between wands and staffs, and they each have their pros and cons. It's theoretically infeasible to create a wand or staff that excels in all areas of casting."

"Just think about it, Ix. It's only been a couple hundred years since Rednoff created the first man-made catalyst. The techniques and tools we use to make things that have been around forever— like houses, swords, or fire—aren't even close to their 'ultimate' form. If you look at wands in the long term like that, don't you think someone down the line will come up with a revolutionary theory that we've got no chance of developing in our time? We can't conceive of it with our current understanding of things."

"But—"

"Besides, Ix," interjected Shuno, holding up a finger and smiling, "there's no point in speculating about what the ultimate wand would be."

"Why do you think that?"

"Well, defining the ultimate wand would be the same as making it, don't you think?"

Their flippant remark caught Ix completely off guard.

Shuno was absolutely spot-on.

But if that was the case…

"That's it…," said Ix.

"Uh, what is?"

"The true nature of the 'ultimate wand' Rednoff left behind. For man-made wands to develop, you would absolutely need a buildup of theories, along with further innovation. The invention of various tools has allowed us to obtain quantitative measurements which, in the past, were gathered with our senses. This has greatly increased the precision of our craft. So if Rednoff did leave something resembling an ultimate wand behind, it wouldn't be an actual catalyst but rather its design. Perhaps it's not even as concrete as a design—maybe it's just the definition or idea of the ultimate wand."

"That's…a perspective I hadn't considered until now." Shuno nodded seriously. "Anyone's free to theorize about things, but no individual can brush aside the limitations of technology. Like, if you wanted to pass hundreds of flow lines through an area the size of your fingertip… You're right. You know what, I think you're really on to something. Come to think of it, it's really strange that a craftsman on Rednoff's level didn't leave any technical documents behind… That's fascinating. Ix, that's really, really fascinating!"

"Not like I have any proof for this theory, though…"

"But your idea is way more realistic than some baseless legend! Man, why didn't I think of that…?"

Inspiration seemed to have struck, so Shuno grabbed a random piece of paper off the floor, then scribbled something in the margins. Then they gave a nod of satisfaction.

"Looks like our conversation veered off course all of a sudden," said Shuno, peering over the sheet of paper at Ix. "Where were we before? Uhhh… Oh yeah. My goal as a craftsman, right?"

"Yeah, there was that," said Ix in agreement, though he wondered why they had to go that far back in the conversation.

"Well, that's, um." Shuno crossed their arms. "I do have one, of course, but, hmm, should I tell you? I've never talked about it with anyone before."

"You don't have to tell me if you don't want to."

"But, I mean, you're curious, aren't you? I don't mind telling you if you're interested."

"You sure? Even though you've never told anyone before?"

"But it's you, so it's different." Shuno gathered up several of the notes on the floor and gently waved them about. "Besides, I think I've found a bit of a clue on how to work it out from talking with you. I'm not telling you this out of gratitude or anything, but—"

Just then, a strong gust of wind blew in from the window and snatched the papers out of Shuno's hand.

"Ah!" They grasped at the air but couldn't stop the sheets from flying out the window.

They went over to the window and saw that the notes had caught on a pile of snow. The pair could tell the papers were getting wet, even from a distance. The characters must have been bleeding so much, they weren't even readable at this point.

"...I—I just looked at those notes, so I remember what was on them. I just need to rewrite them, okay?" said Shuno, slowly turning toward Ix. "A-are you mad?"

"Doesn't really matter. There wasn't anything important on them."

"Well, I think it was plenty important... Hmm? That person..."

Looking down on the street, Ix could make out someone in a dark-colored coat. Two people, in fact, walking side by side.

The person closest to their building was holding one of the pieces of paper. It was still dry. They must have caught it before it landed.

Shuno waved at them and shouted, "Heeey! Wait there just a sec—I'll come get it!"

One of the pair glanced up at the sound of Shuno's voice. The other person tapped them on the shoulder, and they nodded.

They placed the piece of paper on the side of the road and quickly walked away.

"What...? It's going to get wet like that," said Shuno dejectedly. "They just needed to wait a second."

"Must have been in a hurry," supposed Ix as he watched the note that had been placed on the side of the road absorb water and slump as it lost its stiffness.

"Hmm? What's wrong, Ix?" asked Shuno.

"What do you mean?"

"You look really spacey." Their hands still on the windowsill, Shuno peered into Ix's eyes. "Was there something really important written on that piece of paper?"

"That's not it... It's not important."

"If it's not a big deal, you can just tell me."

"...I was surprised is all. I thought I saw someone I recognized."

"Someone you recognized? A friend?"

"No, a customer. I fixed her wand over the summer."

"Ah. Are you talking about the two people who were just here? But I couldn't see either of their faces." Shuno blinked. "Are you sure your imagination wasn't playing tricks on you?"

"Might have been. There's no way she could be here now." Ix shrugged. "Anyway, tell me what you were about to say. What wand do you dream of crafting, Shuno?"

"Huh? Oh yeah. Sure. Right, listen closely," they said, sidling right up to Ix. "I want to make..."

A gentle snow began to fall, and the two looked up into the air, side by side.

"...What?" muttered Ix. Not because he hadn't heard what Shuno said but because he couldn't believe his own ears.

"I want to make a wand that lets you fly. Don't make me say it again. It's a bit embarrassing," said Shuno with a pout.

"Fly...? Why...?" muttered Ix in amazement, but Shuno just looked at him in disbelief.

"Why...? Because it seems like fun."

8

The building stood near the chapel. Both structures looked like they had been built in the same time period. Though the windows of the building offered a good view of the pointed bell tower, night had fallen. Now you could make out only its dark silhouette against the black sky.

Dozens of people were gathered in the room, but the chairs were set a decent distance apart, and the lights were quite dim. Though you could say a room that dwarfed a small number of people implied a level of grandeur, the fact remained that the occupants couldn't see one another's faces very well.

While there was a small gathering here, only about half of the people present were actually participating. The others were attendants or assistants. They were standing at attention behind their masters instead of sitting.

"Are you, sure?"

"About what?" asked Yuui Laika quietly back to the person standing behind her. All with a perfect smile.

"It's not often, you see him. We had time, to say hello at least."

"Were you aware of this, too, Nova?"

"This was, complete coincidence," she responded in a voice that concealed all emotion, in the same way that her bangs concealed her eyes. "I was, surprised."

"Who was the person who called out to us?"

"I don't know."

"And that piece of paper?"

"I don't know," replied Nova tersely. "It appeared to be, some sort of formula. It used symbols, I didn't recognize."

"Write down later what it said."

"Yes."

Just then, Yuui realized that all eyes in the room had fallen on her. She ignored them and took a sip from the drink she'd been provided. This was supposed to be a sign that she didn't want to talk.

"That was quite the feat of athleticism you showed earlier," came the voice of someone sitting diagonally from Yuui. It belonged to an elderly woman with dignity and a strong presence. "Catching a piece of paper tracing such an irregular path through the air looks simple, but it requires masterful control."

Yuui heard clothes rustling behind her; she could tell that Nova had given a silent bow. In a way, she was acting as Yuui's attendant right now. It was the master's job to reply.

"We are honored by your praise," replied Yuui quickly. "I take it you were watching, then?"

"It appears we occasionally pass along the same route," replied Mellay, easily parrying Yuui's jab before moving on. "I must admit to being quite curious about your attendant's background."

"I don't believe this is the right place for that line of questioning," insisted Yuui.

"Ah, of course not. My apologies." Mellay quickly nodded but then continued, as if appending a "however" to her statement. "There is nothing prohibiting us from forming personal connections through these meetings, isn't that right? And to be honest, I am even more curious about the background of someone who has an attendant at such a young age. What do you say, Minaha?"

"I shall leave it to your imagination," she replied, shrugging. Yuui was used to the fake name by now.

"How did you come to participate in these meetings with your entire body hidden behind a coat?" continued Mellay. "I get the impression everyone here wonders, just like I do, where in the world Seyoh found such an intelligent young woman. Some even whisper that you might be the Specter of Estosha."

"A specter?" inquired Yuui, taken aback at the abrupt invocation of a ghost.

"Yes." Mellay seemed pleased. "You can hear their voice and

©Enji

footsteps, but no one has ever seen them. It's a local legend. Are you interested in it? But your lack of awareness means that this is indeed the first time you have set foot in this town. Your Central Standard is so beautifully pronounced, but—"

"Why don't we leave it there, Mellay?" came the low voice of a man, another participant, cutting into the conversation. "You have brazenly pointed out that there are some unusual circumstances regarding Miss Minaha. What the old say in passing, the young take to heart. Or do you not understand that?"

"What a commendable thing to say, Gustavus. When did the man who was brought to court over interrupting a priest's sermon become so gallant?"

"Not this again," said Gustavus with a sigh.

"What do you think, Minaha? Why don't you dine with me below the noon sun, just once?" proposed Mellay, turning back to Yuui. "Please don't worry—I am not making an attempt to discern your true identity. I simply wish to have a nice long chat with you. It's not just me; I'm sure anyone who invited you would feel the same."

"That is not my concern," said Yuui bluntly.

"Cold as always. But that's fine for now. I'm not searching your closet for imra spirits, after all. I do wish for you to actively participate in the meetings, however. Though you have been ardent in your statements lately, which leaves me with little concern in that regard."

"I understand what I am meant to do."

"Then all is well." Mellay nodded in satisfaction.

Just then, the door opened. The light from outside briefly illuminated the chamber but was immediately shut out. The flames in the lamps throughout the room all fluttered in the same direction.

A slender man had entered. His long hair was tied back in a single bunch. He was clad in a dark coat, the same as the other participants, but he took it off at the entrance and handed it to his attendant before approaching the small round stool at the center of the room. That was his designated spot.

A scribe wordlessly pulled out their writing instruments just as the man got up on the stool.

"The 933rd meeting will now come to order," said the man quietly, with no prior introduction or explanation. "The fiftieth edition of the Standards of Faith is scheduled to be distributed shortly. We are on track for submitting it to the spring conference without issue, but it goes without saying that there remain areas into which we must delve further. Do we require a recap of today's topics?"

The attendees shook their heads vaguely.

"Very well." The man nodded. "Additionally, I have an announcement to make before we begin our discussion. As was previously pointed out, we have no wandmaking experts among us. However, I have found an excellent solution to fill that gap, and they are planned to attend the next meeting, which will be the last of the year."

"It's rare to hear praise from you, Seyoh," said Gustavus. "Your playing up their quality leads me to believe they must be famous. Though the only one I can think of in Estosha would be Mr. Coaku Shtah."

"He unfortunately had a prior engagement," said the man, Seyoh, with a shrug. "But they were recommended by Master Coaku himself. They are a very suitable choice. I'm sure that everyone here knows the name of the most lauded wandmaker in the kingdom, Munzil Alreff?"

The crowd gasped, impressed. There was of course no one in that room who hadn't heard the name Munzil Alreff.

"But Munzil has already passed," noted Mellay sharply.

"That is correct." Seyoh nodded slightly. "They studied under him."

Yuui couldn't help turning around and glancing at Nova, who shook her head. *It's just a coincidence*, she seemed to be saying. Yuui decided to believe her, since even Nova wouldn't lie that brazenly.

Yuui turned to face front again and saw that the room was filled with quiet chatter.

"Studied under Munzil?" asked Gustavus again. "Forgive me

for my lack of familiarity with his apprentices, but the only one of Munzil's students I am aware of is Layumatah, and she's based in the capital."

"Just as darkness blots the vision, so does intense light blind the eyes," said Seyoh as he held a hand in front of his face. "I myself am not acquainted with all of Munzil's apprentices, but many are hesitant to make themselves known. Their skills are excellent, but they prefer not to rely on their master's name for work. There are few opportunities to meet with them outside of academic and military spheres."

"Minaha seemed to know something about this," noticed Mellay, suddenly turning the conversation toward Yuui.

"And so the girl gains yet another wrinkle. Acquainted with wandmakers, are you?" murmured Gustavus. He and Mellay were on the same page only at moments like these.

In a reserved tone, Yuui explained, "I have merely heard a few of their names."

But this just seemed to solidify their hypotheses, in light of their previous statements. Whispers of "She knows more than one...?" spread throughout the gathering.

Yuui was frustrated that they'd misinterpreted her words again, though it was true that her relationship with Munzil's apprentices went beyond having *"heard a few of their names."* Her wand had been forged by the man himself, after all.

And when it had broken, Yuui asked one of his apprentices to repair it and even stayed at the shop of a different apprentice in the process. At that moment, it dawned on her that her relationship with Munzil and his disciples was more than superficial. Not that she had any intention of revealing that to anyone else at this point.

"Well, perhaps you know them, then," said Seyoh in amusement. "I have heard that they are particularly knowledgeable about wands and that they always work as a pair."

"There are two of them?" With that information, Yuui had no idea who they could be.

1

The meeting ended in the dead of night. Outside, darkness painted over everything. The majority of the participants and their attendants left the room, leaving only three people behind: Yuui, Nova, and Seyoh.

Yuui remained seated as she stared at Seyoh's back. He was blowing out each and every lamp. Almost all of them were dark, leaving only the one directly in front of her.

Once only one other lamp remained, Seyoh picked it up, flicked his bundle of long hair back over his shoulder, and walked up to Yuui. Amid the darkness, only he was visible, illuminated by the lamp in his hand.

"How do you find being here?" asked Seyoh.

"I can't relax," said Yuui honestly.

"You have my sincerest apologies for that," he said, bringing the light up close to his face. "However, I wasn't able to find any other suitable location to house you. There are no other buildings that I have my eyes on at all times, where I can guarantee your safety."

"I did not intend it as a complaint. You are providing me with room and board, after all." Yuui shook her head. "However, I don't understand why it is necessary to conceal where I'm staying.

It seems like a waste of time for me to pretend that I'm staying somewhere else by going out before each meeting."

"Oh...?" Seyoh's eyebrows arched in surprise. "Yuui, I've arranged it that way based on advice from your own attendant."

"Hmm, is that true?" Yuui turned back.

"Yes," Nova replied with a nod.

"Hmm... Would it not be safer to stay secured in one location?"

"Currently, the greatest threat is an information leak, from the participants," explained Nova. "This is the best way, to deceive them."

"I would have thought there was a greater danger in my identity becoming known when I left."

"My evaluation, is different. Very few people know you are here, Yuui. No, Minaha. People rarely notice, unexpected events. So long as nothing extreme happens, there shouldn't be any issue."

"I think you're being overly cautious..."

Nova, however, didn't seem keen on changing her mind. Instead, she just stared silently at Yuui, neither agreeing nor disagreeing with her.

Yuui did have some idea as to why Nova had grown this concerned. It probably had to do with the incident they'd been caught up in last fall, where a banquet was attacked and its attendees were taken hostage. Yuui and Nova had been there, too.

But the assailants hadn't been targeting Yuui, and the two girls were able to resolve the issue. As far as Yuui was concerned, Nova was being too careful just because of one incident.

There was a knock on the door, and a servant brought in steaming food on a pushcart. They arranged the meal on a table near the two girls. At some point, Seyoh quickly sat down nearby, lifted a dish, and said, "Leave us be for a while."

Nova started eating as soon as the servant left. She was still behind Yuui, however, so she could tell this only from the sounds of her chewing.

A servant brought them food on a pushcart twice a day. Most

of Yuui's time was spent in the chamber beside this meeting hall. In fact, she essentially spent her entire day there. Save for when she would leave and return for nightly meetings, she barely interacted with anyone. The only people she had to talk with were Nova and, on rare occasions like this, Seyoh.

At first, she'd been told it was a kind gesture from the lord of the town. It happened to be pouring rain on the day they were passing through, so they were lent a building that wasn't being used at the time until the weather cleared. But after being kept there for an entire week with the same excuses, Yuui finally realized that there was more to it than that. They weren't going to be able to leave Estosha until at least the end of winter.

Since Yuui wasn't in a position to be making complaints, her only choice was to accept the situation...

And yet..., she thought, her brow furrowed.

She couldn't very well accept the situation she was in if she didn't even understand it.

As Seyoh gracefully handled the dishes in front of him, he noticed Yuui staring at him. He smiled and asked, "What is it?"

"Are you still not going to tell me?" she asked.

"Tell you what?"

"The reason why I was brought here and made to participate in these meetings."

"You still need to ask about that?" Seyoh shrugged as if he didn't know what to say. "That is surprising. I have only ever told you the truth, that I borrow your insight."

"Then you would not have given me such a warm welcome. Now that I think about it, I should have realized something was amiss when you told me the lord was doing this out of the kindness of his heart."

"I swear that is the truth. Were it not for his generosity, we wouldn't be able to hold these meetings. We are solidifying the New Order's Standards of Faith, after all. Doing that in the capital is out of the question, and if the Old Order holds sway, it would mean we'd be unable to have a discussion out of fear of the death sentence. It is only with the protection of a powerful regional lord that we can do this."

"When you swear that to be the truth, does that mean that everything else is a lie?" asked Yuui.

"You are unrelenting," asserted Seyoh with a stiff smile. "It's just a manner of speaking, very common in conversations. Or are you that rigorous with your word usage? Perhaps you've become overly sensitive."

"Better than being oblivious."

"A good response." Seyoh nodded in satisfaction. "It's that clear-mindedness of yours that I wish to borrow. A mind that was able to garner top marks at the Academy."

"My scores were average."

"I need people with keen intelligence and people with different perspectives," continued Seyoh slowly. "Yuui, you have a sharp wit and are not a follower of Marayism. Someone like that is difficult to find, at least in the kingdom."

"I wish you would give it a rest," said Yuui.

She sighed.

Ever since she'd come to Estosha, she'd been showered with undeserved praise. Perhaps this was due to her age, or perhaps the fact that her true identity was hidden made her seem more significant than she really was. Whatever the reason, the comments were completely off the mark and left her feeling constantly uncomfortable.

"I understand how you feel. But even if I was to speak from a place of objectivity, the truth is clear. The Standards of Faith, which we thought were complete, have already been rewritten based on your comments. That is a fact." Seyoh brought his hands together. "The Old Order has failed to put out a unified interpretation of their doctrine, instead leaving it riddled with inconsistencies. Though they may not make their voices heard publicly, there are many members of the clergy who have questions, even among those who are highly educated. That is why the

New Order must make clear standards of faith and present logical doctrine founded in pure theological discourse. That will lead
us to more followers. And those tenets will act as sturdy support
when we begin our massive revolution. No matter how powerful
the king is, it is the common clergy, along with the people they
teach, who form the backbone of Marayism. *That* is why we need
someone who is deeply suspicious of us like you."

The New Order's need of Yuui aside, that was essentially the
background to what was happening.

Marayism was the kingdom's state religion, but there were
many different interpretations of its scriptures and doctrine,
which had led to a number of internal disputes throughout history. The current denomination in power was the Old Order,
though naturally, they didn't refer to themselves as that. But now
there was a new force vying for that power: the New Order. The
sect's current plan was to infiltrate the kingdom, grow their follower base, and stage a peaceful revolution.

The meeting from earlier was just another component of
that plan, a religious debate intended to bring together the New
Order's arguments and solidify a unified doctrine.

Reforming the leading faction of an entire country without
the use of force required a plan of immense proportions. Theologians and clergy members were invited from all over the country
to participate in these meetings, which had been held continu-
ously over the past five years with an ever-changing selection of
attendees.

Currently, they planned to complete the Standards of Faith
during the winter and submit them to the assembly the following
spring. So why had Yuui been invited to join at this final stage?
No, not invited—deceived and forced to take part.

Yuui Laika shouldn't have been here. She had originally
planned to leave in the fall and spend a year in her home country of
Lukutta, a small eastern nation that the kingdom had conquered.

She had been yearning to be in an environment where she

could let her guard down even a little. Here in the kingdom, this was simply impossible, since she couldn't even walk around with her hood down. Though she no longer had family or friends in Lukutta, at least the people there shared her skin color. Yet, here she was, trapped in an out-of-the-way town in the far reaches of the kingdom.

It was those circumstances that kept Yuui baffled as to why she'd been invited to these meetings. She'd only been brought to this country in the first place because she was Lukuttan royalty. What she did know about Marayist theology and doctrine she'd only just learned in the two years she spent at the Academy.

Seyoh had provided her with a plausible explanation as to why she was participating, but she doubted that was the deciding factor. The long-haired theologian had to be hiding something.

"Hmm, I must say, you hold far too low an opinion of yourself," said Seyoh as he wiped his mouth, having finished eating. "What I value about you, Yuui, is that you view things from an incredibly objective lens."

"That has nothing to do with my abilities." Yuui shook her head. "Any nonbeliever would be able to examine Marayism objectively."

"That's not true at all." Seyoh smiled. "You see, people will inevitably subscribe to different religions in areas where Marayism isn't practiced. I daresay they even have different gods. Your homeland, Lukutta, is the same, isn't it?"

"Yes, it is."

"With that in mind, you would think people with different beliefs would attempt to denounce Marayism. Just as we denounce the religions of other areas. I'd assumed you would be particularly inclined to think like that."

"What is that supposed to mean?" asked Yuui sharply.

"Oh no, I don't mean anything by it." Seyoh shrugged. "Anyhow, denial, just like agreement, is the furthest viewpoint from objectivity one could have. But you don't do that."

"Then allow me to denounce Marayism here and now. Your god does not exist," Yuui enunciated clearly. "...How is that? Has that stripped me of value?"

"...Now then."

Seyoh slowly stood, rubbed his hands together, and moved directly in front of her.

"May I ask you a question?" he inquired, his hands clasped before his chest. "Why do you believe God doesn't exist?"

"There is no evidence your god exists," she replied immediately.

"God created this world, life, and gave birth to humanity. The fact that we exist is proof of God's existence."

"You could make the exact same argument to prove the god of my land is real," countered Yuui quickly. "How can the same evidence lead to two different conclusions? It can't, which means it doesn't support either alternative."

"Precisely." Seyoh nodded. "I believe they provide that argument at the Academy, don't they? Although it might not be the most, um, logical."

"That is not a counterargument."

"It's not, because I have no need for a counterargument." He shrugged. "Because your original argument that there is no proof is a false counterargument in and of itself."

"What do you mean?"

"You are the one who must provide evidence, Yuui. Do you understand?"

"That's..." Yuui's eyes opened wide. She immediately understood what he meant, but the argument came from an unexpected direction. "But...that is not an academic stance. You can't demand I first give proof your god does not exist..."

"Is there any need to give proof of the sun?" Seyoh pointed to the ceiling. "The moon? How about the stars? I don't think I have to go so far as to say it's clear that they exist. But if someone insisted that the sun did not in fact exist, you would demand they provide proof, wouldn't you, Yuui? That is what I mean when I say your argument is false." He spread his arms slightly and looked at Yuui. "To us, God's existence is obvious. We have no need to provide proof."

"Your logic is circular," pointed out Yuui in a calm tone. "Saying 'God exists because God exists' does not change anything."

"Unfortunately, the same applies to you. You are simply insisting that God doesn't exist because God doesn't exist. Am I wrong?" Seyoh smiled.

Yuui looked down, her mouth shut. She needed just a bit of time to think.

Feeling someone approach, she looked up to see Seyoh had come closer to her.

"Yuui, you have acknowledged that our arguments are perfectly parallel. This silence of yours was a few seconds for you to accept that, yes?"

"I suppose you could call it accepting, yes," she agreed with a grimace. "Because they each carry the same level of validity, there is no point in further discussion."

"And that is what makes you special." Seyoh moved another step closer and placed his hands on the armrests of her chair as he gazed into her face. His face, covered in shadow, moved along with his words. "Most people are incapable of that. Even if they understand it, they cannot accept it. It is more common for people to think, *I'm still right*. Even I, as I say these things, believe I am right, that God does exist. Emotions come before reason. Yet, you are capable of easily throwing aside your own opinions and looking from a higher perspective. You treat the assertion that God exists and the assertion that God doesn't exist as equal. Was there something that triggered such a holistic perspective in you?"

"Nothing comes to mind..." Yuui cocked her head.

She couldn't remember any obvious event that would have triggered it; she'd just come to learn how little value her own thoughts had in the time she spent in the kingdom. Biases occur when you tried to force two things together, things that couldn't understand each other. It was better to treat them as things that stayed beside each other.

"At any rate, it is that ability of yours to view even yourself objectively that led me to invite you. I believe that you will look at the situation from a higher perspective and see that you are not my prisoner," said Seyoh with satisfaction before picking up the lamp and walking to the door. Just before passing through, he turned back and said, "If you like, you should accept Mellay's invitation. There are a variety of opinions among us believers. I'm sure you will learn something."

The door closed with a heavy thud. The flame in the single remaining lamp flickered before Yuui.

She sat in complete stillness for a while until Nova urged her to leave. Then every lamp in the room was at last snuffed out.

Her room had a single window, but all she could see out of it tonight was falling snow hiding the sky.

Yuui was lost in thought the entire time until she fell asleep. First the thoughts were about God, but when she tired of that, she thought of ways one would prove the existence of the sun, moon, and stars. Lastly, she wondered when Nova slept, since she was keeping guard outside Yuui's room.

2

The meetings weren't held every day. Outside of those meetings, Yuui spent all her time in the room given to her, with nothing but books on Marayism. She had Nova to talk to, but she would disappear at times as well. Yuui didn't know what she was doing. When she was gone, the room was as silent as a grave.

But it was loud that morning.

A whole week had passed since the last meeting. Normally, breakfast would be delivered to Yuui around this time, but no knocks came at the door. She got out of bed and thought vaguely to herself about how it should be anytime now.

Outside the light was growing. The entire town sparkled from the light reflected off the snow piles that had grown over the night. Yuui liked the sight. There wasn't any snow in Lukutta. She hadn't gone outside much during her first winter in the kingdom, so she struggled to learn how to walk across the snowdrifts.

Peering out the window, Yuui listened to all the different noises that drifted to her.

There was the sound of a door opening and closing, someone walking quickly, a voice meant to be heard by others. The sounds continued through the morning. This was the first time anything like this had happened since Yuui had come here.

She didn't know how many people were in this building, but she guessed based on its outside appearance that it was used for more than just the meetings. Considering it was managed by the lord, she imagined it could be a public meeting place or some sort of government building. Its historical air was the perfect decoration to show authority.

Outsiders who viewed her might assume she was of a significant position, considering she lived in this room, but that couldn't be further from the truth.

It wasn't the normal servant who brought food in the end. It was Nova.

"The servants seem busy, so I did it," she said as she closed the door and placed a bowl on the table. "Good morning."

"Has something happened?" asked Yuui.

"Yes." Nova nodded.

"What happened?"

"First," said Nova as she pointed toward Yuui. It was rare for her not to respond immediately.

"What?"

"Your soup, it's getting cold."

"Oh, I suppose that is true."

Yuui nodded and took the bowl.

Nova stared at Yuui, or at least that's what it looked like. Her bangs were in the way, meaning Yuui didn't know where Nova was looking.

But... Yuui stopped eating for a moment.

What did Nova think about her job?

Though she was currently acting as Yuui's attendant, her real assignment was to surveil Yuui while serving as her guard. Those two duties essentially amounted to the same thing, but it seemed absurd to be put in danger protecting the very person you were monitoring. Yuui wondered if her friend, who never showed her own will or emotions, might not be frustrated.

"An anonymous letter was delivered," said Nova abruptly, just as Yuui was finishing her breakfast. Yuui realized this was a continuation of their earlier conversation, but she needed time to swallow the last piece of bread she was chewing before she could respond.

"An anonymous letter...I see." In other words, Nova was explaining that the delivery had been the source of the racket this morning. Now that Yuui understood the situation, she considered what she should ask next. "Who was it addressed to?"

"Seyoh, along with the lord of Estosha." Nova's lips were the only part of her that moved as she replied. "It seems it was placed outside the entrance, this morning."

"What did it say?"

"That they would blow it up."

"Blow what up?" Yuui cocked her head.

"This building." Nova pointed toward her feet. "It also said it would end, the heretical meetings."

"That's not an *'anonymous letter,'* that's a threat."

"Whoever sent it, claimed they were in the criminal group planning the attack. But that the closer the deadline came, the guiltier they felt, so they sent that warning."

"So it's a warning letter," said Yuui as a filler comment before taking a sip of tea. "Am I right to guess you would like to leave this place immediately, then, Nova?"

"Yes."

"Perhaps…" Yuui placed a finger on her chin. "You have already suggested this to Seyoh, and he refused to allow it?"

"Yes. He said it would be dangerous, to make unnecessary moves. He also said, the enemy could be trying to force us out of here, or that it was simply a prank."

"There is some logic to his argument. A single letter is very weak evidence. We don't even know if these people are our enemies at this point. If we are to believe what the letter says, they may actually be our allies."

"At the very least, the enemy knows about the meetings," said Nova, refusing to call them allies. "They know what is being discussed, where they are being held, and who participates. And this is all, despite the fact the existence of the meetings has been, concealed. This is not just a prank."

"No matter how hard they try to hide these debates, they've been going on for five years. The details might be hard to come by, but I bet there are many people who have an inkling about what's going on. Perhaps the Old Order is feeling threatened by the Standards of Faith nearing completion and sent a fake letter to break down the meetings. That seems the most likely explanation."

"I can see that, but…" Nova looked down for a moment, then faced Yuui again. "But if they were trying to prevent the meetings, it would have been more effective to send an anonymous tip to the central authorities than sending a letter here. Besides, I don't see any point in preventing the debates, at this point. The Standards of Faith are almost finalized."

"Which would mean…" Yuui stood. "Where is Seyoh?"

"I'll take you." Nova opened the door in a single fluid motion.

Yuui left the room, her coat on and hood already pulled down over her face.

They walked through the frigid halls of the building, no

different in temperature from the air outside. Servants passed them a few times, but they always turned away when they did, acting as if they weren't looking at Yuui and Nova. They'd been trained well.

None of the people they encountered were in any rush, as most of them were inspecting the walls or floor. Someone was even leaning out the window to chat with a person outside.

Yuui and Nova climbed the stairs, which crisscrossed twice as they continued to the top level. Seyoh's room was at the back of the floor. It was the first time Yuui had been up here.

The door to his room was cracked half-open. Through the gap, Yuui could make out a maid whispering something to Seyoh, whose back was turned. Nova walked ahead of Yuui and knocked on the entrance.

"Ah, it's not often you come to visit me," he said, turning toward them and smiling.

The maid bowed and passed Yuui and Nova as she left the room, remembering to shut the door as she left.

"It seems you've already heard...," said Seyoh as he gestured to a chair in front of him.

Yuui sat there. Nova remained standing in front of the door.

It was a small chamber. Facing the entrance were Seyoh's desk and chair. There was also a chair for visitors, the one Yuui was using now, which was turned toward the desk. The walls were almost entirely covered by shelves lined with neat stacks of yellowed papers. The only sections free of shelving were the fireplace and the window, each casting different-colored light into the room.

"I am not underestimating the danger in any way," remarked Seyoh gravely as he pulled out his chair. "However, I would like you to understand that regardless of the letter, this is the safest location I am aware of within the city. We are taking the utmost precautions with security, and the building itself is incredibly sturdy. That's how it has persisted after so many—"

"Actually, I haven't come to complain about your handling of the situation," interjected Yuui with a slight smile. "I believe your decision is the logical one. If we panic and move locations, our security will almost certainly be compromised. It would be far more dangerous if we were attacked in that situation. Besides, the enemy would need the kind of firepower on par with a military-grade wand to blow up this building. It would be impossible for them to prepare something like that in secret."

"My thoughts exactly. Additionally, I just received a report stating that there are no signs of intruders in town. I believe there is no immediate threat. I've explained the situation to the servants and allowed any who wish to leave to do so. Nevertheless, I will continue to reside here. I can handle myself."

"Yes, and I hope that I may continue to impose upon your hospitality. It would be more difficult for you to spy on me if I was to relocate, after all."

"Oh, come now." Seyoh gave a pained smiled. "You say such things every now and again, and your overly polite language only makes it sting all the more."

"I know no other way of speaking." Yuui shrugged. She had only been learning Central Standard for two years. "One damages themselves by constantly speaking too low of themselves."

Seyoh nodded in acceptance. He clasped his hands together on top of the desk, then settled his gaze on Yuui. "Will you tell me the reason why you're here, then?"

"Before I do, there is one thing I would like to ask." Yuui held up a finger. "What do you make of this situation, Seyoh?"

"I am not in a position to be able to make judgments."

"I don't mind if it's simply your personal evaluation—"

"I don't have one. Putting my thoughts into words could influence the investigation. It is best in situations like this to distance ourselves from our preconceptions and consider every angle. If I had to give an opinion, it would be that."

"Then...have you considered that the culprit could be one of our own?" inquired Yuui. Seyoh was silent for several seconds. Yet his gaze never wavered, instead staying firmly on Yuui as she repeated herself. "There is a possibility the threat is coming from inside. The participants of the meetings know everything about them, from where they are located to what they hope to achieve. They would have no difficulty sending such a letter."

"Yes, of course I have," said Seyoh, wording his answer deliberately. "Though I don't like to consider it, I must not rule out the possibility. However, I do believe the probability of it being an inside job is low."

"Why is that?"

"Because they wouldn't have a reason to send the letter. What possible motive could they have for hindering the meetings? They came all the way to this city, heedless of their own safety, for the sole purpose of aiding the New Order."

"What if—"

"Please don't suggest one of them could be a mole for the Old Order," said Seyoh as he held a hand up to stop Yuui. "All the current participants have made immeasurable contributions to our cause. Simply refusing to attend would have done far more damage to the meetings than sending a threat letter."

"I suppose..."

"Which is why you shouldn't worry—"

"What concerns me isn't anything important like that," said Yuui as she got up. She slowly walked over to the window. It seemed like this room was almost directly on top of hers. The view was the same here, just from a higher vantage point.

The road in front of the entrance to the building was an unbroken sheet of white, save for a series of small footprints. She looked farther ahead and found two children running across the snow.

Yuui turned back to Seyoh, who had a questioning look on his face.

"No, what worries me is our current topic of debate," she said, turning her eyes back to the window. "I know you would like to keep the discussions purely theological, but regardless of how the debate unfolds, or even if it comes to a deadlock, the revolution will have a massive impact upon the world. Both financially and militarily."

"I am aware of that," came Seyoh's voice from behind her. "But—"

"I do not believe the current participants in these debates desire wealth or power. But even if they don't, surely the people around them do. Those kinds of obstacles will appear whenever members of the clergy interact with the public."

"And you believe that drove one of the participants to do this?"

Yuui didn't answer. She returned to the window and watched as the children disappeared into the shadow of a building.

Voicing suspicions about other people was fairly difficult for her. Yuui had been taught from a young age that it was an incredibly dishonorable thing to do.

But...with so much on the line...

She turned back again and said, "I have decided to accept the invitations of Mellay and the others."

"...Are you trying to discover who the culprit is?" asked Seyoh with a sudden smile, after a moment of silence.

"I do think there may be certain things I can learn from one-on-one conversations."

"Yes, I think that's a good idea. I have been suggesting you do so for a while now anyway, and I feel they'll be more comfortable opening up if it's you they're speaking with."

Yuui nodded in thanks and glanced beside the door. "Nova, is this all right with you?"

"Yes," she said, nodding as she always did.

Seyoh bowed and told her he would make arrangements immediately. Meanwhile, Yuui and Nova walked back down the hall, passing a few servants on their way.

Yuui saw snow fluttering about when she looked out the window again and wondered how much would fall this time around.

She turned toward Nova, who was walking behind her at an angle, and said, "I'm sorry for making that decision without asking you."

"It's all right."

"Will it inconvenience you?"

"I will go along with your decision," Nova said. But after they descended the staircase, she asked, "What's so important about the current topic, though?"

"The current debate?"

"As far as I can gather from what I've heard while standing behind you, it's a discussion on people and beasts."

"It is."

"But you said it would have, financial and military repercussions."

"Ah, that… That's because of the topic that will inevitably come up when we debate the current one. That will be an issue, which is why the participants have requested experts on the subject."

"And what, is that topic?"

"Uh, well…" Yuui gazed at the ceiling, wondering how best to explain it. She stumbled upon a good explanation just as they arrived in front of the door to her room. "Simply put, it is the question of whether wands should come under central control of the church."

3

The duo didn't manage to make a trip out that day, but they did end up going to meet Mellay the next morning. They would be meeting neither at the church nor Mellay's home, as she wasn't a resident of Estosha.

The address they were given was that of a modest mansion in the city, squeezed between two tall buildings. Though *"modest"* may have been an understatement—it was still of significant size. Yuui would later learn that Mellay didn't own the place and was simply borrowing it from an acquaintance for the winter.

Though snow was piled on the roof and windows, it had been neatly swept to the side in front of the entrance. It seemed Mellay was expecting company.

When they knocked, it took mere seconds for a servant to come to the door and lead them into the house without a single word. Their face was completely expressionless, though in a different way from Nova's typical inscrutability, and their mouth was set in a firm line that never once opened. The servant seemed like they knew why the two girls were hiding their faces.

Normally, someone would offer to take your coat when you entered a manor like this, but that didn't happen this time. Yuui had been hesitant to enter with her jacket on, since she didn't want it to drip on the floor, but the servant didn't seem to mind. They simply opened the door ahead and walked farther into the building.

"This is the person, who stands behind Mellay at the meetings," murmured Nova as they followed along.

"You can tell?" Yuui asked back.

"From the way, that they walk."

The servant stopped momentarily, perhaps having overheard them, but immediately began walking again. Either that or they had determined the girls' identities using the same method.

After passing several chambers, the servant opened the door to one. Instead of entering, they stood to the side of the entrance, their hands clasped as they looked at Yuui and Nova.

"Thank you," said Yuui before she headed into the room.

They were greeted by the sound of a crackling fire. It kept the room pleasantly warm, but not stuffy. The furniture gleamed in the light. It all looked brand-new, without a speck of dust in sight. When Yuui inhaled, she caught a pleasant scent wafting from somewhere. This room was so comfortable, you would almost think spring had just arrived. It was like a completely different world from the world outside.

An old woman was standing in the center of the chamber.

"Welcome. Thank you for visiting," she said as she spread her arms.

"Thank you for allowing us to visit on such short notice, Mellay," said Yuui with a bow.

Obviously, she had never seen the old woman's face. All she knew was the sound of her voice in that dark room. Even so, the moment Yuui saw her, she instinctively recognized that this woman was Mellay. She had her same air of dignity.

The door behind them closed quietly, and Nova stood beside it, like always.

Yuui turned toward Mellay, who stared straight back and asked, "Is this your first time meeting someone like me?"

"No, I've met one other," replied Yuui as she adjusted her hood.

"Oh really? And is this person doing well?"

"Yes, though I haven't spoken to them much lately."

"I am happy to hear that one of my kin is doing well," said Mellay with a couple of blinks. "At any rate, you must be surprised."

"I know it's rude to be, but..."

"Rude? Not at all. It's to be expected. Women in the clergy are rare enough, but on top of that, I am the only vukodrak to ever attain this high a rank in the church. Unfortunate though it may be."

Long silvery fur covered Mellay's entire body. Fangs glinted in her jaw. She smiled gently at Yuui with her green eyes, but it wasn't the sort of smile you'd expect from a sweet old lady. It was the sort of grin a powerful person makes when they know they have the advantage.

She was a vukodrak, a member of a species whose lands had been invaded by the kingdom in the past before eventually being incorporated into its domain.

"I'm afraid I can't provide much in the way of refreshments, but I do have some tea and sweets. Please take a seat over there and make yourself at home," said Mellay as she pointed farther into the room. "I'll bring the tea; we can savor it together."

Several chairs, their backs tall and covered with soft leather, had been arranged around the fireplace.

Mellay bowed slightly and left the room.

Yuui scanned the area as she softly stepped closer to the fireplace. She sat in a chair that faced the fire at an angle. Then she looked to her side and nearly stopped breathing in shock.

There was a person there. Two, in fact.

A pair of men were sat on a double-seated sofa right in front of the fire. Yuui hadn't noticed them before because they'd been hidden from behind by the back of the sofa.

One of the men had his eyes closed, his mouth hanging half open. He looked like he was asleep. He was resting his head on the other man's shoulder. Though this man appeared to be awake, he must not have noticed Yuui, because he hadn't budged an inch. The light of the fire reflected in his eyes.

What surprised Yuui even more was that the two men looked exactly alike, in both face and build. Their slightly wavy blond hair and the construction of their features, what with their high-bridged noses, looked practically identical. Yuui couldn't tell what their eye color was, but she suspected they were the same. The only difference between the two was their expressions. The easygoing look on the sleeping man's face was the complete opposite of the severe look on his awake counterpart.

As Yuui stared at them, the sleeping man mumbled in his

sleep and twitched before his breathing started to sound like he had woken up. Yuui saw Nova move out of the corner of her eye. She must have noticed the men's presence as well. She drew forward slowly, until she came around behind Yuui.

"Mm...mm." The man who had been sleeping half opened his eyes and stretched his arms out high toward the ceiling. He yawned as he turned his head side to side, where his eyes met Yuui's.

"H-hello...," she somehow managed to stammer out first.

"Oh, visitors!" remarked the man in a clear voice. It was hard to believe he'd been snoozing a moment before. A huge grin appeared on his face. "Don't be so shy. We're visitors, too, so we're in the same boat! Hey, you don't mind that I dozed off for a bit there, do you? I mean, when I came to this room, it was so nice and toasty, you'd think it was made just for napping! Hey, Hemsley! You were awake, so you should be saying hello first. Or did you already do it?"

Yuui was taken aback by the flood of words coming from the man's mouth.

The other fellow, Hemsley, frowned and said, "Cram it."

"Now, now! All right, guess I'll do the introductions. This guy's Hemsley, and I'm Rolphie. Nice to meet you, person whose face I can't see!" he continued. "Did that old lady call you here, too? She's pushy, huh? I have no idea where she heard about it, but there was a servant standing outside our hotel the day after we were invited to the meeting. Man, this is the worst. I was planning on doing a whole lot of nothing this whole winter!"

"U-uh-huh...," responded Yuui vaguely. "So you will be attending...that meeting?"

"Oh, so you're going, too? Yep, we are. Not like I asked to go, but they're paying, so I can't complain, I guess. Not much to it besides showing up and talking, yeah?"

Rolphie jabbed Hemsley with his elbow to elicit his agreement, but Hemsley just glared back at him.

In an attempt to cut off Rolphie, who seemed on the verge of babbling even more, Yuui asked, "You wouldn't happen to be the wandmakers who were invited to the meetings?"

"Yep, that's us," he answered with a bob of his head.

"Which means…you were apprentices of Munzil?"

"Ha-ha-ha, I'd rather not hear that old fart's name. Be careful, 'cause I'll sock you the next time you mention him!" Rolphie smiled as he continued. "Uh…"

"Oh, I'm sorry, my name is—"

"Ah, it's fine, it's fine! To be honest, I don't care about your name!"

"O-oh…"

"But you've got some guts mentioning that old fart in front of me! Speaking of, I've got a question for you. You," he said, his eyes narrowing slightly, "have met other apprentices of his, haven't you? Who were they?"

Yuui was left speechless before his direct stare. How had he been able to intuit that much from this conversation? Not that it could even really be called a conversation; it was more a one-sided stream of words.

But Yuui had seen enough of their mannerisms to be certain these two were Munzil's apprentices. They gave off a very particular impression. You could say they had a peculiar air about them.

"It was a while ago, but I met Ix," said Yuui carefully.

"Oooh, Ix the moron!" cried Rolphie loudly, then held his sides like he couldn't stand how funny that was and said, "Did you hear that, Hemsley? Ha-ha-ha, Ix! The moron!"

"Be quiet," demanded Hemsley bluntly.

"How's that numbskull doing? Actually, don't answer that. I couldn't care less if he's alive or dead!"

"So why did Mellay have you over?" asked Yuui, forcing a change in topic. She'd already realized there was no point trying to have a real conversation with this guy. "Have you heard what will be discussed at the next meeting?"

"What are you talking about?" Rolphie shrugged. "How the hell would I know what they're going to talk about at the next debate or whatever? I don't even know what these things are. I'm just going to answer whatever questions people ask me!"

"That...is..."

Yuui shuddered, impressed by how fast Mellay worked. She had already anticipated the issue that would be raised at the next meeting as well as the questions that would be asked of the wand-makers. That's why she must have found them and posed the same questions to them beforehand. She would be at an overwhelming advantage next meeting if she already knew the answers.

"What exactly did she ask you?" inquired Yuui.

Rolphie jumped to his feet and exclaimed, "You've got some funny questions!" He stepped toward Yuui and held his right hand out to her.

"Um, what is this?" she asked, confused.

"My knowledge isn't so cheap that I'll just give it away for free." He flashed a carefree smile. "I'll tell you if you pay up. The going rate's about..."

There was no need for Yuui to check her coin purse. The price Rolphie put forward was so steep that she would never be able to afford it.

Yuui shook her head, to which he shrugged with an "oh well."

"All righty then. My nap's over, think it's about time we head back." Rolphie pivoted away from her, then pulled up the other man by the arm. "Righty-o, see you later, uh... You know, I don't care about your name! Right, Hemsley?"

"Don't talk to me," he snapped.

With that, the duo made to leave the room. Just then, however, Yuui suddenly called out to stop them. "W-wait a moment."

"What?" Rolphie turned back only partway, showing his smooth features in profile. "We're busy, yeah?"

"Did you speak with Mellay about what will be discussed next meeting?"

"Come off it. I don't care about that."

"If you're a wandmaker, your interest should be piqued," said Yuui slowly. "We will be talking about wands, after all."

Rolphie cocked his head to the side and stared at her. His eyebrows came together in a questioning look.

After staying like that for a moment, there came the sound of a chuckle from deep within his throat. He was guffawing. His laughter grew until it seemed loud enough to rattle the building.

"Ha-ha-ha-ha! What are you saying?!" He spread his arms and looked up at the ceiling. "I don't have any interest in wands!"

"Uh..." Yuui was taken aback, while Rolphie laughed even more.

"I don't give a flying flip about them! What I'm interested in is the massive profits that they bring! That's it!"

"Wh-what?" Yuui would never have expected that kind of statement to come from the mouths of the wandmakers she'd met so far. It left her flabbergasted. "Wh-what about you, Hemsley? You are a wandmaker as well, yes?"

"I don't care," he spat back immediately.

"Ha-ha-ha, this guy, he's the exact opposite of me. He's only interested in stuff that comes before the wand!" said Rolphie as he slipped an arm around Hemsley's shoulder. "He only ever thinks about the wood and trees we use to make 'em! A bit of an oddball, isn't he?"

"I'm hot, get off me," barked Hemsley coldly.

"Anyway, that's just how it is," said Rolphie.

"But...," started Yuui, trying to stop them somehow.

Rolphie, who had already stepped out of the room, looked back and sighed in exasperation. "You still going on? If you're about to ask if we're twins, we're not."

"Oh, really?"

As she was unexpectedly brought back to her first question about them, the door closed.

Into the now-silent room stepped Mellay, a tray in her hands. "Oh, did they leave?"

4

For once, Nova didn't taste the tea and sweets that were served to check for poison. She must have been cognizant of the fact that they weren't served for her, and it would be rude of her to do so, considering they'd been invited.

"I hear quite the letter has been delivered," said Mellay before Yuui could bring it up.

"What do you think of it?" she asked the old woman.

"I haven't the foggiest. Who are they? And what are they after...? Even if the accusations were true, no one would benefit from such a violent act."

"Sometimes people act illogically. Are you aware of what transpired in Leirest?"

"I am. And it was members of the New Order—our order— who were responsible. How foolish. What on earth did they think that would change...?" Mellay stared off into the distance. "You may be right that it's the same now. If these meetings or I went up in smoke, it would amount to a tiny portion of the New Order disappearing. In the grand scheme of things, the attack would have zero impact. But perhaps it would bring them...hope. Hope to people who feel trapped."

"Do you feel threatened at all?"

"Of course I do. But at my age, danger becomes a part of everyday life. I'm more likely to meet my end by slipping in the snow tomorrow than being blown away with the building like the threat claimed."

"While that may be true, it is a peculiar way of thinking..."

"What I mean is that the letter doesn't particularly bother me. It's probably best just to think of it as one of the ghost's pranks."

"Ghost...?" murmured Yuui. "You mentioned that before. An old tale in town, yes?"

"Oh, is that what you came to ask about?" Mellay's eyes widened in surprise, and she chuckled. "I see... Indeed, if an old person like me was to tell a story while sitting in front of the fireplace on a day like today, then it should very well be a fantastical one."

"Is it a well-known tale?"

"Unfortunately, I'm not too knowledgeable about it myself, but it is quite famous around these parts," said Mellay. "Night after night in Estosha, you can hear voices, footsteps, groans, and screams. It does not matter if it's in a mansion or in a small home; the sounds can happen anywhere. But there's never anyone there. There's nothing in the bushes, nothing in the attic... That's what they say. It is supposedly the work of the ghost, slipping in unannounced. There aren't too many mentions of the specter these days, but long ago, there were many people who claimed to have heard it."

"When did these stories start spreading?"

"That I am not positive about... Though, thinking about the customs, I would guess it was around when Rednoff was here. It's such a strange tale."

That would mean this legend had been told for hundreds of years. Quite an old yarn.

And Rednoff...?

For a moment, Yuui wondered if the story had anything to do with wands. Her interest was piqued, since it would have been created around the advent of man-made magic catalysts.

Next, it was Mellay's turn to change the subject. "I heard your conversation earlier while I was in the kitchen. They're an amusing pair, aren't they?"

"Huh?" Yuui looked up. "Yes, I suppose you could say that..."

"Please don't misunderstand, I'm not trying to uncover your true identity," said Mellay as she placed her teacup back on the table and looked at Yuui. "But I must be honest, Minaha, I've become even more curious about you after hearing that. You've realized that the next topic of debate will be how wandmakers are handled after the revolution, haven't you?"

"It is the obvious conclusion based on the current flow of the discussion." Yuui nodded. "You went to the trouble of asking craftsmen here, after all."

"Most of the participants likely believe that is for a different and trivial point of discussion. Yet it is interesting, questioning a wandmaker in Estosha of all places."

"What do you mean?"

"Oh, it's not important." Mellay shrugged. "So then, Minaha, how did you come to believe that wands would be an important point of discussion?"

"Because it is an issue of classification," said Yuui immediately.

"Yes, exactly." Mellay smiled. "This topic is particularly important to me. The scriptures only clarify a distinction between *humans* and magic beasts. But then what is it that separates us vukodrak from simple wolves? We must solidify a definition."

This was the topic they were currently debating.

To Yuui, the fact that the scriptures mentioned only humans was explained simply by the fact that it had been authored by them. But to the others, it was a serious dilemma.

The Old Order had their own general explanation for that.

"I thought that was already explained, that anyone who is capable of understanding Marayism is a person, and everyone else is a magic beast?" asked Yuui with a tilt of her head as she stared at Mellay.

"It's too narrow and contradictory a definition." The old woman shook her head. "If someone didn't believe in Marayism originally but became a follower partway through their life, did they transform from a magic beast to a person? As the scriptures say, the whole world is the child of God. We must not spread mistaken interpretations of the scriptures."

She rubbed her hands together and looked directly at Yuui as she said, "Even without forcing an explanation onto it, there is still one very suggestive depiction in the scriptures. You've realized what that is, haven't you, Minaha?"

"The 'five-legged beast.'"

Mellay nodded. "Do you know the details?"

"*The two-legged beast knew God's grace and thus created the third arm. In its jealousy of those people, the four-legged beast stole God's arm and thus created its fifth leg. The beast was banished into eternal damnation...*," said Yuui, reciting the scripture from memory without hesitation. "Generally, the passage is a way of expressing how sinful it is to deceive God."

"You are very well-read on the matter," said Mellay as she clasped her hands together in glee. "In other words, the real demarcation is 'whether or not they can create the third arm.' That is the standard that separates us from beasts. If you analyze the scriptures logically, you naturally come to that conclusion. And, of course, we must interpret the 'third arm' as spells and, at the same time, wands. With that, history also makes complete sense, don't you think? The ancient forest sages lived in the woods of the kingdom, and Rednoff, the person who invented man-made wands, was a kingdom citizen. The kingdom was the first country in the world to gain the technology needed to make wands *because* of our faith."

"But that does raise another issue." Yuui held up a finger. "With how important catalysts are... The Church cannot possibly leave the craftsmen who make them to run loose. Don't you agree?"

"'*Run loose*' isn't the most positive way to put it," said Mellay with a pained smile. "But yes, you are correct. We cannot allow a technique God gifted us to spread so easily to other nations. Ideally, the Church would absorb the Guild. And I'm sure you know what would be required to do that, Minaha. That was the only thing I confirmed with that pair beforehand."

Seeing Mellay's smile as she spoke, Yuui realized that the old woman had received the answer she'd been hoping for. That was why her next words weren't a question but a request for confirmation.

"There was no flaw, yes?"

"No, there was not. Making wandmakers members of the clergy would not cause any hindrance. That allows us to wrap up the scriptures without contradiction."

Yuui had predicted this was exactly how things would go. That was the only possible way of sorting things if the scriptures upheld wands as holy objects. At the very least, that was what Mellay was going to lead the meeting to conclude.

Yet, Yuui still considered it strange.

If you thought things through logically, you would arrive at the conclusion that wandmakers would have to become part of the Church. That's how Yuui was also able to hit on the answer. She didn't know how wandmaking would be adjusted to conform with the scriptures, but that wasn't the issue.

The issue was everything outside of Marayism. Wands were high-value items, and a massive market, encompassing everything from procuring their materials to selling the actual product, had developed around them. The majority of buyers were nobles or powerful merchants, people with influence. And when you considered the fact that wands were also used in the military, the question of wandmaking extended all the way out to the country's security. Mellay had suggested that the Church would absorb the Guild, but things weren't that simple. It would take a while for the Guild to be integrated into the Church. And even if that could be accomplished, it would have huge ramifications on the kingdom and its citizenry.

But based on Mellay's tone, those issues seemed to be none of her concern. It was almost as if she thought everything besides consistency with the scripture was irrelevant.

Yuui had hoped to delve further into the topic with Mellay, but the old woman didn't seem willing to show her hand any more than that. She smiled as if to say they would continue that discussion at the meeting, then steered the conversation to trivial gossip.

Yuui and Nova left Mellay's mansion before noon. She'd offered them lunch, but Yuui politely declined.

"Is it, for Ix?" asked Nova suddenly as she walked behind Yuui on the way back.

"Huh? Is what?" she asked, turning back.

"Is he why, you're so concerned about this?" continued Nova, her expression as blank as ever. "If being a member of the clergy is added as a requirement for being a craftsman, that would be quite hard on Ix. Is that why, you're trying to prevent it?"

"No... I think you are reading too much into this." Yuui shrugged. "You should know, you've been with me for this long. I am a simpler person than that. My only real motive is to help people if I see them in need."

"Is that, so?" Nova nodded slightly, without indicating whether she'd accepted Yuui's words or not.

The noon bell rang. It sounded incredibly loud because they'd made it back far enough to be close to the Chapel. Yuui had long grown used to it since coming to Estosha. A high-pitched tone echoed across town as the bell chimed, a significant pause hanging between each note. Even the air seemed to tremble as if numb during this time.

As the third note rang out, Nova suddenly came up from behind Yuui. She grabbed Yuui's right hand and pulled her forward.

"What is it?" asked Yuui.

She could see Nova's mouth moving, but she couldn't make out what Nova was saying between the clangs of the bell. Giving up, Nova shut her mouth and pulled Yuui around a corner.

The fifth note rang out, and since they had gotten closer to the Chapel, it sounded even louder.

They immediately turned another corner onto a wide road. Nova stopped and pushed Yuui against the wall of a building. She brought her mouth to Yuui's ear and began to speak, but the other girl still couldn't hear anything. Nova shook her head.

The bell rang again.

Yuui touched the wand inside her pocket. Nova wasn't the kind of person to do something without reason. She'd likely sensed danger. Someone following them or an assailant. With how urgently the girl was acting, the latter seemed very likely. Nova hadn't struck back because she wasn't sure how many enemies there were.

Ahead of where Yuui was looking, the snow at the base of the corner they'd rounded a moment earlier burst into the air. It flew skyward in a wide area, turning to mist and revealing the ground below.

Since the sound of the bells had smothered the noise of the spell, this looked as though it had played out without a single sound.

Yuui moved on instinct, but Nova held her back.

That's when she realized their assailant had lost sight of them.

But the attacker was casting such daring incantations. Yuui and Nova couldn't just hide to deal with this kind of opponent. If they weren't going to launch a counterattack, then their only option was to flee.

Farther down in the direction they were facing stood the building where the meetings were held, which would be their best option from a defensive standpoint. But Yuui was concerned the enemy would tail them and discover where they were living. Nova shared the same uncertainty.

Snow erupted into the air again, this time exposing the ground directly in front of them. Clods of white struck their faces. The enemy was closing in.

©Enji

Nova put her hand in her breast pocket and pulled out her wand.

Then she leaped out into the middle of the road in time with the chime of the next bell.

It was a split-second decision. Yuui jumped right behind Nova. She slipped her hand around Nova from the back and covered the girl's eyes. Yuui squeezed her own eyelids shut tight and pointed her wand toward the sky.

The white flash was so bright, it still dazzled her through her eyelids.

Immediately, she lowered her wand and removed her hand from Nova's eyes.

For a brief moment, Nova looked like she wanted to say something, but then quickly took Yuui's hand and plunged into the mist of snow they'd created a moment earlier.

Yuui didn't know if her plan had gone well, but she assumed that the enemy had been focusing on Nova the moment she leaped out from her hiding spot beside the building. If the light she'd produced met their eyes, they would be temporarily blinded.

The enemy had blasted the snow into the air to conceal their own approach, but that was now working in Yuui and Nova's favor. The snow would conceal their footprints once it fell back down.

They made it back to their home building, nearly slipping and falling several times on the way. The pair burst into the entrance, out of breath, and the servants regarded them with furrowed brows as they passed through the hall.

5

Yuui and Nova informed only Seyoh about the attack.

He told them he would go investigate where it happened, but

it seemed to be a dead end. A few days later, he showed up, shoulders slumped, to reveal that he hadn't turned up anything. Not a single clue. After this, he informed the other participants in the meetings and warned them to be cautious. The enemy's motive was still unknown.

Anyone would guess that the person who sent the threat, or the group that person belonged to, was responsible for the attack, but that was unlikely.

Yuui thought it over several times, but all she found were questions. Who would stand to gain from eliminating her? She was the least important person in these debates. And the fact that they'd come after her in broad daylight made it difficult for her to believe they had any real intention of killing her.

Though Yuui had been invited to speak with some of the other participants besides Mellay, there was no way she could accept them after this incident. In the end, she spent every day like she had before—holed up in her room, bored.

During one of those days, she learned that Gustavus, another meeting participant, was close by. Seyoh visited her room to tell her.

"What do you mean by that?" asked Yuui.

"He's at Estosha Chapel," he replied. "What will you do? Are you going to meet him?"

"What do you think, Seyoh?"

"Would my opinion have an impact on your decision?" he asked, raising his eyebrows in surprise. "I will neither force you to go nor stop you from attending. I have tried to maintain the same stance ever since I invited you here."

"What about you, Nova? Do you think it is much of a risk?"

"The Chapel is right across the street, and many people are, gathered there. I think, there is no danger of attack," she replied flatly.

"Would you like me to accompany you?" asked Seyoh.

Yuui declined and went with Nova alone.

The early-winter sunset was approaching. The sun dipped down, slowly changing the color of the sky. Unlike usual, however, an atmosphere of excitement was wafting through the street. Large groups of people seemed hard at work around where the Chapel was located.

As they entered the grounds, Yuui and Nova came across a group of people wearing clerical vestments. There was a pile of what looked like construction materials on one section of the ground, which the workers were carrying around. Several of them were building something. They seemed to be engaged in some sort of construction work or preparation.

One of the people who happened to be near Yuui and Nova noticed them and drew closer. He was a boy with freckled cheeks. When Yuui told him they'd come to see Gustavus, he ran into the Chapel.

Not long after that, another person in clerical garb emerged from inside the building. He was a middle-aged man. His hair was thinning slightly, and he wore a warm smile on his face.

"You must be Miss Minaha, correct?" He spread his arms out as he walked toward them. He sounded just like the Gustavus she'd heard in the meetings. "I didn't expect we'd meet in a place like this, though."

"I was passing through and thought I would drop by to say hello," said Yuui, bowing.

"It's cold out here. I wish I could invite you inside, but the Chapel is in the middle of preparations right now... My apologies."

"That is all right—here is fine. I don't plan on taking too much of your time."

The three of them moved to a section of the Chapel grounds. Nova stood a slight distance away, scanning the area.

"Now... I'm glad you've come. I've been hoping to have an opportunity to speak with you like this," said Gustavus as he rubbed his hands together.

"I have as well," said Yuui.

"Ah, you've met other participants besides me, haven't you? I mean, outside of the meetings, of course."

"I spoke with Mellay."

"Mellay... I see." He grimaced momentarily. "Though, yes, that isn't surprising. She is the most prominent participant in the debates. Speaking with her first would be the right way to do things."

Yuui was aware that Gustavus was the only person who directly opposed Mellay in the meetings. She couldn't help but notice that he always spoke without hesitation toward her, despite their slight difference in age.

Whenever Seyoh brought up an issue, Mellay and Gustavus would plead their cases, while the other participants expressed support for one side or the other. That was the normal flow of the debates. Mellay would often point out inconsistencies in Gustavus's positions, which meant she would come out on top, but that didn't change the fact that the pair comprised the core of the meetings.

That was why Gustavus had been one of the participants Yuui was most eager to speak with, along with Mellay.

"What is everyone doing right now?" she asked.

"Hmm? Oh, preparing for the festival," said Gustavus.

"A festival around this time... That would be Heaven's Worship, yes?"

"Indeed. The current plan is to hold the festival on the same day as the next meeting. I would love for you to attend as well, Minaha."

"Ah... I will consider it."

"Oh, don't be so strict. It's not like other festivals—there's no alcohol or food going around. It's a small event that doesn't need any fancy equipment or special rituals. All you need to do is go outside and gaze quietly up at the sky. That actually means the work we're doing now isn't strictly necessary. There are just a few odd jobs we need to take care of, since so many people will be coming to the Chapel."

"Gustavus, is this city your home?"

"It is for now. I'm close with the priest of Estosha. He sometimes calls me over and makes me do things like this."

"But I thought the priest of Estosha was Old Order? And the New Order dislikes these sorts of festivals and events, and normally it should be the monks who come to assist, yes?"

The monastery was an Old Order institution, which would be eliminated when the New Order took power. That was because one of their core beliefs was that the average citizen could accomplish in their daily lives what the monks were doing at the monastery.

When Yuui spoke, Gustavus suddenly laughed.

"That sounds like something Mellay or Seyoh would say. I see, so you're that kind of person as well, Miss Minaha."

"That kind of person?" asked Yuui, her head tilted.

"An academic type. A clerical person like me can't think like that."

Yuui suddenly looked around and saw that the monks who were working were glancing their way. They seemed interested in her, this mysterious figure who'd suddenly appeared to engage in a lively discussion with Gustavus. It wasn't surprising, considering her face and general form were concealed. They probably hadn't realized she wasn't even an adult, and they definitely hadn't clued in to the fact she was an easterner.

Gustavus held up an open hand toward them and smiled.

"I have been a member of the clergy in cities for a very long time now. I only have what I know. Instead of staying in one area, I went to all sorts of different places whenever I was told to. I've met many priests and the people who listen to them. And what I've come to understand is that theory is not compatible with practice. The academic type may tout their theory, but the clerical type follows practice," he said, explaining what he meant by clerical. "Of course, theory is still important, in both doctrine and theology. But it is convincing only to a handful of people, namely the clergy and theologians like us. This in no way means that the average person is a fool. Rather, it means that even if most people understand theory, they require a massive amount of knowledge to find it convincing. They don't have the time to learn all that. Do you get what I'm saying?"

"I think I do...," said Yuui vaguely with a nod.

"Let me give you an example. Something we're often asked is, 'Why doesn't God fix the world's misfortunes and absurdities? Why are honest and good people so mistreated while evil people are so prevalent?' So then, Minaha, how would you answer these questions?"

"I would say that humans are incapable of understanding God," responded Yuui immediately.

"That's theory," said Gustavus, his breath turning white. "Humans, whose knowledge is limited, couldn't possibly understand the will of our omniscient Lord. The fact that we ask 'why' is in itself proof that we don't understand God. And that answer would satisfy Mellay or Seyoh. It's the correct answer from a purely theological standpoint."

"I see... Ordinary citizens certainly wouldn't accept the response I just gave."

"It's a given. The people want an explanation, not theory. They'll assume that if they can't understand God, they don't have to follow the teachings. But that's a problem for the priests who are meant to teach and guide them. And that's why people try to come up with some sort of explanation. Such as, 'Take joy in your poverty. The richer you are, the closer you are to corruption, and the more you will be tested.' Theoretically, that's incorrect. But we give that answer because it's necessary in practice."

Gustavus's stance in the meetings finally made sense to Yuui.

What Seyoh and Mellay were after was a purely theological argument. They were focused entirely on the scriptures, so their field of view was rather narrow. That was precisely what allowed them to make clear assertions about their stances, which in turn allowed them to easily gather support from the other participants.

Gustavus, on the other hand, was approaching the debate from a wider vantage point. This inevitably made his arguments vaguer and created contradictions. Even if his position matched the real-life application of Marayism, it was disadvantageous in a debate setting.

"I can't go saying this too loudly," said Gustavus as he lowered his voice, "but I'm not that optimistic about the New Order's current policy. Obviously, I agree that we need to pull together clear doctrine, but it will absolutely diverge and become distorted once the revolution comes. It's easy for the New Order to say they'll abolish the monasteries tomorrow once they gain power. But what about the monks who actually live there here and now? The fact is, even if you've got your perfect armchair-theory revolution, it won't be that simple to actually execute it. I am well aware of that."

He brought his hand to his mouth and gave a wry grin as he said, "Listen to me now. That's enough to make me sound like I'm the one who sent that threat letter."

"What do you think about that, Gustavus?"

"Ah..."

Some pickets were being put up on the Chapel grounds. Four or five men got in a group, counted to three together, and placed them into the earth.

Yuui guessed it was probably a bonfire. Heaven's Worship was held at night. It would be dangerous to have crowds of people gathering in the dark.

The men smiled at one another. Their project had gone well. A few of them looked up at the sky. Yuui followed their gazes, but at some point, gray clouds had filled the sky, concealing even the sun.

"I think the threat is meaningless, regardless of whether it is part of a real plot or if it is just a prank. From a theoretical standpoint, at least," said Gustavus gravely. "But this is reality. In the real world, meaning is found only within the individual. We shouldn't take the letter lightly. Since these meetings are being kept under wraps, there's a high chance it came from someone on the inside. You suspect as much, don't you?"

"Ah, well, I..." Yuui fumbled for her words.

"It's fine. It's just, this sort of situation makes me feel like speaking my mind. I'm sure Mellay is the same."

After that, they made some small talk.

Though she hadn't asked Gustavus about this in detail, Yuui was certain that he would oppose Mellay at the next meeting. Though having wandmakers become members of the clergy might not have been inconsistent with the scriptures, it was infeasible in practice. He wasn't the sort of person to let that slip by.

Gustavus walked Yuui out of the chapel grounds. Just as they were saying good-bye, she happened to remember something and asked, "Gustavus, have you heard of the Specter of Estosha?"

"Hmm? Did Mellay tell you about that?"

He explained the ghost stories to Yuui. His account was largely the same as what Mellay had told her, albeit more detailed. When Yuui asked Gustavus how he knew so much about the tales, he told her there was a book that recorded testimonies of the people who claimed to have heard the ghost's sounds.

"That is incredible... Where can I find this book?" asked Yuui out of sheer curiosity.

"Seyoh has it right now," said Gustavus with a nod. "It's not particularly interesting from a narrative perspective, but it's fine reading for staving off the winter boredom."

"Yet it seems somewhat strange that these ghost stories would spread across the entire town...," she said, bringing a hand to her cheek. "Almost as if there are people who truly believe them."

"Ah, well...," said Gustavus, a strange expression on his face for some reason.

"What is it?"

"No, it's just, the ghost stories of this town aren't completely ungrounded in reality. They're just tricky for followers of Marayism to talk about. People avoid telling them aloud, so a lot of people have forgotten them…"

He looked side to side, checking they were the only ones there. Then he whispered, "Dragon."

"Huh?"

"Once, a dragon appeared near Estosha and created life with its magic. That is the specter. That's the legend from way back when."

"About how long ago was that…?"

"It's just a tale."

Yuui wanted to ask for more details, but Gustavus said he'd see her at the next meeting and cut off the conversation.

"You'd better go home soon. With these clouds, it looks like we might have a blizzard," said Gustavus as he pointed to the sky.

As Yuui stared at Gustavus and the clouds moving quickly across the firmament, she suddenly remembered people talking about how the sky was always clear on the night of Heaven's Worship.

6

The clouds had looked menacing since the night before, but Ix and Shuno paid them no mind as they walked to the monastery.

But the snow and wind grew stronger in the afternoon, turning into a violent blizzard before they knew it. Earlier in the day, they'd stepped out to check the weather, and it still seemed fine, but when next they went outside, everything was coated in white.

Ix stared out the window as he swept up the wood fragments on the floor.

He thought about how it was white both inside and out.

Life here was pure white.

Nothing of note ever happened. He woke up at the same time every day, did the same work, ate the same food. There was no color. Like a canvas painted with white.

In reality, three weeks had passed since he and Shuno had begun making the staffs. Ix hadn't even noticed it until he counted the days. Each had gone by so fast.

The job was going well. In fact, it was going significantly faster than normal, probably on account of the environment. It had been a while since he'd carved wood, but it was as pleasant as ever.

Both Ix and Shuno had already become a part of this small world. They came at the same time every day and continued their work in the same room. Even problems and their solutions were worked into their daily existence.

"You two are practically one of us," said Beter once.

"What do you mean by that?" asked Shuno in response.

"I just thought you seemed like monks. I can tell that both you and Ix are really devoted to your work. The only difference is that you don't live in the monastery."

"You think so?" asked Shuno as they tilted their head. "I've never studied Marayism, though."

"That isn't a joke. I'm mostly serious," he said, dropping his voice low. "Ix, Shuno, I can make some introductions for you at a monastery if you'd like."

"Why are you bringing this up all of sudden?" asked Ix in surprise.

"When someone isn't suited to life in the monastery, they're completely mismatched. I've seen so many cases when someone comes in and leaves a few days later, or even that very same day. But then there are people who grow accustomed to this life. Even if they have to leave for some reason, they always come back. I can kind of see that personality in you two... Sorry if I'm too much of a busybody."

The conversation ended there, but as Ix thought back to what Beter had said a number of times since, it struck him that his client Yuui had also said something similar to him.

She'd told him craftsmen were like devout believers.

Now Ix was starting to think she might have been right. His lifestyle aligned with the monks'. Or perhaps it was better to say they led his ideal lifestyle.

But there was one critical difference. The monks worked to please God—that was everything for them.

But what about him?

For what purpose did he make wands?

It was a question that had plagued Ix ever since that day.

That day, that evening.

Ever since Shuno had revealed they wanted to craft a wand you could fly with.

They were already thinking through the theory needed to make it and would surely accomplish it someday. Or at least they had said as much, their expression full of excitement as they did. Ix had thought up a concept for that type of wand but immediately gave up on it.

Considering this hadn't made him feel like Shuno was a genius.

Instead, it forced Ix to realize that he'd been arrogant for believing he was on Shuno's level.

They were a craftsperson in an entirely different league.

So then, what should he do?

Long ago, his teacher, Munzil, had said that Ix had a talent for making catalysts. He said that because he had lost magic, he could step outside of a wand. But Ix knew that he hadn't gained any ability in exchange for his magic.

He could never forge the ultimate wand, or a wand that soared through the sky.

Was he just going to keep cranking out wands to make a living?

His whole life? Without any goal?

And that led to…

White.

If that was what his life was going to be, then maybe there would be some point in going into a monastery, reading the scriptures he was so unfamiliar with, and making catalysts for God. That was where Ix's mind was going.

As Ix stared outside and mindlessly went about his work, Beter came into the workroom.

"We've readied your lodgings," he said.

"Thank you," said Shuno as they turned around to face Beter, a broom in their hands just like Ix. "Sorry, we would've gone back to our hotel if the blizzard had let up just a bit."

"No, you wouldn't have to go to that trouble…"

While they did have the no-women rule in the monastery, that wouldn't change the weather. That noon, the two apprentices had been informed they would be allowed to stay in the monastery for the night.

"Oh, by the way, listen to this," said Beter, his expression quickly changing to the innocent smile of a young boy. "I went to Estosha Chapel yesterday."

"Oh, that's good," said Shuno with a smile. "You've been saying for a while you wanted to go. Were you running errands?"

"Yep, I went to help with preparations for Heaven's Worship. It really had nothing to do with me; the abbot just happened to ask me to take care of it… But it was incredible," said Beter, his eyes closed, overcome with emotion. "You've seen it before, right, Ix?"

"I only really saw the bell tower from the outside," he replied.

"The facade is incredible, but the interior is marvelous. I'd been meaning to take a look ever since coming to Estosha."

That's right. While Ix had thought nothing in their lives had changed here, there was one thing that had: their relationship with Beter.

In the beginning, the pair had talked to him only when

necessary or explained things about staffs when he asked. But at some point, their relationship developed to the point where they would just chat without pretext. They'd gotten into a routine of talking like this once they finished working. There weren't many people as young as him in the monastery, which was probably why he'd taken a liking to them.

"But yeah, I was in charge of stuff outside the Chapel but just happened to get a chance to go inside. I got a whole lifetime's worth of looking at it," he continued, seeming quite fulfilled. "But I didn't find the underground room. Guess a story's just a story."

"Story? Is there something in the Chapel?" asked Ix.

"Oh, you don't know?" Beter scrunched his eyebrows in surprise. "Huh... I guess that makes sense, actually. It's not something you tell outsiders. Though it does sort of have something to do with wands."

"Well, now I'm interested," said Shuno as they listened. They leaned their broom against the wall and took a seat. "Tell us, Beter. Is there an underground chamber there?"

"Uh, well, I guess it should be fine to tell you two. It's not that big a deal anyway," he said with an uneasy grin. "One of the older monks told me this... Apparently, when the Estosha Chapel was being constructed, the lord of the city at the time summoned a particular wandmaker and told him, 'I want you to make the ultimate wand to fortify the protection of the monastery.' Relations with the neighboring country weren't good at the time, and it seemed that they might be engulfed in war at any moment."

"Huh? That's—" murmured Shuno.

"Let Beter finish first," urged Ix.

"The craftsman refused initially, so they imprisoned him for a fabricated crime. They shut him into an underground room under where the monastery is—though it hadn't been built at the time—and forced him to make the wand."

"Urgh, this isn't a happy story." Shuno grimaced. "So did the craftsman finish it? Or was he executed or something?"

"That's the interesting part," said Beter, his fists clenched in excitement. "When they opened the door to the underground chamber again, *all they saw* was a single wand."

"All they saw... So then, the craftsman...?" Shuno cocked their head.

"Obviously, there was a divine miracle. He hadn't failed in his trials—he was allowed to slip away for crafting a wonderful wand." Beter's cheeks flushed as he continued. "When the lord saw God's power, he started shaking and ordered the entrance to the room sealed. But that didn't stop him from fearing for his life. Apparently, he died young."

Beter wrapped up the story, saying that was the gist of it.

Ix and Shuno were silent for a moment. They glanced at each other and shrugged over who would be the first to speak.

"So, Beter...," said Shuno, "what you just told us, isn't that the legend of Rednoff?"

"Rednoff...?" asked Beter in confusion. "Uh, sorry, I can't say for certain, but wasn't he a famous wandmaker?"

"You could say that..."

Ix and Shuno looked at each other.

While Rednoff was a person whose name didn't need repeating to a wandmaker, it seemed he wasn't a household name to people outside the field. In Beter's defense, it wasn't like Ix knew any of the names of the Marayist saints.

Nevertheless...

There were too many commonalities between the legend of Rednoff and this tale. The mention of "the ultimate wand" and the fact that this wandmaker went missing at the end were a perfect match.

"But anyway, I never did find the underground room. A story's just a story, right?" said Beter as he brought a hand to his head and finished the conversation.

"Why is that story a secret?" asked Ix. "If a miracle did occur, you'd think trying to spread the word about it would be a good thing."

"Well... It's because the Chapel is a symbol of the Estosha. It would get a bad reputation if people heard it was built on that sort of sacrifice. Which is why I'd appreciate it if you didn't tell anyone about it."

Just then, someone called Beter's name from down the hall. He responded, then bowed to Ix and Shuno.

"That's right, there's actually a different ending to the story I just told," said Beter, glancing up and placing his hand on the door.

"What's that ending?" asked Shuno.

"In the alternate version, the craftsman isn't saved in the end. He dies in that underground room. But afterward, he comes back to life as a spirit in order to exact his revenge. The lord seals the chamber so his ghost can't get out."

"Huh. Is that story a secret, too?"

"Not quite a secret... But it's probably just a tale that some monk made up a long time ago. It's mostly used to scare new monks. You know, like what happened in the cafeteria before."

"Ah..."

It wasn't an urban legend so much as a story shared in this sole location. Even if it caused an uproar, it would be out of more amusement than fear. The monks were surprisingly mundane in some respects.

Beter said his good-byes and left the room.

Once Ix and Shuno finished cleaning, Coaku got up from where he'd been sitting in front of the fire. "That was an interesting story," he said before leaving. The two of them were shocked; they'd completely forgotten the old man was there.

Ix hadn't seen Riess since the day of the ghost uproar in the cafeteria. Perhaps she had things to do in the city, or maybe she just found the monastery boring. Neither Coaku nor Shuno seemed to mind, and Ix decided it would be odd to go out of his way to ask about her, so he still didn't know why she wasn't here.

"Maybe we should go back to our rooms, too," suggested Shuno with a huge yawn. "And we won't be able to talk tonight. The rooms are too small, and the monks will probably get angry at us if we do."

"Yeah, seems that way," said Ix.

"But we should be able to get plenty of shut-eye. There won't be any drunks around, unlike at the hotel... What'll we do if there's someone who snores really loudly, though?" said Shuno while flashing a grin.

Ix didn't say anything, only shrugged. He was already used to these kinds of crude conversations. Though he did agree that they would be able to sleep soundly in the monastery.

But that night, something happened.

It was deep in the middle of the night. Ix was asleep. Initially, he'd been very cold in the frigid air, despite cocooning himself in his blankets. Eventually, however, his body heat began to warm the bed, and he even got used to the sound of the blizzard. He slipped quickly into sleep when he closed his eyes.

Suddenly, Ix felt someone shake him. He half opened his eyes.

"I-I-Ix... W-wake up...," came a voice.

Something hot tapped his nose, and he reflexively leaned back. He cast his eyes toward the entrance and saw that the door was open. *That's right*, he remembered. He wasn't in his usual hotel lodgings. The monastery bedrooms didn't have locks.

"All right, I'm awake; let go of me for a sec," mumbled Ix quickly. He brought a hand to his nose and found a drop of water on it.

"A-ah, sorry," Shuno said, immediately drawing back.

The two apprentices sat on the bed side by side, Ix with a blanket wrapped around his shoulders. They only had a single candle for light, but for as dark as it was, Ix's eyes had adjusted, so he could see well.

Shuno had calmed down and was no longer weeping.

"No, I wasn't crying," they denied, crossing their arms. "Come on, Ix—I know you've just woken up, but there's no way I'd be crying."

"What happened, then?"

"Oh man, so the thing is, it was…" Shuno cleared their throat in an overexaggerated fashion and continued. "I saw a gh-gh-ghost. I thought I should let you know."

"……"

"What? Why are you staring at me like that?"

"…You had a bad dream."

"It wasn't a nightmare! There really was someone there!"

"Then it was just a person, not a ghost."

"What? Uh, well… No, no. Come on! Just listen to me before you say anything."

Ix nodded reluctantly and Shuno began their story.

They'd woken up just a few minutes ago. They were thirsty, so they went down to the cafeteria to get a drink.

With nothing but a candlestick in hand to rely on in the pitch black, they made their way into the cafeteria. That was when they heard a sound in the kitchen. It wasn't the sort of noise a mouse or the wind made—it was clearly the sound of footsteps.

Wondering if someone else was up, Shuno went into the kitchen to take a look and found…

"No one was there. There aren't many things you can hide behind in the kitchen, so I know they weren't out of sight. But I still heard the noise. It was even closer." Shuno wrapped their arms around their body. "So that means…"

"The kitchen? That's the same place as the commotion from before?"

"Yeah! Exactly! You remember, right?" Shuno pointed at Ix.

"But it was just a noise. It's not something to cry over."

"I tooold you, I wasn't crying. Are you actually listening to me?" Shuno got up a bit to readjust their seat on the bed. "So then,

I tried calling out, 'Is anyone there?' And what do you think happened then?"

"No clue."

"It stopped! The sound went away! I didn't just mishear something; there really was *something* in the kitchen."

"Still..." Ix looked doubtful.

If what Shuno said was true, it wasn't a ghost they should suspect but a robber. Except he was hesitant to inform the abbot about it, considering it was only just some noise in the night. The fact that Shuno hadn't seen anyone just made the story all the weirder.

As Ix thought this over, they glanced at him and said, "Anyway. It doesn't matter if it's scary or not, you at least get how it's strange, yeah? That's why you should come with me back to the kitchen."

"...Why do you have to go back there?" asked Ix with a frown.

"To see what's going on!" said Shuno, spreading their arms and looking slightly irritated. "I was so shocked, I dropped my candle and left it behind when I came running back!"

7

There was no one else walking around the monastery at night. It was even quieter than at noon. This was in total contrast with the blizzard raging outside.

Ix held his candle out as he and Shuno walked down the hall. They couldn't even be certain where they were placing their feet in this kind of darkness.

They arrived at the cafeteria with no real issue, other than the danger of descending the stairs.

"I don't...hear anything," whispered Shuno from behind Ix.

Ever since they'd entered the cafeteria, Shuno had been practically glued to Ix's back, so he was having difficulty walking.

"It doesn't matter if there's some noise, so long as it doesn't directly hurt us," said Ix with a snort.

"I-is that the problem?"

Ix entered the kitchen as Shuno directed. They really couldn't hear anything.

Ix bent over to bring his candle closer to the ground and quickly found the candleholder Shuno had dropped. The flame must have gone out when it fell to the floor. He saw where the candle itself had rolled a short distance from that.

"Here it is. Can you get off me now?" Ix said as he passed the candleholder over to Shuno.

"O-oh, th-thanks…," they said awkwardly.

Just as Ix bent down to pick up the candle, he stopped moving his hand.

"Hmm…?"

"Wh-what?! Don't scare me like that!" cried Shuno, their voice wavering.

"It's nothing…," said Ix as he illuminated the ground beneath the candle. "There's an underground room here. It's probably just a cellar for food storage, though."

A section of the floor was differently colored than the rest. There was a narrow crack around this section in the shape of a square. It had to be a door.

"Huh, you're right," said Shuno as they peered over. "…An underground chamber? Is it big enough for someone to crawl into…?"

"I doubt it's very large. Maybe it's just a little storage space or something," mused Ix as he picked up the candle.

"R-right… Oh, light my candle, will you?"

Ix did as he was asked and lit Shuno's candle. Though they now had the light of two candles, the room didn't seem that much brighter. The kitchen was as dark as ever.

Since they'd gotten what they came for, Ix thought they should head back straightaway, but Shuno wasn't budging for some reason. Instead, they were staring at the kitchen floor.

"What's wrong? Can I go on back without you?" asked Ix.

"H-hey, Ix. Hold on a second. Can we look under here?" Shuno pointed at the floor Ix had seen earlier. "I mean, I know there's probably nothing down there. But I just want to double-check to make sure there really isn't anything..."

"All right. Let's check really quick," said Ix with a sigh.

The two of them lifted the conspicuous section of flooring. Though it had appeared to be a thick slab of stone, it was actually light enough that they could lift it instantly. They slid it to the side to reveal a square hole.

The two fell into silence as they stared inside.

"...I-it's surprisingly deep," noticed Shuno.

"Yeah."

Pitch darkness blotted out the depths of the hole.

Attached to the edge of the entrance was a wooden ladder, and they could tell it descended deep into the chamber. That meant the room was large enough for a person to enter.

The two stared at each other for a few seconds.

"O-okay, how about this?" said Shuno, holding up a finger. "I go first and check it out. If there aren't any issues, I'll call you down."

"You sure you're okay with that?"

"O-of course. Who do you think I am? In times like this, the more experienced person should go first, right?"

"That's not what I meant."

"Huh?"

"What do we do if there is a problem down there?"

"Oh... R-right, uh..." Shuno grimaced slightly. "O-okay, if you don't hear my voice...first put the cover back on, then go and get help. How 'bout that?"

"Right... Okay. Don't slip."

"S-stop. I mean, not that it's actually bothering me! All right, here I go. It's not like this is going to turn out to be a big deal or anything, ha-ha-ha…"

Shuno placed a foot on the ladder with an empty laugh. They descended dexterously, the candleholder still in hand. Ix watched them from above.

"Urgh, it's so cold down here, Ix…," came Shuno's quiet voice.

"If it's too much, just come back."

"Huh, what did you say? Speak up."

"……"

"Oh, here's the ground. Heeey, I made it to the bottom!"

Shuno's voice echoed up from the hole, but Ix could see only a faint orange glow from the candle amid the darkness. He could make out neither Shuno's face nor anything around them. It didn't seem as deep as they'd thought, though. You could probably jump down the entrance and land without injuring yourself.

"Whoa, it's bigger than I expected. But it does seem like it's used for storage. I'm going to check it out a bit," said Shuno.

The light disappeared from Ix's view for a moment. Shuno must have moved farther into the room. They came back quickly and called up, "No problems!"

Ix descended the ladder just as Shuno had. In contrast to when he'd been staring down at the cellar from above, the darkness of the hole made it seem like the ladder went on forever. Ix got the impression he was descending into the belly of a massive creature.

The underground chamber was larger than expected but still only about the size of one of the monastery bedrooms. All it contained were two rows of shelves packed full of preserved foods. Not even a ghost could hide in a room like this.

"I bet they store this food for when there are blizzards, like now," mused Shuno. "Hmm, I'm surprised how clean it is. There's not even any dust on the ground. It's pretty interesting. With how cold it is… I wonder if it was built to be like this or if it's just because it's winter? Or maybe both?"

"Let's get back soon. We look like thieves," said Ix, standing right by the ladder.

"Hmm? Thieves?" Shuno turned back toward him to ask what he meant but stopped moving the moment they turned to him. "Ix, your..."

Shuno pointed at him. Ix followed his finger and also froze for a moment.

The flame of the candle he was holding was flickering slightly.

If they hadn't come at night and if they hadn't been together, they never would have noticed it.

If you came down here during the day, you wouldn't have to go to the trouble of bringing a light with you. The sunlight from above would be enough to see. And if you went in at night, but alone, you wouldn't thoroughly inspect the flame in your own hands.

But right now, the fire on Ix's candle was flickering, even though he wasn't moving a muscle. Where was the draft coming from?

Ix carefully searched the area with his candle and concluded that air was blowing in from below. He brought his face close to the ground and indeed felt a slightly chilly breeze brush his cheek.

The floor of this room was composed of wooden planks. Ix decided to test the strength of the boards by pulling on one where the breeze was strongest. It came up easily.

"Uhhh... So what does this mean?" murmured Shuno.

"I think we've got a winner," said Ix, though he was still half stunned at this turn of events.

Below the planks was a space large enough for a person to stand and walk around in.

Ix peeked in and could tell it extended quite a distance for the exact same length in all directions. There was no way it was a naturally occurring cave.

It was a deliberately constructed passage. A tunnel that connected the monastery to some other location.

Ix jumped down and felt an even stronger draft. It was quite a large space.

"H-hey, Ix?" Shuno placed their hands on the floor and looked down at him.

"What's wrong?"

"*'What's wrong?'* ...Don't just plunge in without saying anything first! You scared me...," muttered Shuno as they jumped down, too. "What now? Are we exploring?"

"Huh?"

"I mean, you're gonna poke around a bit, aren't you? We did find this place, after all. Wasn't that why you came down?"

"No, I didn't really have that in mind. Do you want to check it out, Shuno?"

"Uh, well, I, uh... Yeah, yeah I do." Shuno puffed out their chest. "I always wanted to do this kind of thing. Adventuring and whatever. It's exciting, isn't it? I doubt the monks even know about this place."

"I doubt it. We might get in trouble if they catch us. Maybe even get kicked out."

"It's fine, it's fine. We'll just check it out a bit, then come back. It's the middle of the night, so we've got nothing to worry about if we come back partway."

"But..."

"What is it, Ix? Are you scared?"

"I'm not scared."

"That means you agree with me, then! Let's go! Ah, let's close the hole in the ceiling there and just put a mark for us to remember. Blow out your candle, too. If my candle looks like it's burning low, then I'll light yours, and we'll switch to that."

Shuno ended with that, leaving no room for argument, and Ix just went along. Though to be honest, he was genuinely curious himself. That's why he'd jumped down before Shuno.

As you might expect, what they'd heard from Beter was in the back of Ix's mind, the tale of a room below the Chapel and the disappearance of Rednoff. Surely Shuno was thinking the same.

But there was one concern that Ix hadn't communicated to the other apprentice: Why was this underground space clean?

Obviously, the hardworking monks must have tidied the cellar every day, but did they really venture down to this incredibly inconvenient place? It was odd that there was no dust anywhere.

It would be a different story, however, if someone had been coming and going through here recently. If someone lifted that floorboard, only a portion of the dust would fall into the hole. The rest would spread around the area. They must have cleaned it to avoid being discovered...

That's what Ix imagined anyway, but he shook his head and decided he was overthinking things.

Shuno had walked on ahead but had stopped to wave at him.

"Heeey, Ix. What's up? You can hide behind me if you're scared. I am your senior, after all."

Ix quickly caught up with them instead of answering. It wasn't because he was afraid; if he got separated, he wouldn't have any light.

1

The dark passage seemed to go on forever. It didn't shift up or down; it just continued on ahead. Though it was a relief to know they didn't have to worry about getting lost, there was nothing to suggest they should turn back, either. They just continued trudging through the darkness. Shuno walked in front with Ix trailing behind, same as when they'd set off.

Shuno had seemed nervous initially but must have gotten bored of the place after a while, because they'd started chatting with Ix.

"That's right, you worked at the front of a wand shop... Must have been tough," said Shuno with a serious nod after asking about Ix. "You could say you were born into being a wandmaker. Guess that's the opposite of me."

"So you only recently became Marlan's apprentice?" asked Ix in surprise.

"Well, I'm not sure *'recently'* is the right way of putting it...," said Shuno, leaving a lot unsaid in their embarrassment. "For a long time, everyone thought I'd take up the family business. I apprenticed under my dad. But our line of work wasn't doing so great. After waffling for a bit, I suddenly made up my mind and switched careers to wandmaking. That's why I notice my attitude is usually a bit different compared to the people around me. I've never had that devotion to wands so many start out with."

Ix could hardly believe his ears. How could someone with their history become such a gifted craftsperson? Up until now, Ix had assumed Shuno had been studying for ages.

"So then...why'd you become a wandmaker?" asked Ix. "I'm sure there were plenty of other options."

"It didn't come down to anything serious. I guess I had a bit of a rivalry."

"Rivalry?"

"Man, this passage is so long. I know I'm the one who suggested we go, but I can't believe nothing's changed yet..." Shuno sighed. "Where the heck does this lead?"

"Estosha, probably. It's heading in the right direction."

"Uh... Ummm, the kitchen faced that way, and the building faces that way...," muttered Shuno as they crossed their arms, then brought a hand to their forehead. "If it goes directly to town, then yeah, it's going to be pretty far."

"We walk this distance back and forth all the time. And since it's direct, it should be a bit shorter. If there's an exit on the other end, that is."

"Don't say such horrible things." Shuno slumped their shoulders. "You know, Ix, I bet you were thinking the same thing as I was, but I'm honestly doubtful now."

"Why now?" asked Ix with a frown.

If a craftsman were shut up in an underground room, it would be quite plausible for him to escape via a secret passage.

"Just look at it. There's no way a single person could dig a tunnel as long as this on their own. And it would take time. You'd need a significant amount of authority and money to build this. And the fact that one entrance is from the monastery means someone with influence in the Church probably commissioned it. You wouldn't do all this to save one measly craftsman. I'm more inclined to believe it's a passage for the lord to escape. This city is on the edge of the kingdom's border. It could become the target of a siege at any time," explained Shuno like it was nothing. "And most importantly, this passage is so boring! It just screams 'for military use.'"

"Which would mean the other end spits out at the lord's manor or thereabouts?"

"Exactly. There's no sign it's been used until now, either...," said Shuno, sounding bored. "But there is one thing I don't understand: How did they dig this passage?"

"...There is that." Ix nodded.

Ix hadn't noticed it until Shuno pointed it out, but they were right. He really didn't know how someone would go about making such a long and straight passage. It would take incredible amounts of labor if done by hand, but you would imagine it would result in some slight curves at least. The workers would run into rocks and other obstacles.

While digging a perfectly straight tunnel wasn't physically infeasible, it made you wonder why they went to the effort of finishing the passage.

"What about with magic? Would that be possible?" asked Shuno with a raised finger.

"Depends on the period," replied Ix. "If it was with wands made in the past couple of decades, then yes, it's conceivable. Any further back than that, though, and the efficiency wouldn't be good enough."

"Right..."

There was almost nothing in the passageway, save for some rags and broken wooden boxes.

But after continuing on for a while, they came across a row of medium-sized wooden casks lining the walls of the tunnel.

Curious as to what was inside them, the pair got closer to take a look and found that one of the lids was broken. The crate had been filled to the brim, and a small portion of its contents had spilled out.

Ix scooped up what had fallen to the floor and cocked his head.

"Is this sand?" he asked.

He couldn't make out what color it was due to the darkness, but it felt exactly like sand. It was damp and contained a few hardened lumps but still had a distinct gritty texture.

Why was this here? And how much was there? It was a complete mystery.

But as Ix stood there confused, Shuno brought some of the substance to their nose to sniff it, then suddenly backed away from the casks, the flame of the candle in their hand wavering.

"Ooooh…that scared me," said Shuno, their back pressed hard against the opposite wall and holding a hand over their heart.

"Does it smell that bad?" asked Ix in confusion. "Or is it dangerous?"

"Uh, w-well, I guess so. Though, not really. It just surprised me. Let's go, Ix."

"Huh?"

By the time he turned to look, Shuno had already left him behind and was walking ahead. The flame of the candle was fading into the distance.

"What's going on?" asked Ix as he rushed to catch up. "Aren't you curious, Shuno? Who would put that stuff down here?"

"Figures you would keep thinking about it…," said Shuno, their voice trailing off. "This place is protected from the wind and rain down here, so I bet some people stumbled on the passage and just started living here. Though it's pretty dark for that."

There were no sources of light in the tunnel. They could only rely on the glow of their candle. But they also didn't know when a breeze might blow through and snuff out the flame. If it came down to it, Shuno could light a spark with basic magic, but their training as a wandmaker wouldn't change the fact that they were a beginner at magic. The duo couldn't get too comfortable.

"The heart of defense is below...?" remarked Ix, suddenly remembering something.

"Huh, what are you on about?" asked Shuno, glancing at Ix.

"It's something Riess said before, that the heart of Estosha's defense is below. I don't know if that referred to the room under the Chapel or this passage, but I bet whoever coined that phrase does."

"Huh... By the way, who's Riess?"

"What?"

Shuno should have met her at the monastery, but maybe they hadn't asked the girl her name.

"But anyway, defense..." Shuno continued, clearly more interested in the previous topic of conversation than Riess. "If, say, invaders took over the city, the people of Estosha could do more than flee with this tunnel. They could also launch a counterattack from here. It'd throw the enemy off if Estosha soldiers showed up out of nowhere in the city."

"Are you saying that this tunnel could allow Estosha to rebound from being sacked?"

"Well, I'm not sure... But this is an absurd line of defense. There's no way the labor that went into this thing is justified."

Ix agreed with that. He didn't think the passage would be all that useful in war. Shuno had probably been right when he'd speculated about it being a way for the lord to escape. Or that it was constructed for some other purpose...

After going ahead for a while, Shuno cried out.

"Oh, that section's different from all the others!"

They examined the wall and found that one section was a different color from the rest. At first, Ix thought it was just a trick of the light, but upon closer inspection, he realized it really was distinct. In fact, this was...

"A door, it's definitely a door," muttered Shuno as they brought the flame closer.

Before them stood a small door designed to blend into the wall.

There were narrow slats cut into it at eye height and near their feet. Unfortunately, however, it was pitch-black inside, so they couldn't see anything.

The entrance didn't have a doorknob, but it would defeat the purpose if it had been designed to be pulled. Shuno placed a hand on the section of wall, and it swung inward with surprising ease.

"Oh, it's open," they said, stepping inside.

Ix had assumed there would be a tiny chamber on the other side, but it was actually quite large. The candlelight alone wasn't enough to reveal the entire space.

"This is amazing. What is it?" echoed Shuno's voice from farther in the room. The walls and floor had been carved out of stone. "Get in here, Ix."

Ix stepped in, and the door swung shut by itself. It must have been set on an angle.

A quick investigation revealed that the chamber was circular in shape. It wasn't exactly huge, but it was equivalent in size to a room in a fancy manor. However, there wasn't much in the way of furniture, just a small bed and table, along with some small wooden boxes attached to the walls.

Actually...that wasn't all.

In the middle of the room—in the dead center of the circle—was a pillar. The thing was crooked despite being made of stone, and it had a strange, slouching form. Considering the size of the room, it had to be holding up the roof. Or so Ix and Shuno thought at first.

But once they approached it, they saw that some of the stones of the pillar had been chipped away to reveal the interior.

They brought the light closer and stared inside.

In the center of the pillar was a very neatly worked, long, thin log.

"Is that...," started Shuno, like they couldn't help themselves, before trailing off.

©Enji

"We can't tell yet. Not unless we take detailed measurements," said Ix, forcing himself to remain calm.

"Y-yeah, of course..." Shuno nodded a few times. "Right, so what do we do? Go back to the monastery and...grab our tools?"

"Yeah, let's do that," said Ix.

"But c'mon, that's the only thing it could be."

Ix and Shuno continued this vague back-and-forth for a while. Both of them were struggling to take it all in. They had entered the passage with a glimmer of hope, of course, but they weren't prepared for a discovery of this magnitude. They thought they were just going for a little stroll.

Ultimately, they concluded they should head back to the monastery for the time being, so they rushed toward the door.

But Ix came to a halt in front of it.

"What's wrong? Do you want to check it out a bit more before we go?" asked Shuno from behind him.

"No..." His eyes drifted skyward as he spoke. "You're the one who opened the door, right, Shuno?"

"Yeah, it was me."

"Did you push it open?"

"Yeah, you have to push it, since there's not a doorknob...," said Shuno, trailing off.

There was a silence as Shuno waited for Ix to contradict what they said.

"W-w-wait, Ix, you can't be telling me..."

Ix let out a slight sigh and flatly said, "Yeah. There's no door-knob on this side, either."

2

Every attempt to open the door failed.

That being said, there weren't all that many methods to try

out in the first place. The entrance was completely flush with the wall. There was nowhere to grab onto it with your fingers. Even when they tried slipping their hands through the holes in the door, their knuckles wouldn't fit. They could get their fingertips to wrap around to the other side, but that didn't let them apply enough force to open the door.

Ix wondered if Shuno could do something with magic, but when he asked them, all they said was, "With how heavy it is... Uh, I-I'm not sure...," so Ix dropped it there. If Shuno ran out of mana, then they wouldn't even be able to light the candle.

They struggled with the door for about an hour, but it gave no indication of budging. They could find no avenue of escape, almost as though the room had been designed to trap them.

At first, Ix had managed to keep cool, but as it dawned on him that there was no way out, a disgusting sweat began to run down his forehead. While he did manage to keep his panic from showing, that was primarily because Shuno was doing enough for the both of them.

"C-c-c-calm down, Ix. It's all over if we lose control. We have to, have to keep calm. We got in here, so there's got to be some way out. And besides, I bet someone will pass through the corridor while we're in here," said Shuno while nodding furiously.

"Down this tunnel?"

"Sh-shut up. Do you want to help or not?"

"Of course I want to help."

"Then stop being so pessimistic. Just wait—I'll come up with a way to get us out of here..."

Ix looked around. It was even more silent down here than it was aboveground. He realized he was still wearing the outfit he'd gone to sleep in. He didn't even have a coat on.

And even though he'd just shot down Shuno's hope of someone coming to their rescue, they really had no other options but to wait for that to happen, since there was no way for them to open the door themselves. The monks would notice their disappearance from the monastery come morning. They'd left the cover to the storage room open, so there was a chance someone would discover the passage.

Either that, or there was that other possibility that had struck Ix when he and Shuno first entered—that someone had used the passage recently. It was their only other hope, but there was no guarantee that person would be willing to lend a hand.

Regardless, they needed to accept they would be there for quite a while. With that in mind...

Ix looked at Shuno, who had their back to him and their head in their hands, and said, "Why don't you sleep for now?"

"Wh-what?" They turned toward Ix. "What are you even saying? How could I ever relax enough to sleep in a situation like this?!"

"The thing we most want to avoid right now is wearing ourselves out," stated Ix, lowering his voice. "As we noticed earlier, there are strange objects in the passage and signs of someone having used it. Obviously, formulating a way to open the door would be best, but right now, all we can do is wait for someone. Our best option is to take turns sleeping while we pass the time."

"I guess so... But if that's the case, you should rest first."

"No, you first." Ix shook his head. "You're the only one who can use magic. I don't know what we can use it for, but we need to have you at full strength just in case."

"Uh... Okay. Not that I'll be able to sleep in a situation like this..."

Shuno wobbled unsteadily over to the bed in the chamber and lay down.

Ix sat on the floor, leaned against the door, and pulled his knees up to his chest.

He blew out the flame on the now-quite-small candlestick, and the room plunged into darkness.

No matter if he opened his eyes or closed them, all he could see was a world of black.

It struck him that the world above was white, and the world below was black.

"Hey, Ix," came Shuno's voice from the darkness. "I actually... was planning on opening a shop in this town. My master introduced me to an old shop. So once this job is over and my craftsman qualification is figured out, you should come, too."

"Yeah, I'll come visit if I get the chance."

"That's not what I mean. I'm inviting you to work with me. You shouldn't let talent like yours go to waste working as an apprentice."

"Together?" Ix raised his head and blinked. "...But just being employed at your shop wouldn't guarantee I could become a craftsman."

"That's true, but..." Shuno muttered to themselves for a moment, then let out a cry of consternation. "Fine. I'll just be straight with you. I want to collaborate with you. Don't you feel the same?"

"......"

"...Right. Well, just give it some thought, will you?"

Ix heard Shuno roll over, and he quietly replied, "Okay."

Perhaps as a consequence of being wound up for so long, the sound of snoring soon came from the bed. Now that he thought about it, Ix realized they'd left the monastery in the dead of night. Sleepiness hit him all at once, as though he'd only just remembered to feel it.

What time was it anyway?

He felt like they'd spent an incredibly long time here, but assuming they were below Estosha, their walk here couldn't have taken very long. Adding that to the time they spent panicking would mean it was still the middle of the night.

Ix let out a heavy sigh.

The two of them had decided together to go into the cellar and explore the passage. But it was clearly his own fault they'd gotten trapped here.

He should have remained outside when Shuno went in. Or he really should have figured out how the door worked the moment he noticed there wasn't a knob. But instead, he'd entered it thoughtlessly…

Moron was hardly a strong enough word to describe him.

And while it would be perfectly natural to shout insults at Ix for what he'd done, Shuno never did any of that. In fact, Shuno went so far as to say they would find a way out. Somehow, they seemed to think this whole thing was their fault.

Ix thought about what would happen if they couldn't get out. It didn't matter what happened to him, but Shuno was absolutely going to be a craftsperson someday. How could he ever apologize to them?

"What are you doing?"

Ix suddenly thought he could hear someone's voice.

He jumped in surprise and swung around to face the door.

"Just now…," he said hoarsely.

"Ix?" answered a young girl's voice.

"I know that voice… Riess?"

"Correct," replied her cheerful voice, unsuited to the situation. Ix could see the flickering light of her lamp through the hole in the door. "I can't believe we'd meet in a place like this. I'm a little disappointed, since it doesn't seem like you were coming to see me. But still, I'm happy. I haven't seen you in so long."

Ix didn't say anything for a while, only wondering what the heck she was talking about.

"…Do you know the story about the ghost?" he finally asked after a moment's confusion. For some reason, he suddenly suspected that Riess herself was the specter.

He was obviously aware that this was a ridiculous idea to entertain, but upon further consideration, he couldn't help feeling like it all made sense. The commotion about the ghost in the monastery had happened the day Riess visited. Hadn't she eaten lunch that day?

And there were a few other strange things. She'd known who Ix was from the moment he set foot in town. She seemed oddly friendly toward him and showed off a breadth of knowledge you wouldn't expect from a child. It was also weird how she would appear out of nowhere only to disappear the same way. Now she'd even manifested in this secret underground passage. And Shuno didn't seem to know anything about her.

"Of course I do," answered Riess.

"...Riess, what are you doing here at a time like this?"

"Taking a walk."

"Huh?"

"It's cold and dangerous outside. Down here, there's no snow on the ground, and no one will find me and scold me," she said with a bitter chuckle. "Ah, but you found me. Can you keep it a secret? In return, I'll tell you about the ghost."

Ix was taken aback, unable to press her on the topic more.

"...Okay," he said.

"It's a famous story in this city. It's a tale that everyone's heard at least once but no one tells."

"No one tells?"

"Yes," murmured Riess. Then, as if reading aloud from a book, she said, "Long, long ago, there was a couple who desperately wanted a child but were never blessed with one, no matter what they did. With no other options, they named a doll carved from wood and doted on it like it was their own. But then one day, they encountered a dragon. The dragon was curious about the couple who treated this doll like their offspring. And the couple asked a favor of the dragon. 'For a child, you ask? No, not that.' They asked the dragon to give life to the doll. As requested, the dragon brought it to life. It moved. But the couple had made a mistake."

Ix listened silently to Riess's fluid storytelling.

"It was only a single mistake. They'd asked for life; they hadn't asked for a soul. Without a soul, the doll had nowhere to go once its body rotted away. Now, it wanders the town, as it will for all eternity. That's why people hear things sometimes—it's the ghost crying out in lament..." Riess's voice dropped there. "But this story is also a secret that doesn't leave this place. You can't accidentally tell it to the people at the monastery who belong to the Church. Because only God can grant life."

Once she finished speaking, the howling of the wind down the passage seemed to grow louder.

Ix couldn't help thinking about how strange the tale was, because he had a connection to dragons. He hadn't even been chasing after them, yet he still found himself running into their footprints, even here...

Before he could say anything, Riess's voice came from the other side of the door again.

"But how'd you find this place? The entrance on the monastery side is pretty well hidden."

"Is this place...the heart of defense that you mentioned before?" asked Ix, getting swept up by what she'd said. "It looks like you could use it to escape the city if it came down to it..."

"The important thing is that it makes you think there's something here," said Riess, as though she was lecturing a small child. "Secrets always get out. To prevent that, you have to poison the secret. It doesn't matter if this passageway gives you the impression they made an escape route or makes you speculate they built a defense system; both draw you in. That's why they put in a trap here."

"A trap? I didn't see anything like that."

"Of course you'd think that. You wouldn't know much about that."

"How do you know about this place, Riess? You're talking like you're well-informed."

"Because I've gone to the monastery so many times as an assistant," she answered bluntly. "There's nothing there, so it's boring. Sometimes, I play hide-and-seek by myself there. Though I didn't get in here from the monastery today."

"There's another entrance, right? Where is it?"

"You're always so full of questions," said Riess with a giggle.

"...Why haven't you been to the monastery in a while?"

"Don't ask rude questions." Now she sounded like she was pouting. "Even kids have things to do. I can't go there every day. How's it going over there anyway?"

"Do you mean with me? Or Coaku?"

"Coaku, of course. I am his assistant."

"It's mean to say this, but I honestly have no idea why he even bothers coming," said Ix frankly. "He just sits in front of the fireplace sleeping the whole time. He's never given us advice or corrected us. Did the monastery know he's like this and invite him anyway?"

"Really? That's weird."

"What is?"

"Well, I listen to Coaku every day, and he always tells me about how you and Shuno work. He says you'll both make really good craftspeople."

"...He's just saying what he's expected to."

"I don't think so."

"Anyway, Riess, stop chatting," said Ix, having remembered the situation he was in after a moment of silence. "Right now, we're—"

"I know, you don't have to say it. You're shut in there, right?" said Riess, taking the words right out of his mouth.

"Y-yeah. Can you open the door from that side?"

"Sorry, I'm not strong enough. I'll go get help, though. Can you sit tight until then?"

"We can probably manage that long."

"Okay. See you in a bit, then."

The light flickered on the other side of the door, and he heard the sound of soft footsteps. But after a few beats, they suddenly ceased.

"By the way, do you have an answer to my invitation? Did you think about it?" asked Riess.

"Huh?" Ix could only blurt out a confused noise in response to the abrupt question.

"Ah, you forgot... Don't say anything. I'll be waiting at the Chapel on the night of Heaven's Worship."

"No, it's just this isn't—"

The footsteps moved away before Ix could finish his statement. Upon further reflection, he realized he hadn't heard her coming in the first place.

That aside, it seemed like he and Shuno would make it out after all. That thought caused the tension to suddenly drain from Ix's body. He sat on the ground, laid his face between his knees, and let out a heavy sigh.

After that, he drifted off. Then he heard the clear sound of footsteps and snapped back to consciousness. Two or three people were approaching.

The moment Ix got up to look at the door, a blinding light shone into his face.

"Ah, it's true... Are you all right? I'm opening the door now," said a man with a concerned expression. His long hair was tied back behind him. He had two people with him, one on either side. They looked like attendants of some sort. They were carrying lamps. "There should be another person with you, yes? A woman?"

"Yeah, they're sleeping in the back," said Ix with a nod. "Did Riess tell you?"

"Hmm? What was that?" asked the man with a tilt of his head. "No, one of my attendants heard voices coming from the tunnel. I couldn't believe it, but I came to check just in case..."

That was how Ix and Shuno were rescued, but the man didn't chastise them at all. He was actually surprised by the two of them. And once he learned they were both wandmaking apprentices, he smiled.

"No, I don't think there really is a need to keep this a secret. It is actually quite well known by anyone related to the Church with a significant enough position of authority," said the man. They walked down the passage in the same direction Shuno and Ix had originally been traveling, away from the monastery. "Though I'm not so sure the monastery is too happy with the situation, which is why you really should be reprimanded, but... It does make me happy, though, to have such enthusiastic young folks find this place, even if it was by chance. I do think it's something young wandmakers such as yourselves should see."

"By '*it...*'" said Shuno, whose face had been one of sleepy contentment until recently, "do you mean the room beneath the Chapel?"

"Oh, you know about that as well? It seems you are doing quite the excellent job at the monastery," said the man as he looked back at them. "You're exactly right. That is none other than the ultimate wand left behind by Rednoff. The Chapel is actually there because the wand supports it."

"Really? How do you prove something like that?"

"I-Ix!" cried Shuno as they covered his mouth. "That's not something you say to the person who saved us!"

"No, it's a perfectly reasonable question," said the man with a strong nod. His long bundle of his hair bobbed up and down. "Even the people who knew of the underground chamber lacked any certainty over whether the story of Rednoff they'd known for so long was fact or fiction. They even questioned if it really was a wand. But once, a renowned wandmaker came to town. They showed him to the special underground room and asked him to inspect the wand, on the condition that it be kept secret. And so he did. Apparently, he took a look at it and said, 'This is the ultimate wand.'"

"Huh. Who was the craftsman?" asked Shuno.

"I'm sure you'll have heard the name. It was Munzil Alreff."

"Huh...?" Ix couldn't help gaping.

His master had really said that...?

"Th-that's a seriously big name...," said Shuno, shrinking

their shoulders as they were overcome by shock for different reasons than Ix.

As they walked forward, the man cheerfully added, "And then just the other day, I discovered there are craftsmen who apprenticed under Master Alreff in town. I showed the two of them that room as well, and they said it was, without a doubt, the ultimate wand."

"Wait, there were two of them?" said Ix suddenly in a loud voice. "What are their names?"

"What? Oh, you probably haven't heard of them. They're called Rolphie and Hemsley."

"Them too...?" Ix cast his eyes down and brought a hand to his mouth. Those were the names of Munzil's third and fourth apprentices.

Ix was more shocked by what they had said than the fact they were in Estosha. Even more so that it was those two, of all people. Out of all Munzil's apprentices, they were the least invested in wands. Would they really say something like that? Something that you'd normally expect from a stereotypical wandmaker?

Ix took a whiff of fresh air. He looked up to find stairs a little ways ahead. One of the attendants went up ahead to open the door, letting in blinding light that stung his eyes.

They'd made it outside.

At some point, morning had come. Gold light spilled over the tops of the buildings. The wind had calmed, and Ix could see wisps of clouds in the sky. It was cold out, and a breeze more frigid than the one underground swept by.

This exit wasn't located on the grounds of a building; instead, it led directly into the street. Normal houses lined either side of the road.

"Good work, you've made it to the exit," said the man, turning back from where he'd stepped out. His form was obscured by shadow, backlit as it was. "I would ask that you keep this entrance a secret. The Church pretends it is just storage. You must be tired.

If you'd like, please join me at the building I live in. I would very much like to speak with the both of you."

Ix was so lost in thought that the invitation didn't even reach him.

But that was to be expected.

After all, to his eyes, the "ultimate wand" in that underground room appeared to be nothing more than an ordinary log.

3

The blizzard calmed, and the quiet light of winter spilled into the room. Nova hadn't arrived yet.

Since morning, Yuui had passed the time reading. Specifically, the book that Gustavus had told her about, the one with the ghost stories. Though he'd called it a book, it wasn't actually bound, so it was really more like a diary or set of notes.

"It's something the priest at the time wrote down," said Seyoh the night before when she'd visited his room. He happily lent it to her. The bundle had been stored on top of a shelf, so it took some time for him to find it.

"It looks quite old…," remarked Yuui as she stroked the cover sheet.

"It was written just after the Chapel was completed." Seyoh clasped his hands together and nodded. "Though you should know it's not particularly interesting. I haven't read the whole thing."

"Why do you have it?"

"Hmm… I'm not sure there is any particular reason," he said with an uncertain smile. "It's not useful, but I'm hesitant to throw it away. It's essentially the result of two acquaintances trying to push it on each other."

Yuui had fallen asleep that night but quickly picked the book up the following day, as she had nothing to do.

She took a look into the book and found that the priest had written an introduction: *Recently, I have heard several odd tales. They all resemble one another, so I have decided to record them here.*

That's what it said. In light of his position, the priest must have frequently given the townspeople advice.

Once Yuui got into the book proper, she found a stream of short, concise paragraphs, perhaps a reflection of the author's personality. They were almost all written like an itemized report, listing the person's name, occupation, and what they were seeking advice about.

Just as Gustavus and Seyoh had told her, it wasn't an entertaining read. The entries were barely distinct.

For example:

Rodak, tailor, female, early morning. Went out to get water from the well where she heard people talking. They were all male voices. Was unable to see the speakers. The voices moved away.

Ulaft, glove maker, male, night. Heard footsteps during a drinking party with friends. Stepped outside but saw no one. The footsteps continued for some time.

Filrin, blast wandmaker, male. Heard the voice of someone he knows who had moved to a nearby town. Evening.

Azzie, carpenter's wife, female. Heard something that sounded like crowds of people passing by the house in the middle of the night. Went outside with husband to look but found no footprints.

All the statements were short like the above. They were very similar, essentially just people hearing voices or footsteps during the night until dawn. The accounts went on and on, spanning dozens of people.

It was obvious that Seyoh was right, and this was written by someone from a long time ago. The age of the actual pages made it feel historical, but so did the vocabulary and grammar usage. It was fairly difficult to read and, had she been in any other situation, she would have tossed it aside herself as well.

However, as she absentmindedly turned the pages, she eventually found herself entirely absorbed.

This wasn't her first time looking through records of normal people. There was one time before when she'd read such daily accounts, so it reminded her of the excitement she'd felt then.

The people who produced this sort of writing were almost always in the Church or held a position of authority, and their work usually focused on their peers. Obviously, this book was also written by a priest, but the content was different. It focused entirely on the people who lived in Estosha. While there was very little information in each small account, that only made her imagination run wild, which she enjoyed.

It was only because she'd been reading so intently that she realized something.

Here and there in the book were oddly thick pages.

Thinking this strange, Yuui closely examined the pages from the side and saw two pages stuck together. She had no idea how long they'd been like that, but a gentle tug told her they weren't about to come apart easily.

With no other option, Yuui took out her wand and cast the smallest spell she could. This sort of incantation required significantly more delicate control than casting something powerful. At the same time, there was rarely a use for a spell so fine, so the Academy didn't even bother to teach this kind of magic control. Yuui had read about it in a book and used it several times to test the limits of her wand.

The first cast was too weak. The second one, though, proved fruitful after some adjustment. The corners of the pages separated slightly. She grabbed onto that part and carefully pulled apart the pages.

They must have stuck together because of the ink that was used at the time. It wasn't suited to the paper and would cause the pages to affix to each other if they were pressed together for a while. It happened sometimes with older books. The characters on one of the pages she'd pulled apart had transferred to the other, leaving it incredibly difficult to read despite the simple, itemized writing style.

Now having gotten into the swing of things, Yuui was able to immediately pull apart the next set of stuck pages she came across. The content was exactly the same as the rest of the book. She smiled ironically as she thought that only someone as bored as her would go through all the trouble to pull these pages apart and read them.

But something was different about the last page in the book.

That page was also stuck, so just as she'd done before, she pulled it apart with magic. To her surprise, however, she found a long paragraph instead of a list of itemized accounts.

The characters on this page had also bled over, making it more difficult to read than any of the previous ones. Yuui gave up trying to interpret the words and instead copied them one by one onto another sheet of paper.

She frowned as she looked at the passage she'd created. It seemed to be a postscript from the priest.

> **This is only a small portion of the stories that have been brought to me by those seeking advice.**
>
> **The first thing I can say is that it is evident ghosts do not exist. The scriptures speak of no such thing. After death, the soul ascends to heaven and is handed a fate of either eternal life or eternal death. There are**

©Enji

no exceptions. It is not possible for a soul to remain in our world.

Despite knowing this, I did not refute the existence of ghosts. The reason I did not was because there are some things more sacred than the honesty of a priest, and I had to protect their honor.

It is no surprise that the blast wandmakers were angry. The tunnel extension would not have been possible had it not been for their utmost efforts. Without their help, we could not have completed excavation in such a short span of time. We were able to fulfill His Lordship's excessive request.

However, what awaited them once their work was complete could only be called betrayal.

In the underground space that they'd so labored over, a magic wand was placed.

I am pleased that His Lordship is so passionate about defense, but I never expected he would go so far as to invite Rednoff. Even I have heard tales of that man.

In reality, I am still skeptical of that wand's power. Everyone who has used it sings its praises, yet I still feel that the power and utility of blast wands surpass it.

But there is no doubt that both blast wands and magic wands are wisdom bestowed upon us by the Lord. It is not my place to personally choose which to stand behind. Nevertheless...

It seems that Rednoff, too, has lost himself slightly— no, significantly—in his old age. One might almost be inclined to believe he *wanted* to be imprisoned in that underground room. I personally heard him say, "Thank heavens no one can disturb me here."

According to the people who watch over him, he spends the majority of his days crafting wands. And when he is not crafting wands, he is jabbering nonsense. He speaks not to himself but to someone the observers cannot see. Almost as if he were conversing with a ghost...

I met Rednoff last night as well.

He grinned at me and said, "I can make the ultimate wand."

I cannot determine whether or not he is still sane. But that is nothing more than a triviality in the face of the blast wandmakers' wrath. If we are to take the ghost stories at face value, then they have clearly placed a trap within the passage.

I hope my suspicions on what they are plotting are nothing more than a misperception on my part, but we must verify it before we are thrown into a situation that cannot be undone.

Before it is all blown away.

A knock at the door brought Yuui back to herself. The light shining through the window had shifted far away. Noon had passed before she realized it.

She set the book on the table and called "enter" toward the door. Nova entered. She didn't often show up around this time of day.

"They have decided, to hold dinner. It was, Seyoh's suggestion," she said. She'd come to inform Yuui.

"Dinner? Not the meeting?"

"No. The meeting participants, were all invited. That includes you, of course."

"I thought these were supposed to be secret gatherings? That's why we hold them in the middle of the night…"

"It is a dinner, and nonparticipants were also invited. Not people entirely, unrelated, though. Those two wandmakers, and some others, apparently."

"Some others?"

"Yes. Some others," said Nova curtly. "Anyway, not many people move around, during winter. Holding the meetings during night or day, has negligible effects on their secrecy. And the need to use lamps at night, renders the difference pointless."

"Perhaps… When will it be?"

"Tonight."

"And when was it scheduled?"

"Five days ago."

"I see…" Yuui let out a little sigh, but she'd become used to this sort of sudden development. "All right. I will attend."

"Okay." Nova nodded. "I also, have information on the investigation."

"Huh? What investigation?"

"Into the threat letter from the other day, as well as the attack on you," said Nova emotionlessly. "First, I don't believe, it had anything to do with Old Order forces."

"How can you be certain?"

"I investigated."

"How?"

"I spoke to members, of the Old Order."

Yuui waited for further explanation, but Nova didn't give any. She seemed to think this was a sufficient explanation. Yuui decided to just interpret that as Nova doing Yuui a favor in her absence.

"Ummm…" Yuui collected herself and asked, "You said 'first.' What else do you have to report?"

"Yes. There are some among the participants, who are voicing suspicions that it is an act, that it's far too convenient."

"An act... By whom?"

"Seyoh."

"What?" Yuui was disappointed.

"He told the others about the threat letter. They seem to believe, it doesn't actually exist, that it would make sense if it was a hoax he concocted."

"That's baseless conjecture. What could he possibly gain from doing that?"

"Yuui, didn't you suspect someone, on the inside?"

"Uh, well... Yes, I did. I just think Seyoh doesn't have much of a motive. Would he really try to destroy the meetings he's worked so hard on?"

"They're saying it's actually the opposite, to move the meetings along," countered Nova quietly, wary of who might be outside the door. "Make the participants feel threatened, to light a fire under the debates. They are saying, his enthusiasm went too far."

"Huh... Then they'll probably question him at the dinner."

"It seems to me like Seyoh himself, is aiming for that," said Nova with a tilt of her head. "He is creating a situation where he can defend himself, since the meetings won't happen so long as there are suspicions."

Yuui nodded as she listened, though she still felt some of what Nova had described didn't add up.

"But if the threat letter was a result of Seyoh's overzealousness, then that doesn't explain the attack on me. Or do they suspect I am collaborating with him?" she asked.

"They say, Seyoh launched a pretend attack. He is near that location, and there isn't anyone else who could accurately target you."

"What was his goal, then?"

"You've drawn the attention of everyone. They would all band together if you were in danger."

"That seems like a stretch."

She didn't know who'd claimed that, but she doubted even they believed the ideas they were putting forward. These monotonous winter days were amplifying their worthless imaginings.

With a condescending smile, she asked, "And who exactly was it who said these things?"

"Rolphie."

"Huh?"

"Or perhaps it was Hemsley. But he doesn't seem like the kind of person, to offer information."

"Uh, no, that wasn't what I was concerned with..."

Yuui had just been taken by surprise at hearing the unexpected name.

She started to wonder why someone who hadn't even attended the meetings yet was saying that but quickly stopped herself. She knew from experience there was no point in speculating about the behavior of Munzil's apprentices.

4

Yuui and Nova left the building temporarily before the dinner that evening. They made it look like they were coming from a different location, the same as they did for all the meetings. Though Yuui didn't understand why the charade was necessary at this point.

This time was different because they went to Mellay's manor first. Yuui had invited Mellay to walk with her and Nova to the dinner. Nova had insisted this would be safer. She had claimed that, while the situation would be the same as it was when they were last attacked, it would be easier to predict the enemy's actions.

"Though if I didn't go outside, I wouldn't require protecting," said Yuui as she looked back. "No one will be suspicious if I just happened to be the first to arrive once in a while."

"You, think?" Nova looked at Yuui.

"Responding with a question...? Yes, I do think."

"People have, different ways of thinking." Nova nodded, expressionless. "You will feel better, if you go outside sometimes."

"What?"

Yuui twisted her head back, feeling like that last statement had come out of nowhere. Yes, it may be healthier for her to go out than to stay shut in her room all the time, but it wasn't something that she could do given her position.

Yuui decided it must have been one of Nova's rare jokes. There was no way the charade they'd been playing out this whole time had been for Yuui's mental health.

They arrived at Mellay's manor, and the old woman immediately stepped out. Her usual attendant was behind her.

"Thank you for coming, Minaha," said Mellay as she walked down the steps of the entryway, holding out a hand in Yuui's direction.

"I see Rolphie and Hemsley are not present today," replied Yuui as she took her hand.

"They were only my guests that one time. I'm sure they've already headed off to the meeting place."

The two of them walked slowly through the snow-covered streets, not bringing up the two wandmakers' suspicions about Seyoh. They were four people in total, including the two attendants walking behind them.

There were other people out and about, perhaps because the blizzard had ended and turned into mild weather. The citizens didn't seem to have any particular destination in mind; instead, they appeared to just be getting some fresh air. Each of them was enjoying the momentary peace and quiet in their own way. The afternoon sun was warm, and the snow on the roads looked to be melting.

"It seems you speak with Seyoh often," said Mellay, as if the thought just suddenly occurred to her. "I also wish I had the opportunity to do that."

"He is looking after me in a way. We naturally have many opportunities to talk," replied Yuui. "And our discussions are rarely of any interest. Primarily just administrative types of topics."

"Oh... That's not quite what I've heard."

"And what is it that you've heard?" asked Yuui with a slight smile, interested.

"For example, that you once said faith is not academic."

Yuui was taken aback to hear the words she'd said but since forgotten brought up again. "That is... Yes, I did indeed say that..."

"No need to be so anxious. I've suspected that you weren't born into Marayism. That's the value you bring, the combination of lack of knowledge of the faith along with objectivity." Mellay smiled. "And I also have no intentions of finding fault in what you've said. I just feel as if you are misunderstanding something, Minaha. It appears as if you have things backward."

"In other words, you mean to say faith is academic?"

"That would not be flipping the order. What I want to say is that academic studies are a religious pursuit."

Yuui couldn't help frowning, though Mellay couldn't see her face beneath her hood. The old woman continued speaking, her words unbroken, since she hadn't noticed Yuui's reaction.

"I am nothing more than a humble member of the clergy, but wouldn't you say that academic study is a human pursuit that attempts to uncover the world's structure and laws?"

"That is how I conceptualize it, yes," said Yuui with a nod.

"But isn't that strange? How are academics capable of such a thing?"

"I don't understand your question."

"Who guaranteed that the world even has structures and laws?"

"......"

"Even the thought that the world has set rules is predicated on the belief that someone—in other words, a creator, a god—made the world. Don't you agree?"

"No... We don't require a guarantee," Yuui argued back. "Both structure and laws are naturally discovered through a series of objective observations. That is the foundation of academia."

"Then why do people conduct those observations? Don't they do so because they believe that the world does have structures and laws?" said Mellay slowly. "Or, if they do discover a law through their observations, what allows them to be certain of it? Do academics not even slightly consider the possibility that it was all some massive coincidence?"

"...I'm not sure I understand what you mean."

"That is exactly why theology is the foundation of all other academic disciplines. It's not a question of which is above the other. Sometimes, we come to better understand the scriptures thanks to the advancement of academic study." Mellay stopped a moment, then said, "But that is why I feel like all academics hold faith deep in their hearts. That faith is perhaps more genuine than that of people like me. It is a drive to reach an absolute truth, like staring into the sky at the stars you'll never reach and praying..."

The word *"genuine"* echoed inside Yuui's mind, while she thought what Mellay said was interesting.

The moment she heard that word, her thoughts didn't turn to priests or academics. She thought of some wandmakers she knew.

They didn't make wands to fulfill their own desires or even as a service to their clients. They made wands for the sheer sake of making them.

Were the stars still the same where they were looking...?

It suddenly dawned on Yuui how you could make wandmakers members of the clergy like Mellay talked about earlier. It may come down to the similarities between the two.

Wandmakers were normally subject to the strict regulations

of the Guild, and they lived lives similar to priests or monks. Which meant that, on the outside, they met the requirements to be clergy. The issue was the requirements on the inside, which was essentially proof that all wandmakers had a devout faith in God. That wasn't all that difficult, either.

All you had to do was create an interpretation where the "ideal wand" that wandmakers pursued and "God" were one and the same. Or you could simply argue that the "third arm" that makes an appearance in the scriptures is God telling the Maray Church to wrap things up quite neatly. That would be all it would take for the Church to absorb the craftsmen.

Once Yuui realized that, she got goose bumps.

She felt like she'd touched on the edge of why Marayism was so widely followed and why the Church invaded country after country.

It was because they swallowed everything.

For example, if some new discovery that created an inconsistency with the scriptures came to light, they wouldn't refute either the scriptures or the knowledge. Instead, they would hold a meeting, just like now. There, they would treat the scriptures as an absolute truth while adjusting the interpretation of them to conform with the times.

The same thing was happening now. There was no resistance to the Church bringing wandmakers into the clergy. And if they needed to, they would "interpret" the scriptures through logic and reason. This was how the Maray Church historically operated.

And then..., thought Yuui, casting her eyes down.

Even your ability to stargaze would be attributed to the existence of God.

They believed in an absolute and unchanging truth. They were convinced that they would someday be able to connect everything into one because the world had been created by a single god. They were trying to absorb everything in the world, along with certainty.

That was the true strength of Marayism. The Lukuttans were completely different. You could never arrive at those same conclusions in the faith from Yuui's homeland.

And there were no stronger ideological grounds in the fight for national supremacy. The people who didn't follow Marayism were just people to be pitied. Marayists didn't hesitate to invade and indoctrinate them.

They arrived at the location of the dinner while Yuui was still thinking, though it turned out it was taking place in the same building in which all the other meetings were held. The same building and the same room. The only difference was how light it was outside and how the furniture was arranged.

5

There was a single long table running down the middle of the room with chairs on both sides. In front of each chair were plates and silverware. Participants were already gathering there, and quiet chatter bubbled up here and there.

Ix and Shuno were led to the seats at the very end of the table. In terms of layout, that meant they were sitting in the spots reserved for the least important attendees, but that wasn't what they had a problem with.

"Wait, wait, wait a second!" said Shuno in a stifled cry, a feat of no small skill. Even so, they sat next to Ix and brought their face close to his. "What's going on here? How many people are attending this meal?"

"Uh...," said Ix as he looked down the table.

"I'm not telling you to count them!" Shuno grabbed Ix's face and turned it back toward them. "Didn't that Seyoh guy say he was inviting us here tonight because he wanted to talk to us a bit? How did that turn into this giant event?"

"He never said we were the only guests," replied Ix, his expression unchanged.

"And who are all these people anyway? Man, we are totally in the wrong place..."

Shuno dropped their head into their hands, which was actually what made them stand out even more. Several people were already staring at them. Some were regarding them with suspicion, almost asking why they were even sitting there. Even the two apprentices didn't know why they were here, so the other guests must have been even more confused.

"Dammit, I thought we were just getting some dinner..." Shuno stared into the distance, their eyes filled with resentment.

Diagonally from them on the other end of the table sat Seyoh, the person who'd invited them. He made no move to introduce the two of them to anyone. He instead simply chatted with a smile on his face to the guests nearby.

The moment Ix walked into the room, though, his attention turned to someone else. They were sitting across from Seyoh, which meant they were on the same side of the table as Ix and Shuno, just with several guests in between. They were the only person in the room whose face was concealed, yet not a single one of the other people in the room seemed to question this. It was strange for someone to wear their coat inside, and they appeared to be a fairly small person.

Ix thought this might be someone he knew well, but the other guests were in the way, so he had no way of confirming.

"Anyway, I think our only choice is to stay as quiet as we can and try not to draw any attention," said Ix.

"I'm with you on that. Don't stand out, stay quiet the whole time." Shuno nodded.

But the moment they decided that, their luck seemed to take a turn for the worse as two far more attention-grabbing people entered the room.

"Ha-ha-ha, I'm here!" came a shout along with the sound of the door opening forcefully.

Everyone except Ix turned toward the door.

Two very similar-looking men stood there as if looking down on everyone in the room. One of them had an arrogant smile plastered on his face, and the other wore an irritated frown.

"Oh, come on, don't all stare at me at once! I'll be making more of a scene later. Just sit back and relax until then!" said the smiling man, not the least bit perturbed by all the attention. "My name's Rolphie! This guy next to me is Hemsley. Have you heard of us? Well, even if you haven't, I don't care, you know?"

Rolphie walked into the room, an arm around Hemsley's shoulder.

But as they were about to pass behind Ix and Shuno, they stopped. Ix's hands automatically clenched into fists.

"Hey, is that the moron?" asked Rolphie. Oblivious to Ix's reaction, he placed a hand on his head without hesitation and leaned over to look at him. "Whoa, it is the moron! Hey, Hemsley! The numbskull's here! You are him, right? What the hell are you doing here?"

Ix's only response was to pull in his chin slightly.

"Ha-ha-ha, your face looks the same as always, like you just got back from a funeral! Are you still wearing your mourning clothes? But you know, since I happened to bump into you, I should tell you...nothing! 'Cause why would I have anything to say to you? Ha-ha-ha!"

This time, Ix didn't react at all. He just let out a slow breath.

"Well, at least take in my awesome figure while you're here! I would've thought even a moron could do that much!" Rolphie lightly smacked Ix's head a couple of times. "Hemsley, you say something, too!"

"Nothing to say."

"Ah well!"

Then the two walked pompously off to their seats almost exactly in the center of the table. Rolphie immediately picked up a utensil at his place, called a servant over, and ordered them to do something.

Everyone else in the room was dumbfounded for a moment, but the chatter resumed with lively force once Rolphie and Hemsley had settled into their seats.

The primary topic was those two, perhaps with a bit of Ix thrown in.

"They're super rude, calling you a moron the minute they see you," whispered Shuno with a frown. "Cheer up, Ix—you're not a fool."

"…We had the same master; they're my seniors," said Ix, managing to get that much out.

"Oh, really?" said Shuno, their fist in front of their mouth. "Then you must have…uh…had a hard time. With stuff."

"You could say that…"

Ix had heard they were in town, but he hadn't expected to run into them this soon. The only good thing was they weren't sitting nearby each other…

Ix didn't get along with those two very well. Well, he didn't really get along with any of the other apprentices, but these two were special. They called him a moron whenever they met, though that wasn't all of it. The real thing was that Ix just felt like they were very different people. He couldn't understand wandmakers who had no interest in wands. He found they rarely understood each other, and he preferred to just not talk to them.

Several other people came into the room and took their seats. A few places were still unoccupied, but the servants came and cleared away the dishes in front of those.

After the drinks eventually came, Seyoh stood.

"I would like to thank you all for responding to my invitation on such short notice," he said, sweeping his eyes about the room.

"I believe you all may be able to guess without my explanation as to why I have decided to hold this dinner. But first, let us eat. The questioning and accusations can come afterward."

While Seyoh spoke, Rolphie stared at him meaningfully. Despite being the target of that look, Seyoh sat down, leaned back in his chair, and gave an unafraid smile.

The food was brought out. Each dish was simple but delicious, in contrast with the extravagance implied by the massive room. Neither farming nor hunting was possible at the moment due to the season, so the dishes all utilized preserved foods. The cook must have been quite skilled to achieve such exquisite flavors with those limitations.

The room was filled with lively chatter, though it was almost entirely idle gossip. Ix could intuit based upon what the guests were talking about that many of them were Marayist. The topic of Heaven's Worship came up, though it wasn't discussed at any significant length.

As the meal continued, the conversations switched to primarily discussions with the person sitting next to you. The atmosphere of the room also seemed to loosen.

"Man, that was nice. I'm glad we came," said Shuno, smiling from ear to ear beside Ix as they brought more food to their mouth. Their nervousness from earlier was completely gone. "Hey, aren't you going to eat?" they said, pointing at Ix's plate. "Oh-ho, do you not like this food? Weeell, I'm not that picky, but I'm pretty sure you shouldn't leave anything on your plate at an event like this. I've got no choice, then, I'll just take—"

"No, I'll eat it," said Ix.

"Really? You will? All of it...?"

"...I guess I'm fine with just one piece. You have the rest for me," said Ix. Shuno was practically beaming.

"Ah, you're really giving them to me?"

"Yeah."

"...Really? You're not going to extort me later?"

"I won't, so just take them already. It's not enough to make up for it anyway."

"Make up for what?" asked Shuno while happily chewing away.

"Nothing." Ix shrugged.

He looked forward again and saw the person sitting across the table staring at him. He was a middle-aged man, his hair thinning slightly. He'd been engaged in a heated discussion with another guest until just a moment ago.

As Ix grew confused, Shuno noticed the man as well. They looked back and forth between Ix and the man, furrowing their brow in unease.

"I-is he angry or something?" Shuno whispered in Ix's ear. "Maybe we're not supposed to give food like that...?"

"It's a possibility," he agreed.

The two of them looked at the man, and he suddenly gave them a gentle grin.

"Ah, apologies for staring. It's rude of me," he said. "The two of you were just making me smile. You must be friends?"

"Y-yes," said Shuno with a glance at Ix. "Right?"

Ix nodded without saying anything.

"Yes, we're close friends," said Shuno boldly.

"And why are you at this dinner? I heard earlier that Seyoh invited you."

"That's right; he asked us here. We didn't realize it was going to be this large of an event, though."

"Oh...?" The man nodded, looking somewhat surprised. "May I ask the reason why you were invited? You don't appear to be from Estosha..."

"Ah, well, the thing is, ummm...," said Shuno, uncertain as to whether or not they could talk about the underground passage.

They struggled to find an explanation, so Ix said, "We've been going to the monastery. To make staffs."

"Oh, I see, that explains it," said the man with a nod, deciding all on his own that that was sufficient. He adjusted his position in his chair and clasped his hands atop the table. "You must be two very promising craftspeople to be taking a job at the monastery at your age. I can understand why Seyoh would invite you. He does like young and brilliant people."

"Th-thank you," said Shuno with a slight bow.

"But if that is the case…are you content not joining their conversation?" asked the man with a hand raised to indicate the center of the table. There were many people there gathered in rambunctious chatter. Both Seyoh and Rolphie were participating. Although whether you could say Hemsley was also joining in was a matter of opinion.

"What do you mean?" asked Ix, turning his eyes back to the man.

"I've been gloriously defeated," said the man with a self-deprecating smile. "It is the inner circle that will attempt to solidify a decision while I'm not there. The majority of people have already been swept up by Mellay's assertions. Even if I tried to make a counterargument, my voice wouldn't reach them from all the way over here on the end. That might very well be the real reason for holding this dinner. In the normal meetings, the participants aren't divided like this. I should have realized it the moment I was led to this seat… All that's left is to determine who was responsible."

Ix and Shuno glanced at each other, not understanding what the man was saying.

"Oh, look at me running off complaining," he continued with a sigh. "They're discussing the possibility of treating wandmakers as members of the clergy over there."

"Wh-what?" shrieked Shuno, but it was blotted out by a laugh that erupted from somewhere else. "Wh-what does that mean?"

"I suppose I can't help but tell you…," he said.

There were a lot of vague sections in his explanation, as if he was trying to conceal something, but the general gist was that some of the members of the Church were debating that topic.

"If that was to happen, you wandmakers would find your-selves under a variety of restrictions. In your shops and in your daily lives as well. You would be significantly less free than you are now," he said.

"B-but it's just a debate, right?" said Shuno. "Even if some-thing like that is decided in a place like this, it couldn't possibly make any difference to all the different places in the country."

"...Of course not. It's best for you to think that," said the man with a sad smile.

"He looks like he's trying to tell us something, but why does it also seem like he's pitying us?" Shuno asked Ix in a quiet voice. "B-but it'll be fine, right? It's not like they can decide something that huge at a meeting in a place like this..."

"Either way, there's nothing we can do about it." Ix shrugged. "Even if the world changes, it's not the kind of problem that peo-ple like us can do anything about. This kind of thing is decided by people in another world."

"What do you mean, 'in another world'?"

"Well, above, probably."

"Above?"

Ix pointed up, and Shuno followed along to stare at the ceil-ing, then turned back to Ix's face.

With a wrinkle between their brow, Shuno said, "There's nothing up there..."

6

Yuui noticed when Ix and the person who'd been with him that one night showed up. She didn't know why they were here, but she was worried he'd gotten himself dragged into something unpleas-ant again.

Currently, however, she was Minaha, not Yuui, so she wasn't

in a position to casually address him. She would put him in greater danger if her true identity was discovered. With that in mind, she kept quiet. It was a blessing that they were sitting so far away from each other. He would surely realize who she was if he heard her voice.

But even if they weren't in this situation, Yuui likely wouldn't have been able to speak with him. It was taking every ounce of her energy to keep up with the debate unfolding before her eyes.

The transition happened naturally.

That was true for Yuui, who already knew what was happening, so the others surely didn't feel any discomfort with it. They probably never even realized that Mellay was shaping the direction of their arguments.

The conversation moved so naturally, almost as if it was to be expected, from idle gossip to the topic of the treatment of wand-makers. There was the discussion of the distinction of magic beasts in Marayism; then the five-legged beast was mentioned, which brought up the topic of wands. The same logic Mellay spoke of before was leading the debate to the same conclusion.

Yuui watched it happen in silence. There wasn't even a tiny gap for her to make a counterargument.

The scary thing was that Mellay looked as if she was almost entirely uninvolved. She offered the occasional remark here and there but kept it to a short comment or a quiet murmur, as though she were only half-heartedly participating in the debate.

But for Yuui, who had been focusing intently on the discussion, it was clear. Mellay's remarks were the turning points that nudged the conversation in the direction she wanted it to go, as if it were gently rolling toward that conclusion.

Actually, she wasn't quite leading the discussion. It was unfolding naturally. Anyone who thought about it would eventually reach the same conclusion. Mellay was more like a gentle wind, pushing on the backs of any who got lost along the way. That was the small amount of guiding she did.

Small amount?

What constituted a small amount?

Yuui wanted to laugh at her own thoughts.

How many calculations and how much preparation had been needed to make that "small amount" possible?

Yuui had spent her life so far being swept along the whole time, wrapped up in the expectations and plans of someone above. She had become just a pawn like that, and all she could do was adapt to the environment she was placed in.

Her life was not her own... She already knew that.

Even so, she'd had this tiny sensation that she'd managed to take back some of that during the events of the summer and fall. She'd expanded the range she could operate in and thought she would be able to do something within that space. If she had to admit it, she actually thought she, too, could join that world above. That was the reason she'd gone along with the suggestion that she return to Lukutta.

But seeing this now, all she could do was laugh. It turned out that the world above, which she's been only vaguely aware of, was a horrifying place.

"But would it be good to make wandmakers clergy? They don't know how to comport themselves as members of the Church," said someone.

"The current Guild lays down strict standards in order for one to become a craftsman. I hear that most of the more unreserved types are turned away," replied another.

"But there is the problem of their faith," said yet another. "Obviously, they are followers of Marayism, but do they have the faith sufficient enough to join the religious bureaucracy?"

They all fell into thought. Eventually, someone said something that acted as a trigger for others to say no not this, no not that, and the discussion grew even more complex.

Once they all finished saying what they wanted to say, there was a moment of silence.

"We do have wandmakers here, after all."

The voice came from that one particular elderly woman. It wasn't something said to the entire group, more like something murmured to the person sitting next to her. But since she said it in the single brief moment when everyone was silent, it seemed to ring out like a revelation.

"That's right, we do," someone said as they nodded.

"Those apprentices of Munzil's could very well act as representatives of wandmakers...," whispered another.

The participants' eyes naturally fell on the wandmakers at the table, on the pair of men who looked so alike, the boisterous one and the reticent one.

The two were engaged in conversation, or rather, there was a one-sided conversation occurring. Then they noticed everyone looking at them, and one raised a loud voice.

"I see, so you want to ask me something? Ha-ha, good! I'll allow a few questions!"

Some of the guests glowered at Rolphie's tone, but it wasn't enough of a hindrance to hold back the current flow of the debate.

One of the theologians cleared their throat and said, "I hope I'm not stepping on any toes if I go first. What do you wandmakers normally hold in your hearts while you are crafting wands? Is it the face of your client? The money you may receive? Or perhaps...your faith in God?"

"Ha-ha, what a dumb question!" cried Rolphie with a laugh. "All craftsmen think of the same thing: the ideal wand, obviously! Right?"

Rolphie hit Hemsley's shoulder, and he nodded.

"The ideal wand...?" The theologian grimaced. "And you are both the same?"

"Well, about that," said Rolphie as he placed the palms of his hands flat on the table, "I'm incredibly interested in how much I could sell the ideal wand for, and this guy next to me is searching for the ideal wood."

"My apologies for adding another question, but what is the ideal wand? What exactly does that look like?"

"Huh, you don't know? The ideal wand's right here in this town!"

"What?"

"Why don't you think about it in that head of yours a bit before you open your mouth?" Rolphie pointed down. "It's under the Chapel! That's the ideal wand, the ultimate wand!"

"That...is true in the stories, but is it actually true?"

"It is," said Rolphie with a self-confident nod.

"In other words, all wandmakers are pursuing that wand?"

Yuui secretly wondered what this wand underground was, but the guests were buzzing. It was probably a story that those connected to the Church knew.

But at that point, a voice came from the opposite end of the table from Yuui.

"Wait."

Looking that way, she saw the gray-haired man stand up, his hands on the table.

Ix..., she thought as she looked at his profile.

"What do you mean when you say that's the ultimate wand?" said Ix, staring directly at Rolphie, heedless of all the eyes that were locked on him.

"...What do you mean, '*What do you mean*'?" parroted Rolphie.

Yuui looked at him and was frightened. There wasn't a single hint of the smile that had been on his face a moment before. His expression was as cold as ice as he stared back at his fellow apprentice.

"Did you actually see that catalyst?" asked Ix.

"Yeah, I did," replied Rolphie with a nod.

"And it's the ultimate wand?"

"Yep."

"How can you say that?"

"You're a moron because you can't figure it out yourself."
It wasn't Rolphie who said that but Hemsley beside him. He was
still looking directly forward, his expression as irritated as ever.
"You'll never be able to see it unless you fix that."

"...Fine."

After seconds that felt as long as hours, Ix quietly took his
seat again.

Yuui felt the tension in her body drain away. It wasn't like
they'd been pointing wands at each other or even really arguing,
but Yuui's palms were slicked with sweat regardless.

It seemed like that might have been the same for the other
guests as well, because many of them were gaping at the two.

Yuui cautiously looked toward Ix, trying to keep the others
from noticing. His expression was as unchanged as ever, and he
was speaking quietly to the person beside him.

Afterward, the debate started up again like people happened to remember it. In the somewhat relaxed atmosphere, it
proceeded largely as expected, as Mellay had planned. They
came to the interpretation that the wandmakers who sought the
ultimate wand were the same as the clergy who held their faith
in God.

"But wands are not God. It would be one thing if God had
given us wands, but it was Rednoff who created them. A human.
To interpret those two as one and the same...," countered one
priest, and a few other attendees nodded in agreement. Even those
who had been pushing that argument so far grimaced at the statement and said nothing.

That's when a white hand rose into the air.

"May I speak for a moment?"

"O-of course, Mellay," said the priest nervously as he gestured
toward her with an open hand.

"Thank you. It has struck me that perhaps you are all forget-
ting the stories."

"Hmm, what do you mean...?"

"According to the legend, Rednoff was alone for a long time in the room below the Chapel where he made wands."

This was the first time Yuui had heard anything about this room below the Chapel or these wands, but she guessed it had something to do with the priest's notes she'd read that morning.

Mellay asked the other guests to think about it, then said, "Below the Chapel. If that isn't a display of faith on par with martyrdom, then what is it? And his success in creating the ultimate wand was nothing short of divine inspiration at work."

Everything clicked for the guess as they listened to what she said.

"Striving for the ultimate wand is, to wandmakers, the same as striving to be like Rednoff," she continued. "Is their drive to emulate his faithful heart at the time not the purest form of faith? That is what I think anyway..."

There was no need to even check. Everyone was completely convinced.

Mellay's tone was hesitant. She'd never broken the illusion that other people were driving the debate, and now it seemed that she was simply mentioning a random thought that had struck her. That actually had the opposite effect of lending her words great persuasive power. Now it appeared that Mellay, who had held back until now despite the authority her voice typically carried, had wrapped up the entire discussion.

No one else voiced dissenting opinions. The next meeting wouldn't have any debate; it would only be for confirmation.

With this, wandmakers would be subsumed by the Church once the New Order successfully stepped into power.

Yuui glanced in Ix's direction again.

Just moments before he had raised an opposing voice against Rolphie. He'd seen this "ultimate wand" or whatever it was.

What sort of wand was it? Was it a marvel of a catalyst worthy of being the target of every wandmaker's aspiration? Or...

7

"All right, let's get to the real topic of the day!"

When Rolphie shouted that, everyone present glanced at him suspiciously, even Ix and Shuno.

The dishes had already been cleared away, and the guests were being served after-dinner tea. Steam wafted up from the hot tea, but the room was already warm enough that drinking the beverage was causing them to sweat slightly.

"Real topic? Does that mean that wasn't all of it?" asked Shuno, their head cocked. "They're making us members of the clergy, aren't they? Whether they actually can or not is another discussion."

"That's what it sounded like to me...," said Ix, just as confused.

Rolphie, acting very casual and in control, crossed his long legs, sniffed the fragrant tea, and took a tiny sip. He returned the teacup to the table and looked around the room.

"Oh, yes. There was still that topic," said Seyoh, clasping his hands together. "I got completely swept away by the other subject, my apologies."

"I don't need your apologies yet!" shouted Rolphie with one arm open wide. "Because soon, you're going to be apologizing to each and every person here!"

Seyoh shrugged and stood.

"As you have all been informed, a few days after the last meeting, a letter was delivered to me. The contents were clear and simple: 'There is a plan moving ahead to blow away this building.' And you likely know this as well, but a few days before, Miss Minaha here," said Seyoh, indicating the person in a coat sitting across from him, "was attacked by someone while traveling down the road. Thankfully, she was unharmed, but we do know that the assailant used magic against her. I have thoroughly investigated both cases but have been unable to determine the culprit. Have I missed anything?"

Seyoh smiled at the room, then continued.

"And what Rolphie speaks of is his accusation that I am responsible for both of these events. Which, if true, is quite a serious issue."

Laughter could be heard in the room from no one in particular. But it died out quickly as strangely loud guffaws burst forth. That was from Rolphie, of course.

"Ha-ha-ha-ha, great explanation!" he said, then stood up forcefully. He started walking slowly around the table. "First just let me say: I have zero interest in this! I don't care who sent the letter or who attacked whomever it is over there! The only reason I'm going out of my way to explain this is because you lot have gotten really pathetic for not realizing who it is by now. Which means I'm saying this all out of the goodness of my own heart! Reflect on that and don't forget your gratitude while you listen very closely!"

His speech was accompanied by overexaggerated gestures and waved hands.

"Despite all that, I don't feel like going into all the annoying details of proof and motive and whatnot! The culprit is obvious even without all that!"

"Obvious...you say," said Seyoh, still standing. He walked down the other side of the table from Rolphie so he was almost directly across from him. "Then let me ask, what leads you to claim that I am responsible for the first incident?"

"Everything. The letter was delivered, right? To this building? Otherwise known as your home. Early in the morning," said Rolphie.

"Yes, that is correct."

"Where exactly was it delivered to?"

"I was told it was placed outside the entrance...," said Seyoh, puzzled.

"You must get tired playing dumb like that all the time."

Rolphie swept his hair up. "So how did you read that letter? A letter that, if placed on the piles of snow, would have gotten so damp you couldn't read it?"

Ix saw everyone's expressions grow cold in that moment.

"...It wasn't that damp," replied Seyoh in a calm tone. "The servants likely picked it up just after it was placed there."

"That is an incredible coincidence!" Rolphie clapped his hands. "But the person who sent it was a serious moron, weren't they? Come on, putting a letter on the snow?!"

"My servants open the front entrance every day at the same time. It is possible the sender investigated before sending."

"Someone who's sending a tip-off letter? That's thinking pretty far ahead for something like that!"

"Or, and I don't say this because I personally believe it, but the culprit may be one of my servants."

"Ah, so then you don't recognize the handwriting of one of the very few servants of yours who can actually write and didn't bother investigating it after the letter was delivered?"

"...Is that all the proof you have for your accusations?"

"Didn't I say that we wouldn't need anything as bothersome as proof? Even a child knows if you put paper on the snow, it'll get wet. There's not any proof of that."

Rolphie and Seyoh glared at each other.

Eventually, Seyoh cleared his throat and said, "Then what about the second incident? Is it obvious that I attacked Minaha?"

"Of course it is! It's even more obvious than the last one!" Rolphie pointed at the person in a coat. "It's not like anyone would attack a person whose name and face they don't even know!"

The room fell utterly silent.

Seyoh blinked in confusion and said, "...Is that your reason?"

"What about it don't you understand? The attack was clearly targeting her specifically, yeah? Only someone who knows what's under the hood would do that. Which is you. Can you think of any other possibilities?"

"I can think of a few."

"Then give them here; I'll shoot down every single one."

"The assailant was attacking at random. The assailant had learned Minaha's true identity elsewhere. The assailant was a member of the meetings and trying to eliminate her despite not knowing her true identity," said Seyoh, listing off example after example.

"Would someone who's intelligent enough to have a wand attack people at random in broad daylight? Nope. You're the only person who knows her identity, so where exactly is someone else going to find out who she is? And seriously? A participant in the meetings? They attacked even though they knew you were on high alert because of the threat letter? Are there any actual morons here? Other than *the* moron."

"……"

It seemed Rolphie had forced Seyoh into submission by refuting his ideas so quickly.

Listening to this conversation was enough to give Ix a general idea of what was happening. As it played out, he'd gone from wondering what Rolphie was blabbering about to feeling like he was actually on to something.

In reality, Rolphie's argument was absurd. Anyone could poke as many holes in the defense as they wanted, but it was Seyoh giving up on defending himself that seemed the most convincing proof.

But just then, a voice came from beside Ix.

"E-excuse me."

Ix looked over to see Shuno timidly raising their hand.

"What now?" Rolphie glowered at the sudden interruption. "Ah, whatever. You can speak."

"Well, according to the conversation from before, you think that the 'blow the building away' thing is just random nonsense, but…I saw it. There's blast powder in the passage below the city."

"Blast powder...?" asked everyone in the room, including Rolphie.

Of course, Ix had never heard of the stuff before. But he did think he knew what Shuno was talking about—the casks they'd found in the passage that contained a sand-like substance.

"Y-yes," said Shuno with a gulp. "It's a specialized powder that will explode when you apply pressure and expose it to flame. I saw it underground."

"Was there enough to provide the force necessary to destroy the building?" asked the man across from them in a calm tone.

"U-uh, well... There wasn't all that much, and it was already damp... B-but it might've been part of some plot."

"Right," said Rolphie, though he nodded in an uninterested way. "Unless I'm wrong, this blast powder or whatever has nothing to do with this incident. Be quiet now."

"H-huh? But—"

"I agree," came a voice that Ix knew well.

It belonged to Minaha, the woman in the coat. She was going by a different name, but her tone of voice and speech patterns were exactly the same as the girl he knew as Yuui.

Everyone turned their attention on her, the girl who hadn't spoken up even when the topic centered on her.

"Are you a blast wandmaker?" she asked Shuno.

"How do you know that name...?" Their eyes grew wide. "N-no, I'm not. I make magic wands."

"In all likelihood, the blast powder that you saw was used long ago when that passage was dug. It's just leftovers."

"H-how can you even claim that?"

"I do not know how powerful blast powder is, and I have never seen that underground tunnel. But I do have one question. During the time when that passage was constructed, by which I mean when the Chapel was built, were magic techniques advanced enough to bore through the earth?"

"W-well, it would be difficult…," said Shuno, their voice growing quieter and quieter.

"Then which do you think is more likely: Someone obtained old technology and secretly transported it underground, or that the materials from that time period were left there? Time passes more gently beneath the earth."

Once she finished speaking in nearly one breath, she held her hands in front of her as if she were handing back the spotlight. Rolphie took the opportunity to start speaking again, waving his arms.

Shuno seemed to almost shrink into themselves as they put their hands on their knees. No one was paying attention to them anymore.

"You okay?" asked Ix. "You were thinking of everyone in the room when you spoke; I doubt they think badly of you."

"Yeah, I'm fine… Actually, maybe I'm not," Shuno said with a weak smile. "Do you mind going outside with me for a bit? It feels really stuffy in here…"

8

When Ix and Shuno stepped quietly out of the room, Ix saw someone he recognized.

People who looked like the attendants of the dinner guests were standing outside the room. Among them was Nova, the girl who had been tasked with monitoring and guarding Yuui.

Ix wasn't sure if he should talk to her, but she nodded slightly when she saw him looking at her, then glanced out the window.

"I shouldn't have butted in…," said Shuno as they walked on unsteady feet. "I'm going to get some fresh air."

"I'll come with you to the entrance," said Ix as he nodded back toward Nova.

©Enji

They descended the stairs and stepped out of the building. The difference in temperature between outside and inside was greater than expected, so Ix pulled his coat tight around him.

Shuno told him they were going to take a walk around the area. Ix waited there and heard the door opening behind him. He turned back to see Nova, expressionless as ever.

"Why is Yuui here?" he asked without any preface. "I thought she went back to Lukutta."

"This was a condition, for her return."

"I didn't hear anything about any conditions."

"No, you didn't."

"...What's the condition?"

"That she participate, in the theological meetings in this town."

"Why?"

"I don't know. But I've been told that once this is over, she really will return to Lukutta."

"I don't get it..." Ix folded his arms and looked up at the sky. "What's the point of making Yuui participate, and with her true identity hidden at that? Since you're here, she'll still continue to cooperate with the New Order, and her having royal blood carries no sway in the Kingdom."

He turned his head and noticed Nova staring at him. Her expression hadn't changed, but she seemed like she wanted to say something.

"What's up?" he asked.

"Did Yuui, tell you?" asked Nova.

"Tell me what?"

"Did Yuui say she had royal blood?"

"Uh, well..." Ix didn't understand the point of the question but brought a hand to his mouth and searched through his memories. "It was...Tomah I heard it from. I think he just told me she had some noteworthy ancestry without going into specifics."

"Which means, she didn't speak to you about it, herself?"

"Nova, what are you asking this for? Are you saying she doesn't really have royal blood?"

"No, she does. But that isn't the reason she's valued in Lukutta. She comes from, another important bloodline."

"Another?"

"Yes, she's…"

When Ix heard Nova's response, he was overcome with a horrible feeling of foreboding.

Though he had nothing in the way of proof to validate his hunch, it all fit together too perfectly.

He glanced around, but Shuno wasn't back yet. He didn't have time to wait.

"Sorry, Nova, I'm going back to the dinner," Ix said as he opened the door. "Tell Shuno that when they get back. They're the person I was with."

"Okay."

Leaving her behind as she nodded, he ran up the stairs and went back in the room they were in before.

Very few people noticed to Ix when he reentered. Most of them were focused on the debate playing out between Rolphie and Seyoh in the middle of the room, the one was already supposed to have been settled.

Rolphie was spreading his arms out and shouting.

"Guys, I'm both screaming and crying here! How the hell did none of you realize such a simple thing?! He wanted someone to figure it out! That's why he was so sloppy!"

"S-Seyoh, is this true?" said one guest with a shake of their head. "Did you really pretend to attack Minaha to see if there was anyone who bore her ill will?"

"It is as you say," replied Seyoh with a smile. "I assumed that if there was someone among the participants like that, they would attempt to contact me afterward. But no one appeared. I do apologize for testing everyone like that, but this means we are finally ready for the next meeting."

"Ready…?"

Seyoh ignored the man who muttered and walked over to stand behind Yuui, the person in the coat. She raised her head but didn't react beyond that.

Everyone there watched him with bated breath.

"There is a debate that we must have—a debate for our future. But it concerns an incredibly delicate matter. Some of you may be sickened at the mere mention of it. But first, I wanted you to trust her."

He placed a hand on her shoulder. Then he slowly rubbed her coat and moved his fingers to her hood.

"Let me introduce the real Minaha: Miss Yuui Laika."

Yuui didn't resist. She kept her hands on her knees and her back perfectly straight as he removed her hood.

Her dark skin, unlike anyone else's in the room, had been exposed.

"I see, so she's an easterner," remarked the elderly vukodrak woman immediately. She waited a few seconds before filling the chamber with her calm voice. "Seyoh, I believe you were overly cautious, but you have magnificently achieved your goal. At this point, no one here has any negative feelings toward her. We can have a rational debate about easterners. Am I incorrect?"

She looked around the room, and everyone nodded. There were murmurs of agreement with Mellay and surprise that Yuui had such a deep understanding of Marayism.

But Seyoh disabused them of their assumption.

"Mellay," he said, "you have come to the wrong conclusion. It is not the easterners themselves we must discuss, but their faith." He smiled as he continued. "What I am most concerned with is how we interpret their beliefs when we enlighten them."

"So then we will be hearing from Yuui herself? About the god they believe in and their doctrine?"

"No. Yuui is an example."

"An example? Of what?" asked Mellay, her head cocked.

©Enji

"A god."

"What?"

Seyoh gestured toward Yuui's face with his left hand. "This girl, Yuui, is a god. She is the descendant of a lineage that has the blood of a deity running through their veins. Or so the people in her homeland believe, of course." He placed one hand on top of the other in front of him. "So then, how do we handle such a person? That is the discussion I wish to have at our next meeting, which will take place on the day of Heaven's Worship."

All eyes in the room were on Yuui.

What emotions were in them?

"...Is it true?" asked Mellay after struggling to find her words for a moment.

And the response:

"...Yes."

When Yuui nodded, no one else chose to speak again.

1

Regardless of what had transpired, Ix still had a job to do. He and Shuno went to the monastery the following day, but he couldn't focus on his work at all. He noticed that his hands had stopped moving, and he'd lapsed completely into thought. It was the first time something like that had ever happened to him.

He hadn't been able to do anything at that dinner.

Of course he couldn't. Considering his low social standing, it wasn't his place to say anything. But even if he had been a participant in the debates, he would have kept his mouth shut.

Ix hadn't known about Yuui. He hadn't tried to find out her secret. His only interest was in wands; he didn't care about his clients' situations, so long as he could keep crafting...

Ultimately, he'd only been able to watch as she was put in danger, then slink back to the monastery to make wands again, like he was running away.

He wondered what would happen to her.

Unfamiliar with the scriptures as he was, Ix did know it was a grave sin to claim you were a god. If they took Yuui to trial for this, she would lose an arm at best. Typically, this sort of crime led to a death sentence.

Chills ran through his entire body as he considered the possibility.

Would she be executed?

Was that why they had brought her here?

Had they tempted her with the prospect of returning to Lukutta only to lead her to the gallows?

"Can I help you with anything?" asked Beter. His face was half-visible as he peered in from the doorway. He was smiling cheerfully. He was blissfully unaware of the meetings in the city and the underground passage. Seyoh had given him a random explanation as to why Ix and Shuno had gone missing.

"No, I'm okay," said Shuno.

"Ix?" Beter looked at him, his head tilted. His table, which would normally be covered in wood shavings by now, was still clean.

Ix almost said nothing was wrong but stopped before he could get the words out. Instead, he brought a hand to his mouth and asked, "Can you...bring the three monks here? The ones I'm making staffs for?"

"Of course, I don't mind at all, but..." Beter blinked, not understanding the reason for his request. "Is there an issue?"

"No, there's not. I just kind of want to talk to them."

"Okay! I'll get them right away."

For some reason, Beter's smile glowed even brighter, and he left the room.

Ix wasn't exactly sure why he'd asked this all of a sudden. But he wasn't going to get any work done today, so he honestly just sort of wanted to hear what his clients had to say.

The first monk came quickly to the room. He'd been in the middle of work, so his clothes were dusty. "Is there a problem?" he asked, furrowing his brows with anxiety.

"It's not that important." Ix shook his head. "Could you take a seat?"

He looked at the monk as he sat down across from him. Ix had gotten into a bit of an argument with him about woodwork on the first day of the job.

"…I'm sorry about before," said Ix, running fingers across his wandmaking tools.

"Huh?" The monk's eyes opened wide in surprise.

"I complained about the treatment on your wood, even though you did your best to research and work it. That was impolite of me."

"O-oh…" The man looked taken aback, his mouth agape. "No, don't be sorry. It was my fault for doing too much without a strong grasp of the fundamentals. Um, is that what you wanted to talk about?"

"No… Let's chat a bit more."

Despite Ix's insistence, he didn't have any specific questions to ask. They spoke about the staff a bit more.

"Honestly, I know how inconvenient this assignment is," said the monk at some point during the conversation.

"What do you mean?"

"I know how much staffs normally cost. The monastery isn't rich, so I'm sure you're not getting compensated enough. I bet you don't often make staffs for regular people like me."

"Well…" Ix brought a hand to his mouth. "The first staff I ever made was for a kid from a regular family; they weren't nobility or anything."

"That's amazing. And did it cost about as much as usual?"

"Uh…yeah."

Ix didn't mention that the order had been canceled due to some special circumstances.

They quickly ran out of things to chat about, so Ix told the monk he was free to go.

"Sorry for interrupting your work; you can head back," he said.

"Ah, okay…," replied the monk. He walked toward the door but then spun on his heel to face Ix again. "Um, thank you," he said with a deep bow.

"Huh?"

"I'm going to keep working hard to become someone deserving of the staffs you make."

Ix couldn't figure out what to say in response, so he just nodded and vaguely said, "Okay." The monk smiled and left the room.

After that, Ix talked to his other two clients. He didn't apologize to either of them, but oddly enough, they both thanked him before they left. Ix had no idea why. It actually made him feel uncomfortable. He hadn't done anything to deserve their gratitude.

Time passed like that until noon came. Just as Ix started to head off toward the cafeteria with Shuno, Coaku suddenly called out to him.

"Ah, Ix, could you stay behind for a moment?" he asked.

"Sure, I don't mind…"

Ix told Shuno to go on ahead. Coaku offered him a seat in front of the fire, which he accepted. He gazed at the old man's face, wondering what he could want. The flames reflected off the old man's glasses, behind which he stared at Ix with narrowed eyes.

"It's good artey, isn't it?" said Coaku. "It's particularly high quality this year."

"Huh? …Oh, yeah. The components are great." Ix was surprised for a moment but nodded. "Coaku, do you use the artey from here, too?"

"I would love to use some, but those trees belong to the monastery." He smiled sadly. "But the wood makes a good sound. And your shavings are smooth. Thanks to all the work you two put in, they'll make for great staffs."

"…You saw our unfinished catalysts? When?" asked Ix with a frown.

"I haven't examined them. I planned on speaking up if there was an issue, but I have no doubts about either of your skills. A glance was enough to tell me as much. That's let me relax here."

Ix couldn't tell if Coaku really meant that or if he was just saying things while half-asleep. When they first met, they'd only exchanged a few words and a handshake, yet now the craftsman was implying that was all it had taken to evaluate Ix's skills. That didn't seem realistic.

"…Did you want something?" asked Ix, ignoring the other questions he had for the wandmaker.

"Sorry, I've gotten into the habit of prattling on as I've gotten older." Coaku brought a hand to his forehead. "I just wanted to tell you that you pass."

"Huh?"

Ix stared hard at Coaku's face. What was this all about?

But it wasn't just Ix who seemed to think this was strange. Coaku also scratched his head, looking befuddled.

"What do you mean, 'Huh?'…?" He adjusted his glasses and tilted his head. "Perhaps you didn't hear."

"I heard you the first time, but what are you talking about? What did I pass?"

"I approve of your registration as a craftsman."

"…What?"

Ix blinked several times. This was either the cruelest joke ever, or he'd misheard.

But Coaku didn't correct his last statement and simply said, "How odd. The Guild should have told you that this assignment doubles as an exam."

"Hold on a second." Ix turned his face to the side and held up a hand. "I don't understand… Shuno's the one being tested here."

"Of course they are." Coaku nodded. "I decided they passed on the very first day. I haven't told them as much, though."

"Passed…? What are you judging if you haven't seen the finished product?"

"I already told you that you have plenty of skill." He smiled. "There are all sorts of craftsmen. The ones who follow their own ideals, the ones who pursue money, they can do whatever they like. The important thing is to know what you're after. That's the only thing about you that I was uncertain about… But after seeing you today, I realized that wouldn't be a problem."

"Now I'm even more confused," said Ix, staring at the ground. "Today I was less steady than I've ever been."

"That's why. You seemed lost, but you'll probably be fine like that. Because up until now, you've just been drifting."

Ix had no idea what Coaku was saying. He was being contradictory.

Besides, there were more conditions required to become a craftsman than just passing the Guild exam.

"A shop... Yeah, I'm completely hopeless when it comes to having a shop," said Ix, raising his head. "You need one to be a craftsman, right?"

"Which is why I told you I'd give you mine, but it seems you didn't hear that, either."

"Give your store...? To me?"

Impossible. Ix shook his head over and over. He couldn't believe this stroke of good fortune would just fall into his lap. There had to be a mistake. Or maybe it was a trick.

"If you're saying that," said Coaku with a sad smile, "does that mean you don't want to be a craftsman?"

"N-no, that's not it. It's just..."

Ix been aiming to complete his registration as a craftsman for ages. But he hadn't been emotionally prepared for this revelation, so the first emotion to come to him was confusion, not happiness.

Seeing Ix's flustered state, Coaku lowered his brows in uncertainty.

"Well, let's just leave it at that for now," he said as he got up. The craftsman leaned on his cane and bent his knees. "It seems like a good idea to give you some time before I ask for your final decision. We'll both be here for the winter regardless. Take some time to mull it over."

"O-okay."

"To be honest, I would really like to leave my shop in your hands. You apprenticed under a good friend of mine and are a promising craftsman in the making. If there's anything you're unhappy with, or if you have any conditions about our arrangement, please let me know. I'll do my best to accommodate them."

"Yeah…," said Ix, though he was no longer in a state where he could think about anything. He had no idea how to react to this reality.

But just before Coaku left the room, Ix remembered something he'd forgotten to ask.

"Earlier…," he started.

"Yes, what is it?" asked the old man as he stopped and turned his face only to look back.

"You said you contacted me earlier, right?"

"I did."

"Who did you send the letter to? Morna? Or maybe Layumatah?"

When Ix asked, Coaku only looked more confused and said, "They should be in town. Have you not met them?"

"You can't mean…"

"Rolphie and Hemsley. I sent them numerous exchanges. I thought that was the reason they were in Estosha…"

2

Ix grabbed his lunch and went out of the cafeteria to find Shuno sitting in their usual spot. They were sitting in front of the pure-white landscape, silently moving the food around their half-empty plate.

"Hey, what did Coaku want to talk to you about?" asked Shuno as Ix sat down next to them. "He wasn't lecturing you…was he? He seemed so nice before."

"No… I'll tell you about it later. I need some time to sort things out first."

"O-oh? Are you okay? You can always talk to me if you need advice."

"Yeah."

Shuno glanced sideways at Ix several times. Though Ix noticed this, he just didn't know what to say to his friend.

For a while, they ate in silence. A light snow fell to the ground, and a few flakes even landed on the back of Ix's hands. They melted away immediately, as though they were never there in the first place.

"You've been like this ever since yesterday," muttered Shuno. "Something happened when I left the room. Tell me about it."

"…Someone I know is sort of…"

"…You can't seriously think that explanation's gonna cut it. Someone you know is sort of what?"

"Sort of in danger of getting killed."

"Th-that's pretty serious!" Shuno looked around. They were all alone, of course. "A-and? When?"

"What do you mean, 'When?'"

"When are you going to go save them?"

Their quick response left Ix silent.

He couldn't change the fact that Shuno could never truly understand. No matter how much Ix wanted to save Yuui, they were up against powerful opponents. They must have concocted an elaborate scheme to set her up like that. There was nothing a mere apprentice could do to stop them. He couldn't even get into the meetings.

But if Ix explained everything to Shuno, he would get them involved, too. Just as he was concluded that it would be best to gloss over the issue and push it aside, his friend spoke up.

"You've already thought of a way to save them, haven't you, Ix?"

"What makes you say that?"

"You're not the type to show stuff on your face, but I can see that much right now. We're good friends, after all. And because we're so close, I can tell that you don't know if you should go through with this, right? But this is exactly the kind of situation where I step in as your senior. So lay it on me! What do you need advice about?"

"Advice…?"

"I told you, didn't I? That you shouldn't hesitate to rely on me if you're in trouble," said Shuno, smiling proudly as they thumped their chest.

There was something encouraging about their face at that moment.

Nevertheless, Ix stared at the ground through the space between his knees for a while. A thin layer of snow settled on the back of his head before he finally looked up.

"...I would be betraying someone I owe if I go through with my plan."

"Someone you owe? Are you saying it'll hurt them?"

"No, that's not it. This person is no longer with us. But... they're very precious to both the person I know and me. And this will disgrace them."

"Hmm..." Shuno looked up at the sky. "This might be a flippant opinion, but isn't the life of someone who still draws breath more important than the honor of someone who's dead?"

"......"

"Wow, this is quite the trifling conundrum you've got. How very you," said Shuno with a sigh. "...I told you before I was planning on taking up the family business, right?"

"What's this about?" asked Ix in surprise as he looked sideways at Shuno.

"Nothing, really." They smiled wide. "Just...thought I'd distract you with a story. It's about the blast powder from yesterday. You've never heard of blast wands before, have you?"

Ix shook his head, and Shuno grinned like they'd thought as much.

"They've been around for a long time, blast wands. My family's made them for generations. That's our trade, essentially," said Shuno. "You were next to me yesterday when I spoke, so you probably know already, but there's this substance called blast powder. It burns violently when you expose it to fire. If you get a lot together and apply pressure to it, the resulting explosion will be even larger. Depending on how you do it, you can wield some serious destructive force with the stuff. This has absolutely nothing to do with magic, by the way. Blast powder produces the same force regardless of who lights it. Blast wands were a type of weapon that used blast powder."

"I've never heard of them."

"They were deadly weapons back in the day. My dad and his dad were experts in the field. Blast wandmakers were pretty much the only ones who knew how to make them and how to produce the powder for them, plus the only people who understood its effects. They were valued by their countries and treated pretty well, so enemy nations couldn't get them to betray their homelands. That was all until Rednoff invented man-made wands."

"Then the reason your family's business went bad..."

"Was because of magic wands. The business was already about to go under back when I was born."

"I don't want to interrupt, but did demand for blast wands really get that low?" asked Ix, his head cocked. "It sounds to me like they were pretty effective, with no difference in strength between users. Wouldn't people use them alongside magic wands for different things?"

"About that. Blast powder's super difficult to synthesize. You produce it by combining a few different substances together, but one of them is incredibly difficult to get ahold of. Difficult enough that you need the support of a nation to do it." Shuno sighed. "Unfortunately, that support dried up. Besides, the stuff just makes explosions... It can only be used for violence. But magic wands can be used over and over so long as the user has mana left, and they can do all sorts of things. Compared to that, blast wands are nothing. The kingdom went all in on fostering magic wandmakers, exacerbating the transition away from blast wands..."

"But you became an apprentice wandmaker."

"I wanted to learn about them. I wanted to get to know these magic wands that everyone talked so much about. Mom and Dad insisted I was betraying the family... But to me, it was plain as day which was the better of the two. I thought, *Ah, so this is why blast wands are going away,* and wanted to laugh. Ever since, I've been working to improve my craftsmanship.

"But you know. I was a bit happy to hear that conversation yesterday. Blast powder was useful for something, even if it was just digging that tunnel below the city. I'm not obsessed with blast wands or anything; I'm entirely focused on magic wands now. But...I dunno. So... Uh, what am I actually trying to say?"

"I thought you just wanted to distract me?"

"Well, there was that..." Shuno crossed their arms and grimaced. "Oh, that was it. Here's the rub: your senior betrayed their living family. So you shouldn't care about being disloyal to someone who's dead. Or maybe you should care a little... Anyway, maybe it would be best for me to say you should just look the other way this time? When it comes down to it, I'll be with you in front of their grave apologizing."

"What the hell was that?"

Not even Ix could hold back a laugh of surprise at how contrived Shuno's explanation was.

But at the same time, he felt some of the tension slip away.

Seriously... What am I hesitating for? he thought.

He didn't have the sheer goodness that Yuui did, but he should at least be able to take on this much responsibility.

3

The pair moved away so no one would overhear them.

They left the monastery behind and slipped into the artey forest that surrounded it. The branches drooped under the weight of the white snow settled on the dark-green pine needles. Every once in a while, a branch near breaking would bend lower and shudder like a beast shivering, causing the snow to slough off.

"This is a nice forest," remarked Shuno.

"Yeah," replied Ix.

The trees were growing at regular intervals, and they had been trimmed of extraneous limbs. You could tell humans had carefully crafted this place. Ix suddenly recalled the mountain he'd grown up on, though the trees there were completely unsuited to wands, unlike the ones here.

As he reflected on that, he felt a very strange sensation.

Why was he here?

Why was a child who'd been abandoned on a winter's day now walking across the snow in this far-off place?

Ix told Shuno about his plan, though there wasn't really anything he needed from them. After that, he decided to ask more about blast wands. He suspected Shuno's knack for crafting had come from his familiarity with this older style of wand.

Perhaps certain theories applicable to blast wands and weapons that used blast powder were also relevant to magic wandmaking. Maybe Shuno had limitless ideas about crafting because they'd entered the field as an outsider, so they weren't constrained by its conventional wisdom.

"Well, blast wands are a weapon that...," said Shuno, speaking with their hands as much as their words. "You produce an explosion in a very sturdy tube, and the reaction shoots out a rock or something..."

"Reaction?

"It's a secondary effect, yeah?"

It was a strange weapon, this wand that needed an explosive reaction to shoot something. In a magic catalyst, that would be considered a secondary effect. It seemed like blast wands weren't able to shoot out explosive force itself. What exactly did they look like?

At that point, his thoughts caught on something in the back of his mind.

Reaction...?

Shooting something out with a reaction?

He stopped in his tracks.

"Shuno..."

"What's wrong?" they asked after walking a couple of steps past Ix.

"Have you ever tried to make a magic wand using blast wand structures?"

"Bit and pieces, yeah... Which part are you talking about?"

"The 'shooting something out using a reaction' part. Couldn't you accomplish the same thing with mana?"

"Ah... Well," began Shuno with a wry smile, "yeah, I've thought about it. I've put together different types of wood. One stick in the middle, with another around it to make the reactive force. But it doesn't work, and you'd probably arrive at that conclusion yourself if you ran the calculations. The wand isn't sturdy enough. It breaks if you try to output more magic power than it can handle. It wouldn't pan out."

"Oh, right..."

Though Ix nodded along with Shuno's explanation, internally, he was confused.

No—Shuno was wrong.

What were they even saying?

Ix knew the wood wouldn't withstand the blast. But that was only an issue if you were outputting the maximum amount of force. You could put a limiter in the wand to avoid that.

Why hadn't Shuno realized that?

No, that wasn't the question...

It wasn't just Shuno.

This was an incredibly simple structure. Anyone could come up with it. It absolutely was not difficult from a technical perspective. People could have implemented it perfectly well a hundred years ago.

And yet...

Shuno, Ix's fellow apprentices, and all the wandmakers in the world...

Had his own master not even thought of it…?

Ix brought a hand to his mouth.

He was shaking.

If his master had thought of it, he would have tried making it at least once.

But he didn't even do that, despite being so close.

Which meant he really hadn't thought of it.

Ix wondered why not but then shook his head.

Why not?

The reason was obvious:

Because all wandmakers sought the ultimate wand, their ideal catalyst.

Oh…

That's why.

That's why the wand underground was the ultimate wand.

Compared to something like that…

But that was it, wasn't it?

Use a magic reaction and put in something to limit the force.

You wouldn't need the fine skills of a craftsman or a careful selection of materials to produce it.

You could make large quantities of identical wands.

You could make an infinite number of catalysts, devoid of special characteristics.

Craftsmen would find no value in trying to make something like that.

It was worthless.

Or was it?

Was it truly worthless?

You could put that kind of wand in the hands of lots of people for cheap.

Did that really have no value?

Was Ix the only one who considered that valuable?

Possibly... Probably.

There was only a single person in the entire world who saw the worth in a wand like that.

Only a person without magic could understand it.

If he'd known how powerful magic was, he would have sought only to amplify its power further.

That's why everyone had considered the idea of a wand that could be mass-produced but had never tried to actualize it.

It was an idea any other craftsman would subconsciously dismiss.

The tips of Ix's fingers grew cold.

His excitement was drawing the blood from his extremities.

"Ix!"

That voice brought him back to reality.

Shuno was staring, their face right up to his.

"What's wrong?" asked Ix.

"What's wrong...? That's what I should be saying. What's wrong with you? I thought you'd lost consciousness with your eyes still open or something."

"Oh, really?" he asked vaguely with a nod.

Shuno gave him an anxious look. "Are you sure you're all right?"

"I'm fine... I'm fine."

"Maybe you should take the afternoon off from work. Did you get enough sleep?"

"No, that's not it. I just..."

"Just...?" repeated Shuno.

"Just..."

Just what?

Just thought...of what?

"I just remembered something. The esne forest on the mountain I grew up on."

A type of wood that repelled mana.

4

They treated Yuui no differently after the incident. She stayed in the same room as always, and she had her meals brought to her. But now, she wasn't allowed out of her room, and Nova didn't come visit.

Yuui hadn't the faintest idea about what was going on outside her room or what the next conference would hold in store. She passed a day doing nothing but gazing out the window. Those days continued.

And then before she knew it, the time came.

Heaven's Worship. The day of the meeting where she would be tried.

Unlike every other time she'd attended, Yuui was the first person in the hall. The furniture had been rearranged from how it had been the night of the dinner to its typical setup, with chairs scattered throughout the darkened chamber. But there wasn't a seat for her. Instead, she was made to stand beside the wall.

She watched the participants trickle in one by one. As they entered, they would glance in her direction for a brief moment, then look away.

Quite a few had arrived already, but no one was doing any chatting. Mellay's arrival produced a slight murmur, but otherwise the participants kept their mouths shut tight.

Eventually, Seyoh opened the door and entered.

He walked to the small table in the center of the hall. The scribe took out their writing utensils and placed their left hand on the paper.

"The 934th meeting will now come to order," Seyoh announced gravely. "During our last conference, we decided that today's debate would concern the distinction between magic beasts and humans. However, now that we are here, we find ourselves with another topic at hand. I believe this concern to be of great urgency for these meetings and, as such, would like to discuss placing it at a higher priority. Please raise your hand if you have any questions or disagreements."

Seyoh swept his eyes slowly across the faces of the participants, but no one raised their hand.

"Agreed?" he said, this time scanning the entire chamber. "The debate participants unanimously agree to change this meeting's topic. Before we begin, I would like to announce that while I did invite Misters Rolphie and Hemsley to attend, they were unable to do so because of an urgent matter that arose."

No one voiced the suspicion that their absence had been planned from the very beginning.

"Now then, we will discuss how to handle easterners who claim to be descended from a god. Please raise your hand if you wish to voice an opinion."

This time, two or three people shot their hands up immediately.

The debate played out as Yuui had imagined it might. Except now there wasn't anyone guiding it. It was running its natural course.

First, the participants confirmed the severity of the sin that claiming to be a god was in Marayism. Next, they accused Yuui of misrepresenting God by claiming to be a deity. The conversation was well laid out and proceeded without issue.

They were about to declare her guilty, with airtight logic at that.

Just as the debate was entering its final phase, there came a quiet knock at the door.

Seyoh, who had been in the middle of a sentence, stopped speaking and turned in the direction of the entrance. The servant standing in front of the door had a quiet conversation through it with whoever was on the other side, then hastily opened it.

"Apologies for interrupting," said a small elderly man as he entered. He was leaning against a cane. From behind his small spectacles, his eyes swept across the faces of each person in the room in turn. "Might you allow me to impose for a moment?"

"Master Coaku?" said Seyoh as he strode quickly over to the

old man's side. Yuui had never heard Seyoh address someone more humbly. "What has brought you here so suddenly? I was under the impression you would be unable to attend today due to work…"

"Well, that was the plan originally, but my schedule opened up," responded the man in his gentle voice.

"I appreciate your coming out of your way to visit us, but unfortunately…," said Seyoh as he rubbed his hands together, "there has been a last-minute change of topic today. We were hoping to hear from wandmakers at the next meeting…"

"Oh?" said Coaku as he shifted his cane to the other hand. "What topic is it, then?"

"The crime of claiming to be God," explained Seyoh shortly.

"Ah, good." Despite the last-minute change, Coaku smiled and nodded. "That's the reason I came, actually."

"Uh…? You came to debate this matter as well, Master Coaku?"

"Oh, no, not me. A wandmaker I know. Come in," he said, directing the last part to someone outside the door before turning back toward the chamber. "I know this is highly unusual, but I hope you'll forgive me. I had to give in when he gave me this condition."

"Condition?" asked Seyoh with a puzzled look.

As they spoke, they heard footsteps approaching from outside the entrance, and a backlit person appeared behind Coaku.

It was a man with gray hair and an uncongenial look on his face. He was immature, with many years yet ahead of him.

Someone Yuui knew well.

Ix…

He passed Coaku and entered the hall. Without stopping, he walked to the center.

Some of the participants must have realized he was the same man who'd gotten up at the dinner the other night.

"Ix…?" said Seyoh as he rushed toward the apprentice wandmaker, his long hair flowing behind him. "What is going on? How do you know Master Coaku…?"

"Sorry for doing this out of the blue. My name's Ix. I'm a

wandmaking apprentice. I came to Estosha to work on staffs at the monastery," said Ix, completely ignoring everything else around him. The participants listened in utter disbelief. "I know this isn't the kind of place someone like me should be. And I think I get what you're all debating. It's something theologians and clergy should be arguing over, not something a wandmaking apprentice should be sticking their nose into."

"So why are you here, then?" asked Mellay. Then she looked around, smiled, and asked, "Well, it can't hurt to listen, can it?"

The confusion gripping the room subsided, giving way to the feeling of a group of adults watching an excitable child. Mellay had deftly handled the crowd.

Yuui couldn't tell if Ix noticed that change in the atmosphere or not; he just kept talking in a flat tone.

"The reason I had Coaku help me get in here to address you all is because I've noticed something that I can't overlook as a believer living in the kingdom. And that..." His eyes darted to Yuui by the wall for a brief moment. "Has a lot to do with your current topic of debate. Sorry for asking this after I started talking, but I would like permission to speak. It won't take long."

"I see now," said Mellay in a voice mixed with laughter. "A youngster with a straightforward sense of justice is a treasure in any generation. How about it, everyone? I feel we should give him an opportunity to speak."

After she said that, there came murmurs of "That is fine" or "I agree." The voices clearly resembled that of parents watching their child have a hissy fit.

Mellay nodded back in response, then signaled Seyoh with her eyes.

"Ah, well then, Ix." With that glance, Seyoh seemed have wrested back control of the situation, as he returned to a tone even more polite than normal. "Please do speak. We would be happy to hear what you have to say."

"I appreciate it. But I didn't come here to speak," announced

Ix with his arms crossed as he glared at the people around him. "I came to reveal a sin."

"Oh, and what is that?" asked Seyoh, his head tilted.

"Misrepresenting God, of course."

"Ah, right now we are—"

"I'm not talking about the girl standing by the wall." This time, Ix didn't look in Yuui's direction. Instead, he locked his eyes on Mellay. "This misrepresentation of God is far more severe. I have come to lay it bare as a morally upright, devout believer."

"I see. That is quite a serious charge, if true." Seyoh nodded slightly. "Then let me ask: Who have you come to expose for misrepresenting God?"

Almost everyone in the room smiled as they waited for what was to come next.

Ix passed his gaze over their faces, then said, "Everyone here."

5

Ix's voice filled the chamber, and it fell silent. It was now or never.

"There is a story about the Chapel in this town. One where Rednoff, the inventor of man-made wands, stowed away in an underground room to complete the ultimate catalyst. Or so the legend goes." Ix's mouth kept moving as he thought through what he would say. "I get the impression it's a famous story among people related to the Church. From where I sat at the end of the table, I even heard a few people bring it up at the dinner that night."

He glanced at the faces of the people around him. They were staring at him with confusion, or with anger, or as though he was weird.

"The guests at the dinner came to a conclusion," he said, looking back again to the vukodrak named Mellay. "They determined

©Enji

Rednoff locked himself below the Chapel because of his faith in Marayism. They arrived at this without any real proof, but that's what was said. Am I getting that right?"

"Yes, you are correct...," said Seyoh, creasing his brows. "Though I won't accept that it is a claim without proof. The logic stands, and there is no proof to refute it, so we should accept it as true for the time being."

"Does that mean you accept that is indeed the ultimate wand?" asked another man in the crowd. "Aren't you the young man who stood up out of nowhere to ask what Mr. Rolphie meant when he said it was the ultimate wand?"

"That was because of my own lack of experience. It is absolutely the ultimate wand," acknowledged Ix, and the man who had asked snorted. "It is. The question of how Rednoff crafted it in that time period remains, but I'm going to set that aside for now. The problem is that all of the attendees at the time, meaning everyone here now, failed to point out something crucial."

"And what is that?" asked Mellay with a tilt of her head.

"The legend doesn't end there. Rednoff disappeared after finishing the ultimate wand beneath the Chapel. But he didn't just walk away. He vanished from a locked underground chamber. Not one person attempted to explain that mystery in the debate the other night. Why didn't anyone question it?"

"Because discussing it wouldn't accomplish anything," countered Mellay immediately. "Legends are exaggerated and change over time. In all likelihood, someone changed 'disappeared' to 'disappeared from a locked underground chamber' somewhere down the line. It is not possible for someone to disappear from a room when they had no avenues of escape. Or are you trying to say that you can explain this?"

"Yes, I can."

"That is an interesting claim." She clasped her hands together on her lap. "And what is it?"

"Rednoff was a ghost."

A few seconds after he said that, cascades of condescending laughter erupted from various places in the hall.

Ix's expression didn't change as he let the cackles roll off him. It wasn't a problem right now.

He waited for the laughter to subside before speaking again.

"Rednoff was a ghost. That is the only explanation that fits the legend. If you want to refute that claim, then provide me with proof or another possible explanation that is just as believable. That's how these meetings work, right? Saying 'it isn't possible' won't cut it."

"You have to verify the existence of ghosts first," asserted a different member. "What is a ghost? What logic allows them to exist? Answer that first."

"Dragons."

As Ix spoke that single word, the other person's expression turned icy.

It wasn't just that man, either. Every person in the chamber froze.

"There is a legend about a dragon in this town. A married couple asked for a doll of theirs to be brought to life. To a dragon. It granted their wish perfectly. Once the doll expired, it become a specter that haunted the town. I imagine some of you here have heard it," continued Ix.

"That's a ghost story," said Mellay sharply. "Dragons are creatures of legend. There are questions as to whether they ever actually existed. What sort of evidence is that?"

"*Dragons existed*," asserted Ix very clearly. "Dragons existed, and they absolutely granted people's wishes. I expect you to act like that's true unless you have proof to the contrary."

"......" Seyoh glared at Ix in silence. "Fine. What is it, then, that you are claiming based on that legend?"

"That the doll in the tale is Rednoff. He was given life by a dragon. He was a doll that turned into a ghost," said Ix without taking a breath. "That interpretation explains everything."

He stopped speaking and looked around the room.

After checking that no one was going to offer a counter-argument, he continued.

"Rednoff invented man-made wands from out of nowhere." Ix walked slowly around the room. The flames of the candles near him wavered as he passed. "But many questions remain about how he was able to make the first wands. He didn't develop them by synthesizing knowledge from the age of natural wands. And yet, the story goes that a single man came up with the idea for man-made wands, refined his creation to the point it was actually useable, and then even managed to craft the ultimate wand. How could he have managed that? 'Rednoff was a genius.' That explanation is simple, but it isn't very convincing. But if he was a creation of a dragon, it would all add up." Ix held his hands out in front of him. "Giving life to a wooden doll. Doing that is quite similar to how we produce man-made wands by cutting a branch from a tree and endowing it with a pseudo-life. Rednoff himself was the world's first magic wand."

"That's not proof," came the calm voice of a man. Ix looked and saw it belonged to the same man who'd sat across from him on the night of the dinner. "It's just as convincing to say that Rednoff was an incomparable genius, and there's as much proof for that as your claim, too. It can stand as an alternative explanation to what you just proposed."

"But it can't explain how he disappeared from the underground room," retorted Ix immediately. "My explanation can cover that as well."

"...Impossible."

"It's simple. After being locked in that room under the Chapel, Rednoff died. In that very chamber. He lost his life. A human leaves behind a corpse, but that didn't happen with him."

Ix stopped to take a breath.

"Rednoff's consciousness became a ghost, and he left a magic wand behind."

Maybe that was enough to get Ix's point across. The participants should have all realized by now. If the ultimate wand was actually Rednoff's body, then it rendered the debate at the dinner entirely pointless, or at least cast serious doubt on it.

Ix remained monotone as he finished.

"The first wandmaker was a magic wand created by a dragon." He shot a glance at Yuui. "That is the only explanation that perfectly fits the legend's mysteries."

At the dinner party, the attendees had made Rednoff out to be a devout believer. They'd argued he was a craftsman who locked himself in that chamber out of his dedication to God and continued to make wands. He was spurred by faith to craft the ultimate catalyst. Hence you could argue that all wandmakers who sought that same wand were faithful members of the Church... That was the explanation they had come up with.

By that logic, the ultimate wand was nothing short of a gift created by God.

But...what if that was wrong?

What if Rednoff had been a doll, and the catalyst in the underground room was his corpse?

That would mean a dragon had created the ultimate wand.

"I came here to expose your sins. Every person who agreed with Mellay at that dinner was treating God and dragons as one and the same. Therefore, you are the sinners who misrepresented God."

Having said that, Ix closed his eyes.

It was his only gambit.

If they denied that they'd misrepresented God, if they defended themselves and said it wasn't true, then Ix could borrow their defense to insist that Yuui hadn't committed a crime, either.

If they accepted their sin and said they would accept the punishment, then Ix would borrow that logic as well, though he wouldn't believe it. He would have Yuui accept her sin and the punishment. But no matter how severe a sin misrepresenting God was, they wouldn't agree to the death penalty, since they would have to face the same fate. That way, he could at least save her life.

This was the only way of protecting her.

Of course, his gambit wasn't a guaranteed success. The participants could simply ignore everything Ix had said. They weren't required to take stock in the words of a layperson. He was hoping to rely on Coaku's name to get him that far, but it wasn't certain to work.

Ix opened his eyes again and saw Mellay right in the center of his field of vision. She was smiling unconcernedly.

Then she gave him an entirely different response than he had expected.

"You are completely right, Ix," she said, as if to agree wholeheartedly.

"Huh?" The reply slipped from his mouth.

"I am amazed you were able to glimpse such a profound truth from only the slightest of legends. I am even more convinced of the value of young people who bring new insights with each generation."

Ix couldn't understand what she was trying to say.

The rest of the meeting participants were exchanging puzzled glances; they were as clueless as he was.

Only Seyoh concurred with Mellay.

"Absolutely," he said with a strong nod. "Perhaps concealing that underground room was a mistake. I can't believe you discerned this much with just a glance."

"What are you saying...?" asked Ix.

"This is such a wonderful opportunity that I must say something. Everyone, this is a common misunderstanding even among the clergy," added Mellay slowly. "It is true that there is a legend here in Estosha about a dragon. In that tale, the dragon grants a doll life. However, past Church members have avoided speaking on this story, as it carries great risk. Do you understand why?"

Everyone in the room gave a vague nod.

"Yes, God created the world and the life in it. The Old Order teaches us that this is proof of God's existence. Which is why you could use a legend about an all-powerful, life-granting dragon to deny God. But that is only if you overlook a crucial part of the story. Seyoh, do you know what that is?"

He smiled when his name was called and said, "The dragon granted the doll life, but not a soul. Is that correct?"

"Yes, precisely." Mellay clapped her hands. But they gave no sound, however, as only the thick fur on her palms touched. "Why did the dragon only give life? Is it because the people in the tale asked for nothing more? No, that's not it. Souls are inseparable from life. That is why every one of God's creations possesses both life and a soul and why none has ever become a specter. I imagine you understand what that means. Even you, Gustavus," she said as she looked to the other side of the room.

"I'm not sure why you'd mention my name there…," Gustavus said. "I assume you are essentially saying that the dragon lacked the ability to make a soul."

"Yes, that is exactly what I mean." She nodded. "As you can tell from that, dragons and God are not the same. Dragons can create life, but only God can create souls. Dragons are mighty, but God is almighty. Which means…"

She turned back to Ix and said, "Dragons cannot create dragons. God can create dragons."

So that was a valid interpretation?

He'd worked so hard to bring his theory together, but they'd neither refuted nor accepted it. They approached it from a whole different plane and slowly consumed it.

"Everyone," said Mellay, "we should thank young Ix. He has shown us a hole in our interpretation and led our debate to even greater completion. It wasn't Rednoff who created the ultimate wand—it was a dragon. And of course, it was God who birthed those creatures. And why did the ultimate wand born of a dragon choose the Chapel as its final resting place? When you think on the reason for that, I'm sure you will come to realize that the ultimate wand was indeed a blessing from God."

She spread her arms wide as the attendees hurled fervent praise at Ix.

Ix accepted cries of "Incredible!", "You've taught us much!", and "This is what a true believer looks like!" as the Marayists swallowed his goals, his plans, his everything, whole.

He stumbled backward on unsteady feet, almost shoved by their cries.

Seyoh raised a hand, and someone quickly brought a chair over for him. They wouldn't let him leave. He was trapped within Marayism.

He sat there, dazed.

His voice wouldn't come out at all.

There was nothing else he could do.

He'd come here with the intention of saving her, but...

Ix naturally looked for Yuui by the wall, but all he saw was the wallpaper.

He panicked, trying to figure out where she had gone. Had she guessed that Ix wouldn't be able to save her and made a last-ditch attempt to escape? But that would be the worst possible choice. Maybe she'd managed to contact Nova somehow...

Just then, he heard a voice from above.

"Thank you."

"Huh?"

The petite girl was standing directly in front of him, looking down.

He couldn't see her face because it was in shadow, but he could tell she was clapping her hands.

The others quickly noticed her. The applause stopped, and commotion grew. No one understood why she would be coming forward at this moment.

"Everyone...," announced Yuui as she turned around. Ix could see only her back now. "Please forgive me, but I simply could not hold back my emotions. I was seized by the urge to tell something to you all, so I leaped forward... Seyoh, may I please be granted permission to speak?"

She looked at him, and surprisingly, he nodded immediately. "Yes, go on," he told her.

"Thank you." She nodded once. "As you all know, people treated me as a descendent of a god in my homeland. However, that description has always felt odd to me. I never felt as if I had the blood of a deity running through my veins." Her voice was filled with emotion as she spoke. "However, now, just now, I have become convinced of something as I listened to what this man had to say."

She stepped forward and gestured toward Ix.

"The gods of my homeland, Lukutta, are similar to the '*dragons*' of which he speaks. They are mighty, but not almighty; they cannot create their own. To be honest, I do not know if I have the blood of a deity in me, but I do know one thing: The gods of Lukutta are also creations of the true God who you all believe in."

There was a gasp from the crowd.

Everyone turned their eyes, filled with anticipation, upon the girl who was about to be converted to their religion.

"I plan to return to my homeland after spending the winter here in Estosha. And upon my return, I hope to spread word of God to my people. I want as many of my kinsmen as possible to know the wonders of Marayism. However...I am only a child. I still know too little about this faith and, until just recently, I misrepresented myself as a descendent of God. I understand that you are unable to trust someone like me. I am sure that your concerns are greater than I can know. But my passion also burns far more brightly than you can imagine. Like the first light that Saint Anma saw...or the lava pool into which Saint Irobai fell."

She moved to the center of the room as she implored the crowd.

"Which is why, please... I beg of you." She bowed her head low. "Please grant me permission to spread the word of God throughout my homeland."

It was her only remaining road to salvation.

But no one in the crowd would have suspected that from her performance. That, or they knew this and chose to ignore it.

Either way, the result was the same. A woman who was a symbol in her homeland had become their missionary.

After a drawn-out silence, the hall erupted in thunderous applause.

Mellay stood and spread her arms in an attempt to draw Yuui into a hug.

The ovation didn't end; Yuui bowed over and over to the crowd.

She had been dragged to an enemy country, had her freedom and future stolen from her. And now, they had even claimed her spirit. Yet Ix saw a smile on her face.

That smile never turned toward him.

6

Yuui glanced out the window and saw a dim glow.

She imagined there must have been bonfires in the streets below. The normally quiet streets were now filled with people walking about. She could hear their voices.

Heaven's Worship had begun.

There was a bustle in the building as the meeting had only just finished, but everyone was likely to go to the Chapel soon. Yuui was relieved because it seemed like no one had seen her head back to her room.

She heard the door to the room open and turned her head to look.

"Thank you for your work, Nova," said Yuui when she saw who was there. She bowed her head. "My stay here has gotten difficult."

That was the kind of thing that Nova would always say "yes" back to, but she didn't say anything. She simply stood in the doorway, staring at Yuui.

"What's wrong?" Yuui asked.

Instead of responding, Nova walked up to Yuui. In the darkness of the room, she drew so close that she nearly ran into her. Yuui saw herself reflected in Nova's emotionless eyes.

"There's something, I don't get," said Nova quietly.

"What is that? I will explain it to you if I understand it…"

"It's about the dinner, from the other night. The group decided that Seyoh orchestrated, both the threat letter and the attack on you. He even admitted as much."

"He claimed it was to draw attention to me, but, well, that is quite an annoying story," said Yuui with a shrug.

"But it, is strange."

"Why do you say that?"

Nova blinked for a moment.

"Because, I saw the threat letter," she continued in a flat tone. "It was an envelope that was slightly damp and mushy. The writing was running a bit, but you could still read it. If it was an act, he wouldn't need to do something like that. He could just tell others, that a threat letter had been delivered."

"It is somewhat perplexing…," conceded Yuui, placing a finger on her cheek. "Seyoh is very thorough, however, so perhaps that was intentional. He wouldn't know who might say they wanted to look at the real letter, after all."

"Wouldn't doing that mean he wanted to stop, the meetings? Doesn't that motive contradict why he attacked you?"

"I thought Rolphie explained that."

"He didn't," said Nova immediately. "All he did was use process of elimination, to claim that Seyoh was the only person who could have done both. He didn't focus on the consistency of motive, at all."

"Then perhaps we should allow for some contradiction. If there is only one possibility, we must accept it even if it is somewhat far-fetched…"

"No." Nova shook her head and stared at Yuui. "There are two, possibilities. It could be that the person who sent the letter, and the person who attacked you, are different parties."

"What leads you to believe there is another possibility?"

"Because I am aware of someone who knows what time the servants open the front door every day, and who could have placed a letter there immediately beforehand."

"…And who would that be?"

Nova didn't reply. She walked over to the window and looked down.

From that small window, you had a clear view of the building's entrance. They weren't so high up that you couldn't open the window and drop an envelope at the doorstep if you aimed well.

Nova turned back to Yuui.

"Will you tell me, why?"

"Why?" Yuui tilted her head.

"You managed to get out of it, this time. Seyoh decided it was better to cover for you, than to keep others from ever knowing the culprit. But it wouldn't have gone like this, if they'd realized you actually sent the letter. You would have been tried, as a real criminal. Why would you do something so self-destructive?"

Yuui moved closer to the window. She stood beside Nova and looked down. There were so many people milling about it made you wonder where they normally were.

"Hey, Nova," said Yuui. "Why do you think I was invited to these meetings in the first place?"

"To discredit the Lukuttan faith. To make clear their attitude toward the countries they've conquered, by declaring you a sinner and executing you."

"That is very unlikely." Yuui smiled and shook her head. "If that was their goal, they could have exposed who I was my very first day at the meetings. They would have no reason to go to the trouble of forcing me to participate. I think Seyoh had only one goal in mind from the start."

"And what was that?"

"To convert me and make me a missionary in Lukutta."

Nova stared at Yuui in silence.

"The potential of converting other nations is a pressing issue in Estosha because it borders other nations. They want someone on their side who is from Lukutta, especially if they are in a position of religious power. They want it so badly, they'll do anything. The impact on the Lukuttan people will be huge when they learn I've converted to Marayism. Obviously, my conversion doesn't need to be true in my heart. But they forced my hand into declaring my intention to convert. Now that I have said that, I have no choice but to proselytize when I return to Lukutta since the kingdom could execute me whenever they wanted. They are monitoring me, after all."

Yuui's words came smoothly.

"That is why Seyoh made me participate in those meetings, made me learn about Marayism, and made me gain the trust of the debate attendees. That was the only thing Seyoh wanted to accomplish in these winter meetings. Just as Mellay put everything into making wandmakers members of the Clergy."

"Were…," started Nova, who had been listening in silence, "were you aware of this? And still did as he wanted…?"

"I had no choice. This was the only possible outcome from the moment I came to Estosha. He'd prepared everything so thoroughly. If I tried to run, I would only be restrained even more tightly."

"But, why…?"

"There is no way I can resist them outright. But if I go along with their plans for me, the ropes binding me will loosen. In that situation, I can move at least a finger, and perhaps I can guide things just a little."

"Guide?" asked Nova, blinking a few times.

"Seyoh must have immediately clued into the fact I had sent the threat letter. He probably suspected I was trying to stop the meetings after I realized what he was up to. But he couldn't pin the blame on me because it would put more crimes on my head. And then I would no longer be just Yuui Laika, the morally upright girl descended from a god. He could have chosen to ignore the threat letter…but someone with a mind like his would actually choose to use it to his advantage."

Yuui paused to take a breath.

"He pretended to attack me and made an even greater issue out of the threats. Even if Rolphie hadn't accused him, Seyoh would have implicated himself. Either that or he would have prepared another 'culprit' to take the fall. Regardless, his plan subsumed mine. Since he showed me his ability, I would have no choice but to go along with his plan even if I knew what it was…"

Yuui held up her palms.

"But what about it? What would the other participants in the meeting think?"

"…What, do you mean?" asked Nova.

"Wouldn't they think it was strange? 'Why would Seyoh test us?' 'Why did he lie in the beginning about the letter and the attack?' They might start to feel suspicious toward him." Yuui brought a hand to her chest. "And they might start to feel just a little bit sorry for me, because he used me. They would go easy on me. Actually, both Mellay and Gustavus spoke to me after the meeting. Those are the two I visited under the pretext of discussing that threat letter. They both promised me. They said they wanted to give me near-complete freedom in regards to the spread of Marayism in Lukutta."

Nova opened her mouth but then closed it again. She stopped blinking and stared at Yuui.

"The meetings went exactly as Seyoh planned. But at the same time, his compatriots lost a tiny bit of trust in him, and I gained some from them. And what will come of that, you ask?" Yuui held up a finger. "When the New Order seizes power, they will hold off on taking over Lukutta. So long as I am there, they will decide it will be fine to leave it alone. I will act in a way that makes them think that. And that will buy Lukutta time. Time. That can change everything."

Nova took a step back as she listened to Yuui's smooth explanation.

"I…," she started to say. "Aren't you afraid, that I'll tell the higher-ups about what you just said?"

"It would make no difference if you did," said Yuui with a smile.

©Enji

"But as your friend, I would warn you that I think it's unlikely you will be able to get them to take it seriously. I am merely a pawn to those above. They don't believe I have the power to change anything. Look at what happened this time—I played exactly into Seyoh's hand. I doubt they are interested in the thoughts of a puppet..."

Nova was quiet for a while. This was normal for her, though this silence seemed different than usual.

"I am, monitoring you," she said.

"Yes, you are."

"I'll likely be kept in this position, even after going back to Lukutta."

"That does seem likely."

"But, I'm going to submit a request, to be reassigned."

"Why now, of all times?" asked Yuui. "Are you fed up with me?"

"No... Because I, can't keep up with you."

"I don't think your request will be approved, though."

"...I agree." Nova nodded once, her voice the same emotionless tone as always. "Yes. I look forward, to being with you longer, Yuui."

7

Once the door to the meeting room opened, the people left, their expressions cheerful. The hall filled with the sound of chatter, which quickly grew into a ruckus.

Ix was swept along with the tide of people toward the front entrance of the building, but Shuno was waiting right beside it. Their face lit up when they saw Ix, and they pulled him by the arm to drag him into a corner of the hall. As Shuno tugged him along, several of the meeting participants tried to talk to Ix. They were all smiling. He looked for Rolphie and Hemsley in the crowd, but he didn't see them anywhere.

It didn't take long for the people to disappear. The hall quickly emptied, returning to silence.

"Everyone's going to the Chapel across the street," Shuno told him. "The attendants waiting in the hall told me. There's going to be a service in the Chapel; then everyone'll go out to the grounds for the Heaven's Worship ritual. Anyone can join that, I guess, so do you want to wait a bit before going?"

"I don't mind, but...," said Ix with a sigh.

"Why're you so down?" asked Shuno in confusion. "I was only listening through the door, but you were amazing, Ix! I can't believe you revealed what the ultimate wand really was! Man, I had absolutely no idea. A wand made by a dragon, that's so cool—"

"It was a lie."

"Huh?" Shuno looked blankly at Ix.

"It was all a lie. The dragon, Rednoff, it was all just bullshit I don't have any evidence for. Besides...that thing isn't the ultimate wand."

"W-wait a second, Ix." Shuno quickly held up a hand. "A-a lie? But Munzil Alreff and his own apprentices all agreed it was. I mean, I don't have any clue how it's used, but—"

"That's right, Shuno," said Ix. "No one can use it, and there's nothing it can be used for. That's exactly what makes it the ultimate wand."

"...What do you mean?"

"How many times have the two of us talked about it? Speculated about if it's possible to forge the ultimate wand or what it would even look like if you could make it? I bet every wandmaker in history has thought the same. They dream about the ultimate wand and try to get just a little bit closer to it. That passion drives the development of catalysts, and it hasn't died down, hundreds of years later. Even if they're not moving forward as fast as before, even if Munzil dies...wandmakers like you will come along. Craftspeople with passion, who'll move the ages along. And there's probably a reason for that."

"Stop complimenting me here," said Shuno, a flash of anger crossing their face before they returned to normal. "So you're saying the reason is—?"

"The ultimate wand," said Ix with a nod. "Everyone believes that someday we'll produce a single wand to end all wands. Because there's a legend about the first wandmaker creating it. That's why everyone's so obsessed with advancing the craft. It doesn't matter if the ultimate wand really exists or not. Just having the name out there means that magic catalysts will continue to evolve forever. It's the same with stars. You feel safe reaching your hand out toward them 'cause you'll never reach them."

"Okay, okay, what about Rednoff, then? Where did he disappear to?"

"Not a clue." Ix shrugged. "Maybe he died in that room, and they kept it a secret, or someone secretly helped him escape… Even if we try to imagine what happened, we don't have enough information. Perhaps he felt guilty about putting all the blast wandmakers out of business and just disappeared."

"……"

After listening to Ix's explanation, Shuno turned away, frowning. They blinked several times, appearing uneasy.

"…Right," murmured Shuno after a while. "I get it, Ix. It's going to take time for you to digest it all… Got it."

"Sorry for dragging you into this."

"Not a problem at all. But I get it. That's what you meant when you said you were betraying someone, right? Saying it was the ultimate wand even when you knew it wasn't true?"

"That's…"

Ix couldn't help falling silent.

That wasn't true. Because what he'd betrayed was the honor of the dragons no longer here.

But Shuno's voice quickly turned cheerful again.

"Well, if you don't want to tell me, that's fine. At least for now, it looks like your friend was saved."

By now, Ix knew that was Shuno being nice.

He had no idea why they were so kind to him, why they were still smiling at him even though he'd gotten them into this mess. He didn't understand it, but it made him so very happy. So happy he nearly wanted to cry.

He looked at Shuno while thinking that, only to find a questioning look on their face.

"H-hey, Ix, are you okay? Does your stomach hurt?"

"No, it's nothing."

"Really? You're making an expression I've never seen you make before; seems like something to me."

There was barely anyone in the hallway at this point. The service in the Chapel was probably well underway, Ix guessed.

But out of the corner of his eye, he saw two small people appear and walk toward him.

"Ah, there you two are," said one of them.

"Oh, Master Coaku," said Shuno, noticing them as well. "And you... Ummm, I'm sorry, I didn't ask your name."

"Nova," she said with a slight tilt of her head.

"Nova? I'm Shuno. Thanks for your help before."

"It's, no problem."

Ix had no idea why Coaku and Nova had come over together, but he just bowed wordlessly. Without Coaku, he never would have managed to get into that meeting.

It seemed the old craftsman had been looking for the two of them. He'd thought they would be in the Chapel and went out to search for them.

"Are you two not participating in Heaven's Worship?" asked Coaku.

"Oh, no, we are," said Shuno with a wave of their hand. "It's just, we don't know the rituals, so we were talking about going after they're finished...right?"

Ix nodded in agreement, but hearing mention of Heaven's Worship made him remember something.

"Coaku, sorry for the random question...," he said, "but do you have a granddaughter?"

"No," he said, shaking his head. "There was only my son. I have no grandchildren."

I knew it..., thought Ix as he glanced down.

Yes, there was still one thing he didn't understand.

Riess. The girl he'd first met when he came to the town, who he ran into every once in a while. The girl who he'd speculated was a real ghost.

But Coaku had told him he didn't have a daughter or granddaughter. Now what Ix had imagined up to this point was starting to feel more real...

"But I do have an assistant who's young enough to be my granddaughter," the craftsman continued.

"Huh?"

"Come on out, Riess."

Coaku stepped aside to reveal a little girl. She'd been hiding behind him the whole time.

She was looking at the ground and gripping the edge of her coat tightly.

"Riess...?" asked Ix, and she looked up to meet his gaze.

Her face turned so scarlet so quickly, you could almost hear a sound accompanying it. She turned around and bolted far down the hallway.

"I think that might be enough to tell you... I'm sorry. She's a very shy girl." Coaku bowed his head while looking in the direction she had run. "She doesn't like having people look at her. She causes quite the headache for me, since she still walks around at night even though I told her not to."

"She's shy...?" muttered Ix.

"Please don't misunderstand, though. She is really quite fond of you, Ix."

"Huh...? I don't remember doing anything to make her like me. Did I meet her a long time ago?"

"I doubt you've met. But you have spoken with her," said Coaku cryptically.

"…No, I don't remember at all."

"She'd be happy to hear that," said Coaku with a smile. "Do you remember I sent a letter to your master some years ago?"

"Yeah. We exchanged quite a few. Master had me write them."

"That's correct. But I only sent the first one."

"What about the others?"

"Riess decided to send them all by herself. She pretended to be me so she could talk to a wandmaker she admired. I bet she was disappointed when the letters came back written by a substitute whose name she didn't even know. But she didn't have too many people to talk to at the time. Soon, she became obsessed with sending those letters… And it seems she took quite the shine to you, Ix. I only noticed because she was enjoying herself so much." Coaku rubbed his head. "That's why she was so happy when she heard you were coming to Estosha. It seems like you haven't had much chance to talk, but we'll have many an opportunity to see each other for a long time to come, now, won't we? Anyway, I brought her with me so she could at least say hello, but…that's how she is."

Ix blinked repeatedly, unable to say anything.

What did that mean?

"So what about the ghost in the monastery?" he asked.

"Ghost? What's this about?" asked Coaku, looking puzzled.

"Uh…well, there was an incident in the monastery where someone said they saw something," said Ix as he glanced at Shuno.

"Ah, yeah, there was. I wonder what that was," said Shuno.

The two of them cocked their heads, and Nova slightly raised her hand.

"It was, me," she said. Her tone was so casual that it took a while for Ix to understand.

"Now what are you saying?" asked Ix as he looked her in the eye.

"It was, me," Nova repeated. "I visited the monastery a few times, to investigate the Old Order."

"They don't allow girls there," said Ix.

"Correct."

"...You visited? Through the underground passage?"

"Yes. It was easier to walk down there, than crossing through the snow. I received information, about the passage's existence," she said, her speech fragmented. "We met, at the monastery."

"Huh? When?"

"You picked up, the book I dropped."

"Book...?"

"It's getting late. I should be going. Good-bye," said Nova as she held out a hand toward Ix, who was still confused.

"Uh, yeah...," he said as he reflexively shook her hand.

In his palm was something unlike human skin—something dry and crinkly.

He stared at Nova as she walked away. Just then, a scene replayed in his mind.

That's right, he'd picked up a book...

The first time he went to the monastery, there'd been a monk pushing a cart. Ix had picked up a book for him.

Which meant...

The person Shuno had gotten a glimpse of in the kitchen had been Nova...

And the reason there had been one lunch too few that day was because there really *was* one too many people at the monastery.

For some reason, Ix felt the urge to burst into laughter.

Even though Yuui had just gone through what she had.

Something made the tension drain from his shoulders.

So it had been Nova the whole time...?

Right...

That's all the ghost was, then.

Ix followed the instructions on the note he'd received when he shook Nova's hand. He entered the Chapel alone.

Service had just let out. There had been large crowds of clergy and theologians there a little while ago, but now no one was left. They were all outside, gazing at the stars.

Though nothing was lit inside the building, the moonlight streaming in from the windows was nearly dazzling in its brightness. Thin wisps of smoke rose from the candlesticks in that bluish-white glow.

Ix leaned forward, as if he were chasing the smoke.

And he saw them.

The carvings on the walls.

The paintings on the ceiling.

The stained glass.

Every single one was the product of a craftsperson.

Someone who'd devoted their entire life to a single skill.

A mark left behind by the lives of people who'd lived hundreds of years ago, whose names had fallen into obscurity.

Ix trembled, overwhelmed with emotion.

They had sought it.

They had reached out their hands, even though they knew they would never make it. They had tried to get there, if but for the briefest of moments.

To the place where their sole ideal dwelled.

They'd looked up.

At the stars.

And among those twinkling lights...

Was God.

That was proof of a craftsman.

It was how every one of them was built.

Ix looked even farther up. His tears would stream out if he didn't.

If all that was true...

Then someone who no longer sought the ultimate wand...

Who'd given up looking at the stars...

Him.

He wasn't a craftsman.

"Good evening."

Yuui called out behind him as he stared up at the ceiling.

"Don't turn around, please," she said as she stood, her back to his. "This conversation should not be happening."

"...Long time no see."

"Yes, indeed." She laughed a little, finding it funny that he would say that when they couldn't look at each other. "May I guess what you are thinking?"

Ix nodded, which Yuui felt through her back.

"Is it about wands?" she asked.

"...Yeah."

"I heard earlier. It sounds like you will become a craftsman. Congratulations."

"...I'm no craftsman." He shook his head.

"What do you mean?" Yuui was surprised; there wasn't even a hint of joy in his voice.

"I'm just not a craftsman. I thought of that wand, so I—"

"Wait," she said, cutting him off. "Before you get so down on yourself, would you mind telling me what this is about? From the beginning?"

"...Okay."

And so Ix explained the wand he'd thought up to her.

You could increase its power using a mana reaction. You'd have to limit its maximum output, but in exchange, you wouldn't need specialized skills to produce it. It would be easier to get the materials for it. You could make them in large quantities, sell them cheaply, and put one in everyone's hands. That was the wand he'd conceptualized.

It was the polar opposite of the ultimate wand—a catalyst without value.

After hearing what he had to say, Yuui remained silent for a while, staring at the floor. A number of different thoughts ran through her mind.

Eventually, she asked, "Where do you think God is?"

"God? In the sky, I guess."

"Yes, that is true with the Marayist god. But let me tell you something interesting. They say the blood of a deity runs through my veins. In Lukuttan mythology, there's a tale where a god walks among humans." Her tone turned gentle as she continued. "That deity came from the earth."

"From the earth...?"

She nodded. "The Marayists are not the only ones to speak of a god's teachings. There is a god like the stars, in a place we can never reach. But on the other hand, there is also a god who came from the ground, who interacts with people. So, Ix," she said, smiling, knowing that he couldn't see her, "that is yours alone... Your god, your wand, something that no other craftsman could reach because it came from your perspective alone. Don't you think so?"

She waited for a few seconds, listening for his wordless response through their backs, then said, "Yes, things have gotten difficult all of a sudden. But please remember this. There is a place that would welcome you with open arms. If you ever need to, come to Lukutta."

"To your country...?"

"This is far in the future, of course. You've only just become a craftsman. You'll need money and people to make the wand you just told me about. But if you ever feel you want to, please come."

Yuui was nauseated by her own dishonesty.

That future she mentioned was absolutely going to pass.

She knew it would.

When the New Order seized power, when they made wand-makers clergy, Ix would feel like his freedom was being taken from him. He would butt heads with the various rules of Maray-ism, and he would likely be stripped of his title.

But he wouldn't give up making wands. Yuui knew that much for certain.

When that happened, surely...

He would remember what she'd told him.

Magic wands. The craft and knowledge of those powerful weapons would come to Lukutta.

Yuui was standing on the sidelines despite knowing all this would happen. Even though she knew Mellay's plan to make craftsmen clergy.

In the town closest to God.

In its chapel.

Stood two nonbelievers.

They deceived people; they betrayed God.

The same thoughts were on their minds.

Yes...it had been only a few months since then.

That summer day, and the moment they'd met on that narrow, windswept mountain path.

They'd both had such simple, pure thoughts then. Where had they gone?

The ideals of magic wands that he'd believed in so unquestioningly.

The innocent goodness that she'd championed above her own interests.

Both were long gone...

Eventually, one of the nonbelievers disappeared into the darkness.

The other stood there motionless for a while before he suddenly raised his head and looked toward the entrance.

He opened the door, then turned back to look once more.

He didn't find any of the sadness or dust he'd seen on that day.

He stepped outside and saw his friend among the people looking up at the stars. Nearby was a small girl. The two noticed him and smiled. They waved.

Ix went to raise his hand in response but suddenly stopped to brush his shoulder. There was nothing cold there. The snow had stopped falling long ago.

➤ Afterword ➤

Every reader has the liberty to decide where they begin reading or where they stop reading. However, just as stories are rarely constructed with the assumption that the reader will begin reading from the end, I write this afterword with the presumption that it will be read last (there are many spoilers this time). Please keep that in mind.

As is clear from the title, *Dragon and Ceremony 3: God's Many Forms*, this book is the third volume in the series, following the first and the second. As before, the *Dragon and Ceremony* part denotes the series, while the subtitle accurately describes the content. We have gods, ghosts, and people in the running, but all those words point to essentially the same thing. It felt a bit strange writing this winter tale in the height of summer for a fall release.

Those of you who have been reading from the very beginning (not that I think anyone would only read this specific volume) will be able to tell this novel has a different feel overall. If I had to put it into one word, I would say that Volume 3 is calmer. There wasn't much in the way of skillful research or thrilling action. It was a bit more relaxed and "everyday" than its predecessors. I've been writing about wandmakers for so long, but now the characters are actually crafting them, so you could also say this is a story about work. Or maybe craftspeople? Well, there's probably no real point in making a distinction between those themes.

In terms of keywords, this book is different as well. Instead of the "inside and outside" themes from Volumes 1 and 2, we have the main theme of "above and below." Inside and outside is a separation along a plane, a frame put in place by others. If you think about stepping "outside," you've only got the three-dimensional directions to choose from. So which direction do you go in? No matter which you choose, there will be things you can see only from that point, information you can learn only from there.

Several new characters appeared in this volume, but I'd originally planned on debuting Shuno in Volume 2. There were a number of reasons why I decided to put them in this novel instead. The circumstances around their personal pronouns made some of the prose rather tricky. I got used to it by the second half, but in the beginning, I was somewhat careless with my writing, which made it a bit questionable.

Speaking of people, I originally started writing *Dragon and Ceremony* to try out writing a story in third-person narration. Now that I've made it all the way here, I finally feel like I've given that type of narration meaning (though the perspective in that last scene was just a bit of me playing around). I also feel like I've largely wrapped up the random foreshadowing I threw into the first volume, the application volume, and like I've reached a stopping point in terms of the story.

August 2020, Ichimei Tsukushi